D0514970

IDEAS AND TOOLS
FOR BRIEF COUNSELING

JACK H. PRESBURY
LENNIS G. ECHTERLING
J. EDSON McKEE

All, James Madison University

Merrill
Prentice Hall

Upper Saddle River, New Jersey
Columbus, Ohio

Library of Congress Cataloging-in-Publication Data
Presbury, Jack H.
    Ideas and tools for brief counseling/Jack H. Presbury, Lennis G. Echterling, and
J. Edson McKee.—1st ed.
      p. cm.
    Includes index.
    ISBN 0-13-079985-8
    1. Brief psychotherapy. 2. Short-term counseling. I. Echterling, Lennis G., II.
McKee, J. Edson.   III. Title.
RC480.55 .P72   2002
616.89'14—dc21   2001021416

Vice President and Publisher: Jeffery W. Johnston
Executive Editor: Kevin M. Davis
Associate Editor: Christina M. Kalisch
Production Editor: Linda Hillis Bayma
Production Coordinator: TechBooks
Design Coordinator: Diane C. Lorenzo
Cover Designer: Ceri Fitzgerald
Cover Art: SuperStock
Production Manager: Laura Messerly
Director of Marketing: Kevin Flanagan
Marketing Manager: Amy June
Marketing Coordinator: Barbara Koontz

This book was set in Berkeley by TechBooks. It was printed and bound by R.R. Donnelley & Sons Company.
The cover was printed by The LeHigh Press, Inc.

Prentice-Hall International (UK) Limited, *London*
Prentice-Hall of Australia Pty. Limited, *Sydney*
Prentice-Hall Canada, Inc., *Toronto*
Prentice-Hall Hispanoamericana, S. A., *Mexico*
Prentice-Hall of India Private Limited, *New Delhi*
Prentice-Hall of Japan, Inc., *Tokyo*
Prentice-Hall Singapore Pte. Ltd.
Editora Prentice-Hall do Brasil, Ltda., *Rio de Janeiro*

10 9 8 7 6 5 4 3 2 1
ISBN: 0-13-079985-8

This book is dedicated to our families—
those at home and at work.

PREFACE

Brief counseling is as much attitude as it is technique. The counselor who attempts to use time wisely and well must have a good sense of where to go with the material a client offers. The suggestions offered in this book spring mostly from solution-focused and narrative approaches to counseling, but they are only useful if you pay close attention to your relationship with a client. As most research shows, it is the way you collaborate with your client that does the work. Although the ideas and tools in this book are drawn from what might be considered a postmodern view, you do not have to abandon the rich discoveries counselors and therapists have made during the profession's first century. Brief counseling is not indicated for all people in all situations, but you will find that many of the brief counseling concepts and strategies can enhance your current practice. This book offers a balance between theory and technique, and it is written so that you can take what you find useful and leave the rest on these pages.

Chapter 1, "History of Brief Counseling: The Fly Bottle," offers the rationale for using a brief approach to counseling. Many practitioners in the helping professions are beginning to question the old notions of the mechanistic and medical models that treat clients as defective machines or as pathological protoplasm. These counselors are now attempting to understand the process of change itself and are trying to find ways to tap the natural resources that clients possess. The older humanistic notions of human potential and growth are being vindicated by these new approaches to helping. Today's interveners are reinventing intervention. Instead of engaging in the traditionally intensive process of long-term psychotherapy, counselors are increasingly involved in the minimalist and "just-in-time" process of brief therapy. Their efforts are aimed at building up the client's strengths and resources rather than at remediating the client's problems and dysfunctions. Although most books on brief counseling and therapy emphasize their differences from traditional approaches, we offer a bridge between the past and the future. The postmodern era challenges us to reconsider our beliefs and to do something different than we have done before.

Chapter 2, "Facilitating Change: The One Constant," addresses how you can help clients change unproductive ways of viewing the world so that they can find new, successful strategies. Instead of only assisting clients in finding solutions, you can also help clients in achieving a sense of resolution by deconstructing their representations. You can consider clients' "problems" as their "stuck" or rigidified representations of experience that are in need of change. Through counseling, your client becomes a newly resolute person. Some important clinical issues discussed in this chapter are the death of resistance, the concept of utilization, and clients' lives as metaphors or stories.

Chapter 3, "The Centrality of the Counseling Relationship: No Magic Tricks," points out that any technique will fail unless you have established a relationship with your client. In this chapter, we discuss the various common factors found by many researchers to be indispensable to the counseling process. Such research inevitably leads back to Carl Rogers, who articulated the core conditions for a successful counseling relationship. We discuss the concepts of empathy and acknowledgment and the LUV triangle — listening, understanding, and validating the client's perspective. We also describe Bill O'Hanlon's technique, "Carl Rogers with a Twist," which is a way of adding possibility statements to our reflections of client concerns.

Chapter 4, "Helping Clients Frame Goals: The Pull of the Future," suggests that it is teleology — not etiology — that is the main concern of brief counselors. You start your counseling work with a view to the future rather than to the past. One of the most important activities in which you can engage with clients is helping them to frame their goals. Goals serve as beacons that can guide your counseling work. In this chapter, we discuss how to develop well-formed goals with a client and how to determine whether the client's relationship to you is that of a "customer," "complainant," "visitor," or is involuntary. We also describe how to use the tools of finding exceptions and scaling techniques.

Chapter 5, "Constructivist Counseling: Inventing Realities," offers an alternative way of looking at reality—constructivism, which is sometimes seen as opposed to empiricism. The first assumption of constructivism is that you can never fully know another person's reality objectively. Only by encountering a client in an authentic relationship can you gain an empathic knowledge of that person's experiential world. The second assumption is that ultimate knowledge of a reality "out there" is not possible. Instead of our perceptions providing a veridical copy, or "immaculate perception," of reality, we can only construct our own interpretation of reality. Your goal in counseling is not to get clients to become more realistic, but to help them reconstruct the way they are representing themselves and their world. One of the important tools for deconstructing a client's negative story—and co-constructing a better one—is your use of the question. In this chapter, we offer suggestions on how to use questions effectively, and we discuss some questions you should avoid.

Chapter 6, "Narrative Counseling: Clients' Lives as Stories," focuses on the idea that clients come to counselors with stories that are outdated, tragic, and rigidified. As a result, these clients experience their lives as repetitive, negative, and unchangeable. Your task as a counselor is to help the client construct a new and therapeutic narrative. The technique of externalization seeks news of past successes, whereas the use of hypotheticals encourages clients to create the image of a success in the future. The "miracle question" technique is a way of inviting the client to construct a detailed scene in which the client has resolved the major concerns of his or her life. Each of these techniques is discussed in this chapter as well as how to encourage, rather than praise or reinforce, client behaviors.

Chapter 7, "Managing the Client's Emotional Arousal: Hot-Wiring," discusses the importance of managing emotional arousal in clients. A common misconception is that emotions are messy contaminants to effective problem-solving and good mental health. In fact, discoveries in neuroscience are revealing that emotions are essential to good thinking. This chapter offers a discussion of new ideas taken from recent research into how emotions work and how they contribute to good social judgment. You will learn the techniques for stimulating empathy in your clients, helping them to respond emotionally to positive images, and managing emotional arousal during sessions.

Chapter 8, "Using Mystifying Techniques: Turning Stumbling Blocks into Stepping Stones," offers ideas and tools for creating a "common everyday trance" in clients and for mystifying them into a different perspective. People who are discouraged have foreclosed on their dreams for the future. Nevertheless, their longing for a better life is always there, waiting to be brought out by the counselor. Your job involves tapping into this longing and increasing your client's emotional arousal that is connected to the image of a better future. You will learn to deliver the reframe, to construct an enchanting metaphor, and to write letters using an exotic audience. You will be offered some guidelines for constructing compelling metaphors with "dramatic hold" as you work with your client.

Chapter 9, "Chaos and Complexity in Counseling: Butterflies and Loaded Dice," introduces some of the more controversial approaches to counseling, such as confusion techniques and paradox. Chaos theory suggests that complex systems can be highly unstable and that small perturbations can throw such systems off course. But these small perturbations can result in a large changes, called the Butterfly Effect. People are complex systems—living systems that are adaptive and self-organizing. Instead of falling apart, complex adaptive systems reorganize themselves and grow. When they are perturbed, they put themselves back together in a new way in the process of emergence. In this chapter, we discuss ways of using confusion and paradox in your counseling relationships. We also offer a caveat–use paradox only at certain times and with certain clients.

Chapter 10, "The Reflecting Team, Consulting Break, and Offering Suggestions," presents strategies for the latter portion of the counseling session. We describe the reflecting team, a technique of involving other counselors in your work. We also discuss the distinction between suggestions and advice. Advice is when you "just tell 'em," but suggestions are more subtle and tailored to your client's style. Finally, we give guidelines for offering successful suggestions.

In chapter 11, "The 'Brief Attitudes,' the Second Session, and Beyond," we review the fundamental attitudes of successful brief counseling. Brief counseling is not just a set of techniques to be applied to a problem. It is a way of regarding the world and what clients need to move from a "stuck" position to one of creative possibilities. In this chapter, we describe how you can capitalize on positive momentum once you have completed the initial session with your client. We discuss techniques for deciding when to terminate with clients as well as rituals for consolidating changes that the client has made. Clients sometimes have misgivings at the termination of counseling, so we suggest some ways of dealing with these.

Finally, in chapter 12, "Dealing with Involuntaries and Revisiting the First Session," we discuss in greater depth the challenges presented by the involuntary client. We offer hints on helping this person become a customer and suggestions for dealing with the referring third party. We also present an overview of the process of the first therapy session and summarize the tools that you can use to succeed as a brief counselor. The chapter concludes with a flow chart showing the steps you take as you facilitate your client's progress toward a positive change.

By understanding the ideas and using the tools of brief counseling, you can increase your success as a counselor. In addition to reading this book, we encourage you to attend workshops and presentations on this approach to helping people. We have found that attending workshops with Bill O'Hanlon, Michelle Weiner-Davis, Scott Miller, and others to be inspiring and important in our own development as brief counselors. Many of the people mentioned in this book are actively involved in training. Seek them out. Obviously, reading this book can be only the first step in becoming a successful brief counselor. We wish you much success in your journey.

ACKNOWLEDGMENTS

Many people have supported and assisted us in writing this book. Our graduate students read early drafts and enthusiastically gave us detailed feedback and helpful suggestions. Our colleagues generously offered both their clinical expertise and their personal encouragement. Our families were tireless in their support and forebearance. We gratefully acknowledge their countless contributions and constant encouragement. In particular, we would like to thank Jane Halonen, Barbara McKee, Lin Presbury, and Mary Lou Wylie.

The comments of the following reviewers were valuable: James Archer, Jr., University of Florida; J. Scott Fraser, Wright State University; Samuel T. Gladding, Wake Forest University; Arthur M. Horne, University of Georgia; John M. Littrell, Iowa State University; Chris McCarthy, University of Texas at Austin; Russell D. Miars, Portland State University; Allen J. Ottens, Northern Illinois University; Pepper E. Phillips, University of Maryland; Michael J. Stevens, Illinois State University; Tracy Todd, University of Colorado at Denver; and Riley H. Venable, Texas Southern University.

Discover the Companion Website Accompanying This Book

THE PRENTICE HALL COMPANION WEBSITE: A VIRTUAL LEARNING ENVIRONMENT

Technology is a constantly growing and changing aspect of our field that is creating a need for content and resources. To address this emerging need, Prentice Hall has developed an online learning environment for students and professors alike—Companion Websites—to support our textbooks.

In creating a Companion Website, our goal is to build on and enhance what the textbook already offers. For this reason, the content for each user-friendly website is organized by topic and provides the professor and student with a variety of meaningful resources. Common features of a Companion Website include:

FOR THE PROFESSOR—

Every Companion Website integrates **Syllabus Manager™**, an online syllabus creation and management utility.

- **Syllabus Manager™** provides you, the instructor, with an easy, step-by-step process to create and revise syllabi, with direct links into the Companion Website and other online content without having to learn HTML.
- Students may log on to your syllabus during any study session. All they need to know is the web address for the Companion Website and the password you've assigned to your syllabus.
- After you have created a syllabus using **Syllabus Manager™**, students may enter the syllabus for their course section from any point in the Companion Website.
- Clicking on a date, the student is shown the list of activities for the assignment. The activities for each assignment are linked directly to actual content, saving time for students.
- Adding assignments consists of clicking on the desired due date, then filling in the details of the assignment—name of the assignment, instructions, and whether it is a one-time or repeating assignment.

- In addition, links to other activities can be created easily. If the activity is online, a URL can be entered in the space provided, and it will be linked automatically in the final syllabus.
- Your completed syllabus is hosted on our servers, allowing convenient updates from any computer on the Internet. Changes you make to your syllabus are immediately available to your students at their next logon.

FOR THE STUDENT—

- **Counseling Topics**—17 core counseling topics representing the diversity and scope of today's counseling field
- **Annotated Bibliography**—seminal foundational works and key current works
- **Web Destinations**—significant and up-to-date practitioner and client sites
- **Professional Development**—helpful information regarding professional organizations and codes of ethics
- **Electronic Bluebook**—send homework or essays directly to your instructor's email with this paperless form
- **Message Board**—serves as a virtual bulletin board to post—or respond to—questions or comments to/from a national audience
- **Chat**—real-time chat with anyone who is using the text anywhere in the country—ideal for discussion and study groups, class projects, etc.

To take advantage of these and other resources, please visit the *Ideas and Tools for Brief Counseling* Companion Website at

www.prenhall.com/presbury

BRIEF CONTENTS

CHAPTER 1   History of Brief Counseling: The Fly Bottle   **1**

CHAPTER 2   Facilitating Change: The One Constant   **19**

CHAPTER 3   The Centrality of the Counseling Relationship: No Magic Tricks   **39**

CHAPTER 4   Helping Clients Frame Goals: The Pull of the Future   **59**

CHAPTER 5   Constructivist Counseling: Inventing Realities   **81**

CHAPTER 6   Narrative Counseling: Clients' Lives as Stories   **100**

CHAPTER 7   Managing the Client's Emotional Arousal: Hot-Wiring   **121**

CHAPTER 8   Using Mystifying Techniques: Turning Stumbling Blocks into Stepping Stones   **143**

CHAPTER 9   Chaos and Complexity in Counseling: Butterflies and Loaded Dice   **164**

CHAPTER 10   The Reflecting Team, Consulting Break, and Offering Suggestions   **184**

CHAPTER 11   The "Brief Attitudes," the Second Session, and Beyond   **206**

CHAPTER 12   Dealing with Involuntaries and Revisiting the First Session   **224**

REFERENCES   **247**

INDEX   **255**

CONTENTS

CHAPTER 1   History of Brief Counseling: The Fly Bottle   1

Chapter Goals   1

Story   1

   Reflecting Questions   2
Overview   3
   An Era of Change   3
   Our Goals   3
Ideas   4
   A Rationale for Theory   4
   "A Rose By Any other Name. . ."   5
   A Brief History of Brief Counseling   7
   Experiencing This Idea   13
   Success Strategies   13
   Reflecting Questions   14
   Implications of These Ideas for the Counselor   14
Tools   16
   Reflecting Questions   16
   Experiencing This Idea   17
   Listening in on a Session   17
   Using These Tools   17
   Segue   17
   A Guarantee   18
Segue to Chapter 2   18

CHAPTER 2   Facilitating Change: The One Constant   19

Chapter Goals   19

Story   19

   Reflecting Questions   20

Overview   21

Ideas   21

  Something about Change   21
  Changing Minds   22
  Experiencing This Idea   22
  Brief Counseling as a Strategic Approach   22
  Resolution as Reconstruction   24
  Experiencing This Idea   25
  Why Use Brief Approaches to Counseling?   26
  Efficient versus Brief Counseling   27
  The Death of Resistance   28
  Dealing with "Resistance"   29
  Utilization   29
  Implications of These Ideas for the Counselor   30
Tools   31

  Metaphors and the Stories of Our Lives   31
  Using This Tool   31
  "Rigid" and "Fresh" Metaphors   32
  Using This Tool   33
  Life Stories and Meaning   33
  Using This Tool   33
  Listening for Client Metaphors   33
  Using This Tool   34
  Listening in on a Session   35
  Reflecting Questions   36
  Working with Client Metaphors   36
  Using This Tool   36
  Capturing Client Metaphors   37
  The Charismatic Use of Metaphors   37
Segue to Chapter 3   38

CHAPTER 3   **The Centrality of the Counseling Relationship: No Magic Tricks**   **39**
Chapter Goals   39

Story   39

  Reflecting Questions   40
Overview   40

Ideas   41

  A Riddle   41
  Experiencing This Idea   42
  Reflecting Questions   42
  Magic Tricks and Miracles   42
  Common Factors   43
  A Caveat: Listen to Your Clients   44

Rogers Rediscovered 45
Empathy as Technique 46
Implications for These Ideas for the Counselor 48
Tools 49
Establishing the Counseling Relationship 49
"Carl Rogers with a Twist" 50
Listening in on a Session 52
Reflecting Questions 53
Using This Tool 53
Deconstructing Client Complaints 53
Reflecting Questions 53
Listening in on a Session 56
Reflecting Questions 57
Using This Tool 57
An Important Reminder 57
Using This Tool 58
Summary 58
Segue to Chapter 4 58

CHAPTER 4   **Helping Clients Frame Goals: The Pull of the Future**   **59**
Chapter Goals 59

Story 59

Reflecting Questions 60

Chapter Overview 60

Ideas 61
What Are Etiology and Teleology? 61
Experiencing This Idea 62
Reflecting Questions 62
A Teleological Theory 63
Overcoming Blocks to a Hopeful Future 63
Implications of These Ideas for the Counselor 64
Tools 64
Inviting Clients to Set Goals 64
Well-Formed Goals 65
Using This Tool 68
Clients Commitment 68
Listening in on a Session 70
Reflecting Questions 71
Third-Party Goals 71
Framing the Third-Party Referral 72
Paths to Story Revision 74
Looking for Exceptions 74
Listening in on a Session 76

Reflecting Questions 76
No Problems Are Ever Fully Resolved: Scaling 76
Do Not Scale "SUDS" 79
Listening in on a Session 79
Reflecting Questions 80
Using This Tool 80
Two Closing Comments 80
Segue to Chapter 5 80

CHAPTER 5   **Constructivist Counseling: Inventing Realities**   **81**

Chapter Goals 81

Story 81

Reflecting Questions 82

Overview 83

Ideas 83

A Mental Reality 83
What Is It That Exists? 84
Constructivism 85
How People Construct a World 85
A Constructivist Way to Proceed 86
Rationalist Versus Developmental Pespectives 87
Intervention in Counseling 88
Experiencing This Idea 89
The Client's World as a Foreclosed Story 89
Understanding the Client's "Preferred View" 90
Implications of These Ideas for the Counselor 91

Tools 92

Deconstructing and Co-constructing the Client's Story 92
The Question: A Major Deconstruction Tool 92
Questioning the Use of Questions 93
Questions You Should [And Should Not] Ask 94
Useful Start-up Questions 95
Listening in on a Session 96
Reflecting Questions 96
Using This Tool 96
"Getting-By" Questions 96
Listening in on a Session 97
Reflecting Questions 98
Using This Tool 98
Circular (or Relational) Questions 98
Using This Tool 99
Presumptive Questioning 99
Using This Tool 99
Segue to Chapter 6 99

CHAPTER 6 Narrative Counseling: Clients' Lives as Stories **100**
Chapter Goals 100

Story 100

Reflecting Questions 101
Overview 101

Ideas 102

The Problem of Meaning 102
Two Kinds of Knowing 103
Outdated, Rigidified, and Tragic Stories 105
Narrative Therapy 106
Experiencing This Idea 107
Who Is Responsible?108
Implications of These Ideas for the Counselor 109
Tools 110

Externalization 110
Listening in on a Session 111
Reflecting Questions 112
Using This Tool 112
Fantasy and the Hypothetical 112
Pretending Miracles 113
Listening in on a Session 114
Reflecting Questions 114
Using This Tool 114
The Interpersonal Perspective 115
Using This Tool 115
Encouragement Versus Praise 115
Compliments, Praise, and Encouragement 116
Using These Tools 117
When a Client Focuses Positively (The Encouragement Triad) 117
Using These Tools 118
Finding the Pony 118
Listening in on a Session 119
Reflecting Questions 120
Using This Tool 120
Segue to Chapter 7 120

CHAPTER 7 Managing the Client's Emotional Arousal: Hot-Wiring **121**
Chapter Goals 121

Story of Carla 121

Story of Bob 122

Reflecting Questions 123

Chapter Overview 123

Ideas   124

   Emotions and Thought   124
   A New View of Emotions   124
   The Case of H.M.   126
   Attaching Emotions to Success   127
   Experiencing This Idea   128
   Positive and Negative Affect   128
   Reverse Empathy   129
   Emotional Arousal and the Yerkes–Dodson Law   130
   Implications of These Ideas for the Counselor   132

Tools   133

   Managing Emotional Arousal   133
   A Reminder about Acknowleging Feelings   133
   Lowering Emotional Arousal   134
   Assessing the Client's Level of Arousal   134
   Listening in on a Session   135
   Reflecting Questions   136
   Using This Tool   136
   Stress-Reduction Techniques   136
   Raising Emotional Arousal   137
   Memory of an Emotion versus Emotional Memory   137
   Inherent Arousal in the Counseling Situation   138
   Evocations and Explications   139
   Evoking Emotional Arousal   140
   Listening in on a Session   141
   Reflecting Questions   142
   Using This Tool   142

Segue to Chapter 8   142

CHAPTER 8   **Using Mystifying Techniques: Turning Stumbling Blocks
into Stepping Stones**   **143**

Chapter Goals   143

Story   143

Reflecting Questions   145

Overview   146

Ideas   146

   The Transderivational Search   146
   The Common Everyday Trance   147
   Experiencing This Idea   148
   Mystification   148
   The Zeigarnik Effect   149
   Experiencing This Idea   150
   Longing as "Unfinished Business"   150
   Enchantment and Moments of Inspiration   152
   Implications of These Ideas for the Counselor   153

Tools   153

Delivering the Reframe   153
Using This Tool   155
Constructing an Enchanting Metaphor   155
Metaphors with "Dramatic Hold"   156
Listening in on a Session   157
Reflecting Questions   159
Get It in Writing   159
Using This Tool   160
A Protocol for a Follow-up Letter   160
Listening in on a Session   161
Using This Tool   162
A Letter from an Exotic Audience   162

Segue to Chapter 9   163

CHAPTER 9   **Chaos and Complexity in Counseling: Butterflies and Loaded Dice**   **164**

Chapter Goals   164

Story   164

The Counselor Who Cured Childhood Psychosis with a Baseball   164
Reflecting Questions   165

Overview   165

Ideas   166

Chaos and Order in Counseling   166
Chaos and Complexity   167
A Little More Chaos   168
Complex Adaptive Systems   169
The Emergence of Something New   169
Implications of These Ideas for the Counselor   170

Tools   170

Techniques for "Butterfly" Perturbations   170
Confusion   171
Deautomatization and Reorganization   172
Experiencing the Following Idea   173
Ambiguous Function Assignments   173
Listening in on Several Sessions   174
Reflecting Questions   175
Paradox as Confusion   176
Therapeutic Paradox   176
Prescribing the Symptom   179
Using This Tool   180
A Caveat on the Use of Paradox   180
Using This Tool   181

Story   181

Segue to Chapter 10   183

CHAPTER 10   The Reflecting Team, Consulting Break, and Offering Suggestions   **184**
Chapter Goals   184

Story   184

Reflecting Questions   186
Overview   186

Ideas   186

The Reflecting Team   186
The Consulting Break   188
The Suggestion   189
Experiencing This Idea   190
Symptom Substitution?   190
Advice Versus Suggestions   191
Implications of These Ideas for the Counselor   192
Tools   193

Successful Reflecting   193
Listening in on a Session   194
Reflecting Questions   195
Using This Tool   195
Task Assignment   195
Delivering Suggestions   196
The TFA Matrix   197
Delivering the Suggestion–A Protocol   199
Listening in on a Session   200
Reflecting Questions   200
How to Select Suggestions after the Break   200
A Task Construction Paradigm   203
Listening in on a Session   203
Reflecting Questions   205
Using These Tools   205
Segue to Chapter 11   205

CHAPTER 11   The "Brief Attitudes," the Second Session, and Beyond   **206**
Chapter Goals   206

Story   206

Reflecting Questions   206
Overview   207

Ideas   207

Brief Ideas and the "Brief Attitude"   207
Change is Inevitable   208
Small Change Leads to Big Change   208
Clients Don't "Resist"   208
Clients Have All They Need to Resolve Concerns   208
Meaning is Co-constructed   208

Actions and Descriptions are Recursive 208
If It Works, Don't Fix It 208
Stuck? Do Something Different 208
Keep it Simple 209
Approach Each Session As If It Were the Last 209
There Is No Failure, Only Feedback 209
Don't Go "Sightseeing" 209
Your Client Determines the Goal 209
Slow Pitching 209
Label Jars, Not People 209
Listen for Client Intrigue 209
Custom Design Interventions 210
Teleology, Not Etiology 210
Use What Is Already Being Done 210
Work with the Client's World 210
Watch Your Language 210
Go for the Goal 210
Major Life Concerns Are Never Solved 210
Communication Is in Context 211
Systems Have Rules 211
People Punctuate Reality 211
"Problems" Are Maintained 211
Like Painting, Brief Counseling Requires Detail Work 211
Client's Metaphors Are Bridges 211
Clients Have Tried Solving Their Concerns 212
All Client Behaviors Make Sense 212
All Counseling is Collaborative 212
Create a Difference That Makes a Difference 212
Be Positive, Resolution-Focused, and Future-Oriented 212
Exceptions Are Clues 212
Experiencing These Ideas 213
Reflecting Questions 213
Implications of These Ideas for Counselors 213
Tools 213

What Next? 213
Consolidating Change 214
Notice Small Changes 215
Listening in on a Session 216
Reflecting Questions 217
Using Client Feedback as Clues 217
When Should You Stop? 218
Termination and "Flight into Health" 218
Dealing with Client Misgivings 219
Keeping Changes Going 220
Making Saying Goodbye Work 221
Segue to Chapter 12 223

CHAPTER 12 Dealing with Involuntaries and Revisiting the First Session   **224**

Chapter Goals   224

Story   224

    Reflecting Questions   225

Overview   225

Ideas   225

    Who's the Client?   225
    Cooperating with Both Primary and Referring Clients   227
    What Does an Involuntary Client Want?   228
    The "Client–Therapist–Goal Relationship"   228
    What If the Involuntary Client Remains Involuntary?   230
    Listening in on a Session   230
    Act II   231
    Act III   231
    Act IV   231
    Act V   232
    Reflecting Questions   232
    Implications of These Ideas for the Counselor   233

Tools: The Flow of the First Session   233

    1. Starting Out   233
    Using This Tool   234
    2. Acknowledging   235
    Using This Tool   235
    3. Offering Carl Rogers with a Twist (O'Hanlon, 1995)   235
    Using This Tool   236
    4. Deconstructing Complaints   236
    Using This Tool   237
    5. Using Metaphors   237
    Using This Tool   237
    6. Waiting to Be Invited   237
    Using This Tool   237
    7. Seeking Goals   237
    Using This Tool   238
    8. Using Hypotheticals   238
    Using This Tool   238
    9. Scaling   238
    Using This Tool   239
    10. Looking for Exceptions   238
    Using This Tool   239
    11. Asking for Other Views   239
    Using This Tool   240
    12. Asking the "Miracle Question"   240
    Using This Tool   240
    13. Externalizing the Problem   240
    Using This Tool   241

14. *Finding the Pony* 241
Using This Tool 241
15. *Offering Encouragement* 241
Using This Tool 242
16. *Taking The Break* 242
Using This Tool 242
17. *Analyzing Your Relationship* 242
Using This Tool 243
18. *Deciding on a Task Type* 243
Using This Tool 244
19. *Doing a "Preflight" Test and Offering a Suggestion* 244
Using This Tool 245
Continuing to Use These Tools 245
A Final Review 245
Segue to Your Own Next Chapter 246

REFERENCES **247**

INDEX **255**

CHAPTER 1

History of Brief Counseling: The Fly Bottle

[My aim] "is to show the fly the way out of the fly bottle."
Ludwig Wittgenstein

CHAPTER GOALS

Reading about and experiencing the ideas in this chapter will help you to understand the following concepts:

- Counselors who understand theory are likely to be more flexible, creative, and effective in their use of techniques.
- The history of brief counseling has involved the collaboration of many original thinkers and resourceful therapists.
- Actively using the tools in this book will help you to gain a greater experiential understanding of the concepts and to develop skills in doing brief therapy.

STORY

In this book, we want to underscore the place of narrative in successful brief therapy. We see our task with clients as one of helping them to find their voices and tell their stories in ways that lead to healing, growing, and achieving goals. In keeping with this emphasis on narrative, we have decided to tell the story of this book's creation.

Like most stories, this one begins with some foreshadowing of things to come. As therapists and counselor educators, we had grappled with the challenges and frustrations of managed care, heard the many calls for brief interventions, and felt tempted by the appeal of promising new therapeutic approaches. We also were intrigued by the possibility that the counseling profession was on the verge of a major paradigm shift. At the same time, we had serious doubts and concerns. Over the years, we had developed a healthy skepticism about the therapeutic fads that pop up far too frequently in the counseling field. After observing this cycle—initially unrealistic promises, rumblings of misgivings, disappointing findings, and ultimately discarding—take place time and time again, we assumed that if the claims for a counseling technique sounded too good to be true, they probably were. In addition to these doubts, we also had concerns that these techniques might sabotage the counselor's ability to be authentic, warm, and accepting—the foundation, as we saw it, of any effective counseling. To us, many of the brief therapy strategies smacked of manipulation and seemed almost Machiavellian in their emphasis on maneuvering clients and orchestrating change. Nevertheless, in spite of our strong ambivalence, we decided to pursue our interest in brief counseling.

Early in our investigation, we attended a workshop on solution-focused brief therapy. We became quite excited by this way of working with clients, and we asked the workshop presenter about the theory behind the techniques she was presenting. Her reply was startling, "We don't care how this works. We just know that it does." As we discussed her answer among ourselves, we came to the humbling realization that our own behaviors reflected a similarly cavalier attitude regarding theory. We became troubled by our sense of sloppy thinking as we had continued to add techniques without considering their implications on our fundamental assumptions about people and change. We began looking for ideas that could inspire and inform our tools, rather than tools that would mold our ideas or, worse yet, muddy our thinking.

As we reflected on how the counseling and psychotherapy profession had changed over the years, we recalled reading *On Becoming a Person* (Rogers, 1961) and *Client-Centered Therapy* (Rogers, 1965) in graduate school. At the time, we wondered how we would ever learn to be the kind of therapist Carl Rogers described and seemed to personify. We were fortunate that many of our mentors, professors, and supervisors were skilled therapists, but their expertise seemed beyond our reach. They appeared to be guided by an inner peace or set of principles that allowed them to be approachable and nonpretentious. Even though they often ventured into new and threatening territory, they had an air of confidence—even serenity—about themselves as they engaged with clients by caring and not giving answers. They had a way of being intensely interested in people, tuning into the rich themes of their stories, and communicating a profound faith in the ability of clients to change, grow, and heal. They were patient and accepting and did not feel compelled to comment just to fill the silence. When they did talk, almost everything sounded profound. We listened, learned, and discovered, in our encounters with them, that we actually knew more than we thought we knew about the therapeutic process.

Decades after our own graduate training, we found ourselves in another period of doubt, turmoil, confusion, and self-examination with regard to our identities as practitioners and trainers. Will we be able to use—and teach—brief techniques and still be true to ourselves? Are those lessons about the importance of the relationship, core dimensions, and common factors in therapy that we learned years ago still valuable to counseling trainees of today?

After months of reading the philosophical and counseling literature, thinking about these concepts, talking—and arguing!—with one another, counseling clients, and training counselors, we agree that our answer is an enthusiastic "Yes!" Our hope is that reading this book will enlighten, assist, and encourage as much change for you as writing it did for us.

Reflecting Questions

1. What are your own reactions to our story?
2. How does our initial ambivalence regarding the idea of brief therapy compare with your reaction?
3. At this time, what is your vision of yourself in the future as a brief therapist?

OVERVIEW

An Era of Change

It is now a cliche to say that we are living in an era of change, but this axiom is especially true for those of us who are in the business of change. Counselors, psychotherapists, and other change agents are abandoning once popular theoretical stances, moving out of their offices to work in new settings, reaching out to new populations, and addressing new challenges and concerns. Third-party sources of revenue are seeking quicker results and greater accountability from counselors. And clients are becoming more sophisticated consumers of mental health services, demanding greater quality of care from their counselors and psychotherapists.

The so-called postmodern era is also upon us. It appears that no area of human endeavor has been left untouched by this emerging paradigm. The arts, the natural sciences, and the social sciences are questioning their fundamental assumptions regarding the nature of reality, the impact of culture and technology, the essence of our humanity, and the meaning of our lives. While some would say that we have lost our way, others rejoice that we now find ourselves in a time when we can redefine what it means to be human.

Many practitioners in the helping professions are beginning to question the old notions of the mechanistic and medical models that treat clients as defective machines or as pathological protoplasm. Instead, they are now attempting to understand the process of change itself and trying to find ways in which to tap the natural resources of those we are attempting to help. Paradoxically, older humanistic notions of human potential and growth are being vindicated by postmodern notions and new approaches to helping. Simply put, today's interveners are reinventing intervention. Instead of engaging in the traditionally intensive process of long-term psychotherapy, counselors are increasingly involved in the "minimalist" and "just in time" process of brief therapy. Their efforts are aimed at reinforcing the client's strengths and resources, rather than remediating the client's problems and dysfunctions.

Our Goals

Throughout this book we emphasize the fundamental centrality of goals in all effective interventions; therefore, we want to begin with a statement of our own goals. First, we wanted to create a book that is well grounded in theory. Many books on brief therapy emphasize the practice of techniques without a serious consideration of the ideas, concepts, and philosophical assumptions that offer a foundation and a meaningful framework for these strategies. Of course, we want intervention strategies that are useful and effective, but these techniques ultimately must be based on a supporting theory if our interventions are to make any sense to us. Our aim is to strike a balance between theory and technique by providing a rationale for the various interventions and by offering you opportunities to experience these ideas through activities and practice. It is our belief that theory without application is only a meaningless light show and that technique without a guiding theory is merely a shot in the dark.

Our second goal was to produce a book that is truly integrative. While some other books on brief approaches emphasize their differences from traditional counseling and therapy, we wanted a book that offers a bridge between the past and the future. The postmodern era challenges us to reconsider our beliefs and to do something different from

what we have done before. It does not require, however, that we abandon the rich discoveries counselors and therapists have made during the profession's first century.

IDEAS

A Rationale for Theory

> "I came to theory because I was hurting."
> *bell hooks*

Steve de Shazer (1991) has maintained that precisely how the therapy works is something we cannot know. "One can only know that it does work. . . . Make up your own
explanation; it is as good or better than mine" (pp. xvii–xviii). At de Shazer's invitation,
we shall attempt in this book to delve more deeply into an explanation that will place
this type of work in a theoretical context and that will explain why the techniques appear to be effective.

While a technician without a theory is groping in the dark, it is also true that one
should not let grand theories become the driving force in their work with clients. It is
most important to remain open to what is happening in your relationship with a client,
whether it fits the theory or not. As Bill O'Hanlon (1995) has said, "It's O.K. to have a
theory, so long as the theory doesn't have you."

Many members of the counseling profession—students, practitioners, and educators—seem to place little value in theory. When you enter a professional counselor's office, you will likely find plenty of books about counseling techniques, professional issues, and client problems, but rarely more than a couple of books on
theory. When you attend a professional counseling conference, you will notice that
the program also reflects this bias. The program is packed with presentations and
workshops on counseling strategies, practice concerns, and policy issues. However,
it is rare to find a session that deals only with ideas, concepts, or theories. You may
see yourself as sharing this attitude. After all, you are studying this field because you
want to do *counseling,* not *theorizing.* Like someone who "fast-forwards" a videotape
to "the good parts" of a movie, you may find yourself skipping the theory portion of
a book to find "the good stuff"—the actual counseling techniques. Or, you may consider the act of reading a theory section to be so tedious that you endure it only in
the hope that eventually there will be some payoff for your pains, in the form of a
powerful counseling method.

Our experience as counselors has taught us two fundamental lessons that run
counter to this prevailing attitude about the place of theory in our therapeutic work. The
first is that we are all theorists; the second is that there is no fundamental gap between
theory and action. As Immanuel Kant (in Kolb, 1984) put it: "Thoughts without content are empty; intuitions without concepts are blind" (p. 106).

You will find a lot of theory in this book. We make this statement not as a warning,
but as an invitation, because we truly believe that the theory offers you new and exciting ideas, with important implications for counseling. This theory explains the changing view of how things in the world function and how change itself takes place. Our science and art are entering a new paradigm, which calls for innovation and fresh view of

the world. It is our hope that as you gain a better understanding of the ideas that are behind the tools of brief counseling, you not only will know why you do what you do, but
also know how to decide what to do next. In other words, engaging in theory helps you
in your counseling—and engaging in counseling helps you in your theory.

"A Rose By Any Other Name . . ."

Practitioners in the field of counseling and psychotherapy today find themselves sur-
rounded by a dizzying array of new approaches to helping clients with their personal
concerns. A virtual explosion of new counseling methods in the past two decades has
filled the literature with titles such as: Competency-Based Future-Oriented Therapy
(Hoyt, 1994), Constructivist Therapy (Neimeyer & Mahoney, 1995; Prochaska &
Norcross, 1999), The Miracle Method (Berg & Miller, 1992), Narrative Therapy
(White & Epston, 1990), Post-Modern Therapy (Mahoney, 1995), Possibility Therapy
(O'Hanlon & Beadle, 1994), Solution-Building Therapy (DeJong & Berg, 1998), So-
lution-Focused Therapy (de Shazer, 1985, 1988), Solution-Oriented Therapy
(O'Hanlon & Weiner-Davis, 1989; Weiner-Davis, 1993), and Time-Effective Therapy
(Friedman, 1997).

These approaches are all related in that they stress the goal of helping clients
change within a limited period of time. In this sense, all these models could be considered to be oriented toward "brief" counseling. In addition, each of these approaches stresses searching for better outcomes in the future, rather than digging up
the problems in the past. This change of emphasis has marked a significant departure
from the orthodoxy that has informed counselors for the past century. This dramatic
turn of emphasis appears to have begun with the work of Steve de Shazer and his colleagues at the Milwaukee Brief Family Therapy Center (BFTC). Most of the new
counseling approaches mentioned above have borrowed liberally from de Shazer's
ideas, which had, in turn, evolved out of the ideas developed by the people at the
Mental Research Institute (MRI).

Sir Isaac Newton stated, with uncharacteristic humility about his discoveries, that
he had merely stood on the shoulders of giants. The truth in that statement is that no
ideas arrive *ex nihilo* (out of nothing). Like a group of good friends, in developing theory and practicing science, everybody borrows from everybody else. However, when dramatically new discoveries are made, they usually represent a surprising turn on former
ways of thinking. The people at BFTC began with the ideas of Gregory Bateson and
Milton Erickson, as formulated by the people at the MRI in Palo Alto, and pragmatically
arrived at a new way of viewing the counselor–client relationship. Steve de Shazer
(1982) offered a statement reminiscent of Newton's as he addressed the issue of owner-
ship of the ideas contained in what later became known as solution-focused brief therapy (SFBT): "If new ideas can be *owned* . . . then this [BFTC] group is the collective
owner of the ideas. I, the author, am but a technician, a voice of the chorus" (p. ix).

The above remarks were written just prior to the formal establishment of SFBT as
a counseling approach. Since that time, many writers have elaborated, added to, and
sought to place their own stamp on the SFBT model. Noting this, de Shazer (personal
communication, 1998) cautioned that some of the ideas claiming to be based on SFBT
were becoming a bit unorthodox. In fact, while the original notions that de Shazer and

the Milwaukee group established remain foundational, the field is continuing to evolve.

The authors of this book acknowledge Steve de Shazer and his colleagues as the originators of this particular way of viewing counseling relationships. However, with so many other contributions to this literature, it is difficult to refer to these collective approaches as a coherent body of knowledge. Instead of collecting and presenting a hodge-podge of brief counseling techniques without any theoretical framework, our aim in this book is to synthesize these ideas into the conceptual themes that, like grand musical themes, have inspired so many variations. One of these fundamental theoretical themes in the brief therapy literature is that of the centrality of *resolution* in any significant change. The concept of resolution reflects the emphasis on encouraging a *sense of resolve* by helping clients to recognize the personal strengths and resources that they bring to the current situation. When people can gain the resolve necessary to face their difficulties with determination and hope, the problems can be transformed into challenges. Resolute people realize that life is never free of adversity, but they are also confident that they possess the resources necessary to deal with whatever comes.

At the beginning of this introduction, we noted that the philosopher Ludwig Wittgenstein once said that his aim in doing philosophy was to show the fly the way out of the fly bottle. In Vienna, where Wittgenstein lived, people trapped flies by putting some honey in a vinegar bottle. The fly would smell the honey, crawl into the bottle, and either remain stuck in the honey, or fly in circles until it buzzed to death. "To 'show the fly the way out of the fly bottle' was not to *solve* . . . problems, but to *dissolve* them" (Palmer, 1994, pp. 329–330).

The concept of resolution also reflects the focus of brief therapies on helping clients in achieving a better outcome—a *positive resolution*—in the future. Although the term *solution* has been most commonly used in the literature to describe the better outcome that is the focus of brief therapy, we see resolution as being a more comprehensive theme. The counselor's goal is to help clients toward resolution of the fundamental issues they face in life—not merely to find solutions to their problems. As Gilligan (1997) put it, you can assume that a client is "stuck in a narrow understanding of, or limited connection to, his or her potentiality. Identifying resources and activating them are seen as central to helping the client" (p. 6).

When you come together with clients, you have certain options as to how you will view them. You could, for example, see them as defective, ignorant, or ill. Many traditional psychotherapies adopt these views. The counseling ideas and tools described in this book are founded on the assumption that people are inherently healthy and that they are capable of dissolving their own "stuckness." Instead of viewing problems as merely fundamental flaws in their character or biology, you can view their problems metaphorically as being stuck in the fly bottle. The events and circumstances leading your clients to this fly bottle may have been unavoidable and even traumatic. However, their current sense of hopelessness and stagnation is a fly bottle that they themselves have constructed. If the constraints of the bottle are removed, their concerns will dissolve. You do not need to fix their wings or teach them how to fly. If you can help them find their way out of their entanglement, they will fly free on their own—and achieve resolution.

A Brief History of Brief Counseling

In order to understand how the ideas and tools contained in this book have evolved, we will trace for you the roots of the brief-resolution counseling movement. This is by no means meant to be an exhaustive history, but in the spirit of being brief, we wanted to give you the high points that have brought us to today. Since the end of World War II, there have been significant changes in thinking about pathology versus health, catharsis versus encouragement, problems versus resolutions, and looking toward the future versus digging into the past. Some of these newer notions may, at first, seem counterintuitive to you and difficult to accept, while others will appear to be just good common sense.

The Cybernetics Connection. In 1948, Norbert Wiener coined the term *cybernetics,* which he took from the Greek *kybernetes,* meaning steersman. A cybernetic system involves a purposeful, self-organizing entity that is heading toward a goal. While people have often been characterized in psychology as simply passive reactors to their environment, the idea of purpose and goal-directedness began to cast human striving as teleological—working toward a desired state. The central idea of cybernetics is the feedback loop, "by which a system gets the information necessary to self-correct in its effort to maintain a steady state or to move toward a preprogrammed goal" (Nichols & Schwartz, 1991, p. 106).

People can be thought of as cybernetic entities who seek to transcend their current situation and achieve future goals, while, at the same time, they seek to preserve themselves in a steady state. The concept of "resistance" is sometimes viewed as a person's tendency to maintain a steady—or homeostatic—state. For therapists who view resistance in this way, a great deal of time is spent interpreting reasons for such "blocks" to progress in therapy.

As brief-resolution counselors, we are most interested in finding out how people change their current state and move toward goals. We are change agents who seek to help people move from unproductive homeostatic patterns of thought and behavior to new, emergent patterns that will enhance their lives. The notion drawn from cybernetics is that certain kinds of feedback will provide the information necessary to change the unproductive system. This means that the system must be "perturbed" so that static patterns can be broken up, allowing the change to take place. As Haley (1973) put it, "To change a stabilized, miserable situation and create space for individual growth . . . therapists often must induce a crisis which creates instability" (p. 18). To purposely make a system unstable seems counterintuitive to most people because of our implicit belief in the notion of entropy—that a destabilized system will fall apart. But people are not mechanistic systems. They are self-organizing, and we can trust that with the right amount of perturbation they will destabilize, but then reorganize—and something new will emerge.

Gregory Bateson: Founding Father. Gregory Bateson was enthralled with the cybernetics idea and began to translate the concepts of engineering and mathematics into the language of the behavioral sciences (Becvar and Becvar, 1993). He was invited in 1949 by psychiatrist Jurgen Reusch to join in a study of human communication in psychotherapy. Before that, Bateson had not been especially attracted to psychotherapy, having already achieved fame as a cultural anthropologist along with his former wife, Margaret Mead. But he, together with Reusch, became interested in the difference that context makes in the interpretation of a communication. For example, Reusch (in Lipset, 1980) posed the following question: Imagine a man is peeing in the woods and he thinks no one can see him. The man does not intend to send a message by his urination. But this act would have a somewhat different meaning if someone were watching him, even if he does not know it. The meaning would be further changed if the man knew he was being watched. Finally, "what sort of message is it, in the case of mutual knowledge, when both the actor and the observer know of each other's presence?" (p. 187).

On the face of it, this does not appear to be very exalted wonderment, but the idea that messages are changed by their context was to become a major influence in the field of brief and narrative therapy. Bateson interviewed many psychiatrists in order to understand the communication processes that took place in a psychotherapy session, but he found their explanations to be filled with jargon and abstruse ideas. So Bateson turned to the work of Norbert Wiener and attempted to bring psychoanalytic processes under the heading of cybernetics.

In 1952, Bateson received a large grant to study communication. He needed good researchers to help carry out the project. The first person he hired was John H. Weakland, who was one of his former students. The next person was Jay Haley, then a graduate student at Stanford studying fictional films. Haley recalled, "I went over to talk to Gregory about it, to get an advisor. We had a big argument and he hired me on the project" (Lipset, 1980, p. 200). Later, Bateson hired Don Jackson to serve as psychiatric consultant on the project. Jackson was a psychiatrist of a different stripe, having studied under Harry Stack Sullivan, who introduced him to the idea that all mental disturbances were relational in nature (Teyber, 1997).

Early on, these researchers were concentrating their efforts on the paradoxes that arise in communication. Their investigations were rather wide-ranging. For example, they studied the communication involved in the training of guide dogs for the blind, messages exchanged between a ventriloquist and his dummy, communication in films, and the communication patterns of otters. The most fruitful of all their projects began when Weakland and Haley decided to study the hypnotic therapeutic techniques of Milton H. Erickson. The interest in hypnosis came from Bateson and Mead's studies of trance behavior in Bali.

In 1956, the group published a paper on the effect of what they called the "double-bind" communication on schizophrenia (Bateson, Jackson, Haley, & Weakland, 1956). Assuming that communication has many levels, they believed that inconsistency in these levels created confusion in all of us, but especially in people with schizophrenia. The double-bind theory of schizophrenia since then has been largely disputed, but all people seem to relate to the idea that if verbal communication does not match its nonverbal accompaniment, the listener can become vexed.

After the double-bind paper was published, the Bateson group devoted nearly all its efforts to the study of family communication and psychotherapy. At about the same time, Don Jackson began to establish an institute in Palo Alto. It became known as the Mental Research Institute (MRI), and it attracted a number of interested participants, including Virginia Satir and Paul Watzlawick. Weakland and Haley acknowledged their indebtedness to Bateson as their "teacher and guide," but they also drifted away from his research program and into the MRI.

The MRI Influence. In 1967, Watzlawick, Beavin, and Jackson published *Pragmatics of Human Communication*. In this seminal work, they analyzed human communication and laid the groundwork for subsequent theorizing in brief therapy. Also, during that same year, the Brief Therapy Center was opened at MRI when Paul Watzlawick joined Arthur Bodin, Richard Fisch, and John Weakland in the investigation of communication patterns in human relationships (Weakland & Fisch, 1992). Weakland and Jay Haley jointly initiated visits to Phoenix to discuss hypnosis with Milton Erickson. Fisch was trained as a psychiatrist in the Sullivanian, rather than the Freudian, tradition. He later took some training at MRI and found himself influenced by their approach. He was especially attracted to the ideas of Jay Haley. When he learned that Haley had gotten his inspiration from Erickson, Fisch attended a couple of workshops with Erickson.

The most significant work performed at MRI, which has also been called the "Palo Alto Group," was the emphasis on communication and change in psychotherapy, which was distinctly different from the personality and pathology emphasis in the prevailing psychiatric and psychological communities. The question they asked was not about etiology—the historical cause of the client's problem—but, rather, what elements of human communication contribute to change. Then, in 1974, Watzlawick, Weakland, and Fisch published *Change: Principles of Problem Formulation and Problem Resolution*. In this volume, they drew on the principles outlined in *Pragmatics* and offered a model for brief therapy based on their view of how specific types of communication can be employed to interrupt problem patterns. Rather than search for *causes* of dysfunctional communication patterns, the MRI group thought it more productive to understand what might be *maintaining* the problem and to, somehow, interrupt it. The idea of defining problems in detail turned out to elicit "problem-saturated talk" from the client and focused undue emphasis on the complaint. Since investigating the layers of the problem serves only to reinforce such thinking in the client, it was decided to minimize this aspect of the work.

Earlier, Haley (1973) had stated that psychotherapy should be "strategic." Counselors must be intentional in their approach and attempt to design a situation in which solvable problems are identified and definite goals are stated.

> Strategic therapy is not a particular approach or theory but a name for those types of therapy where the therapist takes responsibility for directly influencing people. (p. 17)

In this passage, Haley displayed the influence of cybernetics on his thinking: that therapy should be purposeful and directed toward a goal, making corrections according to whether the therapy is on course. A strategic approach would keep the goal in mind and do what was necessary to arrive at that goal.

Milton Erickson: The Practical Therapist. Milton Erickson was born in a small mining town in Nevada. He was still a young child when the mine went broke, and his family traveled east to a Wisconsin farm in a covered wagon (Haley & Richeport, 1993). During his elementary-school education, he appeared to be dyslexic. To overcome this, he taught himself strategies for recognizing letters: for example, he learned to differentiate an "m" from a "3" by imagining a horse grazing for "m" and a horse rearing up as a "3." This was apparently the beginning of the "utilization" technique that would later distinguish his therapy.

In his teens, Milton contracted polio, which left him paralyzed from the neck down. Later, when he had recovered the use of the upper part of his body, he embarked alone on a thousand-mile canoe trip with only a few dollars in his pocket. At the beginning of the journey, he could neither walk nor carry his canoe. On his return, he could swim a mile and he could walk. Perhaps this experience, more than any other, shaped his belief that one cannot dwell on the past or on what doesn't work, but, rather, must find a way to overcome difficulties through ordeal. This became the guiding philosophy of his therapy.

While Erickson achieved a certain level of fame as a medical hypnotist in his psychiatric practice (he was the founder of the American Society of Clinical Hypnosis), his true legacy was established late in life, after he moved to Arizona because of his allergies. He set up a private practice in his tiny home in Phoenix. A recurrence of his polio symptoms left him in a wheelchair during these latter years, and he dealt with his great pain through autohypnosis.

It was while he was in Arizona that Erickson was first visited by Jay Haley in 1953 (Bloom, 1997). Through many hours of recorded conversations and editing of numerous papers written by Erickson, Haley was able to extract and systematize the major ideas behind the work, which Erickson called "common-sense therapy." After two decades of collaboration with Erickson, Haley established his own approach to therapy. He labeled Erickson's therapy as "Uncommon" (Haley, 1973), and his own approach as "Strategic." Haley interested many other therapists in Erickson's way of working. Regular pilgrimages to Erickson's small home in Phoenix were made by a number of ambassadors from MRI, and Erickson's ideas, which seemed to dovetail nicely with Gregory Bateson's, became the foundation for modern brief therapy. Fisch (1982) described some of the important contributions made by Erickson. For example, when starting a session with a client, Erickson would not ask for a lengthy history or encourage the client to express feelings. He refrained from interpreting a client's resistance and actually used the resistance to the client's benefit. "He simply did not waste time arguing with patients, focusing instead on the task the patient was to perform to resolve his problem" (p. 159).

In the strategic form of therapy, which Haley derived from Erickson's work, "the main therapeutic tool is the directive, which is to strategic therapy what the interpretation is to psychoanalysis" (Madanes, 1990, p. 18). Bloom (1997) identified two types of directives: voluntary and involuntary. In the first, clients are asked to do something that is under their control, such as sit down, look at a certain spot, or concentrate on a certain image or idea. In the latter, they are asked to do something seemingly outside their control. They are asked to feel better, free associate, see something that isn't there, or not see something that is. Obviously, the apparent absurdity of the involuntary form of directive will bring about a certain resistance on the part of the client. Erickson often dealt with such resistance by cooperating with it, by using it as part of the therapy. For example, if Erickson sensed that a client wished to withhold information from him, he might direct the person to be sure to not tell him everything. If he sensed that a certain directive might not be readily accepted by the client, he would suggest that they might find themselves wishing to engage in another (therapeutic) behavior instead. He might, on occasion, encourage a relapse when he felt the client was resisting through a "flight into health," and he might say that it would be good for the client to have a recurrence of symptoms, because it would not be good to improve too rapidly. "I want you to go back and feel as badly as you did when you first came . . . [and tell me if] . . . there is anything from that time that you wish to recover and salvage" (Haley, 1973, p. 31).

"Erickson's First Law," as de Shazer (1982) called it, was: "As long as they are going to resist, you ought to encourage them to resist" (pp. 10–11). Whether giving direct instructions to a client, or seemingly capitulating to the client's resistance, Erickson seemed to maintain his control of the client's behavior. While this may seem devious and manipulative, keep in mind that Erickson's only motive for such behaviors was to influence the client to change for the better.

Seeing the impact of Erickson's influential techniques on clients, Haley conducted extensive studies into the nature of influence. In his 1969 book *The Power Tactics of Jesus Christ,* Haley stated that the most obvious way of displaying power over someone is to order that person to do something. But there is also a great deal of power in being passive. "One man can order others to lift and carry him, while another might achieve the same end by collapsing" (p. 36).

Milton Erickson's contributions, drawn from his trance work, together with his life-long attitude of looking for possibilities rather than pathologies, have had a significant impact on the field of brief therapy. Erickson died in 1980, about the time when his ideas were beginning to take hold, but his influence can be seen in the adoption of his beliefs and intervention techniques by the brief therapy movement.

The Evolution of the Brief Therapy Center. John Weakland died in 1995, but research into communication and therapeutic techniques at the Brief Therapy Center (BTC) is ongoing and productive (Fisch & Schlanger, 1999). Despite some changes in their approach resulting from careful scrutiny of their many cases, the "Brief" model continues to focus on each client's problem. This focus is due to the belief that the client's attempted solutions to the stated problem become part of the problem itself, and therefore the heart of the work. "Thus, the thrust of the therapy is not to get the complainants to *do* something so much as to *stop* what they have been doing about the problem" (p. 2, emphasis in original).

Problem-identification was seen as the crucial first step in helping clients overcome their difficulties, to the point at which therapy was impossible without a clear problem definition. Some cases at the Brief Therapy Center were terminated when therapists were unable to determine precisely what the client's problem was. Fisch and Schlanger (1999) concluded, "Thus, we did not get to the point of eliciting the client's attempts to deal with whatever the problem was and to intervene in that attempt (p. 147).

As you will see in the next section, Steve de Shazer, while originally attracted to the BTC approach, later decided to bypass the problem-identification phase and to focus instead on solutions. This would prove to be a profound change in the method of working with clients briefly.

One major modification made by Fisch and his group at the BTC over the years was to spend more time carefully listening to clients. Fisch and Schlanger (1999) stated that some of their cases had not turned out well because of "our jumping too quickly into suggesting some action to clients . . . and our not recognizing or eliciting clients' position or frame of reference regarding their problem" (pp. 147–148). They now believe that it is important to carefully acknowledge clients' feelings, because otherwise it would be difficult to gain compliance. In a later chapter, we will discuss this point in greater detail. For now, we would like to focus on how to find solutions in problems.

Steve de Shazer: The Shift from Problem to Solution. Steve de Shazer and his colleagues began to develop the solution-focused approach to therapy as a promising method for brief marriage and family therapy (Bloom, 1997). de Shazer described his therapeutic lineage as proceeding directly from the work of Erickson, Haley, Bateson, Watzlawick, and others of the MRI. While living in the Palo Alto area, de Shazer became a close friend of John Weakland and, as a result of their many discussions, was influenced by the brief therapy approach of the MRI group (de Shazer, personal communication, 1998). According to Weakland and Fisch (1992), de Shazer was associated with the people at MRI from 1972, when he took a workshop, there. The difference between the MRI approach and the ideas later developed by de Shazer was the approach to solutions. "[Weakland and Fisch] focus on attempted solutions that do not work and maintain the problem, but with some attention to noting and promoting actions that have worked; de Shazer . . . has the inverse emphasis" (p. 317).

Later, working with a small group of creative family therapists, de Shazer helped to found the Brief Family Therapy Center (BFTC) in Milwaukee, with the idea that the Center would be a place for both service and research into the efficacy of their methods. The Center became a Mecca for young psychotherapists who wished to be trained in nontraditional approaches to therapy.

During the early phases of the BFTC research, the consulting break was developed. The therapist would leave the consulting room and meet with colleagues who had been watching the session from behind a one-way mirror. Ideas contributed by the observers were then brought back to the family by the therapist and discussed. Originally, as is typically done in "live supervision," the observers would simply phone in a suggestion for the therapist to follow. One day, as de Shazer (1982) put it, the barrier between the observers and the therapist–family relationship broke down. The therapist had disagreed with a suggestion and decided to leave the room to speak with the observers. Together, they designed a plan that the therapist brought back to the session. "From this beginning, a 'consulting break' became routine with the group. It was seen as a vast improvement upon the telephone communication system" (p. xi).

The consulting break seemed to have the effect of compressing the therapeutic movement and making the treatment briefer. As this technique was elaborated on, more strategies were added to the "after the break" part of the session, and it was found that certain rituals on the part of the therapist seemed to be effective in moving clients more rapidly to a better place.

It was not until around 1985 that the solution-focused model was first enunciated by de Shazer, with its emphasis on solutions, rather than problems. Today, de Shazer's own work is still in the process of evolution, and it has proliferated into a number of variants with many different names. Hoyt (1994) attempted to capture the essence of the approach by referring to it as "competency-based future-oriented therapy." There is likely to be a continuous evolution of solution-focused brief therapy, and it will be its genotype that endures, no matter what form its phenotype may take.

In rejecting the first premise of the MRI approach—that the problem must be understood in order to be disrupted—de Shazer stated that one does not have to know very much about a problem in order to solve it. Furthermore, he asserted that the solution that solves the problem may not bear much resemblance to the problem itself (de Shazer, 1991). He believed that our time with clients is best spent looking for "exceptions" to the litany of grief. As the counselor attempts to shift the client's narrative from symptom to solution focus, goals must be established for the client's work. According to de Shazer, workable goals must:

- be small,
- be relevant to the client,
- be specific and behavioral,
- be achievable,
- involve the client's "hard work,"
- be the "start of something," and
- involve new behaviors.

The work of the people at BFTC, with their emphasis on solutions rather than problems, has greatly influenced the practice of brief counseling. O'Hanlon and Weiner-Davis (1989) referred to this group of people as "The team that made Milwaukee famous," after an advertising slogan for a brand of beer.

Experiencing This Idea

Have you ever wondered how the computer can scan and make sense out of those universal price codes that are now on every product we buy? To help you learn about solution-focused therapy, we are giving you a problem. You have one minute to find the solution in Figure 1-1.

Success Strategies

Perhaps you were able to find the solution below, but many people are not successful at first and become frustrated with this task. Below are some reminders to help you recall the success strategies that you have used before to deal with similar rid-

FIGURE 1-1　Universal Price Code.

dles and problems. You can read each of the success strategies below and then return to the figure to try it. As you know from your own past experiences, sometimes you can find the solution by using a tactic that is counterintuitive, so we encourage you to try one even if it does not make sense.

"**Rely on Your Strengths.**" Many of your successes in life have been due to taking full advantage of your own competencies, instead of trying to be something that you are not. In dealing with this problem, however, you might first have tried to mimic a computer by counting the dark lines and dots in order to break the binary code or find the algorithm. Instead of acting like a computer, take another minute to rely on your reading skills to find the solution before reading the next paragraph.

"**Look for a Solution by Taking a Different Point of View.**" With the reading strategy, you may have found the solution. However, if you have not yet found it, then you may want to remind yourself that many solutions have appeared to you in the past when you have taken a different perspective. In the case of this problem, you may have assumed that the best way to view the figure is in the way that we have presented it to you. Instead, you may want to rotate the book sideways 90 degrees to the left and see how your perception of the figure changes. After using this additional strategy for another minute, you may want to go on to the next paragraph.

"**Do Something Different.**" In your life, there certainly have been times when you have successfully solved a problem by making a simple change in what you were doing. In this case, you may be looking at the page the way that you look at any typical page— straight ahead, 12 to 18 inches away, and with both eyes open. Instead, to find the solution, you may want to bring the page nearer, close one eye, hold the book sideways, and alter the angle of the page by tilting it slowly until it is lying almost perpendicular to your eye.

"**Seeing the Goal Can Help You Achieve It.**" As you look back on your life, you may have found that one of the best ways to succeed is to clearly see the goal. In the case of this problem, the solution you are seeking is, in fact, the phrase "The Solution." Now that you see the goal, see if you can successfully find "The Solution" in Figure 1-1.

Reflecting Questions

1. What were your first reactions to the problem?
2. What would your reaction be if we had only reflected your feelings or suggested that you talk about other times when you were unable to find a solution?
3. How did you find the solution?

Implications of These Ideas for the Counselor

The ideas of Bateson, Watzlawick, Erickson, Haley, Weakland, and de Shazer (see Figure 1-2) have important implications for your day-to-day work with clients:

- Engaging in theory can help you in your counseling.
- Working toward goals in counseling can improve your effectiveness as a counselor.

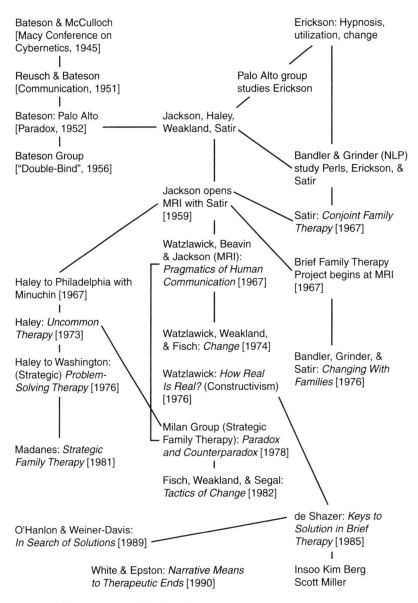

FIGURE 1-2   The Bateson/Erickson legacy.

- Knowing how a client can change is more valuable than knowing how a problem began.
- Encouraging a client to focus on solutions can lead to greater change than prompting a client to concentrate on problems.

Tools

We have designed this book to provide you with plenty of opportunities to become skilled in using the tools of brief therapy. We strongly believe that the format and style of a book should have a working symmetry with the therapeutic approach it presents. Because we emphasize that every intervention should be goal-oriented, we begin each chapter with a statement of the chapter's goals. Because we promote a narrative perspective in counseling, we include in each chapter a story that portrays the concepts. Many books open with a number of chapters that focus entirely on theory and do not deal with practice until the ending chapters. Consistent with our belief that theory and practice are intertwined, all of our chapters include both ideas and tools.

We invite you to engage with us actively as you read our book by doing more than merely underlining sentences or highlighting words. Instead, we encourage you to make the most of this book in the following ways.

Collaborate with Us on this Book. Rather than just reading "Ideas and Tools for Brief Counseling," we would like for you to join us as a coauthor in creating a *personalized* book that is custom-designed for you. For example, you can jot in the margins your reactions to what we say, outline the material in your own way, critically evaluate our arguments, and even pose some of your own reasoning. You may want to keep a journal of your own epiphanies ("aha experiences"), creative observations, personal growth experiences, and possible therapeutic applications. By the time you finish reading this book, it will become a truly collaborative venture that adds an important chapter in your own life narrative.

Get Involved in the Stories. As we said earlier, we find the idea of narrative to be an exciting recent development in counseling theory. In each chapter, we tell stories from our own personal and professional experiences. These are not neat and tidy scenarios with two-dimensional characters who simplistically personify the concepts. Rather than skimming through these stories looking for "the point," we suggest that you read for meaning as you would a short story, poem, or biography. Throughout each chapter, you will be returning to the story in order to gain a deeper understanding of the ideas portrayed in the story and to practice the tools of brief counseling.

Participate in *All* the Activities. There are five types of activities. The first activity that you encountered in this book was the section of "Reflecting Questions" at the end of the story. "Experiencing These Ideas," the second type, provides opportunities to gain a deeper awareness of the concepts. "Listening in on a Session" is the third kind of activity you will find in this book. These boxes provide you with an opportunity to hear brief therapy in action. "Using These Tools," the fourth type, offers chances for you to begin practicing the skills of brief counseling. The final activity you will encounter is on the page at the end of every chapter—a "Segue" or transition activity.

Reflecting Questions

This activity invites you to explore some of your thoughts and reactions regarding the chapter's story and other activities. We realize that it is tempting to answer these questions quickly and then immediately move on to the next section of the chapter. However, we strongly encourage you to write down your reflections. The very act of writing—of putting your observations and reflections into words—can not only help you to articulate your ideas, but can also encourage you to explore the nuances and intricacies of your reactions.

Experiencing This Idea

Each of these sections includes an activity that involves you in using an idea in several possible ways—to gain a richer understanding of the chapter story you read earlier, expand your own self-awareness, or increase your insight into the change process. These activities can help you to really "get" the concept and "burn in" the idea by using it in meaningful ways. For example, earlier in this chapter, we gave you a problem and asked you to find "The Solution." At the start, we tried to mislead you by mentioning computers and universal price codes when we introduced the problem. Then we invited you to recall your own past success experiences and apply those strategies to this problem. This experience has important parallels with that of a client trying to find the solution to a problem. As you can see, we are challenging you to become an active participant in this process.

Listening in on a Session

These activities offer the opportunity for you to hear how a brief counselor can work with the people whose stories you read at the beginning of the chapters. As you read these dialogues, keep in mind that these are not scripts or "magic words" to memorize. Instead, remind yourself that this is *one* counselor's way of using brief therapy strategies with a particular client. Instead of passively reading through the dialogues, we invite you to place your personal mark on them by reviewing the process, reflecting on the dynamics, using your own words, and proposing your own interventions.

Using These Tools

These structured activities for practicing the techniques of brief therapy include designing intervention strategies for the characters you met in the chapter story, applying these approaches to your own experiences, or practicing these techniques with others. For example, in each of the remaining chapters, we ask you to join with two colleagues to form a small practice group. One of you volunteers to be a client seeking counseling to address a particular concern. Another volunteers to serve as the brief counselor who uses the tool presented in the chapter. Finally, the third person serves as the recorder who observes the activity, leads the feedback discussion, and reports the group's experience to other colleagues.

Remember the "wax on" and "wax off" drills from "*The Karate Kid*" movie? Conscientiously doing those drills helped the protagonist to build a foundation for successfully performing martial arts. It is the same for successfully learning brief counseling. There is no better way to gain these skills than through practice. It is only by performing these techniques—again and again—that they can become second nature to you as a brief counselor.

Segue

The purpose of this activity is to get you in the right mood or the appropriate frame of mind for the concepts and techniques that you will be learning in the next chapter. By taking some time to experience these segues, you can gain a sense of the cohesion and interconnectedness of the ideas and tools presented throughout this book.

A Guarantee

There are few guarantees that can be offered in the counseling profession, but we can confidently guarantee that the more active you are in reading this book and participating in these activities, the more knowledge and skills you will gain.

Segue to Chapter 2

Heraclitus, a Greek philosopher, once said, "You cannot step into the same river twice." It is also true that you cannot encounter your same self twice. Waking up this morning, having something to eat, and even reading the previous sentence are now part of your past. In what ways are you different from the person who woke up as you this morning? What has contributed to these changes? Is this amount of change typical in your life?

CHAPTER 2

Facilitating Change: The One Constant

"I think, therefore I am."
Rene Descartes

"I think, therefore I err."
J. E. McKee

"As long as they are going to resist, you ought to encourage them to resist."
Milton Erickson

CHAPTER GOALS

Reading about and experiencing the ideas in this chapter will help you to understand the following concepts:

- Effective interventions are oriented toward the future, focused on achieving resolution, and based on the client's personal agency.
- Change is always happening. As a change agent, you are merely facilitating this change process by helping clients to alter their perceptions, revise their representations, and expand their openness to possibilities.
- Metaphors are not just tools for poets and artists. They offer you ways to understand how clients perceive the world and to respond to clients empathically.

STORY

James's opening line to his counselor was, "I'm basically here because I think of myself as damaged goods." A week ago, when he had finally made the decision to seek counseling, James found himself mentally preparing for what he imagined would go on in the therapist's office. His image of counseling was based on the occasional scenes of therapy he had seen on television and in the movies. He thought it was a narcissistic detective story, a self-centered process of searching for clues from one's own past—for the repressed memory or traumatic incident—that could solve the mystery of a screwed-up psyche and discover the reasons for a person's inappropriate actions. If a mystery is a "whodunit," he thought, maybe counseling is a "why-I-dunit." James had serious reservations about embarking on such an endeavor, but he could no longer tolerate the sense of anguish that dogged him.

Walking into the counseling center's waiting room, a parlor of an older house cluttered with old magazines and mismatched furniture, James recalled an event from his childhood that he hadn't thought about in years. He had spent most of his summers at an old cabin with a front porch that was just as cluttered as this waiting room. The cabin, which had been owned by the family for three generations, was situated on the bank of a small river in the Shenandoah Valley. One hot, sultry day when he was 5 years old, James had chased his cousin into the enclosed front porch, letting the screen door slam behind him—even though he had been reminded countless times to close the door quietly. His startled grandfather, who had been peacefully napping in the porch hammock, growled in exasperation at the boy's forgetfulness, "James Matthew! Let me ask you something, boy. Did you ever fall on your head when you were a baby?"

James had stopped in his tracks, intrigued by this seemingly irrelevant question about his medical history. With a perplexed expression on his face, he had felt his head for any tenderness and swelling, before giving his diagnostic opinion, "I don't think so, Grandpa," and then immediately resumed the chase after his cousin. His grandfather later told the story at the family dinner, to the amusement of the other relatives.

Now, as James waited to begin his counseling, he mentally checked himself for psychological wounds that would indicate trauma. However, looking back on his life, he couldn't lay his finger on any dramatic instance of abuse, threat, or shock. Of course there had been tough times, painful losses, and ongoing hassles. But instead of any sharp specific pain, he felt only a dull, hollow ache as he reflected on the fact that as he neared his 35th birthday, he still felt that he was somehow an intruder on life. He was not sure of his welcome after barging in on the lives of others, and felt he was never able to please the people who meant the most to him.

Contrary to his opening statement in the session, James certainly did not appear damaged to the counselor. James was a well dressed, nicely groomed, and ruggedly handsome man who spoke with a bit more heartiness and self-assurance than required. The counselor was reminded of salespeople and "greeters" in discount stores. At first glance, James's manner, lifestyle, and circumstances seemed to epitomize the American dream. He had a good job managing a local grocery store, a fine family, a comfortable home, and the family cabin by the river for holidays and weekends. However, as the counseling session progressed, his hearty manner grew more forced, as if he were the host of a dinner party, responsible for keeping the mood light and cheerful for all his guests. In spite of James's efforts to appear confident, halfway through the session, he tilted his head slightly in a pensive manner, exhaled with a sudden sigh, and slumped back in his chair like a rag doll cast aside by a disinterested child.

Reflecting Questions

1. What were your reactions to this story?
2. What would it be like for you to work with this client?
3. What are the strengths of this client?

OVERVIEW

For centuries, people have been intrigued with discovering the secrets of the change process. If there is one central idea in the counseling approach we are offering in this book, it is that your focus should be on *change*. In particular, you are in the business of helping a mind to change. When people stubbornly resist change, they often say, "My mind is made up." Reluctant to change their minds, they then repeat the same behaviors over and over—with the same results. If they are getting the results they desire, they do not view themselves as having a problem. But often people repeat behaviors that do not get them what they want. Freud (1922/1961) called this "repetition compulsion."

Successful counselors help clients change unproductive ways of viewing the world so they can find new behaviors that are more likely to yield desired results. While most of the techniques or tools that we recommend are drawn from the various brief approaches, particularly the solution-focused approach, we recommend that you not think of client concerns as "problems" in search of "solutions." Instead, we suggest you consider client "problems" as their "stuck" or rigid representation of experience that is in need of change. Rather than solving a problem, you are helping a client to resolve the "stuckness." By deconstructing the client's representations, you help the person achieve a new *resolution*. As a result, the client becomes a newly resolute person, with his or her mind made up in a more useful way. As a brief counselor, you are working to accomplish this task in the most efficient way possible. Brief counseling is done "on purpose." In other words, it is a method in which you guide or engineer change, rather than taking a nondirective approach. Such an intentional way of working will inevitably be briefer than if you were to wait for the client to attain a corrective emotional experience or breakthrough insight.

Some important clinical issues discussed in this chapter are the "death of resistance," the concept of "utilization," and clients' lives as metaphors or stories.

IDEAS

Something about Change

Early Greek philosophers wondered how things could come into being that seemed not to have been there before. They also wanted to understand the processes of growth and metamorphosis. These philosophers thought that there must be some basic substance at the root of all change, some hidden cause of all change in nature (Gaarder, 1994). In the segue to this chapter, we quote the famous saying of one well-known philosopher, Heraclitus: "You cannot step into the same river twice." If Heraclitus is right, then change is all there is. Nothing stays the same. This means that a client who is resisting change is swimming against the current—it is actually easier to go with the flow of change than to try to stay in the same place.

Your job as the counselor is not to motivate, but to help a client to engage successfully in the natural ongoing process of change. Many clients are reluctant to change because they are afraid that change brings chaos. They follow the saying, "Better the devil you know than the devil you don't." Still others desire change, but they feel stuck, believing that change for the better is not possible. Such clients need a change of mind.

Changing Minds

What does it mean to change a mind? A change of mind is a shift in someone's pattern of thought. It is an alteration in a person's way of representing the environment. A dramatic shift, such as a sudden burst of insight, a creative illumination, or a religious conversion, is rare. However, for the people experiencing such shifts, nothing is ever quite the same again. This does not mean that these people have suddenly forgotten the way they formerly thought. This change of mind may be more aptly characterized as moving a former pattern of thought into the background and bringing a new conceptual framework to the foreground. Such a change of mind has been described as overcoming an outmoded mind-set, or as a reframe.

Experiencing This Idea

A good example of this phenomenon is a Necker cube. Stare at the Necker cube in Figure 2-1 and try to find the two ways in which it can be viewed. Once you have done this, try shifting the patterns back and forth. You can generally do this by willing it to happen. Then try holding only one view for a long time. This, you will find, is something that you cannot do. As hard as you may try to maintain only one perspective, the face of the cube that you are viewing as the closest will suddenly jump to the back of the cube. You can bring it to the front again, though. Once again, concentrate and will it to happen.

You may be wondering, "So what?" Well, the pattern you saw the first time you looked at the cube was your automatic response to the situation. But when you took the time and tried to see another possibility, you were able to pull a different pattern from the cube. Did the cube itself change? No. *You* experienced a change of mind.

Once you have willed the two patterns to present themselves, you know that there will always be more than one way to see the cube. Even though you will have a tendency to see only one face of the cube when you next observe it, you are now armed with the knowledge that you may see the other face if you wish. What was once a fact is now a choice.

Clients come to counseling having fixated on only one view of their situation. You can help them change their minds by loosening this singular view, making it possible for them to see things another way—even if the situation itself doesn't change.

Brief Counseling as a Strategic Approach

The counseling approach offered in this book is an amalgam of many of the most recent brief approaches to counseling and psychotherapy. Central to many of these recent ap-

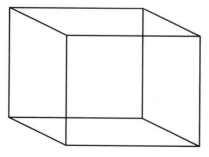

FIGURE 2-1   The Necker cube.

proaches is the notion that solutions—not problems—should be the focus of our work with clients. The idea that counseling can be done efficiently and, therefore, briefly is also a defining characteristic of these models. These interventions are brief because they are done in a deliberate manner—the counselor helps engineer a change in the client's thinking and subsequent behavior. In this sense, brief counseling approaches are cognitive. They also are strategic (Haley, 1973), meaning that the counselor has an outcome in mind for the therapy. *Webster's New World Dictionary* defines *strategy* as a "skill in managing or planning, especially by using stratagem." The word *stratagem* comes from the Greek "to lead." Brief counseling, in other words, is *not* a "nondirective" model of counseling.

In recent years, the strategic approach to counseling has been criticized as manipulative and deceptive. The strategic counselor has been portrayed as an expert with a bag of tricks designed to leave clients disoriented, but changed, in spite of themselves. For example, Efran, Lukens, and Lukens (1988) complained that strategic therapists played "fast and loose" with language in using the technique of reframing. They saw the strategic approach of Haley and others as therapy "done to" clients instead of the counselor "being with" the client. They decried the hierarchical relationship between the counselor and client, calling for a more cooperative approach. "We are interested," they said, "in simplifying and demystifying life's problems, not in adding additional layers of counterintuitive, half-believed, poorly substantiated mumbo jumbo" (p. 34).

The approach to counseling we are presenting in this book is not strategic in the above sense. It is a collaborative, respectful, and open way of working with clients. We use the word *strategic* to mean that you can know *generally* where you wish to go with clients—this is not a "clueless" form of counseling. At the same time, you can adopt with your clients what has been called a posture of "not knowing," with respect to their unique lives (DeJong & Berg, 1998). You cannot possibly be the expert on how your clients view their world and the meaning they place on their significant experiences. But counselors *are* experts on knowing how people can work toward resolving their life issues. So this approach is strategic in that you introduce techniques that will increase the chances that you will be helpful to clients. As Eron and Lund (1993) put it, the use of the term *strategic* does not mean "the prescriptive, impositional sense that has come to be associated with the method, but in terms of having a clear therapeutic direction in promoting change" (p. 291).

Whether explicitly stated or not, problem-solving has traditionally been the focus of many counseling models. For example, the medical model of therapy involves a differential diagnosis of the client's symptoms in order to arrive at the proper treatment plan. The client's situation in this case is a syndrome, or collection of problems, and the therapist's job is to figure out which disorder the syndrome represents. Once this task has been accomplished, the major step of the detective work has been completed and treatment will be dictated by the diagnosis. Thus, the problem has been solved. In contrast, DeJong and Berg (1998) adopt what they refer to as the "solution-building" approach and state that client concerns are not puzzles to be solved because "the difficulties brought by clients to helpers bear little resemblance to the diseases for which the medical model was designed" (p. 9).

The common theme in the "solution" approaches to counseling is that it is the solutions—not the problems—that should be investigated. Resources—not deficits—

should be probed. And outcomes—not histories—should be sought. An emphasis on solutions rather than on problems is not simply the other side of the same coin. Seeking positive outcomes, rather than probing symptoms, is often misconstrued by those who are new to the idea as "looking on the bright side" therapy. Similarly, the notion of brief therapy is often misconstrued as "get over it" therapy. The full potential of counseling, however, goes beyond merely finding the solution. Instead, truly successful counseling is a process of seeking resolution. Lest you think we are merely quibbling over semantics, let us elaborate. *Webster's New World Dictionary* defines *solution* as "the act, or method, or process of solving a problem . . . the answer to a problem." The term *resolution* is defined as "the act or process of resolving . . . deciding . . . a resolute quality of mind."

Resolution connotes the arrival at a new realization or the formation of a new gestalt, once the old view of the situation has been perturbed or deconstructed. In addition, *resolution* refers to the developing of a newly resolute, or determined, state of mind. Someone who becomes resolute is no longer in a state of indecision or uncertainty. The client has replaced an old way of viewing the world with a new and more successful way. Thus, the resolute person is confident, hopeful, and focused on future goals, rather than discouraged, disheartened, and haunted by past and present concerns. Instead of identifying problems and seeking solutions, the successful brief counselor works to promote this process of resolution—the way clients change their minds, themselves, and their lives.

Resolution as Reconstruction

Prochaska and Norcross (1999) have suggested that the newer forms of brief counseling should be categorized as "constructivist therapies" (p. 437). They see constructivism as a higher-order concept that can subsume the solution-focused and narrative approaches to counseling. We will discuss constructivism in greater depth in Chapter 5, but it is useful to state here that constructivism is a philosophical position on human knowing. Constructivism's fundamental position is that the knower does not—in fact, cannot—achieve knowledge of a reality that is independent of the knower. In other words, while there may be a reality "out there," we can't know exactly what it is or how it works. Instead, it is our constructed representation of reality that is real for us. Representations of reality exist in our minds, so the focus of the counselor's work is on deconstructing unproductive representations so that a client can construct new and more successful ones. In other words, old representations are dissolved so that a new resolution can be achieved.

While most of the assumptions of the humanistic movement regarding the nature of human beings and their ways of knowing are consistent with the constructivist approach, the models of therapy offered by the humanists would not qualify as strategic. For example, the original "core conditions" claimed by Carl Rogers to be "necessary and sufficient" are regarded here as necessary, but not sufficient for helping people change. The humanistic models of counseling often stress the importance of allowing the client to lead and for the counselor to follow and wait for opportunities. In this sense the counselor would be a "reactor" rather than a "conductor." In the brief constructivist model, the counselor encourages the client to focus on images of success and to recover forgotten resources. The counselor in this mode is much more of a "conductor." The basis of such counseling is the intentional, goal-directed attitude of the counselor. It is counseling done "on purpose."

The humanistic emphasis on the here and now often leaves both counselor and client unsure of where they are going. The counselor who has a strategy is focusing on the future. Without a goal in mind, and some idea about a possible path to that goal, the counseling process heads out in no particular direction, with the hope of getting somewhere. Lewis Carroll (1991) made a similar point in Alice's conversation with the Cheshire Cat:

> "Would you tell me please, which way I ought to go from here?"
> "That depends a good deal on where you want to get to," said the Cat.
> "I don't much care where—" said Alice.
> "Then it doesn't matter which way you go," said the Cat.
> "—so long as I get **somewhere**," Alice added as an explanation.
> "Oh, you're sure to do that," said the Cat, "if you only walk long enough" (pp. 64–65).

It is clear from Carroll's account that if you do not know where you are headed, you will surely do a lot of inefficient traveling. If, on the other hand, the purpose of the counselor/client journey is to help clients get somewhere that is a better place than where they currently are, a little planning is required.

Experiencing This Idea

Suppose a salesperson must travel to five cities to display his or her product to potential customers. One of the cities is the salesperson's hometown, but all others must be visited by car. As shown in Figure 2-2, the cities lie at varying distances from each other.

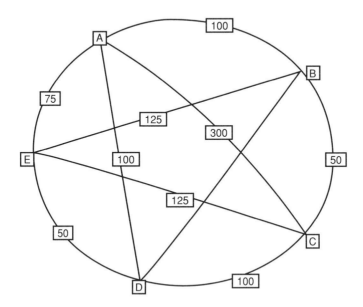

FIGURE 2-2 The Traveling Salesperson Problem. (After Luger & Stubblefield, 1993, p. 84.) Which would be the best path for the traveling salesperson to take when visiting the five cities (A–E) and returning to the starting city? What assumptions do you make when solving this problem?

The cities are indicated by the letters A, B, C, D, and E. The distance between each of the cities is indicated in miles. The salesperson would like your help in planning the itinerary. What would be the best route for the salesperson to travel? Once you have planned the trip, then read the next paragraph.

We're betting that as you did this exercise, you attempted to find the shortest route for the traveling salesperson to follow. It makes sense that if time and money are involved, then the shortest route would be the best route. However, if sightseeing is your aim, then time is less important. When clients come for counseling, they generally do not have unlimited amounts of time, money, or emotional stamina. They usually would prefer to get somewhere with the least amount of travel.

Why Use Brief Approaches to Counseling?

A counselor's first responsibility is to the client. Yet, you may hear that the reason the profession seems to be moving toward brief approaches to counseling is that caseloads are becoming too large or that insurance companies are growing stingier. Both of these may be true. More people value counseling as a useful way of working through their concerns. In schools, agencies, and hospitals, where resources remain limited while the demand continues to grow, counselors are asked to do more with less—especially in less time. Third-party payers (insurance companies) are also demanding more results in less time. With the advent of managed care, a counselor who wishes to be paid through the client's insurance must state an explicit plan. The counselor will then be allotted only a limited number of visits in order to accomplish the goals for counseling.

But neither the supply-and-demand argument nor the managed-care argument can be the primary reason for adopting brief methods in counseling. Both rationales are external to the client, to whom counselors are primarily responsible. If we use brief methods because of the money, then we are mercenaries. If we sell out to the marketplace, then we are prostitutes. We must always do what we do because it is in the best interest of our client.

If all counselors were independently wealthy and there were enough of them to give clients all the time they requested, would we ever consider using brief methods? O'Hanlon (1995) cited a number of studies that suggested that "brief" is what we do anyway. For example, one study (Garfield, 1978) concluded that in both private practice and community mental health centers, the average duration of therapy was five to eight sessions, regardless of the theoretical orientation of the therapist. Another study (Lambert, Shapiro, & Bergin, 1986) suggested that 75% of the clients who benefit from therapy do so within the first 6 months, and that the major positive impact of therapy takes place in the first six to eight sessions. Several other studies indicated that the most common length of treatment is a single session. Seventy-eight percent of clients in one study stated that their problem was "better" to "much better" after one session, and that they had gotten what they wanted from the counseling (Talmon, 1990). School counselors know that one session is often all they will get to work with a student, and that sometimes they have to do their counseling "on the run"—in a vacant classroom, hallway, or cafeteria. If we are going to see clients for such short periods of time anyway, why not adopt brief and strategic ways of dealing with their concerns?

Parkinson's law states that a task will expand to fill the time allotted to it. If we could offer our clients unlimited counseling—as many sessions as they wanted—would they benefit more, or simply take longer to get better? We don't have the answer to this question, but it does seem clear that a counselor can ethically adopt a "brief" attitude toward counseling, and that this can be for the client's benefit, and not for the insurance company, the demands of the marketplace, or for any other external reason.

Efficient versus Brief Counseling

In 1966, Richard Fisch proposed the establishment of a research project to study the change process in counseling and psychotherapy. For want of a better term, the research group referred to its model as *brief therapy* (Watzlawick, Weakland, and Fisch, 1974), and the institute they established became known as the Brief Therapy Center of the Mental Research Institute (MRI) in Palo Alto. The term *brief* caught on and came to be regarded by many as the primary emphasis of the work. The MRI researchers, however, were never really comfortable with this emphasis:

> The name is unsatisfactory because "brief" therapy often refers to some sort of stopgap, superficial, or first-aid measures undertaken provisionally until "real" long-term therapy becomes possible (p. xiv).

Brief is now a term considered to be "delicious" by insurance companies who pay for counseling services, and "disgusting" to many therapists, who view it as merely a truncated version of real counseling. It is unfortunate that the term *brief* is associated with the various models of counseling that have evolved from this original approach. *Efficient* better describes the use of time in this type of counseling session, and even then, efficiency is simply the byproduct of a planned, strategic approach.

Effectiveness, not efficiency, should matter more. The fact that the idea of "brief" has currency in the marketplace is both a blessing and a curse. Counselors who claim to work briefly seem to have fewer problems dealing with HMOs and other managed-care agents. On the other hand, there seems also to have been a counselor backlash to the notion of working briefly, and the term *brief* for many counselors is anathema. The approach to counseling offered in this book is designed primarily for its effectiveness in dealing with most issues brought to the counselor's office. Fundamentally, "brief" is an attitude. The counselor who begins the work intending to be successful, while also being scrupulously efficient in the use of client's time, will likely require fewer sessions to get the job done.

Parkinson's law is also a principle in physics. For example, if you open a container of compressed gas, the gas molecules will spread out to fill the room. The inverse of this situation is the fire block traditionally used by many Africans. It is a device made of wood with a cylindrical hole drilled into it. The second component is a stick of wood that fits so snugly into the hole that it must be pounded to be driven all the way into the block. When someone wishes to start a fire, some bits of straw are placed in the bottom of the hole and the stick is inserted. The stick is then driven all the way to the bottom. The sudden compression of the molecules of air inside the hole heats them up so fast that a fire is ignited in the straw. The stick is quickly removed and the burning straw is poured onto a pile of twigs and the cooking fire is begun. If this aspect of Parkinson's law holds in human terms, reducing the amount of time in which the therapy is to take place will "heat up" the work, and more will be accomplished than if the time had been left open-ended.

Much of the folk wisdom in counseling would seem to suggest that counseling must be long-term in order to be effective. Occasionally, counselors can be heard saying to clients, "It took you a lifetime to get this screwed up, so it may take an equal amount of time to undo it." Counselors who work efficiently have a different world view. They believe that, with proper engineering of the counseling situation, seeming miracles can happen. Time spent getting "screwed up" does not have to be matched by time in therapy. Breakthroughs, in the form of reframes, can bring about sudden and lasting changes in people's lives. Like reports of "seeing the light" in a religious context, people can change rapidly under certain conditions. If you want to be an efficient counselor, it helps to believe in miracles. As Carl Rogers taught us, the counselor's belief in people and their ability to change themselves is essential to this work. After all, a miracle is simply a change that cannot be explained by conventional wisdom.

The Death of Resistance

In 1984, Steve de Shazer declared resistance to be officially dead. He said the concept of resistance was the result of a wrongheaded notion that clients would naturally resist changing and the counselor would have to devise heroic strategies for overcoming the client's natural tendency to stay the same. For de Shazer, this was thinking based on the old mechanistic notions of physics. He quoted Maruyama (1963), who contended that a "second cybernetics" operated on principles that later became known as chaos, the butterfly effect, and complexity. When a system is given sufficient push or a kick in the right direction, it will enter into a deviation-amplifying process, resulting in change that is disproportionately large, compared to the initial perturbation. According to de Shazer, we do not pay sufficient attention to the fact that whatever behaviors are exhibited in a counseling session take place within a system that includes both the client and the counselor. If the client is thought to be resisting, this behavior occurs within a "resistive" atmosphere. Instead of *resistance,* de Shazer preferred to speak in terms of *cooperation.* Change is inevitable. Clients do the best they can to cooperate in the change process. If change does not appear to be taking place, then the counselor has not initiated sufficient "push"—that is, the counselor has not introduced a "difference that makes a difference."

The chief benefit of declaring the death of resistance is an alteration in the counselor's attitude. Instead of viewing the client as resistive and seeing the overcoming of this resistance as combat, you can view the client as not having yet reached escape velocity from his or her troubles. The staff of the Milwaukee Brief Family Therapy Center, headed by de Shazer, apparently considered the death of the idea of resistance to be so important that a funeral was held to mark its passing (O'Hanlon & Weiner-Davis, 1989; Young, 1998). We could not find this funeral ritual cited in de Shazer's writing, but we thought it was a great story that dramatizes the importance of this change of attitude. In order to satisfy our curiosity, we emailed de Shazer, who responded by saying that they had indeed conducted a funeral for resistance and that they had buried it in their back yard. They even erected a tombstone, but someone stole it (de Shazer, personal communication, 1998). He went on to say that they had not publicized the event because they did not want people to think they had murdered resistance; it had died a natural death.

Many psychodynamic and cognitive approaches to counseling have suggested that we must somehow seek to break through the client's resistance. In this attitude, the counselor musters a set of tactics designed to defeat the client's stubbornness. Contrary to this, de Shazer believes that "resistance" can be used in ways that improve the therapeutic alliance and lead to better outcomes.

Dealing with "Resistance"

Dolan (1985) recounts the story of a man watching a butterfly emerge from its cocoon. The man, impatient with the slow progress of the butterfly, determines to help by prying away the impediment of the shell and thus allowing the butterfly its freedom. He fails to recognize the protective nature of the constricting "resistant" cocoon. The butterfly, with the man's "help," is set free in the cold air prematurely. Deprived of adequate time to make the necessary adjustments within the cocoon, it crumbles into a helpless suffering heap. The therapist must have reverence and appreciation for each client's personal rate of change, idiosyncrasies, difficulties, vulnerabilities, and resources (p. 3).

Milton Erickson viewed resistance as an aspect of the client's total picture of symptoms and found ways to use it to the client's benefit. Like the butterfly's cocoon, while resistance may temporarily slow a client's progress, it simultaneously expresses a protective wisdom that cannot be fully verbalized. If asked about their reluctance, clients can only say—if they can speak of it at all—that for some reason they are frightened to go farther or to talk of certain things. The butterfly's helper would see this as a moment when stronger intervention is required—tearing open the covering and exposing the interior is considered by many to be the most efficient and useful thing to do. At such times, the techniques of interpretation or confrontation or immediacy are employed in order to strip the client of old, atrophied, and confining impasses from which the client needs to break free. Without a doubt, if the moment is precisely right and the client is ready to deal with the realization that such measures bring, these techniques can be profoundly effective. The problem is that the helper more often risks forcing the client into a premature insight that may not then become fully integrated into the client's experience, because the idea seemed more the counselor's than the client's. And the worst-case scenario would be that the client, not ready to face whatever shame or terror might be associated with the sudden realization, would collapse into an emotional heap. The paradox is that often the counselor's efforts to speed up the therapeutic process produce the opposite of the desired effect. As Erickson (1975) put it, for the therapist to know the correct treatment is not sufficient for success. The client must also be "receptive of the therapy and cooperative in regard to it. Without the patient's full cooperativeness, the therapeutic results are delayed, distorted, or even prevented" (p. 212).

The Ericksonian notion is that the resistance of the client should be honored and that the counselor should go with the client's flow and pace, rather than rush the process. Not only will this lead to better understanding on the part of the client, who then discovers everything for himself or herself, but it further cements the bond between counselor and client, making them allies rather than adversaries. Attempting to match the client's pace also has a paradoxical effect. While it may seem like a waste of time to the counselor, it is probably more efficient, because less time is lost attempting to get the client to see things the counselor's way.

Utilization

"Too many psychotherapists take you out to dinner and then tell you what to order" (Erickson & Rossi, 1973; quoted in Dolan, 1985, p. 6). Following Erickson's metaphor, we must make sure that we allow the client to slowly peruse the menu, selecting only those items that seem palatable. We may wish that clients order full-course meals when they desire only appetizers or desserts. We may worry that clients will not be getting all the essential food groups, but if we allow them to be the experts on what they need, they may eventually end up eating nutritious and satisfying banquets.

Utilization is the Ericksonian term for taking whatever the client brings to the table and using it. This must be done without direct or implied criticism of the client's style or choices. Dolan (1985) suggested three requirements that utilization must meet in order to be helpful. First, you view the client's resistant behavior as a communication about the way the client views the world. Second, you welcome the resistant behavior as a valuable therapeutic resource. Finally, you communicate that the resistance is honored and respected. Resistance is the client's way of defending against unpleasant realizations. Much care and creativity has been invested in these defenses, so you should appreciate the client's artistry in erecting them. To disrespect a resistance is to disrespect the person who created it.

As Dolan states, it is useful to assume that resistant behavior plays some functional role for the client. Siding with the client's resistance is often the most useful behavior you can display. Rather than "getting clients to change," you must find ways to allow them to change—their way. According to Dolan (1985), a counselor can fully accept the client only if he or she is willing to set aside personal judgments and view the client's model of the world as a valid and accurate representation of the client's experience. "By accepting and thereby symbolically joining the client in his or her model of the world, the therapist enables the client to feel safe enough to make contact" (pp. 9–10). It is only when we understand the client's need to remain the same that we can help the client change.

Implications of These Ideas for the Counselor

The above ideas regarding change, resolution, strategies, and resistance have a number of important and practical implications for how you can successfully work with clients.

- If you believe that change always happens—and sameness never does—you will not need to see counseling as motivating clients to change. You simply take a seat alongside them.
- Though clients are constantly changing, they may fail to see new possibilities because they keep reconstituting their visions of discouragement. Your job as a counselor is to seek the overlooked background information that will help to deconstruct this recycled tale of woe and create a new mental representation of the client's experience.
- Client concerns are not problems to be solved. They are, rather, dilemmas in which clients have become stuck. Problem-solving is a logical process, while the resolution of dilemmas sometimes is not logical at all.
- Brief counseling works best when you and the client have both a destination and a plan to arrive there without extraneous sightseeing.
- Your focus should be on the client's world. This world is the client's construction of experience, rather than the so-called real or objective world.

- When you counsel deliberately, you tend to be briefer. Your aim is to be both effective and efficient, successfully achieving therapeutic goals without wasting the client's time or money.
- When a client resists your attempts to engineer change, it is because you have failed to communicate your respect for the resistance. In metaphorical terms, you have prematurely tried to pull the butterfly out of its cocoon. You should then try to join the client in his or her view of the world before trying once more to influence change.

TOOLS

Metaphors and the Stories of Our Lives

People use metaphors to help shape their experiences into the stories of their lives. When you first begin to engage with your clients, they typically want to tell you their stories of tragedy and despair. Your initial task is to listen carefully, acknowledge their stories empathically, and look for the metaphors they use to describe both their pain and their longing to find relief.

But just what is a metaphor? How does it differ from a statement of fact? What is the use of a metaphor to anyone other than a poet or artist? According to Sheldon Kopp (1985), there are only three basic ways of knowing. The first is rational, which involves our use of logic and scientific reasoning. The second way is empirical, which is achieved through our sense perceptions. And the final way of knowing is metaphorical, which offers an intuitive grasp of situations and their coexisting multiple meanings.

Typically, people think of metaphor as a literary device in which one thing is expressed in terms of another. For example, one person may be described as having "a heart of stone," while another is "a breath of fresh air." Metaphors are comparisons that illuminate. They have a figurative, poetic quality about them. While English teachers may decry our lack of precision, we lump all these comparisons, such as similes and analogies, under the general heading of metaphoric language.

Metaphors are, by definition, "fuzzy" thinking and are literally false (MacCormac, 1985), but "like poetry . . . metaphors can express emotive meaning; the tension that they produce is the very expression of meaning" (p. 26). If a person suspends disbelief, a metaphor can have the ring of truth and the clarity of real enlightenment. A cardiac specialist, for example, can assure us that test results prove that someone does not have "a heart of stone." However, if we have experienced this person as unfeeling, unloving, and uncharitable, we will stand by our metaphor as true, even if it's not medically accurate. Another important point about metaphors is that their meaning may not be obvious, and their initial ambiguity is often the source of metaphors' emotional clout. The evocative nature of metaphors compels one to reflect and mull over their message until they are "digested"—or incorporated into the experience of the listener.

Using This Tool

You can sensitize yourself to metaphoric speech simply by making it a habit to "tune in" and listen for metaphors in everyday conversation. However, metaphors may present problems for those who wish to think precisely. If you are, as we might say in politically correct terms, "metaphorically challenged," you can loosen up and stretch your thinking a bit by using the following recipe for constructing a metaphor.

Remember that a metaphor is simply associating one idea with another that is normally not considered to be related. For this exercise, join with three or four colleagues to form a small practice group. Take turns selecting one of the concepts below and linking it to a different object in the room. Once you have paired the concept with an object, explain to your colleagues the metaphoric relationship. For example, you might say, "Depression is like that reclining chair, because the longer you lie in it, the more difficult it is to get out of." Or, you might say, "Anxiety is like this carpet, because you worry what sort of vermin might be lurking in it." Continue taking turns until you have completed the entire list.

Problems are like _____, because _____.
Solutions are like _____, because _____.
Counselors are like _____, because_____.
The future is like _____, because_____.
The past is like _____, because _____.
Relationships are like _____, because _____.
Worries are like _____, because_____.
Parents are like _____, because _____.
Friends are like _____, because _____.
Happiness is like _____, because_____.
Anger is like _____, because_____.

Once you have completed this activity, take some time with your colleagues to discuss the experience. What was it like to make these links? What reactions, such as curiosity, emotion, surprise, or laughter, did you have to the metaphors of others? What intriguing parallels did you discover? How would your group process have differed if you had engaged in a rational or empirical discussion of these concepts?

"Rigid" and "Fresh" Metaphors

As you listen to clients tell you their stories, you can begin to see that it is the "stuckness" of their metaphors that forestalls possibilities in the way they view their lives. In other words, clients often "think themselves into a corner." The metaphors they use to describe their experiences reinforce the representations they have in their minds about how the world is and what kind of persons they are. When they develop rigid representations—hardening of the categories—many things that do not fit easily into their representations pass unnoticed, many doors seem closed, and many opportunities are viewed as impossible.

Your job as a counselor is to help change clients' rigid representations that have narrowed their world so much that they feel discouraged and hopeless about the future. If you are successful, their worlds will be transformed and their futures expanded in a hopeful manner. Of course, nothing in their worlds will have actually changed, but *they* will have changed, so to them it will seem that their worlds have changed. They will have created fresh metaphors. It is as the poet T. S. Elliot (quoted in Siegelman, 1990) put it:

And the end of all our exploring
Will be to arrive where we started
And to know the place for the first time. (p. 67)

Using This Tool

Return to the case story at the beginning of the chapter and underline all the metaphors you can find. Put a minus sign by each metaphor that may sabotage a sense of personal agency and hope for the future. Put a plus sign by each of the positive metaphors. Now consider how you could change the negative metaphors into positive ones.

Life Stories and Meaning

As we reflect on our life stories, we tend to view ourselves as the protagonist. Life itself, in order to be successful, must be lived meaningfully. Truly fulfilled individuals not only participate fully in life, but also strive for personal understanding of "what it's all about." Religion and science can provide helpful guidance and information for us along the path, but in the final analysis, we make our own life—we write our own story.

Stories are, by their very nature, metaphors. Metaphors have a loose structure, so that an individual can supply the meaning. The metaphor is a powerful teaching tool because it invites the listener to bring his or her own emotional experience to the understanding of it. Jesus, for example, used metaphors as devices with which to teach. "Instead of putting forward his teachings in scholarly texts, Jesus spoke in metaphors and parables. Bible scholars counted 65 of them in the four gospels" (Ehrenwald, 1986, p. 257). Parables and allegories are useful ways to teach moral lessons. They exist in many forms of literature, from mythology to Aesop's fables. When Shakespeare said "All the world's a stage, And all the men and women merely players," he opened up a parallel system for understanding the structure of events that take place among humans. It is when metaphors parallel life events that they add to our meaning.

As you begin to listen to your clients' stories, they will, at first, be teaching you about their lives. Later, as you employ their metaphors in the deconstruction of the stories, you will be opening up their restricted accounts so that there is room for fresh meaning and new realizations.

Using This Tool

Writing down a client's metaphors is a useful strategy so that you can use the exact words when acknowledging his or her concerns. The main thing to remember is that you are not collecting facts or data in the way a scientist would, but rather, you are collecting metaphorical insights into your client's world. Even though you may find that taking notes during a counseling session is awkward and distracting at first, we encourage you to keep practicing until it feels natural to you.

Join with two colleagues to form a practice group. One of you should talk for about 5 minutes about a recent experience that stirred up some emotions, either positive or negative. Another should actively listen for metaphors and take notes. The third person serves as the recorder, who observes the activity and leads the discussion of the process. Now switch roles until everone has had an opportunity to practice.

Listening for Client Metaphors

The personal metaphors adopted tend to color everything that takes place in a person's life. Think for a minute about the root metaphor you use to summarize life. What is it? Here is a list of some of the positions that people might adopt. Life can be viewed as a . . . trial, mythic quest, cross to bear, accident of nature, box of chocolates, battle, journey, veil of tears, bitch and then you die, gift, curse, mystery, problem to solve, learning process, blessing, or losing proposition. Is your own metaphor for life among these? Perhaps just considering this list will help sensitize you to the fact that each of us carries with us, in the form of metaphor, a summary idea for our lives, our problems, our hopes and dreams.

Most of the time we are unaware of our own metaphors, and we are even less conscious of those of others. We must deliberately listen for the metaphors of our clients in order to truly hear their experience of the situations they are reporting to us. As Siegelman (1990) put it:

> They talk of feeling trapped, of having a wall go up, of being fenced in or of being suffocated. They talk of a breakthrough. In listening, we often do not see the metaphor but look through it or past it, to the content it appears to address. These cliches may have been born out of bodily experience that was once vivid and compelling. But now the figures appear worn out—like coins so thumbed one can scarcely distinguish the buffalo's head on the old nickel. (p. 45)

Client metaphors can range from "pale" to "vivid" in terms of the emotions they summon for the person using them (Wright, 1976). A pale metaphor has become a "cliché," a French term that refers to a stereotype plate used in printing multiple pages. In other words, a pale metaphor is one so worn and familiar that the meaning and impact may be lost on both the client and the counselor. But even such automatic metaphors may simply be slumbering (Siegelman, 1990). Your job as a counselor is to listen for, and note, the metaphors used by your clients as they describe their concerns and to employ their exact terms in your feedback, while seeking alternative metaphors that will enhance the possibility of turning around client's negative narratives.

When client metaphors turn from negative (narratives of discouragement) to positive (what we call metaphors of longing), it becomes your job to attempt to capitalize on these novel metaphors and help expand them. Siegelman (1990) calls such novel turns "key metaphors" and she suggests that you need do little more than to stay with these metaphors to encourage their continued use in the client narrative.

> Metaphor often carries not only affect but insight as well, so that the therapist needs to do very little. It is more a question of attentive receptivity. I often feel I am functioning as midwife, "catching" the psychological baby as it emerges. (p. 78)

Using This Tool

In order to give you a better idea of the terms you will be looking for in client-talk, we have put together a short list of metaphors that clients sometimes use to depict themselves. These are such common expressions that you can complete them by filling in the blanks.

> "I don't have any more options. My life is a _____ end."
> "People have been treating me like a _____ mat."
> "When I get so tense, I gotta blow off some _____."
> "I'm so overwhelmed. I can't keep my head above _____."
> "I'm caught between a _____ and a _____ place."

Listening in on a Session

Review the story at the beginning of the chapter. A resolution-focused counselor might engage with James by using the client's own metaphors in communicating empathic understanding.

> **Counselor:** (*After introducing herself and inviting James to have a seat in her office, the counselor sits and looks expectantly at the client.*) James, what changes would you like me to help you make in your life?

> **James:** (*He pauses, takes in a deep breath and exhales as he leans forward, hands together in a posture that evokes in the counselor an image of someone preparing to dive into a swimming pool.*) I'm basically here because I think of myself as damaged goods.

> **Counselor:** (*She is struck by the metaphor of "damaged goods," particularly since James' appearance and manner seem to be those of a confident and successful person.*) It sounds like you've been through some tough times, and now you're wanting to see about repairing the damage.

> **Client:** Well, not exactly. I was just thinking about this in your waiting room, and I'm definitely no poster boy for victims. To tell you the truth, I had a pretty happy childhood. My parents never beat me and I was never traumatized in a war or anything like that. I've got a great family and a nice job. It should be a good life, but I feel like one of our dented canned goods items at the store. You know, the ones we have to mark way down to unload 'em and even when somebody does finally buy one, they aren't really all that thrilled with what they bought. If people could afford it, they'd take the can that's in great shape and not put up with damaged goods.

> **Counselor:** So getting the dent itself isn't what's so bad. It's how people don't realize that what's inside is still just as valuable.

> **Client:** Yeah, I feel like I've gotta work extra hard to show people that. In your waiting room, I was just thinking about this river cabin that's, well, been in our family for four generations. About 10 years ago, a flood carried it off. I was all for selling the property, but my dad had his heart set on rebuilding. So, I worked like a dog helping him—weekends and evenings—for the better part of 5 years. It's been more trouble than it's worth, if you ask me, but now I own it 'cause my folks signed it over to me before they moved to Florida last year. Now the whole damn thing's on my shoulders.

> **Counselor:** So, you've carrying this heavy burden on your own now.

> **James:** That's part of it, but it's even more complicated than that. It got flooded out again 6 months ago and I was feeling so fed up that I didn't even want to go out to survey the damage, but I got a call from Ben, the guy who lives year-round in a neighboring cabin. All he says is, "James, you'd better get down here quick," and then hangs up. He's always been a peculiar old bird, a real character, but I decide I'd better see what's up. When I get there, Ben's eyeing me like a judge about to sentence a child molester. "I found your dog, James. He's dead." (*James points his finger accusingly to punctuate each word now.*) "You let him die!" he says.

Well, of course, we didn't have a pet at the cabin, but there was a stray dog that came by sometimes and we took pity on it and threw it some scraps. Ben must have thought it was ours. I spent an hour trying to convince this stubborn old mule that we didn't own that poor mutt. What really gets me is that there I was—with a cabin I didn't want that's been washed away and a dog that's not mine that's been killed— and I'm feeling that it's all up to me to please everybody, even crazy old fools, and make everything OK, even if it's a mess.

Reflecting Questions

1. Circle the metaphors that the client used in telling his story.
2. What metaphors did the counselor use in responding to the client?
3. Write a possible counselor response to James's last statement.

Working with Client Metaphors

As clients tell you their stories, the narratives will usually be saturated with rich metaphoric imagery. Your job is to learn their metaphors so that you can use the same or similar terms when communicating your understanding. Generally, clients will offer metaphors without being fully aware of all that they are communicating. When you embed the same metaphoric terms in your responses, clients are more likely to sense that you are resonating with them.

Many client metaphors involve the body. According to Siegelman (1990), the body is equated with the self more than any other object, and this leads to what Lakoff (1987) called the bodily kinesthetic schema of "the container." For example, when we are "full," we tend to be satisfied, but when we are "empty," we tend to feel we are in need. On the other hand, someone else might consider us to be "full" of ourselves or "full of crap." They may also see us as "empty-headed" or in some way deficient—"one brick short of a load."

When we are "hot," we tend to feel unsatisfied. We may lust after someone or we are angry and want to lash out by "fuming" or "blowing off steam." When we are "cool," we are content with our image or we are in control of our emotions—"chilled out." Furthermore, the various sensations involving the locations or positions of our bodies can be metaphors for our psychological state. We may be "backsliding," "falling," "feeling down," or we may be "flying," "lighter than air," or "cruising." We may be "crushed," or "10 feet tall."

Clients will produce such metaphors without fully realizing that these are not literal descriptions. From these metaphors, you will be able to pick up clues as to their experience of the world, and should be able to verbally stay with them much better than if you were to try to reinterpret what they are saying.

Using This Tool

Think of some recent event that stirred up some significant emotions, positive and negative, for you. What are these different emotions and what part of the body might be most involved in feeling or expressing these emotions? For example, expressing anger might be "giving someone a piece of my mind," or feeling annoyed might be considered to be having a "pain in the neck."

Generate a list of five metaphorical phrases that involve emotions and their location in the body. The main thing is to begin to think in metaphorical, rather than logical, conceptual terms. Get loose!

1. _____
2. _____
3. _____
4. _____
5. _____

Opening up your own mind to new possibilities will help the client to do the same. Not only will the client be able to find new cognitive connections, but he or she will be helped to get in touch with his or her emotions in a less threatening way. Metaphors tend to place emotions in an "as if" context and, thus, make them easier to talk about. As Caruth and Ekstein (1966) put it, "like the repartee of the cocktail party [a metaphor], permits a kind of freedom and license which is recognized by both parties to be meant and not meant at the same time" (p. 38).

Capturing Client Metaphors

Emotions are more closely connected to metaphor than to other forms of language. According to Siegelman (1990), this is because the experience of the emotion is bodily and nonverbal in the first place—a primary process experience—and ordinary language is inadequate for its expression. One has only to consider that people rarely speak in complete sentences when making love or expressing rage, to realize the primitive nature of what is being felt. Clients who are in crisis will be experiencing emotions intensely, and their language will not always make sense. As you listen to the metaphors they use to describe their situation, you will discover that they are metaphors of loss, failure, guilt, and anguish. These metaphors will dominate the conversation. You should also expect to hear metaphors of longing: the way they wish things could have been, the way things used to be, or the way they hope things will turn out. You can then use their negative metaphors when acknowledging, and their longing metaphors when attempting to enhance their more positive images of the situation.

In Chapter 10, we will discuss how you can construct a metaphor to use as an indirect influencing technique. This procedure usually comes after the "consulting break." You will find that having taken notes of client metaphors can be helpful at this stage.

The Charismatic Use of Metaphors

Erickson, Rossi, and Rossi (1976) believed that the therapeutic use of metaphor and analogy created a far more powerful message for the client than direct explanation. The mechanism for this was seen as unconscious patterning and the subsequent ability to view something differently. It is important to recognize the metaphors that clients use and to employ them in your feedback. If the metaphors are negative, it might be possible for you to become a "spin doctor" for the client's metaphor. Spin doctors are political spokespersons who follow up on speeches and debates by placing the most euphemistic interpretation on what has taken place. Successful spin doctors, preachers, teachers, and counselors are "charismatic." According to Kopp, (1985), the word *charismatic* comes from the Greek, meaning *gift of grace*. The Graces of mythology were goddesses who brought joy and beauty to human lives. In the New Testament of the Bible, Paul speaks of *charisma* as the possession of spiritual gifts from God, such as prophesy, the working of miracles, and the gift of healing. "But," Paul added, "that which gives these gifts their meaning is not mere wonder of them but how they are used to help other men." (pp. 9–10)

Metaphors can be used charismatically in several ways. First, you can identify the metaphors used by the client in the client's story and employ them in your acknowledgment of client concerns. Second, you may attempt to subtly alter (put a spin on) the client's metaphor, thus changing the client's image of the situation, the client's feelings and attitudes, or the client's description of the behavior of others. Third, you may compare the client's situation and its solution to some well-known situation, for example, to a game of tennis, to rock climbing, to building a house, etc. Better yet, you might find something that greatly interests the client and build a metaphor on that topic. Fourth, you may tell an Ericksonian story that parallels the client's situation and contains a positive outcome. There are many books on how to design such metaphors. One we suggest would be *Enchantment and Intervention in Family Therapy* by Stephen and Carol Lankton (1986).

It is not necessary to get fancy with the use of metaphors. If you are sensitive to the client's metaphors and you think about the client's situation in metaphorical terms, the appropriate metaphors will come naturally. Sometimes phrases from well-known literature or popular songs are found by clients to be compelling, so long as you are not delivering them pedantically.

SEGUE TO CHAPTER 3

You cannot rely on techniques alone to do counseling. Any successful intervention is based on the relationship. Think about the times when you made important breakthroughs in your own life and identify one person who helped you. What was there about this relationship that facilitated the change?

CHAPTER 3

The Centrality of the Counseling Relationship: No Magic Tricks

"My humanity is bound up in yours, for we can only be human together."
Desmond Tutu

"we are so both and oneful
night cannot be so sky
sky cannot be so sunful
i am through you so i"
e. e. cummings

CHAPTER GOALS

Reading about and experiencing the ideas in this chapter will help you to understand the following concepts:

- As a counselor, you do not have a bag of magic tricks. Instead, you have a tool kit, and you practice your craft by forming a helping relationship and using basic tools of change.
- Power and expertise always remain with the client.

Reading about and practicing the tools in this chapter will help you to learn these valuable skills:

- Listening, understanding, and validating to connect therapeutically with clients.
- Deconstructing clients' self-defeating portrayals of themselves and their problems.

STORY

Edra bursts into the school counselor's office right after her second-period English class ends. She tells the secretary that she has an emergency and needs to talk to her counselor NOW! As luck would have it, the counselor has just finished a session with another student and Edra has to wait only a couple of minutes. After she invites Edra into her office, the counselor asks what is troubling her. Red-faced and misty-eyed, Edra takes a deep breath and angry words pour forth from her like lava from a volcano.

"I can't take it! I'm always getting myself into these messes!" Edra tearfully exclaims. "Yesterday afternoon, Todd, he's my boyfriend, borrowed my car and he was supposed to pick me up at 4:30 because my group was meeting at the library to work on our final project for English class. I waited and waited, but . . . like . . . no Todd. I called his house, and one of his housemates said that he was drinking beer with a bunch of guys from his fraternity. Well, that really pissed me off and I started freaking out because 50% of our final grade is based on our group project and my group hates me anyway and Todd picks today to be the frat boy. He's so immature and selfish! Just like a man to let you down right when you count on him to come through for you."

Edra pauses and looks at the counselor expectantly, waits a moment or two, and goes on to sadly confess, "I'm such a loser! I always end up with guys that treat me like dirt. I think I take after my mother, because she's unlucky with men, too."

She hangs down her head, looks out the window, appears to be stuck.

Reflecting Questions

1. If you were the counselor, how would you respond to Edra's statement?
2. What does Edra want from you?
3. How is she portraying herself in her story?

OVERVIEW

In this book we will offer you many therapeutic tools and techniques that may seem as though they will work like magic. We do not wish to imply this; there is no magic in counseling techniques. Furthermore, any technique will fail unless you have established a relationship with your client. In this chapter we discuss the various "common factors" that have been found by many researchers to be indispensable to the counseling process. Such research always leads back to Carl Rogers, who articulated the core conditions for a successful counseling relationship.

In this chapter we discuss the concepts of empathy and acknowledgment, and what we call the LUV triangle: indicating that you are *listening*, communicating *understanding*, and *validating* the client's perspective. We also describe Bill O'Hanlon's idea, which he called "Carl Rogers with a Twist." This technique is a way of beginning to add possibility statements to our reflections of client concerns. As clients begin to inform you of the "problems" in their lives, you subtly "deconstruct" the clients' stories of stagnation and hopelessness by relabeling unproductive descriptions and "creatively misunderstanding" some self-defeating aspects of the stories.

No matter what techniques you use, keep in mind that if clients revert to "problem-saturated" talk, you must then return to acknowledging their complaints. You must take care not to get ahead of where the client is. If you do, all the fancy techniques found in brief approaches to counseling will be of no use.

IDEAS

A Riddle

Here is another riddle for you. Read the following and try to answer the question, "What am I?" Spend some time seeking a solution before reading the paragraph below the riddle, which ends with the answer.

> I'm not in earth, nor the sun, nor the moon.
> You may search all the sky—I'm not there.
> In the morning and evening—though not at noon,
> You may plainly perceive me, for like a balloon,
> I am suspended in air.
> Though disease may possess me, and sickness and pain,
> I am never in sorrow nor gloom;
> Though in wit and wisdom I equally reign.
> I am the heart of all sin and have long lived in vain;
> Yet I ne'er shall be found in the tomb.
> [Lord Byron's *Enigma*]

Before we tell you the answer, we want to emphasize that once you know the answer, the one that was there all along, then you can never *not* know the answer. What clients learn and discover in counseling is like this. Once clients discover the answers to the dilemmas they face, they can never not know these answers. Presuming that the answer to a client's concerns is *within the client* is the most basic tenet in the brief-resolution approach to counseling. Well, the answer to the above riddle is the letter "I." You see?

Answers to human concerns are usually hidden in what people already know. Like the embedded "I" in Lord Byron's *Enigma*, the answer becomes obvious once you have discovered a new way to look at the problem. Answers are often quite simple. Perhaps you have seen a magician perform a magic trick that to you seemed quite impossible at the time, and that later, when the secret to the trick was exposed, you thought, "Why didn't I see it before?" Magicians are masters at keeping your focus on one thing while they, with a little sleight of hand, do something else. In a way, people are like that when it comes to their concerns. They stay focused on the negative feelings and the accompanying immobility while, at the same time, they ignore possible alternative ways of looking at their lives. You could say that they have hidden the rabbit in the hat and forgotten that it is there. And when they finally do realize where it is and pull the rabbit out of the hat, it looks for all the world like a magic trick!

The techniques of brief counseling are not magic. They are not mysterious or secret, and they do not reflect some hidden, special, and spontaneous power within the helper. In other words, as a brief counselor, you do not have a bag of magic tricks.

Instead, you have certain ideas, some fundamental values regarding the dignity of clients, and a tool kit to influence and encourage them to heal, change, and grow. You practice your craft by forming a helping relationship and using basic tools of change. These basic tools, or common factors of effective helping, include the "core conditions" of listening and empathizing. Without communicating to your clients that you are sincerely interested in them and willing to do your best to understand their situation, they will not invite you to help. To paraphrase Scott Miller (1996), you must be invited into the house before you start rearranging the furniture.

Experiencing This Idea

Think about a time in your life when you have made important discoveries. These discoveries may have been how you thought about yourself, your attitudes about life, or your place in the world. Now pick one person who influenced you the most as you went through the process of making these changes—someone who was there for you during this time of change. Recall your experiences with this person.

Reflecting Questions

1. How did this person influence you?
2. What was it about this person's manner, apart from specific words or actions, that you found helpful?

Magic Tricks and Miracles

In 1997, Gale Miller published a book on brief therapy under the misleading title of *Becoming Miracle Workers*. The name would seem to imply that when one learns the tools of brief therapy, one can then do magic and that the tools themselves might hold miraculous powers to change clients and help them out of their misery. It certainly is an appealing idea!

Moore and Gillette (1990), drawing on masculine Jungian archetypes, describe the magician as someone who knows something others do not. People come to him with their questions, pains, and concerns in hopes of a cure. The magician, whether priest or counselor, is viewed by those who seek his advice as someone who can peer into issues that are not revealed to ordinary people. "He is a seer and a prophet in the sense of not only predicting the future but also of seeing deeply" (p. 99).

Without doubt, many men and women in the helping professions have sought to assume the role of miracle worker or magician with their clients. Conventional wisdom has suggested that counselors should be trained to the point of possessing knowledge far superior to that of their clients, so that when dispensing sage advice, they can both capture the client's awe and offer correct information. This belief is the root metaphor of the medical model.

But you have to face facts. You are neither seer nor sage. Although you may continually strive to master the knowledge and skills of the counseling profession, you will never attain magical powers over your clients or become the expert on their issues. Power and expertise always remain in the client's domain. Most practitioners of brief therapy suggest that, instead of adopting the position of a guru or expert with your clients, you must instead adopt a position of ignorance—of not knowing. One of the authors of this book (J. E. M.) instructs his beginning students in counseling techniques to communicate to the client the "I'm not from around here" attitude. By adopting this stance, the counselor cannot assume the position of spectator of the client's world, but rather, must "be with" the client in his or her world. In the postmodern view of science, "the pure scientist's traditional posture of *Theoros*, or spectator, can no longer be maintained: we are always—and inescapably—participants or agents as well" (Toulmin, 1982, p. 255).

Whatever the client may think or do can no longer be considered to simply reside within the client's "bag of skin." On the contrary, what the client may think or do when he or she is with you is a *function* of being with you. Whether you like it or not, you participate in—or co-construct—clients' stories as they tell them. You are in a relationship with the client and the client's world. With this in mind, you must always do your best to establish and maintain a respectful therapeutic or working relationship with your client. If there is any magic in counseling, it is in the relationship that you develop with the client. Without the richness of the relationship, any tools you may attempt to use will be mere incantations cast to the wind.

Common Factors

Years of research on the efficacy of counseling models have found "surprisingly few differences among different therapies; with several exceptions, there is little evidence to recommend the use of one type over another in the treatment of specific problems" (Norcross & Newman, 1992, p. 9). Counseling works, but no particular brand appears to be greatly superior to any other. Borrowing from the dodo bird in *Alice in Wonderland,* Luborsky, Singer, and Luborsky (1975) said that "everybody has won and all must have prizes" (Norcross & Newman, 1992, p. 9).

The reaction to the news that all counseling approaches seem to work—but none appreciably better than any other—brought about a search for "common factors," or those curative elements that might be shared across theoretical schools, regardless of their stated aims. Kleinke (1994) asserted that by 1980, over 250 different psychotherapies had been identified. By 1989, Arnold Lazarus, in an address to the American Psychological Association, had characterized the proliferation of approaches to counseling as a state of "confusion, derangement, turmoil, and bedlam" (Kleinke, 1994, p. 2). In order to reduce the chaos and make sense of these various therapies, Kleinke surveyed authors who had identified common factors in psychotherapy that appear to be shared, no matter what the ostensible focus of each approach might be. Jerome Frank (1985) identified "an emotionally charged, confiding relationship with a helping person" (p. 4) as one of the four major components that appear to be shared by all approaches to psychotherapy. Along with other characteristics, Judd Marmor (1985) considered two to be vital. First, the client must endow the counselor with "help-giving potential" and, second, the client must have the "ability . . . to confide and express feelings to a person whom they trust and count on as being supportive" (pp. 4–5). Finally, according to Nicholas Hobbs (1962), a counselor is most effective when the client experiences the therapeutic relationship as one "in which it is possible for the client to be close to another person without getting hurt . . . [and] . . . The client is helped to develop an acceptable sense of meaning for life" (p. 5).

Regardless of the differences in their approaches to counseling and psychotherapy, all the theorists that Kleinke surveyed regarding common factors agreed that it is the caring relationship that establishes the foundation for effective work. In such a safe and trusting environment, clients can take risks—try new ways of thinking and acting—and can understand their thoughts and actions from a different perspective (Goldfried, 1980).

Fred Duhl, a well-known family therapist, dressed up in hip waders and fishing gear when he addressed a convention of therapists in order to make the following point: "The ways of the fish are more important than the tools of the fisherman" (Young, 1992, p. 32). No techniques can work if you do not first have a working relationship with your client. You might say that the relationship is what "hooks" the client into collaborating with you as a counselor. Furthermore, each client will respond to the techniques you are offering in a different way. Just as an expert fisherman allows the fish to run, rest, and "resist," all the while keeping a tender touch on the line so as to know when to reel the fish in, so does the sensitive counselor remain tuned to the client's moods and moves. This tentative, yet totally involved, attitude on the part of the counselor will do as much to help the client as any technique we can suggest.

A Caveat: Listen to Your Clients

Imagine our surprise when we picked up the July/August 1997 issue of *The Family Therapy Networker* and read that three of the more well-known exponents of solution-focused brief therapy had made the discovery that listening to clients is more important than flashy technique! Our surprise was that *they* were so surprised by this realization. In their article entitled "Stepping Off the Throne," Barry Duncan, along with Mark Hubble and Scott Miller, stated that "when faced with a seeming choice between technique and relationship, a therapist is often better off focusing on relationship" (p. 28). This insight apparently came to these authors as a result of their "impossible cases" study. This study was an attempt to show that the techniques of solution-focused brief therapy could be applied to all sorts of client problems and diagnoses. After absorbing the techniques of Weakland, de Shazer, Erickson, and others, Duncan, Hubble, and Miller wanted to show that the techniques of these master therapists were useful in the most difficult cases for which other approaches had failed.

As a result of their outreach efforts, Duncan, Hubble, and Miller were referred some "nightmare clients" by a local psychodynamically trained psychiatrist, who they were sure was seeking revenge. Ironically, while this trio of therapists eventually were able to report some success with these clients, this success apparently had little to do with their technical skills. What mattered was not the "technical wizardry" of the therapists or the particular therapeutic approach. Their success was credited more to the attitude they brought the therapeutic effort. What these therapists found was that success "is far more heavily influenced by what the clients bring into the room and the relationship that is created there" (p. 24). Realizing what they had lost in their haste to fix their clients and blinded by their "theoretical arrogance," these therapists decided to eschew their therapeutic tactics and, instead, start listening to what the clients were saying to them. Duncan reported that he spoke fewer than 15 sentences in one successful session. "I used no genograms, marital contracting, head tapping, guided imagery, miracle questions, finger waving, trance suggestions, enigmatic Ericksonian prescriptions, lies, manipulations or gurulike pronouncements" (p. 26). Instead, the therapy team "dethroned" themselves as therapeutic experts and began to listen to what clients made of their own situations, what theories the clients had, and how the clients thought that their problems might be solved.

Heeding the advice of the philosopher Pascal, who wrote that people are more persuaded by reasons that they themselves have discovered than by those from the minds of others, the team began to refrain from intervening too soon. Instead, they began listening more and inviting more participation on the part of their clients. They were encouraged both by the positive results in their sessions and by research that suggests "that positive change is correlated with how much clients—but not therapists—say" (p. 26). Specifically, a meta-analysis of over 1000 process-outcome studies (Bergin & Garfield, 1994) concluded that the most important determinant in successful outcomes was the quality of the client's participation. As a result, the team went back to the drawing board for rationales that supported what they were learning from their "impossible" clients. "The work led us in two apparently divergent directions—into a hard-boiled examination of outcome literature and into a rereading of Carl Rogers" (p. 26).

Rogers Rediscovered

It is not unusual for a person-centered therapist to attend a workshop or conference at which people are speaking with great enthusiasm about a new theory or technique that has been developed in their field, only to realize that it is right out of a Carl Rogers book! Often, without credit to Rogers, the new approach has been given a new name and declared a new discovery—much like Columbus "discovering" America in spite of the fact that people were already living there. Rogers's ideas have become so pervasive that their influence is felt in nearly all the newer forms of therapy. What initially had seemed to be his simplistic, overly optimistic, and naive ideas, now are appreciated for their "profound beauty and importance" (Kahn, 1991, p. 35). The notion of the importance of carefully listening to clients is a topic that pervades all of Rogers's writing, but, perhaps, no passage is more poignant than the following:

> One thing I have come to look upon as almost universal is that when a person realizes he has been deeply heard, there is a moistness in his eyes. I think in some real sense he is weeping for joy. It is as though he were saying, "Thank God, *somebody* heard me. Someone knows what it's like to be me." In such moments I have had the fantasy of a prisoner in a dungeon, tapping out day after day a Morse code message, "Does anybody hear me?" And finally one day he hears some faint tappings which spell out "Yes." By that one simple response he is released from his loneliness, he has become a human being again. There are many, many people living in private dungeons today, people who give no evidence of it whatever on the outside, where you have to listen very sharply to hear the faint messages from the dungeon. (Rogers, 1969, p. 224)

Although Kahn (1991) did not see Rogers's methods as sufficient for a complete therapy, he considered their relationship aspects to be indispensable. He wrote that no matter what theory we hold dear, or how we view the human mind, "there is much to be learned by paying careful attention to Rogers's advice about the relationship between therapist and client" (pp. 35–36).

Walter and Peller (1992) are solution-focused brief therapists who have placed little emphasis on building a trusting relationship with a client. They presume that trust simply exists. However, in spite of their lack of emphasis on the Rogerian approach, they specifically cite the basic techniques of Rogers as important to maintaining a working relationship in which the client feels supported and understood. Among these techniques are "reflective listening and empathic listening, the restating what the client said, with the same affect and tone . . . [This remains essential to communicating] initial support of the client's position" (pp. 42–43).

In addition, solution-focused brief therapists O'Hanlon and Beadle (1994) described a therapeutic technique called "Carl Rogers with a Twist" in their book on a specific therapeutic approach called possibility therapy. Following Rogers, they communicate acceptance of their clients. However, "then we add a little twist. We communicate, 'where you are now is a valid place to be, AND you can change' " (p. 15).

Though they cite Rogers in naming their technique, O'Hanlon and Beadle see what they do as an intervention, rather than as an attempt to listen to the client with the intent of encouraging him or her to further explore a concern. The "Rogers" part of the technique is employed as an acknowledgment of the client's concern, while also adding the more important possibility statements that are implied in what the client says. In fact, Carl Rogers himself used the technique of "Carl Rogers with a Twist" on the famous "Gloria" videotape (Rogers, 1965).

Duncan, Hubble, and Miller (1997) have taken the advice of Rogers to heart and now place more emphasis on carefully attending to the client and establishing that crucial bond between therapist and client. They have come to believe that extreme care must be taken to ensure a high-quality relationship after reports from their clients that simple courtesy and confirmation of the clients' position had been experienced as very powerful. Initially, they thought of such behaviors as "foreplay," a way to woo the client into doing the real work of therapy. However, their reading of Carl Rogers convinced them of the importance of the core conditions of empathy, warmth, genuineness, and acceptance:

> Now, we realized that the relationship was, in fact, the therapy. . . . [C]lients are far more likely to consider these "core variables" responsible for their improvement than theories and flashy technique. (p. 29)

By 1997, the "impossible-case" project of Duncan, Hubble, and Miller was 10 years old, and they regarded the project to have been generally successful. But the project's greatest success proved to be in the reorientation of the therapists. The therapy team members reported that now, when they train and supervise others, "we encourage them, above all, to listen and to notice the effect of their words on their clients. . . . [W]e emphasize the factors that are common to all good therapy" (p. 33). A dyed-in-the-wool person-centered therapist might criticize the realizations of these solution-focused therapists as nothing but "old wine in new bottles," but we don't believe Carl Rogers would object. It was never his wish to create a person-centered movement. Rather, Rogers hoped to influence the behavior of therapists in relationship to their clients. He certainly has been vindicated by Duncan, Hubble, and Miller and the "impossible-case" project.

Empathy as Technique

Becvar, Canfield, and Becvar (1997) spoke of the counselor's attitude as one of "beneficence," a term that "dates back at least 2,500 years to the time of Hippocrates in classical Greece . . ." (p. 57). They considered this stance to be the primary moral imperative for the helping professions. *Beneficence* means engaging in acts of kindness and doing no harm. Merely doing no harm, however, could imply mere acts of passive observation, acts of charity, or acts of sympathy. You must do much more than this. You must engage with your client—you must seek to enter the client's world and understand it from his or her frame of reference. This "engagement" does not mean simply being kind. Instead, you must "be with" the client. You must be empathic. This admonition is central to the notion of a therapeutic relationship and is considered scripture among humanists—so much so as to have had its utterance now seem almost clichéd and trite. "Being with" conveys the idea that a counselor must not only empathize, but communicate that empathy for the client's plight.

The notion of empathy is very confusing to beginning counselors. They often think it means becoming so close to the client that the client's pain is taken on or absorbed by the counselor. To do less than this is typically regarded as not caring enough. But too much "caring" of this sort is good for neither the client nor the counselor. Counselors find it difficult to maintain the optimal distance between being too removed from the client and being too close. Welch (1998) offered some useful observations on the empathic nature of the counseling relationship and optimal distance. Although the relationship in counseling is an intimate one, Welsh stated that a certain degree of detachment is necessary. The counselor must remain concerned, while being objective. "Those who err on the side of closeness burn up with the emotions. . . . Those who err on the side of detachment become calloused to the pain of people" (pp. 55–56).

You must always strive to achieve the proper therapeutic distance from the client's concerns. Optimal therapeutic distance means that you maintain a boundary between client and yourself—albeit a permeable one. This separation not only preserves you in the relationship, but serves as a model for the client as well. Clients often come to counseling having been submerged by their concerns and feeling overwhelmed by their emotions. To focus inordinately on pain and confusion only causes the client to sink deeper into discouragement. As DeJong and Berg (1998) put it, "We believe that empathy, like any other skill, can be overemphasized. We definitely do not recommend that you use the type of empathy that is sentimental or that tends to amplify negative feelings" (p. 37).

By maintaining a proper *therapeutic distance* (a term we prefer to *detached concern*), you avoid exacerbating the client's problems. Furthermore, when working in the brief-resolution mode, you invite the client to move away from the pain and problem into a more hopeful realm, seeking to find the survivor in the victim. While the difference between a "therapeutic alliance," in the psychodynamic sense, and a "working alliance" is not completely clear in the counseling literature, we would assert that a working alliance is intended to be somewhat less intimate and of shorter duration. If this works well, aspects of the relationship such as client dependence, transference, and difficulty with termination may be minimized.

The optimal balance between intimacy and detachment is always dependent on the mutually agreed upon contract between you and the client. This contract, however, is largely implicit and is always in flux. Some days the client can tolerate more distance; at other times he or she will demand more intimacy. When attempts are made to influence the client's movement toward a goal, and the client returns to "problem-saturated talk," this is a signal that you must move a bit closer and reacknowledge the client's concerns.

Acknowledgment can be empathically communicated without highlighting the client's negative mood. DeJong and Berg (1998) suggested that, rather than highlighting the client's pain and discouragement in the present, you might say, "Things have been pretty discouraging for you." Then immediately proceed to look for client behaviors that fly in the face of the negative situation. The difference between DeJong and Berg's preferred responses and the ones they consider less useful is that you are suggesting that the client's emotions are situational, relational, and time-limited.

Portraying emotions in these ways has profound implications for how clients view their concerns and themselves. *Situational* concerns do not require that clients get personality transplants. Rather, they are about events that have taken place that can be remedied or transcended. *Relational* concerns imply a contribution on the part of someone else and that the problem exists between at least two people—not within one person. This may relieve the client of some feelings of crushing responsibility. Finally, the *time-limited* connotation of the acknowledgment suggests that the problem will not last forever—without the counselor resorting to trite and obviously empty reassurances, such as, "This is a phase you're going through."

If you have been trained to probe and uncover deeper feelings so that the client might get in touch with "repressed" or disavowed emotions, you may find the above suggested acknowledgment a bit lightweight. Perhaps it is. But whether it is an adequate acknowledgment or not depends on the client. You must remain sensitive to the client's nonverbal communication and to whether the client seems willing to move toward resolution talk. O'Hanlon and Beadle (1994) suggested that clients will send a message if they do not feel sufficiently understood as a result of your acknowledgment. At such times, more acknowledgment is required. Empathy is, after all, the extent to which clients believe they are understood—not the extent to which you believe *you* understand.

O'Hanlon and Beadle (1994) used the metaphor of the sport of curling, in which the participants use brooms to sweep a path for a stone sliding along the ice, to explain how carefully you must move the client toward solutions. A curler sweeps immediately in front of the stone, and so the counselor must sweep directly in front of the client by opening up possibilities. The curler must pay close attention to where the stone is, and less to where it should go. "Translated into therapy-land, that means we'd better pay more attention to where clients actually are than to our theory about where they should be" (p. 11).

Unless the client experiences your empathy—your accurate understanding of his or her world—you will not receive an invitation to help. Unless that invitation is received, clients will appear to resist your best attempts to assist them. You cannot say that the client is noncompliant in such a situation. It is more likely that you have not yet convinced the client that you truly understand. To restate a line from the movie *Cool Hand Luke*, "What we have here is failure to communicate." Communicating empathy is your job, and the communication is never complete until the client gets it.

Implications of These Ideas for the Counselor

Ideas concerning the centrality of relationship in any productive encounter have important implications for your day-to-day work with clients:

- No matter how well informed you become about people and counseling in general, the individual client *always* remains the expert on his or her own experience.
- Whatever the client does in the counseling session is a function of being *with* you. You and the client are both participants in the construction of the client's story.

- The most important aspect of successful counseling is the *relationship*. This means that you must attempt to communicate to the client that you care, that the client can trust you, and that you will do your best to listen and understand. Without this as the basis of your work, the counseling is likely to go nowhere. Counselors must carefully listen to what clients have to say, so you must somehow communicate to the client that he or she has been heard. But this does not mean that you encourage clients to further explore all the nuances of their pain. The notion of "Carl Rogers with a Twist" implies that you also seek to add a possibility statement to your acknowledgment.
- It is important to communicate empathic *understanding* to your clients, while, at the same time, maintaining a therapeutic distance. This means that you do not allow yourself to be overwhelmed by the client's pain.
- Any time you are attempting to lead the client away from a focus on the concern—and the client returns to "problem-saturated talk"—this is your signal to *return to acknowledging* the client's current version of the story.
- Before you attempt to engineer a change in the client's story, make sure you have been *invited* to do so. If your client resists, it means you have been uninvited. Go back to acknowledging.

TOOLS

Establishing the Counseling Relationship

When you begin a counseling relationship, there are two fundamental tasks that you must perform—*attend to* and *acknowledge* the client. According to *Webster's New World Dictionary,* "attend" means to give heed to, be mindful of, minister to, or serve. "Acknowledge" means to recognize as having authority or worth, and accept as being true or having value.

Attending and *acknowledging* sum up well the behavior of the successful counselor in the beginning stages of counseling. But even though they are well-defined terms that convey the proper attitude, they do not immediately imply precise concrete behaviors. We might come closer by stating that there is a triad of behaviors that must be exhibited by the counselor in order to convince the client that the counselor is, indeed, attending and acknowledging. We call this the "LUV triangle" (Figure 3-1). In the LUV triangle, you display behaviors that convey to the client that you are *listening, understanding*, and

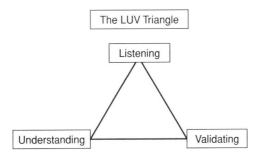

FIGURE 3-1　　The LUV triangle.

validating the client's view of things. Similarly, Scott Miller (1996) uses the acronym "LAV" to describe these behaviors (listen, acknowledge, validate). However, his terms do not all seem to be at the same level of abstraction.

Even with the use of these more concrete terms, it is probably still not completely clear to you what you are actually doing. So let us attempt to further establish what the precise behaviors are that would be called for at the beginning of a counseling relationship. The most important aspect of these behaviors is that the client must perceive that you are attempting to establish the LUV triangle. In other words, these conditions must be communicated to the client. It is one thing to intend to send a certain message, and quite another for the message to be received as planned. This point cannot be overstated.

What does it mean to *listen* so that the client believes you are paying attention? According to Egan (1994), it helps to perform the following behaviors.

- Face the client with an engaged, inviting manner.
- Adopt an open, nonthreatening posture.
- Lean toward the client.
- Maintain good eye contact.
- Keep a sense of poise, and refrain from fidgeting.

How will the client know that you *understand* what is being said? There are a variety of specific strategies that you can use to communicate your understanding.

- Repeat or paraphrase what the client has said.
- Check your understanding by saying what you think the client means and asking for verification.
- Nonverbally match your client's mood and the pace or rhythm of his or her communication.
- Use words, phrases, and expressions that are similar to the client's.

Be particularly alert for the metaphors that the client uses as descriptors of the problem and for what the client hopes to change. At this stage, you stay with the content that the client is giving you, without probing or going beyond the facts that are offered.

Finally, what can you do in order to convey your willingness to *validate* the client? There are a number of simple behaviors you can use to communicate that you support the client and affirm what he or she is saying.

- Nod affirmatively as the client speaks.
- Smile warmly and offer minimal encouragers ("um-hmm," "I see," "yes, go on," etc.).
- Refrain from conveying skepticism, doubt, or the desire to debate with the client.

Of course, you do not ask questions that may indicate repudiation of the client's presentation of his or her experiences; nor do you behave in any way that suggests you are devaluing the client. Instead, by validating, you are indicating, in every way you can, your openness and willingness to believe what the client is telling you.

"Carl Rogers with a Twist"

We find that most people misunderstand Carl Rogers and his way of working with clients. Ask the average counselor and he or she will say that the essence of Rogers's work was the "um-hmm" and the "I hear you saying . . ." phrases. Others, even farther off base, think it is the "How do you feel about that?" question. A close analysis of Rogers's work reveals an extremely subtle maneuvering strategy that influenced clients to center the conversation on themselves and to begin to realize their personal power. If any set of techniques qualifies as "empowering" another person, it is Carl Rogers's way of counseling. Most people understand his approach only superficially and think it is simply being a kind, friendly, accepting person—an attitude sometimes pejoratively known as "Little Bo Peep Psychology"—"Leave them alone and they'll come home. . . ."

O'Hanlon and Beadle (1994) have said that what Rogers did was acknowledge the client. The focus of the acknowledgment was not so much on the client's feelings as on the client's meanings. If the client hears meanings coming back from you that match his or her own, the client feels understood. While many would call this understanding "merely cognitive," it seems to do the job. O'Hanlon and Beadle's notion of "Carl Rogers with a Twist" (which sounds more like a cocktail than a technique) involves doing three tasks simultaneously when you acknowledge the client.

- Feed back the meaning of the client's complaint.
- Place that complaint in language of the past tense.
- Replace client language of "stuckness" or despair with language of possibility.

For example, instead of saying to the client, "You *are experiencing* a lot of *depression* about your *inability* to resolve this situation," you might say, "You've *gone through* some times when you've felt *really down* because you have *not yet* found a way to resolve this situation."

O'Hanlon insisted that we must "watch our language" with clients, and that the use of subtly different feedback—while retaining the client's meaning—can change the way the client views the situation. In the above example, substituting "you've gone through" (past tense) for "you are experiencing" (present tense), and "really down" (a less damning phrase) for "depression" (a diagnosis), and "not yet" (implying that it's a matter of time) for "inability" (a personal flaw), all serve to reframe the situation. You convey the message, in so many words, that the client has been having normal reactions to a situation that has existed in the past, but which will be resolved, offering the client a more positive and hopeful view.

Past Tense Phrases. You can characterize these negative emotions as taking place in the past by using a variety of phrases. For example, you might say, "for a long time you have felt . . .," or "you didn't seem to be able to shake the feeling of . . ." Placing these emotions within a certain time period suggests that these feelings or perceptions were influenced by situations that may have changed. For example, you could say, "When that happened, you felt . . .," or "Because he didn't seem to be paying attention to you, you believed . . .," or "When she would do that, you thought that it meant. . . ." You can even suggest that this feeling or perception may be different now by saying, for example, "Until now, it has seemed to you that. . . ."

Possibility Phrases. Dropping in some suggestions of the possibility of a future resolution is an excellent way of planting the seeds of change. Your reflections may begin with such phrases as, "*So far,* you have not seemed to be able to . . .," or "You have *not yet* been able to accomplish this." Other possibility phrases include, "You *haven't quite* mastered the skill of . . .," or "When this happens again, *you're wondering how* you will handle it differently," or "You're thinking that it might be difficult, but you still *really want* to do it."

Another less obvious aspect to this form of feedback is that a reframe is automatically built into it. When clients tell you how things are going, or what kind of persons they think themselves to be, the opportunity for you to normalize the situation is present. For example, a *loser* is someone who, despite many setbacks, keeps on trying; a *lazy* person is someone who must think about a job for a while before starting it; and a *control freak* is someone who has wonderful attention to detail and works for the best outcome. You get the idea—when clients use damning phrases to characterize themselves, you can modify and loosen the client's construction of the world by feeding back more positive terms as if the client had used those words in the first place. By taking care to communicate your respect, you can successfully carry out this process without coming across as the stern teacher correcting the client on improper word usage.

In addition, you can rephrase client assertions about "the way things are" into more tentative terms. Instead of colluding with the client's absolute pronouncements about reality, you can accept the client's declaration as a point of view or "*one way* to look at it." For example, you can preface your acknowledgments with such phrases as, "So, in your *opinion* . . .," or "The *way you see* it . . .," or, "It *seems* to you that. . . ." Each of these statements suggests that it is the person's *perception*, rather than reality itself, that is being considered here.

"Carl Rogers with a Twist" is a useful technique for simultaneously acknowledging the client's complaint, while at the same time, beginning to deconstruct it.

Listening in on a Session

Review the story at the beginning of the chapter. A resolution-focused counselor might engage with Edra in ways that promote the relationship by using the LUV triangle and "Carl Rogers with a Twist."

> **Edra:** (*After her litany of complaints about the recent events, Edra pauses, looks at the counselor expectantly, and waits a moment or two.*) I'm such a loser! I always end up with guys that treat me like dirt. I think I take after my mother, because she's unlucky with men, too.
>
> **Counselor:** (*Looking directly at Edra and speaking in a calm but concerned tone of voice, the counselor decides to invite Edra in deconstructing her story.*) You've been having to deal with so many problems with Todd lately that you are wondering what it might be like to be treated well by a man.
>
> **Edra:** (*Her voice starts to quiver and her eyes fill with tears as she continues, pausing often to wipe her eyes and blow her nose.*) I really wish I knew. . . . Anyway, Todd finally showed up about 6:00 and tells me he had a flat tire. I screamed and yelled at him for making me late and not calling. Then I got into this huge fight with him and called him a stupid asshole. He just looked at me and walked away. I can't believe what a complete bitch I am! By the time I got to the library, it was closed. I was going to call somebody in my group last night to explain everything,

but I was so embarrassed about screwing things up that I just couldn't do it. So now my group thinks I blew off my part of the project.

Counselor: (*Since Edra has returned to "problem-saturated talk," the counselor returns to the LUV triangle by indicating understanding, nodding her head affirmatively, and speaking empathically, while adding a twist at the end.*) So it must have felt like the whole world has been against you since yesterday afternoon. It looked to you like Todd let you down. Then you thought your group may have gotten the wrong idea about you, too. You've been feeling really upset and now you've come here to find a way out.

Edra: (*Her voice becomes softer takes on a sad quality. The tears begin again and her demeanor and tone of voice suggest that Edra sees herself as helpless.*) Yeah! It's like I'm in really deep water and I can't even see the shore.

Counselor: (*Softly and leaning forward*) Yeah, you've felt that you've been in way over your head lately, and now you're looking for a place to come ashore.

Reflecting Questions

1. Point out the verbal and nonverbal examples of the LUV triangle in the above interaction.
2. Identify the "twists" that the counselor offered.
3. Write another possible LUV triangle statement or "Rogers with a Twist" response to Edra's last comment.

Using This Tool

Form a group of three. One should volunteer to be a client by sharing a situation in which he or she feels stuck. Another volunteers to help by using the "Rogers with a Twist" technique. In other words, feed back the meaning of the client's words, but use the past tense in acknowledging complaints and use the present and future tenses to suggest possibilities of successes. Finally, the third person serves as the recorder, who observes the activity, and leads the feedback discussion.

We believe that the use of this technique is a turning point in the therapeutic relationship. This is the first time that the counselor becomes intentionally influential in deconstructing. Because this technique is so fundamental to becoming an effective brief counselor, you need to do two things. First, practice this technique until it feels as natural to you as the LUV skills. Second, take time in your group to talk about your reactions to being both compassionate and influencing, genuine and intentional, heartfelt and goal-oriented.

Deconstructing Client Complaints

When clients begin to give descriptions of their concerns, they believe that what they offer is a recollection of the facts of their lives. In other words, there are events happening in the real world that have an impact on their lives and they believe these are objective, immutable happenings. You will find in the literature of solution-oriented approaches that how clients talk about problems in their lives is sometimes referred to as "problem-saturated" talk or the client's "complaint." On first reading, you may think these terms are disrespectful or a trivialization of the client's pain, but the words are really meant to remind us that the "map is not the territory." No matter how faithful the client believes he or she is to the facts of the matter, in the constructivist view there really are no facts of the matter.

Client descriptions of their problems are their interpretations of the facts. These descriptions are loaded with personal meaning for the client, and it is usually this meaning—and not the facts themselves—that causes the client to suffer. Milton Erickson is said to have stated that his clients came with problems they couldn't solve, so he gave them problems they could solve, meaning that problems can be deconstructed, or changed into other problems. In other words, problems are negotiable. Your job is to renegotiate the client's complaint so that it is looser and more workable and offers a way out. We hasten to point out, however, that this does not mean you should attempt to turn problems into nonproblems. You are not trying to talk the client out of the problem or to minimize it in the way that a parent might have done. We all can recall examples of those attempts: "You think you've got problems? You should think of the starving people in Africa." or "In a year, you'll laugh about this." or "So what if you missed this one—there are plenty more fish in the sea." If you can vaguely recall any of these parental responses to your complaints, you also realize that they are utterly useless! When you attempt to deconstruct complaints, you are not trying to get clients to "look on the bright side." You are subtly offering another interpretation of the complaint, which you hope will throw the problem into a more workable frame.

Everyone's world is a constructed one. That is, the way we see things and what we view as facts are filtered through our representations and our meanings. When you attempt to "deconstruct" a client's world, you are not simply trying to get the client to see things your way. Rather, you are perturbing the schemes that the client has constructed. This approach is not the "disputation" therapy, as is sometimes seen in the "rational–emotive" techniques. Deconstruction is quite different from disputation. In the latter approach, the counselor actively exposes and corrects the client's irrational, self-defeating thinking. Albert Ellis, who does not mince words, tells us that irrational beliefs "can be elicited and demolished by any scientist worth his or her salt, and the rational-emotive therapist is exactly that: an exposing and nonsense-annihilating scientist" (in Gelso & Fretz, 1992, p. 250).

Instead of viewing clients as having faulty thinking, you validate, rather than dispute, client perspectives. You are not trying to talk the client out of his or her assumptions and into yours. However, by attempting to loosen the client's rigid categories and self-defeating assumptions, you hope to send these constructions into disarray so that the client can rebuild, or reconstruct, a world with more possibilities. In that sense, the client becomes empowered to meet the world head-on and with less trepidation. The client's new assumptions and constructions will be built on the same "facts," but will offer a new way of seeing these "facts."

A client may construct a story that is self-defeating by using dead-end, all-or-nothing, irrefutable, and insoluble complaints that express certain emotions, but also sabotage a search for resolution. Below are some of the most common stagnating portrayals that clients are likely to use. With each of them, we offer some suggestions for deconstructing them. Please keep in mind that these suggestions are meant to be examples, rather than rigid prescriptions for your counseling behavior. You can use your own creativity in deconstructing client complaints, and you must also pay careful attention to how the client responds. Remember the axiom coined by the solution-focused therapists: If your intervention doesn't work, do something different.

The client's complaint is couched as universal. In other words, something is "always" or "never" happening. To deconstruct this portrayal, you can respond by describing the circumstances as possibly *episodic* or *situational*. For example, you might say, "So you've been going through some really hard times recently, and it seems that this problem has been happening nearly all the time."

The client's portrayal is the absolute truth or "reality." The client implies that his or her interpretation is the only valid representation of the events. The basic deconstructing strategy is to respond to these assertions as *perceptions*—the client's interpretation of the facts. In this case, you may be prefacing your responses with, "So it has seemed to you that . . .," "The way it has looked to you is . . .," "In your eyes . . .," or "From your perspective. . . ."

The client heavily relies on a label or diagnosis to characterize self and others. For example, the client announces, "I am an enabler," "My daughter is an anorectic," or "My son has a conduct disorder." Here, you attempt to deconstruct by describing the specific behaviors that relate to the diagnosis, or relabel the behaviors. For example, you may respond to the self-described "enabler" by saying, "So many times when he has wanted money for alcohol, you have let yourself give it to him and then you have lied to his employer about his being sick." To the parent who labels a daughter as "anorectic," you might answer, "So let me check this out. Your daughter has not been eating enough and she has become so thin that it's endangering her health?" And with the parent who diagnoses a child as having "a conduct disorder," you might respond, "So your son seems to be someone who has questioned authority an awful lot."

The purpose of deconstructing stories that rely on such diagnostic characterizations of people is that behaviors are much easier to change than labels.

The client gives a litany of problems. The client presents a long list of concerns, complaints and grievances. Focusing on one concern that seems the most workable or most urgent to the client is a good deconstructive method. You may say, for example, "Wow! It sounds like it's just been one thing after another for you. I can understand how you have felt so overwhelmed. If you could choose only one concern to start with, which would you pick?"

The client portrays himself or herself as a passive victim. As appealing as motivational speakers may occasionally sound, deconstructing a client's self-portrayal as a victim requires more than an inspirational slogan or challenge. Instead, you can offer a deconstructive strategy by externalizing the problem. For example, you might say, "So nearly every time that refrigerator has beckoned to you, you have found yourself listening to that Siren song." or "When that old depression monster began to whisper in your ear and tried to get you down, you decided to give in."

Please note that you should not present an externalization as controlling the client's behaviors, moods, and thoughts, but rather as merely attempting to *influence* the client. In other words, you would not say to yourself, "The devil made me do it," but "The devil whispered in my ear and told me to do it." We will describe the technique of "externalization" in greater detail in a later chapter.

The client speaks in pejoratives by making negative statements about self or others. Working to deconstruct this portrayal involves responding to the pejoratives in a neutral manner, normalizing them, and *separating the behaviors from the labels.* For example, you might say to a client, "So, you have been labeling yourself as 'overly dependent' because you like to rely on your mother for things that you realize you could do for yourself."

The client's rendition of the situation is vague and unclear. The deconstruction process could include engaging with the client to *clarify* the circumstances without probing the feeling level. In other words, you can encourage the client to "video talk" it (O'Hanlon & Beadle, 1994). For example, you might say, "I would like to be really clear on how this has been for you. I guess I'm kind of a visual person. Pretend that we are watching a video of what you are describing and you are the guide telling me what I'm seeing."

The client's concern is stated in the present tense. He or she may be saying, for example, ". . . and so now I'm so fed up with my life, there's no choice but to kill myself." Your deconstructing strategy here is to place the problem in the *past tense* and offer the current conclusion as only one of a number of options. Responding to the above client statement, you might empathically engage in the deconstruction process by saying, "So far, you've felt like nothing has worked and as you sorted out your options, the one that came up first as a possibility was suicide."

The client's complaint is characterized as a state. In other words, the concern is presented as something that is fixed and unchangeable. One promising deconstruction approach with such a characterization is to turn it into a *process*—an ongoing dynamic that is subject to change. For example, you might say to a client, "Yeah, you've really had some tough times getting launched from your family, and you have sometimes wondered whether your autonomy is worth all that effort." Another possible response is reflecting, "It just seems so hard to get through all this rehearsal for being a grownup." or "Sometimes it has looked like you'd have to choose between being adult and being in your family, but what you really want is to find that place where you have both."

The client speaks of the situation as global. The concern is seen as something that happens across all situations. When a client portrays the problem as global, your best deconstructive strategy is to contextualize the problem. This technique involves creatively misunderstanding a statement so that the client will name an exception. For example, you might speculate, "So I guess even when you're in church or at work, you still have found yourself acting that way." Or you may wonder out loud, "I guess when you were at Disney World riding the Tower of Terror, these thoughts were still going through your mind."

Listening in on a Session

Let's go back to this chapter's story and continue with the dialogue between Edra and her school counselor.

> **Edra:**   I guess that I got myself to come here because I can see that my whole life is impossibly screwed-up.
>
> **Counselor:**   Well, with all the frustrations that have piled on since yesterday, it sure has seemed to you like these things have been happening all your life.
>
> **Edra:**   Yeah. And if I weren't such a loser, I wouldn't have been in this mess to begin with.

Counselor: (*Softly and leaning forward*) Let me check something out with you, Edra. When you've been talking about yourself as a "loser," it sounds like you think that you made a mistake about choosing Todd as your boyfriend and you have been blaming yourself since then.

Edra: (*Reflecting*) Yeah, but Todd's not such a bad guy. I just don't think I can depend on him to be there for me even when he makes a promise. Now with everything else that's happening, I don't know what to do.

Counselor: It looks like since yesterday, it's just felt like it was one disappointment after another for you, Edra. With all that has happened, everything must have seemed really discouraging.

Reflecting Questions

1. In what ways has the counselor encouraged the client in the deconstruction process?
2. How has the counselor used the LUV triangle in this interaction?
3. How might you respond to Edra's comments?

Using This Tool

Realizing that you would not try to deconstruct every stagnating portrayal a client offers, choose just five of the many that are embedded in this chapter's story and offer a deconstructing statement for each.

Stagnating Portrayals:	*Deconstructing Statement:*
1. _____	_____
_____	_____
2. _____	_____
_____	_____
3. _____	_____
_____	_____
4. _____	_____
_____	_____
5. _____	_____
_____	_____

An Important Reminder

It should be obvious to you at this point that establishing a relationship in which the client feels you have listened, understood, and validated his or her position is going to take a lot of practice. When you add the attempt to deconstruct the client's story in order to give it more possibilities, you will find yourself walking a tightrope. Turning to the LUV triangle will never fail to help you keep that balance. You can always go back to communicating to the client that you are listening, understanding, and validating. As you add "Carl Rogers with a Twist" and attempt to deconstruct the client's complaint, you must constantly be sensitive to the reaction you are getting: *Anytime the client balks, go back to LUV.* This is true even in later phases of the work. If the client seems to be "resisting," this is a message to you that the client believes you have forgotten to attend to and acknowledge the pain he or she is experiencing, and that you have run too far ahead. After you have returned to LUV for a while and the client seems once more to feel understood, try again to begin adding possibility statements to your feedback and subtly deconstructing the client's complaint. Your client will let you know if he or she is ready to go with you toward resolution.

Using This Tool

Return to your groups of three. One of you should elaborate on your previous client presentation by adding dead-end, all-or-nothing, irrefutable, and insoluble portrayals of your concerns. Another volunteers to help by using any of the above suggested strategies for deconstructing client traps. Finally, the third person serves as the recorder, who observes the activity, leads the feedback discussion, and reports the group's experience to the class.

SUMMARY

The techniques of brief counseling are not magic. They are not mysterious or secret, and they do not reflect some hidden, special, and spontaneous power within the helper. In other words, a brief counselor does not have a bag of magic tricks. Instead, you have tool kits and you practice your craft by forming a helping relationship and using basic tools of change. These basic tools, or common factors of effective helping, include using the LUV triangle and "Rogers with a Twist."

SEGUE TO CHAPTER 4

Think about a time when you were aspiring to achieve something important. How did thinking about this future possibility affect how you were currently acting? After reflecting on your answer, begin reading the next chapter.

CHAPTER 4

Helping Clients Frame Goals:
The Pull of the Future

"The future is made of the same stuff as the present."
Simone Weil

CHAPTER GOALS

Reading about and experiencing the ideas in this chapter will help you to understand the following concepts:

- The future is now. Helping clients to frame goals for the future also changes their current way of viewing themselves and the world.
- The counselor–client relationship may be characterized as that of a "customer," "complainant," "visitor," or involuntary.

Reading about and practicing the tools in this chapter will help you to learn these valuable skills:

- Finding the gaps in the client's story that are the exceptions to the problem.
- Using scaling techniques to help clients recognize that resolution is not an all-or-nothing proposition, envision their goals with greater detail and vividness, and assess their progress in achieving these goals.

STORY

"This is NOT how I want to be living my life," Jamelle muttered as she sat in her car, caught in the 45-minute traffic jam, gritting her teeth and gripping the steering wheel. With a vague sense of dread, she concluded that, if anything, she would be squandering her life even more when she finally did make it to work. Like every other day at her management trainee job, she would endure hours sitting in her Dilbert-like cubicle and performing what seemed to her to be meaningless tasks. She never knew why she was doing the assignments that mysteriously appeared on her computer screen. Nobody could satisfactorily explain to her the purpose of the chores she completed at her computer. On those rare occasions when she did bring up a question or offer a suggestion to one of her supervisors, she was worried that she was being seen as either dimwitted or naive—in either case, definitely not management material. The only certainty at work was that she always felt behind the other trainees.

But work was not the only place where she felt inadequate and behind, like a student who arrives both unprepared and late for a test, or a birthday present that's both cheap and belated. "Who am I kidding?" Jamelle thought. "I'm just as messed up and clueless in my personal life." All her friends were either sprinting ahead on fast-track career paths, happily pairing off in intimate relationships, or having babies—and some were even successfully managing to do all the above. While they were moving forward with their lives, Jamelle was bouncing around like a pinball from one trivial point to another, careening along without any real sense of direction or purpose.

One particularly frantic day, all the management trainees had to attend an intensive workshop on new federal regulations. The red-faced, clenched-jawed workshop leader was like a drill instructor, using the Socratic method of questioning as an attack weapon rather than as a learning tool. The expressions on the faces of everyone else ranged from gaunt apprehension to grim determination as they struggled with the challenging questions and frantically took notes on the complex material. Jamelle was certain that her own face had that frozen, "deer-in-the-headlights" look. Like a threatened animal, she certainly felt that same sickening sense of paralysis. In fact, she was so panicked and flustered that, although her neighbors had several pages of notes by the end of the workshop, her pen had barely moved. After the others filed out of the room, Jamelle remained to jot down as much of the material as she could remember and left feeling relieved that the workshop leader had not targeted her for interrogation. After lunch, the trainees were all scheduled to meet with someone in the company's Employee Assistance Program, so Jamelle found herself sitting in a comfortable chair facing a counselor.

REFLECTING QUESTIONS

1. What do you see as the primary issue that Jamelle faces?
2. If you were Jamelle's counselor, how would you help her to address this primary issue?

CHAPTER OVERVIEW

One of the assumptions of the medical model is that knowing the cause of a client's current symptoms is ultimately necessary in order find a cure. Because the cause always exists prior to the symptoms, taking a client's history has been the traditional beginning of the counseling process. However, in brief counseling, you start your counseling work with a view to the future, rather than to the past. How is it possible for something that has not yet happened to cause a change in someone's present condition? In fact, hope and a sense of purpose—both essential parts of any successful life—are actually rooted in the future. When people act now to anticipate a possibility, their future is affecting their present. This idea, first articulated by Aristotle, is known as teleology, or final cause.

No doubt, at the physical level, we are "caused" to behave. For example, should we choose to jump from the sixth floor window of a building, we will fall. Gravity, of course, is the simple and obvious cause of our fall. But the "why" of our jumping is not a cause, but, rather, a reason. And furthermore, the reason was probably based on our expectation of what would happen after we jumped—the reason would be about our future.

If the future actually played out in a strictly teleological manner, then we would always know with certainty what is going to happen. Human life, however, is more often lived "teleonomically"—that is, we know the general direction of our lives, but we are not certain about the specific circumstances of our future (Mahoney, 1995). Nevertheless, although they are neither definite nor inevitable, goals help us to maintain purpose and hope in our lives.

One of the most important activities in which you can engage with clients is seeking to understand and helping to frame their goals. Once articulated, goals serve as teleonomic guides for the direction of the counseling work. In this chapter, we discuss how to develop well-formed goals with a client and how to ascertain whether your counselor–client relationship is that of a "customer," "complainant," "visitor," or involuntary. Third parties, people who refer clients to you, often have goals that are not the same as those of the client. We offer suggestions for framing the referral and working to align the third-party and client goals. Finally, we describe how to use the tools of finding exceptions and scaling techniques.

IDEAS

What Are Etiology and Teleology?

When someone asks us to explain why we behave in a certain way, we often point to our *past* and offer a *cause* as the answer. We may answer, for example, "I've always done it that way," "That's the way I learned it," or "My mother told me to do it that way." In other words, we see past events as causing our current behaviors. The "past causes present" assumption is common in most people's thinking. When clients come to you for counseling, they often want you to discover what's causing the experiences and behaviors that are vexing them. They have the idea that some past trauma, habit, or unexamined experience is holding them prisoner to a way of thinking, feeling, and acting that is now causing them anguish. These clients want to know the *etiology* of their current situations. *Etiology* is the deterministic notion that is the stock-in-trade of most traditional scientific thought. In this view, all events are caused, and the causes always precede—or come before—the effects.

But is it possible that behaviors in the present could be caused by the future? At first glance, this idea sounds a bit preposterous, doesn't it? Nevertheless, recognizing how the future can cause the present offers a valuable perspective for a counselor. Taking this point of view, your job as a counselor is to help clients construct a future image that will change their current ways of thinking, feeling, and acting. Many people turn to counseling when their present is no longer viable and their future seems grim. It is your challenge to help them imagine a future in which they could be happy and fulfilled, and thus give purpose to their present behaviors.

The philosopher Aristotle, who said that everything is on its way to realizing its potential (Palmer, 1994), originated the idea that present behaviors are attempts to actualize a future goal. In fact, according to Aristotle, the prime motivator in our lives is our striving for a more perfect future. He called this the final cause or *teleology* and said that "everything 'moves' toward [the future] in the way a runner moves toward a goal" (p. 73). *Telos* in Greek means end, goal, purpose, or reason why. In the teleological view of counseling, it matters little how the client got to the present moment. What matters most is where the client wishes to go from here. Teleology—not etiology—is, therefore, the thrust of a brief counseling approach.

In the first half of the 20th century, during the behaviorist hegemony over psychology, humans were portrayed as mere reactors to stimuli that came from the environment. Their behavior had no purpose—no more than a rock falling downhill. Then, in 1948, the behaviorist Edward Tolman suggested that even maze-running rats seem to display purposeful behaviors (Hothersall, 1995). The rats desired a goal and they developed strategies for getting what they wanted. Furthermore, Tolman asserted that rats (and even people!) created "cognitive maps"—mental representations of their environments—that aided them in their movements toward their goals.

Later, in the 1960s, Martin Seligman developed the theory of "learned helplessness," the notion that when an organism—be it rat or human—exhausts all its known strategies to get to a goal, it finally gives up (Seligman, 1974). People who experience learned helplessness come to believe that they are no longer in control of their lives and that their current behaviors have no purpose. Their cognitive maps lead nowhere. As a result, they often grow discouraged, feel depressed, and see little use in trying to alter their situation. Ultimately, they lose hope.

It has been said that we humans suffer only because we have expectations that are not realized; one antidote to suffering, then, is to want nothing. The hopeless person is afraid of wanting something, because such a desire will only increase pain. The discouraged person eventually comes to a place where the only thing that is desired is freedom from the pain. This attitude is why clients often frame their goals for counseling as wanting to make something go away. Your job is to assist your client in formulating a goal that is the presence—rather than the absence—of something, and to help the client feel hopeful about achieving this goal. In this way, counseling becomes the teleological pursuit of a hopeful future, and the client's cognitive map begins to develop paths that are leading somewhere.

Experiencing This Idea

For this exercise, form a practice group of three people. One of you volunteers to share some habit or typical behavior that you would like to change. Another volunteers to serve as the interviewer. The interviewer's task is first to focus on *etiology* by asking questions about the origin of the habit for 5 minutes. For the next 5 minutes, the interviewer's task is to explore the *teleology* by asking questions about how things would be different when this behavior is changed. The third person serves as the timer and recorder, who observes the activity and leads the feedback discussion. Switch roles and engage in the same process until everyone has had a turn in each role.

Reflecting Questions

1. How do the two approaches differ?
2. What differences did you notice in the client's response to these two interview approaches?
3. What possibilities for change emerged with each of these two approaches?

A Teleological Theory

Rychlak (1980) considered teleology to be the essence of our free will. He pointed out that humans possess the ability of "telesponding" to events as well as *responding* to them. To put it more succinctly, what we do now is based in part on how we think things will turn out. Some more ordinary words for telesponding are "anticipating," "planning," and "preparing."

To the extent that we telespond, we are self-determined beings. Moreover, since the future has not yet happened, it can still be changed. Very little can be done about the "facts" of our history, and the contingencies and vagaries of our immediate existence are sometimes temporarily beyond our influence. But the way we self-determine is within our control. We can seize our future—it is only the next moment, day, or year that can really be changed. Ironically, though, changing our future can result in changing our past. What's done is done, of course, but the meaning we have assigned to our past can be changed. "It's never too late to have a happy childhood" (Furman & Ahola, 1992, p. 18) is a statement that may seem to be a bit extravagant. Nevertheless, it is possible to let go of old injustices, grudges, desires for vengeance, notions about our histories as our destinies, and preoccupations with past events that obscure any view we may have of a brighter future.

Alfred Adler (1870–1937) was originally a colleague of Freud, until they parted company over the sexual theory (Schultz & Schultz, 1992). Adler stated that our basic striving was for superiority, not meaning that we want to dominate others, but that we wish to surpass ourselves and overcome our current condition (Prochaska & Norcross, 1994).

Every person is a prophet—we proceed by predicting how events will turn out. Therefore, we are not so much impelled by our instincts or our history as we are compelled by our goals in life and our predictions of the future. Each of us creates an ideal self that represents the person we wish to become, and we establish a lifestyle (Adler coined this now popular term) based on our "fictional finalism." By *fictional finalism*, Adler meant that we live now in light of where we expect to end up, even though we cannot know for sure. Adler was capitalizing on Aristotle's final cause—the teleological reason for living a certain way. While not ruling out ordinary causation, Adler stated that our future is far more causative of our current behavior than is our past. Of course, it is not a real future; it is the story we tell ourselves about where we are going—our mythic quest.

Overcoming Blocks to a Hopeful Future

Your clients who feel dispirited and discouraged are often trapped in a paradoxical state—they desire a change in their situation, but they also fear change. As they contemplate going into an uncertain future, they will tend to cling to the way things are. Somehow, you must help them "tip the balance" (Young, 1998), so that they allow themselves to relinquish the relative security of the present—however unsatisfactory—and take that uncertain path to the goal they seek. As Young put it, "The situations or problems that bring clients for help can be thought of as a temporary balance of driving and restraining forces" (pp. 256–257). For example, people who are suffering from the loss of a loved one may wish to get past the pain and find a way to go on with life but at the same time feel that to do so would be an act of disloyalty, signifying that they did not care enough to continue mourning.

Tipping the balance is not simply a situation in which one weighs the pros and cons of an issue and makes a decision. You must stay with clients and hear their stories until a clear path toward a goal emerges for them. If you can encourage clients to continue this exploration, they will likely open up to new possibilities and become ripe for change. Remember that no matter how well you believe that you are empathically "walking in their shoes," you have never actually been over your clients' terrain. Ultimately, therefore, clients—and not you—determine the goals in counseling. Mahoney (1995) criticized some counselors as attempting to sell maps of the road ahead. "They claim to be well traveled and to know the best route for traveling to the destinations sought by their clients. They are, in a sense, travel agents" (Mahoney, 1995, p. 391).

Unlike Mahoney's "travel agents," to be truly helpful, you must journey with the client, offering compassion and comfort, respecting the client's need to rest, and ensuring the client's safety and well-being. It is at these times when your humanity is much more important than your techniques. But simply resting will not necessarily help the client to construct a new image of the future. While you take your cues from the client as to how to proceed moment to moment, you must at the same time remain strategic, deliberate, and mindful of the need for the client to establish a goal.

Implications of These Ideas for the Counselor

These ideas about teleology have important implications for your work with clients.

- You are not attempting to find the past causes of the client's present concerns. Instead, you are interested in establishing what the client desires for the future.
- The client may indicate that what is desired is for the present situation to go away. You must then help the client find a goal that involves the presence of something they desire.
- People who are discouraged or depressed have lost a sense of purpose and control of their lives. Coming to believe that they can get to a better place will help restore their feelings of hope and resolve.
- People live their lives according to a "fictional finalism." We proceed according to how we expect things to turn out. In this sense, the future causes the present.
- We are not so concerned with whether the stated goal has been accomplished, but rather with whether the client continues to move forward in a hopeful manner.
- Clients are always wavering between changing and trying to stay the same. Your job as a counselor is to "tip the balance" in favor of change.
- It is the client's job to establish the goal for counseling. You can never know the exact path the client must travel, but you can help your client envision a destination.

TOOLS

Inviting Clients to Set Goals

Beginning your goal-setting work with clients involves the simple step of asking them, in one form or another, what they hope to achieve by coming to counseling. The initial goal statements that clients offer in response to your question, according to Sklare

(1997), are likely to fall into one of four categories: positive, negative, harmful, or "I don't know." Each of these responses presents different challenges to your efforts to help clients develop well-formed goals.

Positive goals, the first category, are those in which the client articulates a desire for something that will change the situation for the better. However, the client's initial goal statements are often phrased in vague terms, such as "to be happy," "to have better self-esteem," "to get along with others," or "to have better communication." The challenge here is that none of these statements is a goal for which you can really form a contract. If you do, you have agreed to a trip bound for "Never-Never Land," because such goals are simply too abstract and nebulous.

Negative goals, Sklare's second type, are those in which the client wishes something to go away. This goal statement, which is the most common first response of clients, involves the absence of a problematic condition or situation. Clients typically respond to your question regarding goals with complaints and detailed descriptions of their concerns—"problem-saturated talk"—for example, "I want my parents to get off my case," "I wish that I was less depressed," "I wish people wouldn't reject me," or "I wish that I had a magic wand that would make my troubles disappear." These goals either rely on other people changing their behavior, or they imply that the clients themselves have little or no personal control. Your challenge is to find something the client is willing to do that can improve the situation.

Not infrequently, clients will offer a goal that falls under the third category—harmful. Harmful goal statements involve wishes for outcomes that either put the client at unnecessary risk or sabotage future opportunities for personal fulfillment. For example, it's not unusual to hear adolescent clients wish to drop out of school, have a baby, hurt someone, or run away from home. Once you recover from the initial shock, such statements may entice you into debating the merits of these goals, cautioning clients regarding potential hazards, or skirting the issue of goals entirely. The challenge you face is how to engage in the counseling process with such clients, but not to support goals that you believe to be harmful to them or others.

When your clients offer the fourth type of response—"I don't know"—to your request for a goal statement, they are signaling that they are not yet invested enough to begin the work of changing. Such clients may be in counseling involuntarily, referred by a third party who wishes them to change in ways the clients do not desire. In other situations, clients may be just so discouraged that they cannot seem to muster the energy necessary to become involved in the goal-setting process. In either case, you are well advised to proceed slowly. As the old adage goes, "You can lead a horse to water, but you can't make it drink." Your challenge is to see if you can discover your clients' tastes well enough to get them to "swallow" the notion of working with you toward a resolution of their situation.

Well-Formed Goals

Once a client has started to envision the future, you then will be helping to crystalize this initially amorphous goal statement until it is explicit, specific, realistic, and valued by the client—in other words, a well-formed goal (DeJong & Berg, 1998). DeJong and Berg pointed out that well-formed goals must be "important to the client, small and concrete, and represent the beginning of something different rather than the end" (p. 17). Of course, counseling agencies, psychiatric services, and third-party payers require that you document goals for every counseling client. The rationale for the policy of mandating goals has been to maintain accountability. An unfortunate consequence of this practice is that many counselors do not fully appreciate the tremendous therapeutic power of well-formed goals. In fact, developing a well-formed goal helps clients to create a vivid and powerful vision of their future. By setting such a goal, clients gain a sense of direction and hope, become more motivated and involved in counseling, and increase their momentum toward therapeutic outcomes. You can help clients formulate successful goals by following a few simple principles described below.

Help Create Positive Goals. The first, and most fundamental, principle for forming goals is to encourage your clients to state their goals in the positive, describing what they will be doing or thinking, rather than what they will not. Never accept a contract to work toward the absence of something. If your client gives a negative goal, you can invite him or her to begin developing a well-formed positive goal by using a variety of questions. For example, you can ask what the client will be doing when the negative condition is no longer present. A client may say, "My goal for counseling is that I'd like to stop having these rage reactions." In response to this statement, you could ask, "What will you be doing when you are no longer having these reactions?"

Another strategy for redirecting a negative goal into a positive one is to use terms that encourage clients to see possible alternatives. Beginning your questions with phrases such as "instead of," when you are no longer," "in place of," and "rather than" invites your clients to begin thinking outside the box of a negative goal statement (Sklare, 1997). For example, the opening of the sentence "When you're no longer overwhelmed with depression, what will you be doing?" suggests a positive future, while the ending question encourages the client to fill the void with a positive goal.

Sometimes it is helpful to ask "a circular question"—what others will be noticing or saying about the client when the goal is achieved. This question adds the interpersonal dimension to the client's view of the world and helps to make his or her situation a bit more objective. An example of a circular question is, "When you have changed so that your parents are no longer on your case, how will you be different? What will your parents say that they have noticed about you that allows them to ease up on you?"

Help Clients Create Their Own Goals. The second principle for developing successful goals is to ensure that clients "own" their counseling goals. No matter how well-formulated goals may be, if they are to be successful, clients must embrace these goals.

Working with clients whose initial goal statements seem harmful can be particularly challenging. The first thing you must realize is that such goal statements represent a yearning for thwarted, but unstated, positive goals. The goal to drop out of school may represent a frustrated desire to succeed or to maintain self-esteem. For a teenage girl, the desire to have a baby is often the result of feeling unloved and wanting to have someone give her unconditional positive regard. (Of course, we all know that expecting this from a baby is certainly misguided.) The desire to injure someone is often the result of wanting respect—and not getting it—or the urge to even a score. Finally, the desire to run away from home may reflect seeking more autonomy or a safer environment. Your job in these situations is not only to dig for the positive goal beneath the surface of a harmful goal statement, but also to acknowledge the client's discouragement. People do not move from a discouraged position to a hopeful one without first feeling that someone has understood their pain (this does not mean help them wallow in it). You can acknowledge the client's level of frustration without focusing on it; at the same time, you can slip in a possibility statement. This is where O'Hanlon and Beadle's (1994) "Carl Rogers with a Twist" comes in. You could say, for example, "Wow! It sounds like you have been trying everything you know to get better grades and were even thinking about giving up, because you haven't yet hit upon a way to do better in school."

Finding the goal that exists beneath the goal statement is always difficult. This is where your skill as a counselor comes in. In this book, we can offer suggestions, but they are only guidelines that point out what you must do—find out what the client wants and have him or her state it in useful terms. In order to accomplish this task, you must sometimes use your skills of reflection and interpretation. It is okay to probe for goals and exceptions (the times when the problem is not happening). The point here is that you need to find what the client will be a customer for, and have that stated as a goal that will not be harmful. Remember the rule: If your client will not cooperate with your attempts to move the session forward, then you probably have not acknowledged enough.

Help Create Action Goals. The third principle for forming goals is that you are more likely to develop an effective goal if you avoid nouns, diagnoses, or static words and instead use behavioral terms—such as action words ending in "ing." If, for example, a parent says, "Our goal for counseling is to treat Johnny's conduct disorder," you might ask, "How will Johnny be different when he is doing more of what you expect of him?"

When you ask for a goal statement, your client may answer simply, "I don't know." At these times, you can nudge your client toward a goal statement by inviting him or her simply to guess. For example, Sklare (1997) offered such counselor responses as "If you did know . . . ," "If you did have an idea . . . ," "If you could figure it out . . . ," and "If it weren't beyond you . . ." (p. 27) as possible leads that might set aside the client's reluctance and introduce a hypothetical. By asking the hypothetical "if," you relieve your client of any obligation for knowing the answer. Instead, you offer an invitation to speculate on a possibility. "In some cases, persistent repetition of *if* questions may be needed to ascertain the reasons the client is in the counselor's office" (p. 26).

Sometimes, what is produced is a problem statement instead of a goal statement: "The teacher says I have a bad attitude" or "They say I don't fit into society" or "The judge says I'm mental." In any case, such statements can begin a process that might eventually arrive at a well-formed goal. You might follow one of these statements with something like: "If the teacher doesn't like your attitude, what would she say you would be doing if you had a good attitude?" or "How would you be behaving if people thought you did fit into society?" or "Do you mean that the judge doesn't think you are thinking straight? How could you convince him that you are OK?"

If any of the above queries produces a goal statement for the referring party, you can then follow up by asking, "What part of what they want is something that you also want?" or "How does that fit for you?" Well-formed goals must be the client's—and not the counselor's or the referring third party's—goals.

Be Presumptive As You Help Clients Envision Change. The fourth principle of effective goal-setting is to be presumptive, rather than subjunctive. Word all your statements and questions in ways that suggest that positive change is not only possible, but inevitable. For example, rather than asking, "If the situation changed for the better, how would you be feeling about Johnny?" you would phrase the question, "When the situation changes for the better, how will you be feeling about Johnny?"

Keep It Simple. Finally, your client is much more likely to develop an achievable goal if you keep it simple. Make sure the client's aspirations are concrete, focused, and doable. One common complication is a goal that a client offers, but nevertheless believes to be out of reach. With such a seemingly unattainable goal, you can explore what "on-track" goal would be a "successive approximation." For example, you can ask, "So, if you were already on track to being outgoing, what would you be doing differently now?" The goal should either be behavioral (a change in doing) or meaningful (a change in viewing). A workable goal cannot be pie in the sky.

Even positive goals can be stated in such a way as to not be well formed. For example, the client may say, "I want to be happier," or "I want to be a success in life." These goals are too vague to be useful in the counseling session. If, for example, the client wishes to "be happier," you might help him or her get closer to a well-formed goal by asking something like: "Tell me about a time when you were happier. What was going on then? How were you different?" This exception question might lead to a more concrete description of what it means to the client to be happy; it then might be converted into a goal.

Using This Tool

Form a group with two colleagues. One of you volunteers to be a client by sharing some goal in you life that you would like to achieve. As you describe this goal, however, be sure to begin by making it vague and assuming an external locus of control. Another volunteers to help the client develop well-formed goals according to the principles listed above. The third person serves as the recorder, who observes the activity and leads the feedback discussion. Take turns until everyone has performed each role.

Clients and Commitment

Your job would certainly be easier if all clients came desiring to change, but because of their reluctance to trade the known for the unknown, they may not be willing to take such a chance right away. They may worry that you will judge them negatively or that your diagnosis will be even worse than their own. As you already know from reading the previous chapters, diagnosing problems does not play a part in this approach to counseling. Instead, your counseling philosophy follows an old and anonymous admonition:

> As through this life you wander,
> As through this life you roll,
> Keep your eye upon the doughnut,
> And not upon the hole.

You are looking for strengths—not deficiencies—in the client. You want the client to gaze across the problem space of the hole, scanning for a possible resolution—the doughnut. Once you've helped the client spot promising possibilities, you help con-cretize—make explicit—the desired resolution leading to a contract.

The term *contract* here does not necessarily mean a signed document or even a pledge that is stated out loud. We use *contract* to refer to any agreement, involving mu-tual obligations and benefits, between at least two parties. In other words, each party must put something into it and get something out of it, or it is simply not a contract. For example, "You must get better grades and be better behaved in school because I want you to" is not a contract. Of course, as the counselor, you are receiving some form of compensation for offering your professional services. Therefore, the obliga-tions and benefits on your side of the contract are clear. With each client, however, you must find the unique answer to the question, "What does this person want for in-vesting the time, making the effort, and taking the risks that are involved in counsel-ing?" The caliber of the counseling contracts you establish is reflected by the involve-ment of your clients in setting goals and making changes. If you do not have a good working relationship, or the client seems disinterested and disengaged, then you must renegotiate the contract.

Some solution-focused therapists have come up with a useful framework for con-sidering initial levels of commitment (de Shazer, 1988). This taxonomy is not to be taken as a diagnosis of the client, but rather as an appraisal of your working rela-tionship with a specific client at a particular time. In this classification scheme, clients can be visitors, complainants, or customers in their view of their relationship with us.

A *visitor* (also called a "window shopper") is a client who is currently not com-mitted to engage in counseling. It may be clear to others that the visitor "has problems" but this client currently has little motivation to change. The best way for you to respond initially to someone who is just visiting is to listen respectfully, compliment and en-courage when possible, but offer no suggestions or tasks.

A *complainant* presents problems, either specific or vague, that the person wishes to talk about at some length. Clients who encounter you primarily by complaining often present themselves as helpless victims of their circumstances and see others as respon-sible for making changes. It is not initially clear whether you are being invited to give advice or to help change someone else. In the beginning, your best option is to treat the complainant as a visitor.

A *customer* comes with a complaint, gives a reasonably clear description of it, and is ready to engage in the process of counseling. In this relationship, you can quickly invite the client to move into productive goal-setting and successful change.

School counselors typically receive a referral from a teacher or parent who is a com-plainant, about a child who is a visitor, and the task is framed as turning both com-plainant and visitor into customers. Worse yet, the child is often presented as an *involuntary* by people in authority. The involuntary is countercommitted because to comply or cooperate would be an admission of guilt or weakness—becoming a cus-tomer would be a capitulation for this client. Obviously, the counselor has the most dif-ficult time establishing a contract with the involuntary. This category of client will be discussed in Chapter 12.

Scott Miller (1996) warned that we should remember that any categories of clients we generate are really descriptions of the relationship between the counselor and the client. Some involuntaries, for example, will easily become customers with some counselors, while they never will with others. You stand a much better chance of having customers if you make sure you establish relationships with clients in which they become convinced that you are both competent and interested in helping. You must understand fully the client's goal in being with you, and what he or she might be a customer for. Never assume, for example, that someone referred by a third party is a customer for the same goal as the referring agent.

Listening in on a Session

Review the story at the beginning of the chapter. A resolution-focused counselor can help Jamelle to begin developing well-formed goals by engaging with her in the following way.

> **Counselor:** (*After they shake hands and introduce themselves to one another, they sit in comfortable chairs facing one another.*) Well, Jamelle, what goals would you like me to help you achieve by coming here?
>
> **Jamelle:** (*She appears flustered by the counselor's words. She cuts short her breathing, squirms uncomfortably in her chair, tips her head in a quizzical pose, and softly chortles in a muted, high-pitched manner.*) Mmm . . . my goals? Honestly, right now I'm only concerned about the goals of my supervisors. I don't even know what's going on, much less what people expect of me, around here. I was hoping that maybe you could give me some advice on what to do."
>
> **Counselor:** (*She nods, offers a concerned smile as she leans forward, and uses a wave of her hand to indicate the management training program.*) All the ambiguities that they build into this program have been really baffling and frustrating for you, and it sounds like that now you'd really like to find a way to get a better handle on what it's all about.
>
> **Jamelle:** (*She pauses, crosses her legs, smooths the crinkles out of her skirt, and finally looks up.*) Yeah, that's right. I mean, in less than a month, I come up for performance review and the rumor is that it's an all-or-nothing proposition. It's getting hard for me to sleep at night because I keep going over and over in my mind everything that's going on in my work and life, trying to make some sense out of it. The only thing I do know for sure is that this has been a really stressful time for me. If it's OK to go back to your original question, I guess the goal of this counseling for me is to get rid of this overwhelming stress.
>
> **Counselor:** Tell me, Jamelle, when this overwhelming stress is no longer present for you, what will you be doing differently?
>
> **Jamelle:** (*She starts to answer, hesitates, considers for a moment, and then talks briskly.*) Well . . . um . . . well, that's a very good question. (*She pauses.*) One of the useful things they've taught me here is to use that line when our employees ask us a question that we can't immediately answer. The management trainers call it a "delaying tactic" that gives you some time to pull together your thoughts.
>
> **Counselor:** (*She nods, smiles, and invites the client again.*) You've got that management skill down nicely. So now that you've bought yourself some time to give

that question more consideration, what will you be doing differently when you are no longer overwhelmed by stress?

Jamelle: (*She responds with a rueful smile.*) Maybe I've mastered that delaying tactic, but I don't think it helped me all that much, because I'm still not exactly sure what I would do differently. The one thing that flashed in my mind when you asked me again is that I would be acting more like one of the other trainees—Sophia—who I met here. She's really got a different aura about her.

Counselor: (*She tilts her head in a gesture of curiousity.*) So when you begin to handle work and life more like this Sophia, what will you be saying and doing that will be different?

Jamelle: (*She gazes off, lost in reflecting on this possibility.*) I wouldn't be so uptight and worried all the time like I am now. I guess I would be acting with an air of serenity and a sense of purpose. Do you know what I mean? I'd be relaxed and focused, but still energetic and motivated.

Counselor: When you become, as you put it, "relaxed and focused, but still energetic and motivated," who will be the first person to notice? What will that person see or hear that would be different about you?

Jamelle: My sister Harriet would have to be the one. I've been bugging her on the phone for weeks with all these complaints about stress at work and in my personal life. She would definitely notice if I told her that I decided that I'm going to get something out of this program—and my life—even if I weren't as successful as others seem to be.

Reflecting Questions

1. During this segment, in what ways is the counselor–client relationship changing?
2. In what ways are Jamelle's goal statements changing?
3. Write a possible counselor response to Jamelle's last statement.

Third-Party Goals

You may already have noticed that when someone is referred for counseling, the referral is often saturated with problem statements. Usually, the only goal that is implied by the referring agent—be it a parent, teacher, or court official—is the wish that the problem behaviors be eliminated. Just as you do not accept the absence of something as part of a well-formed goal when speaking with your clients, neither should you accept a list of problem statements without well-formed goals from third parties who refer clients to you. You can begin the relationship with your clients on a more positive note if you can work briefly with third parties to develop well-formed goals. Not only will this help get your counseling relationship off on the right foot, but it will also change the relationship you have with referring agents. It is much easier to chart the progress someone is making toward a goal than to note the elimination of problem behaviors. Besides, some of the problem behaviors cited by third parties may not be seen by you or your client as problems. It will be much easier for your client to contract to work toward a certain goal than to consider making a current behavior go away.

Furthermore, be careful about accepting the client's "problem" as defined by the referring agent. If possible, normalize the problem definition by relabeling it or putting it into a different frame, acknowledge that there is work to do, and talk about goals, rather than problems. Change problem frames into goal frames by finding out what the referring party wants and by minimizing the focus on the undesirable behavior. Whenever possible, change nouns, which label the person, into verbs, which describe behaviors.

Never accept a referral that lists only problem behaviors! When consulting with the referring person to establish well-formed goals (Tohn & Oshlag, 1996), you need to make explicit the target behaviors that will indicate to the referring person that the involuntary client is improving. The following exchange between the counselor and the school official illustrates this point. The counselor, who is to work with a boy named Steve, asks the referring school official how the boy must change in order for the school official to believe that counseling has been successful:

School Official: Staying out of trouble would help.

Counselor: What would be some signs to you that Steve is beginning to do this? (p. 161)

Note that the counselor is not only asking for a specific behavior and the presence—rather than the absence—of a behavior, but also is couching improvement as a "beginning" rather than a miracle cure. This not only helps to create well-formed goals that are clear to everyone, but it also tends to change the referring person's focus toward behaviors that will be improving. Kral (1986) suggested the use of a referral form that encourages the referring person to focus on goals rather than on problems. Figure 4-1 offers an example of a goal-oriented form.

Framing the Third-Party Referral

Iatrogenesis is a term meaning that whatever happened was caused by the treatment. Usually, this is stated in the negative—for example, the medicine the doctor prescribed actually made you worse. Tardive dyskinesia, a Parkinsonian-like disorder of the nervous system, often develops in people who are given major tranquilizing drugs for schizophrenia. People sometimes go to the hospital for something minor and die from something they contract in the hospital environment. But Milton Erickson (quoted in O'Hanlon and Weiner-Davis, 1989) said, "While I have read a number of articles on this subject of iatrogenic disease, and have heard many discussions about it, there is one topic on which I haven't seen much written about and that is iatrogenic health" (p. 51).

Usually, when someone is referred, or the counselor is called in for a consultation, the thing people want to know is "What's the problem?" It is amazing how, once the problem is named, many people seem satisfied, as if something had really changed after a label has been applied to the problem or a cause has been offered. It is not uncommon for a counselor to have a referring agent report that the client improved after he or she had merely been tested or seen in an assessment interview. This situation dramatizes the iatrogenic or placebo power of the referral itself and the referring person's belief that something is being done—whether it is or not. When this happens, you may feel obliged to explain that it is unlikely that anything so far could have made a difference because you have only evaluated, and not yet actually treated, the client. However, you are bet-

DESIRED BEHAVIORS FORM
[TO BE FILLED OUT BY THE REFERRING PERSON]

Directions: Please place a check mark under "Already Doing This" or "More of This De-sired." If more is desired, indicate what this improved behavior should look like ["As ex-hibited by"], so this can be communicated to the client.

Client Name:_____ Date:_____.
Name of Referring Person:_____.

The Desired Behavior   Already Doing This   More of This Desired

1. *Shows interest in school work*...
    [As exhibited by]:
2. *Works cooperatively with others*...
    [As exhibited by]:
3. *Displays self-control* ....
    [As exhibited by]:
4. *Works well independently*...
    [As exhibited by]:
5. *Exhibits leadership skills* ....
    [As exhibited by]:
6. *Shows respect to grownups* ....
    [As exhibited by]:
7. *Uses appropriate language* ....
    [As exhibited by]:
8. *Stands up for self*...
    [As exhibited by]:
9. *Treats others fairly* ....
    [As exhibited by]:
10. *Stays on task*..
    [As exhibited by]:

The main behavior I would like to see more of:

_____

[As exhibited by]:_____

Thank You. Signed:_____School Counselor

FIGURE 4-1   An example of a solution-centered referral sheet (school counselor form). After Ron Kral, 1986.

ter off simply accepting that a change has taken place. You have already accomplished that first step of helping the referring person to notice desirable behaviors in the client that had previously been overlooked.

There is a lot of mythology surrounding counseling. Most laypeople think they know something about it, but as to how it actually works, they haven't a clue. They often just assume it does work. We counselors want to keep them thinking this way! When someone who has referred a client comments that the client is better—accept that person's perception, even if it doesn't match your own, and ask for elaboration on the noticed improvement.

Paths to Story Revision

Walter and Peller (1992) have offered a series of paths that clients may take toward reconstructing their stories. The resolution of rigid, outdated, or tragic stories comes about as the client begins to deconstruct the old narrative in order to make room for a new one. The easiest path, when the client is a "customer," is what Walter and Peller called the "goal statement and exceptions" route (p. 69). On this path, the counselor may ask, "What is your goal in coming here?" and the client might respond with a well-formed goal statement, or one that is fairly easily molded into a well-formed goal statement. For example, the conversation could go as follows:

Counselor: "What is your goal in coming here?"

Client: "I'd like to get better at being comfortable striking up a conversation with a woman."

Counselor: "What is it that will be different about you when you become more comfortable with a woman?"

Client: "Well, I'd talk more and be more confident that what I have to say is important enough to hold her attention."

Counselor: "Tell me about a time when you felt this confidence more than usual and were able to talk more."

In the above example, the counselor did three things to help mold the client's goal statement. First, the counselor asked for more specificity in asking for news of difference—"What is it that will be different . . . ?" Second, the counselor asked for an exception to the problem—"Tell me about a time when you felt this confidence. . . ." Finally, the counselor asked presumptively—not tentatively—for an exception—"Tell me about a time. . . ." Problems never always happen. Exceptions always do.

Looking for Exceptions

Earlier in this chapter, we discussed the importance of looking out for client goal statements that involve merely the absence of something, such as not being angry or not smoking. When you spot these absences, you can encourage clients to formulate better goals that involve the presence of some positive behavior or attitude. Helping clients fill in the blanks of their goals can help them develop a powerful vision of the possibilities in their future. This strategy of looking for absences is certainly important in formulating goals, but it is especially valuable when you are listening to the client's story. In particular, you are searching for the gaps in the client's story that are the exceptions to the problem. Clients come to counseling expecting that all you want to hear about is the problem. In fact, they often describe it to you in excruciating detail. Furthermore, clients may report the problem as constant and unwavering. As a result of this "problem focus," clients tend to ignore, or dismiss as trivial, the times when the problem is not happening. These times "are not seen by the client as differences that make a difference" (de Shazer, 1991, p. 58).

Finding exceptions is the quintessential technique of resolution counseling. The exception—a time when the problem is not happening—is a resolution that the client has already achieved, however temporarily. Therefore, fully realizing an exception is the dramatic moment when the client both understands his or her own resources and gains a more hopeful attitude. The exception is Bateson's (1972) "news of difference"—the lubrication that "unsticks" the problematic story.

In addition to the above path identified by Walter and Peller (1992) is the "problem statement and exceptions" path (p. 71). Trying to get clients to recognize exceptions when they are mostly focusing on problems is tricky. It must be done while still acknowledging the pain of their complaint; otherwise, it trivializes their concerns. Cade and O'Hanlon (1993) suggested that your responses should fit in with the severity of the clients' complaints. For example, you could say to a client, "Given what you have told me about your situation, I am really surprised that things are not much worse. How have you kept going?" (p. 99).

As the counselor, you are much more curious about the strengths, resources and resilience of your clients than you are about their problems and concerns. Remember the Universal Price Code Problem in Chapter 1 and the Necker Cube in Chapter 2? In both cases, you were able to discover another view of the situation by gaining a different perspective. Your clients are coming to you able to see—in discouraging clarity and detail—their problems, personal inadequacies, and failures. However, they fail to notice their personal skills, talents, and resources—the clues for resolutions. By asking questions regarding their successes and competencies, you help clients become aware of these experiences and characteristics. The counselor's statement above invites the client to switch from focusing on problems to seeing possible resolutions. Your job, then, is to capitalize on this opportunity by pursuing a description, at great length, of their exceptional behaviors and the nature of the situations when they were able to handle these problems. Using this technique also encourages clients to recognize their personal agency. It teaches clients that behaviors once thought to be out of control are truly within their control, and, furthermore, that change is actually happening!

Of course, the more straightforward way of seeking exceptions is simply to ask your client. For example, you might say, "Tell me about the times when this problem is not happening." Or you may identify positive circumstances by asking, "What is different about the situations when this is less a problem?" Or you may explore personal strengths by asking, "How are you different when this problem is not happening?" Of course, your questions are presumptive—you assume that there are such times. This should not be asked in a hesitant manner, such as: "Are there possibly times when the problem is not happening?" Clients who are so overwhelmed with the problem will simply say, "No." But, as we have stated, problems *never* always happen! Count on it!

Listening in on a Session

Let's return to this chapter's story and continue with the dialogue between Jamelle and her counselor. Look for ways that the counselor begins sifting through the client's story to find those nuggets of exceptions to the problem.

> **Counselor:**   Jamelle, I'm puzzled about something. Given all the ambiguities in this program, the intensity of your training, and the demands of your supervisors, how have you managed to hang in there and face all these challenges? As you know, a lot of trainees drop out.
>
> **Jamelle:**   I've wondered that myself sometimes because it certainly hasn't been easy. I've thought about quitting dozens of times, but I guess I just decided that some way, somehow I'm going to get something out of this program in spite of my own hang-ups and the craziness and pressure.
>
> **Counselor:**   So your decision to make the most out of this situation, no matter how vague and stressful, has helped you stay determined—not just to finish the training—but also to take something from it. I guess that your use of the "managerial delaying tactice" is one example of what you're taking from the training. Tell me, Jamelle, about a time when you've been able to be more relaxed and focused.
>
> **Jamelle:**   Maybe it's because I've already mentioned Sophia earlier, but one time that comes to mind is when I was talking to her just today after our training workshop. Our workshop leader had been really intimidating, but she stayed pretty cool, even when he was grilling her on new federal policies and procedures. Afterwards, I told her how impressed I was, and she just shrugged, grinned this enigmatic smile, and started to joke about the workshop leader—she even nicknamed him "Old Sergeant Rock"—being so full of it. I couldn't help laughing and joining in with her.

Reflecting Questions

1. During this segment, how did the counselor encourage the client look for exceptions to the problem?
2. What personal strengths and resources emerge from the client's answers?
3. Write a possible counselor response to Jamelle's last statement.

No Problems Are Ever Fully Resolved: Scaling

Since counselors are not healers, you cannot offer an absolute cure to your clients; therefore, you should not contract with clients to resolve their problems completely. If the client believes that the situation will not be improved until all problems have vanished, then you will be working with that client for a lifetime. What you seek in brief counseling is to get clients on the way to a place where they can carry on without you. In other words, you are trying to work yourself out of a job as soon as it's practical.

In working yourself out of a job, one useful strategy is to invite your client to participate in a scaling exercise (Walter & Peller, 1992). Scaling techniques can help clients in three important ways. First, participating in scaling can encourage clients to recognize that resolution is not an all-or-nothing proposition. Second, the activity can help them to envision their goals with greater detail and vividness. Finally, clients can use scaling to assess their progress in achieving these goals. Brief counselors vary the specific details of this activity to fit their individual styles, but one general approach is to ask your client to imagine a scale that ranges from 1 to 10, with 1 representing the situation at its worst and 10 representing the best possible resolution. Of course, self-report scales have been used for years to document perceived change and client satisfaction. Such scales have been part of preintervention and postintervention assessment batteries that evaluate counseling effectiveness. However, our focus here is not on using such scales for documentation and accountability. Instead, we offer scaling as a valuable tool for encouraging therapeutic change.

You can invite clients to scale their current circumstances and then encourage them to explore possibilities. For example, once a client has rated the present, you can ask, "If you were on your way to [the next higher number], what would be happening that is different from now?" Out of such a question you hope to get the beginnings of a goal for your work with the client. Notice that you do not ask what would be different if they reached a 10.

As you attempt to set an expectation for the termination of your work together, you could ask, "When we get to the point at which your problem is under control enough to let us know that we have finished our work together, what will your number be then?" This question has the benefit of communicating to the client that there can be a certain ending point that can be anticipated for the counseling work, and that not everything has to be solved to be good enough.

Virtually anything can be placed on a scale if the number has meaning for the client. You don't need to ask them to explain why a particular number has been chosen, nor do you have to understand the meaning of the number. It is sufficient that a number has been indicated, and this number gives you a starting point in your search for a higher number that would symbolize improvement for the client. This scaling technique can be used for most any content. For example, you can use scaling questions to assess a client's "self-esteem, self-confidence, investment in change, willingness to work hard, to bring about desired changes, prioritizing of problems to be solved, perception of hopefulness, evaluation of progress, and so on" (Berg, 1991, p. 88).

Using scaling questions, you also can "restrain" the client and keep expectations reasonable by saying, "Well, it would be great to go for a 10, but that's a lot to ask. What would you settle for in the next week?"

We have heard of school counselors being able to check in with their clients in the hallway by simply giving a signal that they wish to know how the client is doing today. The client responds by holding up the number of fingers that represent his or her current state. If there is progress, the counselor can give a "thumbs-up" gesture for a job well done. This exchange can all happen without a word being spoken, and this signal conveys to the client that they are in a secret club together, sending messages in code that others do not understand.

The scaling device is also helpful for assessing progress and "taking inventory" with clients. You can ask how the client felt at the beginning of your time together—represented by a 1—and how the client will feel at the end when the goal is accomplished—a 10. Once this scale is established, you can ask, "[W]here would you put yourself at this point?" (Walter & Peller, 1992, p. 107).

Walter and Peller (1992) point out that younger children sometimes have difficulty keeping the scale in mind. In such a case, more concrete devices may be used to help the child retain the idea. For example, you might ask, "If one crayon shows how you have been noisy and acting like you were 5 years old, but this whole box of crayons would stand for when you have been acting grown up and quiet in class, how many crayons did you have in your box this week?" With another child, you might say, "Draw a circle on the board to show me how hard you worked on your studies this week. A small circle would show that you didn't work very hard, and a big one would show that you tried really, really hard."

Scaling is a good technique for helping your client to see progress, and to realize that solving problems is not an all-or-nothing process. Furthermore, when clients are attempting to extinguish a behavior, there is a tendency for it to recur spontaneously. By predicting a relapse, and scaling the subsequent recovery from it, you can help the client avoid discouragement and the belief that he or she has failed. You might say, for example, "From time to time, you may find that you have slipped from a higher number to a lower one. That is to be expected. You know the old saying: 'two steps forward and one step back.' " Or, you could observe, "So you found yourself slipping back from a 6 to a 5 last week, what will it take to get you back up to a 6?"

It is important to convey to clients that being on track toward solving a problem is success. The paradox of this is that, while it is the goal or solution that is being pursued, the real change is taking place in the successive approximation toward the goal. Furthermore, the client will occasionally come up with ideas that could not have been anticipated, because the scaling technique does not dictate that particular events must take place in order to get to the higher number. A wonderful example of the concept is illustrated in the following vignette from Berg and de Shazer (1993):

> [A]n 8-year-old child was brought to therapy following molestation by a stranger at a shopping mall. During the fourth session the therapist drew an arrow between a 1 and a 10 on the blackboard, with 10 standing for the time when therapy was finished. The therapist asked the child to indicate how far she had come in therapy by drawing an x on this line. The child drew her x at about the 7 mark. She was next asked what she thought it would take to go from x to 10. After several minutes, during which time she shifted her weight from one foot to the other, she hit upon an idea and said, "I know what!" "What?" asked the therapist. The little girl replied in a rather somber voice, "We will burn the clothes I was wearing when it happened." The therapist, amazed at this creative idea, said, "That's a wonderful idea!" Soon after this session the child and her parents had a ritual burning and then went out to dinner at a fancy restaurant to mark the end of therapy (p. 23).

Berg and de Shazer (1993) suggest that the language of conversation is a shared misunderstanding. While we normally think of counseling as a conversation in which the counselor helps the client describe more accurately the facts of a situation so that the counselor can figure out what causes lie behind and beneath those facts, this is not the most helpful way to regard language. The traditional Western view, proceeding from the common-sense assumption that there is a reality "out there," sees language as a conveyance in which the facts of the real world are communicated from the observer to the listener. Conversely, the Eastern (Buddhist) view is that language obscures the truth of any situation. Reality, whatever it may be, is ineffable—beyond words. In the scaling technique, numbers are a language that roughly describes ineffable states that the client experiences, or expects to experience, and they do not necessarily point to an external reality. Numbers can stand for something that the client cannot fully articulate. They can possess powerful meanings, and so long as the client is master of the numbers, we counselors do not have to know precisely what the client means by their use.

Do Not Scale "SUDS"

It should be noted that the scaling technique we are advocating here should not be confused with the so-called SUDS (subjective units of distress) technique. SUDS is used by some counselors to get the client to indicate a measure of the frequency, duration, and intensity of distress that they are experiencing. On this scale, higher numbers indicate more discomfort, and the goal would be to get the client to a lower number, at which he or she would be reporting less stress. In this case, 10 would be the most uncomfortable, while 1 would be a state of only mild discomfort, and therefore the goal (Young, 1992).

The problem with the SUDS scale is that it seeks as its goal the *absence of something*. In other words, the counselor tries to get the client to a point at which most of the stress has gone away. This would not fit our definition of a well-formed goal. Our goal is to establish the *presence of something*. The assumption in a resolution-counseling approach is that, as the client achieves more of his or her goal (the presence of something), the less stress he or she will experience. In this model of counseling, the elimination of stress is not the focus of the work. Our belief is that lowering the client's subjective level of distress will be a byproduct of the work. Just as we do not focus on the "pursuit of happiness," neither do we see stress reduction as the focus of our work. We assume that both these states—lower stress and more happiness—will ensue as the result of the client's changing his or her viewing and doing of the situation. The scale we are discussing here would have the opposite values of the SUDS scale. On our scale, 1 is the situation at its worst, and 10 would be the complete resolution of the concern. We work toward higher numbers, but we don't believe anyone ever gets to a 10.

Listening in on a Session

Once again, let's go back to this chapter's story and listen to some more of the dialogue between Jamelle and her counselor. In this segment, see how the counselor uses scaling as a therapeutic tool.

> **Counselor:**   Jamelle, you've been sharing with me in our time together how you have been dealing with the stress here at work and in your personal life. Now I'd like for you to imagine a scale from 1 to 10, where 1 represents you feeling completely overwhelmed by this stress and 10 represents you handling this stress so well that you feel both relaxed and energized. What number would you say represents where you are right now?

> **Jamelle:**   Oh, I guess I'd like to use another delaying tactic, but you're already on to that managing trick. Let's see, it's not as bad now as it was this morning, which was pretty close to being the worst I can remember, but things aren't dramatically better now. That would make it about a 3, maybe.

Counselor: Alright, tell me in what ways you will be different as you go from a 3 to a 4.

Jamelle: If I were going from this 3 to a 4, then perhaps I would. . . .

Reflecting Questions

1. During this segment, how did the counselor use scaling to invite the client to envision resolution possibilities?
2. What details about goals, strengths, and resources emerged from the client's responses to the scaling activity?
3. Write a possible counselor response to Jamelle's last statement.

Using This Tool

Divide into groups of three. One of you volunteers to share some aspect of your life that you would like to change, but in which you feel stuck. Portray your concern in a simplistic, self-defeating way by characterizing it as an all-or-nothing and a right-or-wrong proposition. Another volunteers to listen, understand, validate, and, when appropriate, use the 1 to 10 scaling technique. Finally, the third person serves as the recorder, who observes the activity and leads the feedback discussion.

Two Closing Comments

Have you ever noticed that when you read books like this on counseling or view a videotape of a therapy session, it always turns out well? We've noticed that, too. The vast majority of case studies offered for public consumption seem to be nearly perfect. Although these examples may be excellent models, they imply that, while the rest of us may bumble our way through counseling sessions with clients, the experts never mess up or make mistakes. That belief can be discouraging, so in this book we present excerpts from counseling sessions that may demonstrate specific brief counseling techniques, but do not inevitably arrive at tidy resolutions.

Finally, keep in mind that one of the goals of this book is for you to find your own voice as a brief counselor—not to parrot ours. As you read the sessions in this book, regard the counselor statements as examples to illustrate, not scripts to memorize. Consider each of our suggestions in the spirit in which we offer it—an example of what you might say with a particular client in a particular situation. As you practice the brief counseling skills, you will learn to trust yourself to give expression to these strategies. Successful counseling requires authentic communication—not well-delivered quotes.

SEGUE TO CHAPTER 5

To help you gain a feel for the ideas and tools in the next chapter, do this experiment. The next time you go into a store, pay close attention to the *positive* aspects of your experience. For example, you might notice the helpfulness of a clerk, the cleanliness of the store, or the quality of the products. Ask to speak to a manager or supervisor and offer a sincere compliment. Notice this person's reactions.

CHAPTER 5

Constructivist Counseling: Inventing Realities

"Only a science which is directly related to life is really a science."
William James

CHAPTER GOALS

Reading about and experiencing the ideas in this chapter will help you to understand this fundamental constructivist concept:

- How we represent our experience, and how those representations may restrict or free us, is the focus of the constructivist approach to therapy.

Reading about and practicing the tools in this chapter will help you to learn these valuable skills:

- Asking questions that help the client conjure up images of success, mastery, and new possibilities.

STORY

Her husband used to tease her by saying, "No one could ever claim that gardening is just a hobby for you, Honey. It's clearly a crusade." Of course, Mrs. Thompson didn't have a violent bone in her body, but she certainly assailed weeds, bugs, and other threats to her flowers and vegetables with fervor. Dressed in a dilapidated straw sombrero—a souvenir from Tijuana—a pair of patched Oshkosh ("B'Gosh!") overalls, plaid shirt, and workboots, Mrs. Thompson would march into her garden with a glaring intensity that rivaled General Patton. Her husband used to gently needle her with the comment, "Well, dressed like that, Dear, you definitely don't need a scarecrow." Year after year, she had worked the soil early in the spring, coerced the plants to thrive in spite of unfavorable conditions, and then harvested her impressive vegetable bounty every fall.

On this particular day, Mrs. Thompson attacked the weeds with a ruthless take-no-prisoners ferocity that she had never shown before. She wielded her gardening tool like it was a bayonet, jabbing the dirt with a rhythm that punctuated her mutterings. "What a fool I've been!" she grumbled as she stabbed the earth. "After all that I've done for them, how could they be so mean?" Each time Mrs. Thompson ended the refrain, she ripped the weeds out by their roots and flung them aside in distaste.

These words were the only ones that Mrs. Thompson seemed to be able to form. Each time that the words forced their way through her clenched teeth, Mrs. Thompson felt slapped once again by the stinging, stunning statements of her three grown children at the meeting with her minister. Certain words of her repeated litany seemed to stir up a particular emotion all over again. The word "fool" would trigger another wave of the shame that had blindsided her at the meeting. The word "all" would provoke once again her sense of righteous anger and outrage over the unfairness of it all. But the final word "mean" would bring out emotions that she had rarely expressed during her 72 years—hurt and vulnerability. She found herself emphasizing those three words in her repetitions—"What a FOOL I've been!" and "After ALL that I've done for them, how could they be so MEAN?"

Mrs. Thompson was sure that her youngest daughter had been the mastermind. That realization finally nudged her into a new theme for her mutterings. "That 'mastermind' should've minded her own damn business, instead of poking her nose where it doesn't belong. I'd like to 'mastermind' her for airing all our dirty laundry in front of the Reverend." Mrs. Thompson finally stood up, surveyed the results of her work, massaged her back, and carried her wooden stool and gardening tool to her back porch.

Whoever had been the mastermind, all three children—hardworking, successful, and loving—had shared with their mother AND the minister how concerned they were. They had detailed the times she had been so bitter and sarcastic during the past 5 years. They explained that they had tolerated her cutting remarks because they understood that her forced retirement at 65 and the sudden death of her husband 2 years later had been terrible blows. But neighbors, old friends, and other relatives were not as patient and, one by one, they had drifted away from her over the years. It was only when her children brought out the heavy guns at the meeting that Mrs. Thompson finally agreed to see a counselor. Her children told her that recently the grandchildren had begged to be left at home so that they wouldn't have to endure her caustic and cutting remarks. Mrs. Thompson didn't see how counseling would do any good, but not being able to see her grandkids would be unthinkable.

The following week, Mrs. Thompson steered her vintage, mint-condition Buick Skylark into a parking space behind the community mental health center. As she stepped out of the car, she realized that she was feeling the same queasy apprehension that she had when she faced her last dental appointment. She stalled for a few minutes, unfastening the seat belt, tidying the car, carefully making sure that everything was shut off properly. As she stepped out of the car, she felt an overwhelming urge to flee. As she was reaching into her purse for the car keys, her billfold fell on the pavement and reaching down to retrieve it, she saw the school pictures of her grandkids. Sighing, she muttered, "You big 'scaredy cat'! For cryin' out loud," she reassured herself gruffly, "This counselor's surely not going to take a drill to me."

Reflecting Questions

1. In what ways did Mrs. Thompson create her world?
2. How might you begin your work with this client in her current state of agitation?

OVERVIEW

This chapter offers an alternate way of looking at reality. It is known as "constructivism" and is sometimes seen as being opposed to "empiricism" (Prochaska & Norcross, 1994). There are two important positions taken by constructivists that can have a tremendous impact on how you view counseling. The first fundamental assumption of constructivism is that one can never fully know another person's reality from an objective stance. Therefore, as a counselor, you cannot make sense of a client's experience through disengaged, "objective" approaches involving diagnostic or scientific methods. Only by encountering the client in an authentic relationship can you gain an empathic knowledge of that person's experiential world. The LUV triangle we described in Chapter 3 takes on even more importance now. If all knowledge is relational, then listening to, understanding, and validating not only help you develop a trusting relationship, they also are essential if you are ever to come to know your clients.

The second assumption is that human knowledge of an objective reality is not possible. Instead of our perceptions providing a veridical copy of reality—sometimes called the "immaculate perception"—human beings can only construct their own rendition of "reality." Consequently, when you take a constructivist position as a counselor, your goal is not to get clients to become more rational and better adjusted to reality. You are trying neither to "straighten out" the thinking of clients, nor to dispute the facts that clients offer as their life stories. Instead, you are helping clients to reconstruct the way they are representing themselves and their world. As part of this reconstruction process, you assist clients in recovering hidden facts that suggest a different story. This recovery process is the search for exceptions to the current story plot. In order to carry out this task successfully, you must hear your client's story, while beginning to deconstruct the story's negative and destructive features.

One of the important tools that you can use in deconstructing a negative story—and co-constructing a better one—is the question. In this chapter, we offer you suggestions on how to use questions effectively and we discuss some questions you should avoid.

IDEAS

A Mental Reality

The artist Rene Magritte drew a picture of a pipe with the caption, "This is not a pipe." What could he have meant by that? Was his intent merely to play some paradoxical trick on us, or did the message have a deeper meaning? Goswami, Reed, and Goswami (1993) offered an explanation:

> Suppose that you say: This is a picture of a pipe. That's a good answer, but if you are a true master of tricks, you will say: I see the image caused in my head (brain) by the sense impressions of a picture of a pipe. Exactly. No one ever saw a picture in an art gallery. You always see the picture *in your head* (p. 142, emphasis added).

The question of the location of reality has plagued philosophers and psychologists for millennia. Early on, "scientific" psychology adopted on faith the position that reality exists "out there" and presents itself to us by impressing itself upon us. According to this position, our subjective experiences of reality are copies of this independently existing reality—sort of a mental Polaroid snap shot (Benson & Presbury, 1989). But there is no good reason to believe that reality is as we sense it to be. In fact, there are persuasive arguments to believe otherwise, despite the evidence of our common sense.

Many of us assume that our senses are windows that serve to bring us as much information as possible about the outside world. However, our sensory receptors actually reduce, filter, and exclude much of the information that we receive from the world. For example, the electromagnetic spectrum ranges in wavelength from a billionth of a meter up to more than a thousand meters. But of this immense spectrum, we see only the tiny portion of waves that are between 400 and 700 billionths of a meter. Our eyes are completely insensitive to everything else (Martindale, 1981). Because we cannot see other phenomena on this spectrum, such as ultraviolet light, infrared radiation, x-rays, and radar, our visual apprehension of "reality" is, at best, remarkably limited.

This argument, however, still does not shake our belief in the existence of an objective reality, but only calls into question the limits of our unaided ability to grasp it. While we may even entertain the belief that there are realities existing beyond the limits of our technologically aided grasp, we remain firm in the common-sense belief that the reality we perceive is *real*—existing independently of us and our puny ability to perceive it.

What Is It That Exists?

Ever since the philosopher John Locke asserted that there is nothing in the mind that was not first in the senses, science has concerned itself primarily with the world "out there." The human mind was seen as a passive recording instrument, gathering the facts of the "out there." Furthermore, mental health came to be measured by the degree of correspondence between the individual knower's mind and the facts of this objective world. If the mental representations in the knower's mind matched the facts of the world out there, then the knower should be mentally healthy. If experience were simply a matter of recording the sensations created by the objects in the outside world, then there should be no confusion in the mind—unless the recording equipment was somehow impaired. Therefore, according to this position, if someone is confused about reality, then he or she is mentally ill.

Locke also introduced the notion of "secondary qualities" (Schultz & Schultz, 2000). He suggested that while some qualities of external objects are "primary," meaning that they exist in the objects themselves, he also observed that experience includes "secondary qualities"—the way in which humans experience these objects. For instance, a "tickle" is not in the feather itself, but it is something that depends on us for its existence (if you are not ticklish, then the tickle does not exist at all). Locke proposed a famous example to demonstrate his point. Take three bowls, he suggested, and fill one with cold water, another with hot water, and a third with luke-warm water. Place your right hand in the hot water and your left hand in the cold water. Of course, your right hand feels hot and your left feels cold. However, when you place both hands into the third bowl, your left hand will feel warm and your right hand will feel cool. The sensation of temperature is not a property of the water; it comes from your experience—a secondary quality. The confusion comes when you attempt to determine from your experience what the temperature of the middle bowl *really* is. In this case, your experience creates a dilemma—is the water warm or cool, or both? Would it be mentally unhealthy to say "both"?

The philosopher Berkeley was making a similar point when he asked, "If a tree falls in the forest, and no one is there to hear it, does it make a sound?" Since sound appears to be the product of air molecules striking the eardrum of the person hearing it, Berkeley intimated that no sound exists in the world out there. Berkeley's position was that there are no primary qualities at all (Schultz & Schultz, 1996). Dramatizing this point, Gertrude Stein is supposed to have said that there is no "out there" out there.

According to philosophers, "What really exists?" is the ontological question, which you really don't need to trouble yourself with as a counselor. However, the question of how we come to believe that we know what exists, and how we represent our knowledge, are epistemological questions. Epistemology, not ontology, is the philosophical issue fundamental to helping people out of their dilemmas. The nature of knowing—not the nature of reality—is central to your work with clients. The ways in which your clients experience, assign meaning to, and portray their worlds are your crucial consideration. According to constructivists, people do not discover reality—they invent it (Watzlawick, 1984).

Constructivism

Constructivists claim that objective knowledge of events is not possible. "Constructivism is an epistemological perspective based on the assertion that humans actively create the realities to which they respond" (Lyddon, 1995, p. 69). This constructivist stance is not the solipsistic position that the only reality is one that resides in the mind of each individual. For example, constructivism does not claim, as did Peter Pan, that if you believe you can fly, the law of gravity will suddenly be rescinded. There are always physical constraints involved in your relationship with the external natural world, and so long as your beliefs fit well enough into those constraints, you should not find the natural world objecting to your movements.

According to von Glasserfield (1984), people approach the world out there as a thief deals with a lock—they are looking for a key that fits. Many keys, however, can fit the same lock, so the fact that people can open it does not mean that they know everything about the nature of the lock itself. The key fits, but it's not necessarily a match of reality. Whatever the "facts" of a situation, there is more than one key that will fit those facts. Clients' view may fit the facts of their circumstances, but their interpretations may be so self-defeating that any change seems impossible. In counseling, it is the key—not the lock—that is more important. Because many keys may fit the same lock, successful counseling is helping clients find master keys that can make sense of their current situation and also open doors to successful resolution.

How People Construct a World

Some constructivist thinkers object to the term *representation* as the way of talking about how people construct worlds (Miller, 1997). They associate this term with the Lockean notion that our experience is a picture of reality. Although we acknowledge their concerns, we think the term is too valuable to discard. Instead, we use *representation* to refer to an active process of making meanings, rather than a passive response of recording reality. People organize their experiences and then *represent* these experiences to themselves. A representation, in this sense, is the recycling of experience that can sometimes lead to "hardening of the categories" on the part of our clients.

The re-presenting process begins with the raw material of some experience of the world. That experience may have a positive, negative, or neutral value for us. Automatically, our mind associates the event with previous ones that evoked similar emotions, and stores this new experience with these others. Out of this process of putting experiences together, our minds develop categories that represent reality. These representations are not faithful snapshots of reality, but are the way we reexperience these categories; they are based on the emotional meaning these events have had for us. The representing process continues as we fit new experiences into our established categories.

This description of category construction is, of course, a simplification of the representing and meaning-making process, but it emphasizes the point that we do not passively receive experiences to store in our minds as facts. Instead, we actively create meanings by sculpting the raw material of our experiences. The world out there, whatever it may be, is meaningless in itself. Meaning is a human thing—experiences would not be meaningful if humans did not make them so. When clients come to you in trouble, the difficulty exists in the way they are representing their experiences. Many troubled clients are experiencing "hardening of the categories"—their representations have become so inflexible that they are rigidly representing their new experiences as either negative or neutral. If the representations are negative, clients are anxious or depressed. If neutral, clients feel empty. Therefore, you intervene with these clients by targeting their representational systems—not the world out there.

A Constructivist Way to Proceed

No one can prove that his or her reality is the correct one. If you adopt the constructivist belief system, you must do so as an act of faith. Likewise, to adopt the empiricist position of John Locke would be a similar assumption on faith. We think that the constructivist position is much more useful as a way of working with people. We would like you to consider the following set of beliefs as a heuristic—a way to proceed.

There are two sorts of existence—the world and the individual knower—and the interaction that takes place between the two is complex and rich. Here's how it works. The world contributes stimuli, which the individual receives as sensations. The knower, in turn, contributes perceptions to this process, shaping the world in distinctive ways. Through countless transactions with the world as both an observer and a participant, the knower creates a personal world. Experientially, there is no such thing as *the* world— every knower has a different world.

This process gets sticky because, for the individual knower, some of the objects in his or her world are people who are also knowers who have constructed worlds. But their worlds are not identical to that of our original knower, who has direct access only to his or her own world, and not to the worlds constructed by other knowers. As was pointed out by R. D. Laing, the paradox of human existence is that we live both private and communal existences. Despite the fact that we cannot know firsthand the experience of another person, we still see ourselves as the object of the experience of the other. When two people encounter each other, they can work toward aligning their worlds and decreasing the disparity of their perceptions.

You and your client, who are both knowers and world-constructors, are engaged in coconstructing a world together. You each experience the other, and in turn, experience yourselves as being experienced by the other. By keeping the focus of the dialogue on your client's experience, you can have an impact on his or her world because of the inevitable tension that exists when world views collide. We all feel validated when we meet "like-minded" people who see the world as we see it, but sometimes we will alter our views when this tension of difference is present. Furthermore, you will increase your persuasive power if your client has a positive impression of you. If your client trusts you and perceives you as caring, then you are more likely to influence your client to construct a more hopeful world. While we are sometimes reluctant to think of it this way, there is an aspect of counseling that is "sales work."

Rationalist Versus Developmental Perspectives

When the field of psychology underwent a "cognitive revolution" in the 1960s and the mind once again became a legitimate area of study, there developed within this revolution a divergence among psychologists—and counselors—regarding how to conceptualize mental processes. One group, having assumed that reality is to be copied by the mind, held that an individual's mental representation must be brought into correspondence with the reality out there by a combination of logic and empirical investigation. Another group, having adopted the constructivist position, placed its emphasis on the meaning that events have for the individual. They did not accept mere correspondence to an external reality as the criterion for mental health. Mahoney (1988) called these two views the "rationalist" and the "developmental," respectively.

Albert Ellis and Aaron Beck are two therapists who personify the rationalist view. From this perspective, failure to take a clear picture of reality is the result of a defective lens, bad film, or inadequate exposure. If someone's picture of reality is distorted, that person is thinking irrationally. Your work as a counselor would then be to help this client adjust the photo-taking apparatus in order to obtain a veridical picture of reality. The result would be what Mahoney (1988) and others have called the "immaculate perception" (p. 158). As Mahoney put it, "Rationalists tend to portray the brain as a curator of information gleaned from sense data that reliably reflect an internal order" (p. 162).

Contrasting the rationalist perspective, Mahoney (1988) stated, "Developmentalists and constructivists . . . tend to portray the brain as an active sculptor of experience, proactively 'projecting' its 'expectations' into each next milli-moment of development" (p. 162). Knowledge, in this sense, always implies a participating knower. The rationalist view, as Mahoney characterized it, portrays the client as needing to adjust to an external reality. The developmental view, on the other hand, sees the client as needing to change and grow. Rather than viewing the client's cognitive schema as distorted, the developmentalist might characterize such schema—or constructions—as outmoded.

One important difference between the two views, as articulated by Mahoney (1988), is centered around the relationships among cognition, affect, and behavior. The rationalist position is one of "rational supremacy." The "higher" intellectual processes are thought to rightfully dominate the more primitive functions of emotion and action. Because the rationalists believed that intense emotions can disorganize both thought and behavior, they cast emotions as antagonistic to the good life. On the other hand, people see emotions as giving meaning to life. Even "foolish" love is wonderful while it lasts.

Regardless of our sophistication with psychological theories, we all know the long-standing struggle between head and heart. Speaking for the head, the rationalists claim that stability—with emotions under control—is preferable. Aligning with the heart, the developmentalists would counter this position by suggesting that intense emotions create a positive opportunity for growth—the journey through chaos toward a new level of stability. This does not mean that the constructivist/developmentalist counselor would consider *any* emotion to be useful to the client. When people come for counseling, they usually have hardened their experiences into categories of negative emotions. Your job is to help them reassign meaning to their experiences, and thus change their representation of reality.

To illuminate this point, imagine that two people are looking at a chair. Both could say that the chair is, say, a green recliner with the fabric on the arms slightly worn. One observer, who has never seen the chair before, might be able to comment on whether she finds it esthetically pleasing, but otherwise would likely have an emotionally neutral response to the chair. The other observer, remembering it as the favorite chair of his beloved, and now deceased grandfather, would have an entirely different emotional response to the chair. Each time this observer sees the chair, the emotions associated with grief and loss arise. Same chair—two different representations.

It may be that our second observer experiences only the emotions of sadness, regret, and guilt when he thinks of the lost grandfather. In this case, negative emotions have eclipsed all other emotions—such as fondness, happiness, and comfort—associated with the grandfather. It would be your job as the counselor to help this person find a useful balance in the meaning of the loved one's memory and not become struck within the negative valence.

Intervention in Counseling

Counselors have traditionally argued as to whether it is best to intervene in the client's thoughts, emotions, or actions as a primary strategy. The rationalist position is that thinking is primary, and that a change in cognition will generally effect a change in the other two. Grieger & Grieger (1982) asserted, "Thinking creates emotions. Thoughts, or cognitions, mediate between events or stimuli and emotional responses" (p. 12). Using rational–emotive therapy terms, they explained how a situation leads to certain emotions because of the person's beliefs. If someone is inordinately disturbed by the event, this is because the person misinterpreted the circumstances. Such irrational thoughts do not match the reality of the situation. The important metaphysical position taken by the adherents of this view is that reality "out there" possesses certain qualities. For people to be mentally healthy, their beliefs must correspond to the nature of this reality. Good thinking is logically connected to the inherent reality of the situation. However, clients often distort the incoming messages from the real world because of a tendency to "think crookedly" (Ellis, 1982). At bottom, clients are fundamentally flawed and in need of a cognitive overhaul in order to be brought into alignment with life's realities.

There is another possibility, as indicated in Mahoney's (1988) "developmental–constructivist" view. Rather than assume that there is a single reality to which an individual's cognitions must narrowly align, you can take the position that while a reality is out there, it cannot be fully known and its psychological aspects can be altered by the participant-observer. In other words, the so-called nature of reality comes into being as the observer becomes involved with it. Its "nature" depends on how it is observed. This is not unlike the famous Copenhagen Interpretation that was offered by the physicists Born, Heisenberg, and Bohr (Goswami, Reed, & Goswami 1993) to explain how the observer could influence an electron to misbehave. But a client's world is much more than electrons, matter, and motion—it is a world of meanings. And while meaning may not be capable of moving objects in the world, humanistic thinkers consider meanings to be the main motivational force of humans. Polkinghorne (1988) pointed out that meaning is the most neglected subject matter in psychology. Clients create and store meanings in a narrative form. They come to counseling prepared to tell their stories. If a story is one of tragedy and hopelessness, it is your job as counselor to find overlooked aspects of the story that could turn out to have a different meaning for the client. This is not always easy, but it is a worthwhile search.

Experiencing This Idea

Think of a time when you were watching an activity from a distance and then later became involved in it as a participant. How did your experience of the reality of that event change as the result of your increased involvement?

The Client's World as a Foreclosed Story

There is a well-known phrase that, at the time of this writing, is repeated each week on the Arts & Entertainment channel's "Biography" series—"Every person's life is a biography." Your life is a story—told by you to yourself and others—that is updated each day; it gives your life its particular flavor and meaning. You are the main character, the protagonist, and you have cast yourself in a certain role. There is a cast of characters around you, and you live in a world largely of your own making. You are on a quest, seeking your "fictional finalism," as Adler put it. The way you think, feel, and act are all based on how you believe the story is going, how achievable the goals in this life might be, and what motivates all the characters in the story. If you are experiencing the world as a reasonably hospitable place, in which your efforts are likely to get you what you want, then you are living in a pleasant story. Furthermore, if your story is flexible enough to accommodate change and the occasional negative event, your story remains sufficiently capable of handling new contingencies or unexpected happenings.

Clients often come for counseling because their stories are inflexible to the point that they feel stuck. They have foreclosed on their stories as tales of failed expectations. If, for example, someone creates a story in which possessing great beauty, wealth, or fame would give meaning to life, then this story can end happily only if these stipulations are met and maintained; otherwise, it becomes a story of failure and disappointment.

Most people have more pedestrian stories. They see themselves as finding love, being reasonably successful in some type of work, and possessing enough of life's necessities to be comfortable. This doesn't seem like a lot to ask of life. However, it has been said that "Life is about loss." We all occasionally come up short in terms of our desires in life, and we regularly lose people and things as we continue through our story. If we have foreclosed on our story and will only accept a life in which all our dreams are fulfilled and everything we have attained is forever retained, we will be in trouble. Some people have learned early on that their efforts don't seem to pay off, their dreams are regularly dashed, and their goals cannot be attained. These are people whose lives are centered around an attitude of "learned helplessness" (Seligman, 1974, 1994) and appear to be too discouraged to try. They are stuck in a story that has been foreclosed on unhappiness.

It is common for a client who is not in an immediate crisis to come to you with a story that has, over time, become so inflexible that it seems to hold the person prisoner. This client seems to be living under a "life sentence" of gloom. But somewhere within the client burns an ember of hope. Coming to you is a clear sign that the client still longs for a better life story and believes that there is hope for a reprieve. You must always keep this hope in mind so that you are not seduced into, and discouraged by, the client's foreclosed story of failure and loss. Remember that the client's story—the representation of reality in which he or she lives—is a construction, and the good news is that this reality can be reconstructed. You must first find a way to start deconstructing the negative story in order to open it to new possibilities. You must also remember that the client has adopted an assumptive world view that seems to be "realistic." You cannot simply talk a client out of this perspective. Your methods must be allied with the person's hoped-for view of self and world. At the same time, you communicate respect for your client's desire to cling to the negative narrative.

Understanding the Client's "Preferred View"

Eron and Lund (1993) noted that problems arise for us when we experience contradictions, or "disjunctions," between our preferred view and the way in which we experience others viewing us. These authors cited Milton Erickson as saying that it is important for the counselor to understand how clients wish to be seen by others—their preferred view. The notion of the preferred view was also implicit in the work of Carl Rogers. His research showed that there is a marked increase in congruence between a client's initial view of self and the ideal self during therapy sessions. "Furthermore, Rogers's therapeutic 'unconditional positive regard' is closely akin to what we would call 'joining with a person's preferred view' " (p. 298).

Eron and Lund suggested that a disjunction, or discrepancy, might take place between one's preferred view and the way the person perceives himself or herself as being viewed by others. First, according to Eron and Lund, some event takes place that shakes one's "perceptual moorings." This event awakens a search for new meanings, including a reassessment of how one is seen by others. As this person becomes aroused and vigilant, and starts to scan the environment, he or she may begin to notice or imagine others viewing him or her in a way that contradicts a preferred view of self. He or she may then feel disrespected or misunderstood as a result of this real or imagined disjunction, and may attempt to remedy the situation by demanding more respect or understanding. This behavior is received by others as problematic, and the feedback they give in response is even further away from the preferred view of the person in question, who escalates the situation even more by acting in ways that are—in the view of others—not himself or herself.

From this perspective, people "slip into" problem-maintaining behavior more by accident than by structural or systemic design. Even a seemingly trivial event can trigger the onset of a major problem by jostling the preexisting views of those affected by the event. Steve de Shazer (1985) mentions a similar theme in describing how problems might evolve out of "damn bad luck"(p. 299).

In the approach suggested by Eron and Lund (1993), you endeavor to understand the client's preferred view of self and to align with it. In this way you become a significant other who sees the client in the way the client wishes to be seen. This alliance overcomes a form of resistance that Eron and Lund call a "narrowing of the narrative landscape." When people have constructed a life story that contradicts their preferred view of self and confirms their "problem-saturated" account of events, they are in trouble indeed. They begin to predict future events in terms of this narrative—to expect doom instead of "happily ever after." However, there are many events from the client's past that tell another story. These are exceptions to the tale of woe, which contain images of the client as competent, happy, and helpful. These stories are eclipsed by the current negative frame, and so they are not noticed by the client. "But these stories lie dormant, outside the present negative frame, and are not accessed to explain current events . . . [so your job is to] look for what might help the problem dissolve" (p. 305).

Eron and Lund are correct in drawing connections between their work and that of Carl Rogers. In addition to "unconditional positive regard" being the same notion as "joining with the preferred self-view" of the client, the idea that we must listen carefully to the client's story in order to find clues as to how to bring out that dormant self is crucial. Rogers would accomplish this by first accepting the client's version and acknowledging the client's concerns. But he would also focus on certain things the client said as he reflected the story back to the client. Without overtly adding his own perspective, Rogers would respond selectively to the material produced by the client and emphasize what he considered most important to helping the client toward resolution (Moore, Presbury, Smith, & McKee, 1999). He maintained an ostensible attitude of "not knowing" while, at the same time, he always worked toward therapeutic goals that were inherent in his theory.

Implications of These Ideas for the Counselor

Constructivism has rich and important implications for the practice of counseling. Taking a constructivist perspective opens up a number of exciting possibilities for you as the counselor:

- In this way of working with clients, you are not interested in trying to align someone's thinking with "reality."
- People's realities are constructions based on experiences they have had and the meanings they have assigned to these experiences.
- People form categories for their experiences and there is a natural tendency for their representations to become foreclosed as "hardening of the categories."
- Whatever your version of reality, you should not attempt to sell it to your clients. Instead, you must seek aspects of the client's own story that are more hopeful and more filled with possibilities.
- While "rationalist" cognitive therapies seek to straighten up client's "crooked thinking," the developmental-constructivist approach seeks to dissolve "hardened" or foreclosed stories.

- Rationalist approaches view emotion as distorting client cognitions, while constructivist approaches see emotions as crucial to meaning formation.
- Your client will always have a preferred view of how he or she wishes things to be in life. Your task is to discover this preferred view and to join with it.

TOOLS

Deconstructing and Co-constructing the Client's Story

Any account of historical events is a construction, an interpretation of those events. Even the facts are not always clear, since we all have the tendency to focus more often on events that support our existing world-view. Remain aware that you and your client will be co-constructing a reality as you go over the client's story together. Your challenge is to attempt to deconstruct the story so that the client will see new paths to a resolution of the current story.

It is important to remember that although you are attempting to deconstruct a story and to co-construct a better one along with your client, the client ultimately is the author of his or her life story. You must be careful not to impose your interpretation on the client. This error is common among beginning counselors. They fail to recognize that clients are always the experts on their own life stories. The counselor's expertise involves changing minds—that is, on perturbing the client's representations of the world so that the story of the client's life will have, so to speak, gaps or holes in it that must be filled so that the story is coherent. It is when these gaps are present that the client is open to change—open to what Bateson (1979) called "news of difference."

The Question: A Major Deconstruction Tool

Brief counselors ask a lot of questions. However, these questions are not asked out of idle curiosity or to probe for the "underlying problem." You can use the right kind of questions as tools for steering your client toward positive outcomes and as intervention "wedges" that deconstruct your client's complaint. When you adopt the position of "not knowing," you are then in a position to also "express confusion" as the client tells his or her story (Miller, 1997) or "creatively misunderstand" the client's story (White & Epston, 1990). These two ways of questioning tend to perturb or deconstruct the version of reality the client is presenting.

For example, if your client is talking about becoming very anxious when she attends parties or other social events, she may assume that you will view this as a mental disorder that requires treatment. You might respond, "Maybe I've missed something here. I get anxious at some of those events, too. How is this a problem for you?" With this questioning of the nature of the problem, you normalize the experience and remove the client's expectation that you will view this as a disorder.

The client might then answer your question, "Well, because I get lonely sometimes, and this makes it hard for me to get out and meet people." You now have the opportunity to attempt to establish a goal that involves more of something—getting out—rather than less of something—eliminating the personality trait of anxiety. You then might say, "So, what would be helpful for us to work on together would be your getting out more and meeting more people." By expressing confusion, you have the opportunity to refocus the complaint and to move the concern from one over which your client has less control (anxiety) to one over which she can have more control (getting out more).

Questions are powerful devices in conversation. Most people feel pressured to answer when a question has been asked. Because of this dynamic, questions can be wonderful intervention tools. But their use should include the label "Warning! Questions can be hazardous to your relationship."

Questioning the Use of Questions

Many authors in the field of counseling and psychotherapy have cautioned that the use of questions can be problematic (Benjamin, 1987; Brammer, 1979; Egan, 1986; Landreth, 1991; Purkey & Schmidt, 1996). Sommers-Flanagan and Sommers-Flanagan (1993) have gone so far as to recommend that, because of the numerous liabilities possible, novice therapists should refrain completely from asking questions until such time as they are sensitized to the impact of questioning on the client. They claim that questions often allow the client to become too comfortable, reducing the productive anxiety that less directive techniques often stimulate. This questioning technique can be a good or bad thing. Obviously, in such situations, a question would have the result of soothing the client. The drawback, however, is that "clients end up talking about what interviewers want them to talk about. This is one of the many side effects of using questions in the therapeutic interview" (p. 92). Egan (1986) wrote, "When clients are asked too many questions, it can interfere with the rapport between helper and client" (p. 112).

Questions are characteristically used by counselors to direct the content of the session. They "provide the interviewer with control over the direction and course of the interview" (Sommers-Flanagan & Sommers-Flanagan, 1993, p. 92). You certainly are not being "nondirective" when questioning your client—questions are always more about you than your client.

Counselors sometimes use questions in a self-serving manner. For example, the counselor's anxiety about the interview can be soothed by filling the air with questions. "If you examine random interviews, you will find them so studded with questions that you may begin to think the only thing the interviewer can do or feels comfortable doing is asking questions" (Benjamin, 1987, p. 134). According to Benjamin, we ask too many questions and many of them are meaningless. "We ask questions that confuse the interviewee, that interrupt him. We ask questions the interviewee cannot possibly answer. We even ask questions we don't want the answers to" (p. 134).

Questions emphasize what the counselor considers interesting and important, and clients may react by feeling that their viewpoint is unimportant. Ineffective questioning also sets up the interviewer as an expert who is responsible for asking the right questions and, sometimes, for coming up with the right answers. Consequently, a differential of power, responsibility, and authority is established. Questioning may also make clients feel defensive, especially if they are asked several questions in succession. Questioning tends to make clients less spontaneous. They may sit back and wait for the interviewer to ask the *right* question. This produces a paradox. You began asking questions because you wanted information, but the process of questioning decreases client spontaneity, increases defensiveness, and results in less information being obtained (Sommers-Flanagan & Sommers-Flanagan, 1993).

It appears that the most egregious type of question that can be asked is the "why" question. Benjamin (1987) suggested that clients interpret a "why" question as connoting disapproval or displeasure. Brammer (1979) stated that clients are not completely sure what sort of help they seek, and that they have only vague understandings of "why" they feel as they do, and so will only be made more uncomfortable when asked this question.

Reading all these cautions might leave you believing that questions have no place at all in counseling. This is not the case. The point we are stressing here is that questions—if they are not used mindfully and deliberately—are very powerful techniques that can alter the course of the interview in ways you may not intend. As Benjamin (1987) put it, "The question is a useful tool when used delicately and sparingly. Too often, I fear, it is employed like a hammer" (p. 156).

Benjamin offered some guidelines for the use of questions:

- Be *aware* that you are asking a question.
- *Challenge* the question you are about to ask and weigh carefully the desirability of asking it.
- *Examine* carefully the types of questions you tend to use.
- *Consider alternatives* to asking a question.
- Be *sensitive* to the questions the client is asking, whether he is asking them outright or not.

When working toward resolution and attempting to focus on positive content, avoid asking any questions about the client's trauma, pain, or discouragement. The best questions to ask are about exceptions to problems and visions of success.

Questions You Should [And Should Not] Ask

Walter and Peller (1996) stated that there are kinds of questions that counselors (they prefer to call them consultants) should and should not ask. Counselors *should not* ask questions to:

> Gather information
> Make an assessment
> Validate a hypothesis
> Get the client to do something, or to do something different
> Solve a problem
> Be helpful (p. 19).

We would add that questions should not be asked to satisfy your curiosity or to trap the client into recognizing his or her discrepancies or contradictions of thought (as in the Socratic questioning technique). So what, then, could be considered as good questions? What questions might be helpful to the client in the brief counseling approach? The effects of any question are greatly influenced by the manner in which they are asked. Your style should be low-key, gentle almost tourist-like—"I'm not from around here and I need some help"—as compared with the interrogator's know-it-all, distant, rapid-fire approach. Open-ended questions beginning with "what" and "how" encourage clients to talk more, explain further, and go deeper about their situations and feelings. You may want to consider using an open-ended lead, which is a statement rather than a question.

Open-ended leads also might begin with "I." For example, instead of asking, "How did that make you feel?"—a hackneyed phrase at best—you could say, "I am wondering what that must have been like for you."

Walter and Peller (1996) suggested that questions should be asked "from a position of curiosity about what may be created" (p. 20), rather than to get the client to say something the counselor already knows or to get the client to say something that the counselor already has in mind. In general, questions should be addressed to successes or possibilities. Some questions that should be asked are: (1) What does the client want from the counseling? (2) How will what the client wants make a difference? (3) How will the client know when the goal has been reached? (4) How much of what the client wants is already happening?

Questions are powerful devices. They usually cause clients to pause and consider the question, and give some sort of response—even if it is that they do not wish to respond. Your clients are likely to feel some obligation to search for a response to the question. This increases emotional arousal and sometimes causes the client to have a slightly altered or elaborated experience regarding the content of the question. Questions "dig up" experiences in the client. You want to ask questions that encourage images of success or possibility, rather than frustration or despair. Remember—before you ask that question, think!

Useful Start-up Questions

Bill O'Hanlon (1995) has suggested you should use goal-oriented questions at the beginning of your work with the client. These questions are designed to set expectations for success and to focus the client on solutions, rather than on problems. These might be considered in place of the intake or assessment questions that are usually asked, and which often focus on problem-saturated ideas. Some examples that elicit the client's positive expectations for counseling might be as follows: "When you get to be on track to your goal, and can carry on by yourself, how will we know?" "What changes will have taken place when you get to that place?" "How will you be different?" O'Hanlon suggested that you should ask "for a video description" (1995, p. 6) of the client's image of the successful outcome. By video description, O'Hanlon means to get the client to elaborate the image of successful behaviors in detail; as if the counselor were following the client around with a video camera and capturing the new behaviors that the client will be exhibiting when the counseling has been successful.

There are also questions that can be asked that focus on the resources possessed by the client, and that have, in the past, served to assist the client in dealing with difficulties: "Tell me about a time when you experienced a similar difficulty. How did you handle that problem?" "What about those times when this problem started to come up, but you headed it off so it didn't happen?" "How about a time when you did something positive and you were surprised by your ability to do that?" "When was a time that you acted out of character and it turned out well?"

It is useful to ask what clients have tried in order to resolve their difficulties, because you don't want to offer suggestions for remedies they have previously attempted that haven't worked. O'Hanlon suggested that a good opening line for this inquiry should still focus on the positive: "What medications or therapy approaches have worked best for you, if any?" (p. 6).

Listening in on a Session

Review the story at the beginning of the chapter. At some time during their first session, a brief counselor might use the following questions with Mrs. Thompson.

> **Counselor:** (*He had started the session with an invitation to offer a goal statement. However, when the client quickly turned to her account of how she was encouraged to seek counseling, the counselor listened and validated. He now returns to the future by using the following question.*) Mrs. Thompson, as you were sharing with me the meeting you had with your children and minister and your time in the garden going over all your reactions, I was really curious about something. How in the world did you get yourself to come here for counseling? You've never been to counseling before in your life.
>
> **Mrs. Thompson:**   Well, I may seem like a hateful old bitch to my grandkids, but I actually do love 'em all. The oldest one used to throw a fit if she couldn't come to visit her "Goody Granny"—that's what she used to call me. I'll do anything to change so the grandkids want to see me again.
>
> **Counselor:**   What's the first sign your grandkids will be able to see when things are back to the way they used to be?
>
> **Mrs. Thompson:**   I guess that I'd be able to just keep my damn mouth shut and not nag them about how stupid they look with earrings stuck where they don't have any ears.
>
> **Counselor:**   What sort of things will you say to them instead?
>
> **Mrs. Thompson:**   I'm not going to say *anything,* 'cause everything I say seems to be wrong.

Reflecting Questions

1. In what ways has the counselor used questions therapeutically?
2. How might you respond to the client's final comment?

Using This Tool

Write two *start-up questions* that you could ask the client in the story. In order to increase their power and impact, make the questions specific to the story. Remember—a useful constructivist question is one that helps the client conjure up images of success or possibility.

"Getting-By" Questions

Miller (1997) suggested that sessions might begin with the use of "getting-by" questions. He borrowed this idea from Berg (1994) and Weiner-Davis (1993), who claimed that two-thirds of the clients they saw in the first session had already begun to improve the situation that brought them to counseling. Sometimes, asking about changes that happened before the first session took place "is a way of speeding up the therapy process by focusing the conversation on changes that are already working. It is also a way of helping clients redefine themselves as problem-solvers" (Miller, 1997, p. 77).

Even if clients cannot come up with anything, you can imply that it is there, but they simply have not yet noticed the change. This focuses the session on change and on the notion that it is the client who is to bring about the change.

In the case of the survivor of a crisis situation who is still focusing on himself or herself as a victim of the event, you can assume that they have surely done something right or you wouldn't be speaking together. The rape survivor was not murdered, the flood survivor did something to avoid being drowned or perhaps was able to save some prized belongings, the person who is the survivor of the death of a family member [notice that in the obituary, they always say the deceased is survived by . . .] has probably found a way to take care of funeral arrangements or financial affairs. In these cases, the "getting-by" question—"How did you do that?"—can be asked with genuine astonishment by the counselor who, imagining himself or herself in the same situation, is not sure he or she could have done as well.

Listening in on a Session

Let's return to the session with Mrs. Thompson. Continuing with their interaction, the counselor can turn to "getting-by" questions.

> **Counselor:**   You know, Mrs. Thompson, one of the amazing things I have found in working with people on their concerns is that by the time they come for the first session, they have already started something new that seems to be helping. What is some small thing that you have noticed yourself doing differently between the time you made the appointment and now?

> **Mrs. Thompson:**   It's interesting that you should ask me that question because I honestly do believe that I've been making an effort not to be a pain-in-the-butt with my grandkids. I dropped off a birthday present for one of them and he grabbed it, tore off the paper, and ran off playing with this electronic toy he had wanted without thanking me. In the past, I would have yelled at him to march right back to me, give me a hug and a kiss.

> **Counselor:**   (*Leaning forward to listen more closely and pausing to invite her to continue*) And instead . . . ?

> **Mrs. Thompson:**   Well, instead, I just tried to keep my thoughts to myself. I didn't like being ignored, but then again, I seem to stick my foot in my mouth every time I try to help. Heck, I wasn't that careful with my own kids and they turned out all right.

> **Counselor:**   I'm still back to when you said that you would have yelled at your grandson. I could tell by the way you just said it that you had really strong feelings at that moment. I don't know many people who pulled that off. How did you get yourself to do that?

> **Mrs. Thompson:**   I just reminded myself that it's HIS gift and not MY present. After all, he's only 8 years old—what do you expect? I mean, I can feel good that he's so excited about it—even though he didn't use good manners—and be satisfied that at least I picked out a good gift.

Reflecting Questions

1. In what ways is the counselor continuing to use questions?
2. How might you respond to the client's final comment?

Using This Tool

Write two *getting-by questions* that you could ask the client in the story. In order to increase their power and impact, make the questions specific to the story. Remember—a useful constructivist question is one that helps the client conjure up images of success or possibility.

Circular (or Relational) Questions

The idea of the circular question comes from Gregory Bateson's notion of "double description" (Penn, 1982). By this, Bateson meant that an individual's world must be described and understood not only as the person's unique perspective, but also from the views of others (relational). This means how they see themselves being seen by others, and how they see others constructing their worlds. Family therapists have long used the technique of the circular question in order to make sense of the interactions within the family system and to add a dimension of understanding within the family system. For example, the family therapist might ask a child to describe the relationship between the mother and father, or between her mother and another child. On hearing the description, the other family members are forced to take into account another perspective on their family's problem and perhaps to alter the meaning of their family's interactions. This alteration might be called a change in the "family self-concept."

Solution-building counselors (DeJong & Berg, 1998) use similar questioning techniques, which they call "relational questioning." In this sort of questioning, the clients are asked to take the perspective of a significant other person in their lives and to see themselves through the eyes of the other as the clients change for the better. The result of this type of questioning can be the elevation of the client's self-concept. The difference between this and the standard circular question is that the client will produce the images of how he or she will be seen differently by others when a positive change has happened. This is "double description" from the inside out. If the client can imagine someone seeing them in a better light or saying positive things about the change, then the client will be simultaneously changing a meta-perspective: the way of seeing himself or herself in the eyes of others will have changed for the better.

In order to be helpful in this process, ask the client things like: "When this change in your life has happened, who will be the first person to notice? What will he or she say is different about you?" or "If your mother were here and I were to ask her what had changed about you, what would she say?" or "When I talk to your teacher and she tells me that you are doing better, what exactly will she talk about?" or "What will your boss say you are doing more of than before?" or "What will it take to convince her that you are a changed person? What will she have to see to be convinced?"

All these questions are designed not only to concretize the goal statements of clients and to give a clear picture of the desired behaviors, but they also offer the opportunity for the client to begin to see others seeing him or her differently. As the client's behaviors (the doing) come into alignment with the images of success (the viewing), the client's belief in the way in which he or she will be seen, and positively valued by others, is strengthened. We might call this a change in the meta-viewing.

Using This Tool

Write two *relational questions* that you could ask the client in the story. In order to increase their power and impact, make the questions specific to the story. Remember—a useful constructivist question is one that helps the client conjure up images of success or possibility.

Presumptive Questioning

In the literature on brief therapy, there appears to be some disagreement as to whether questions should be put to the clients in a presumptive manner. Our position on this is that open-ended questions that presume strengths and resilience are powerful change devices. For example, if you were to ask "Is there a time when the problem is not happening?" the client is able to take the easy way out and dismiss your question with a simple "No." However, if you were to ask "Tell me about a time when the problem is *not* happening?" the client will likely feel more pressure to come up with something. We think that presumptive questioning should be used anytime that you wish the client to search for exceptions to the problem (a time when the problem is not happening) and when you are asking for the client's vision of success: "When this is no longer the major problem for you that it is now, how will your life be different?"

Using This Tool

Write two *presumptive questions* that you could ask the client in the story. In order to increase their power and impact, make the questions specific to the story. Remember—a useful constructivist question is one that helps the client conjure up images of success or possibility.

Segue to Chapter 6

To help you gain a feel for the ideas and tools in the next chapter, think of a time when you were hoping to gain something. In other words, you didn't have it yet, but you had the hope of getting it. How were you different while you had this hope?

CHAPTER 6

Narrative Counseling: Clients' Lives as Stories

"O wad some Pow'r the giftie gie us
To see oursels as others see us!"
Robert Burns

"He who has help has hope, and he who has hope has everything."
Arab proverb

CHAPTER GOALS

Reading about and experiencing the ideas in this chapter will help you to understand the following concepts:

- Creating meaning is one of our fundamental characteristics as human beings
- A narrative perspective is valuable in understanding how people see their world

Reading about and practicing the tools in this chapter will help you to understand these valuable skills:

- Externalizing the problem
- Using the miracle question
- Helping clients to view resolution from different points of view
- Using the encouragement triad

STORY

"William" was the name that appeared on his birth certificate, but people never called him that. His mother, who was notorious for giving nicknames to her children, decided that this youngest child—the runt of the family—was much too short for the seven-letter name they had selected originally, so she started to call the baby by his initial—"W." But even this abbreviation, with its three syllables, seemed too long and cumbersome for such a tiny thing, so she quickly shortened his name even more, to the single syllable "Dub."

Even when he had grown to a lanky 6 feet, 2 inches, a height that certainly could justify a longer name, people continued to call him "Dub." Dub never actually complained about his nickname, but he began to resent it when he was 13. One day, he had realized that his name was distinctively odd. Sure, many of his friends and relatives had nicknames that often bore no resemblance at all to the names that appeared on their birth certificates. But "Dub" was different because it wasn't a word. In fact, it wasn't even a letter—just a sound that started a letter. It was as if he wasn't worth more than just an simple utterance. Dub thought about asking people to call him "William," but it seemed such a minor issue to trouble others.

Since graduating from college a year ago, Dub eventually came to the realization that the nickname issue—what to call himself—was only part of much larger and more fundamental questions. Who was he? What did he want to do with his life? Where was he heading? Dub really had no idea. He was working as a waiter, but that was just to support himself until he found some answers. He had lived much of his life without thinking about these questions, but now they intrigued and even obsessed him.

Dub had never before been introspective. Instead, he had been an outgoing guy who was more interested in tinkering with motorcycles than in figuring out what made himself tick. For some reason, however, he lately had been keeping to himself, playing his guitar, and making up song lyrics. Coming home from work, Dub would squat on a tiny wooden stool he had kept from his childhood days, hunker over his guitar as if he were cradling a baby, and experiment by combining different chords with his lyrics. After several hours, he sometimes would throw aside his guitar, disgusted with himself when the words rang so maudlin and his fingering seemed so awkward that they would never capture the depth and intensity of his feelings.

Many of Dub's friends were also in temporary jobs, taking it easy and biding their time, keeping their lives on hold. They seemed to enjoy the respite from the grind of school and were in no hurry to enter the real world of adulthood commitments and responsibilities. But Dub began to feel a sense of urgency tugging at him and distracting him as he waited on tables. Even partying, which used to be so much fun, now seemed to be just a diversion that left Dub feeling even more empty and dissatisfied with his life—and wondering if he would ever be able to change it. In fact, it was after a party that he decided to make an appointment to see a counselor.

Reflecting Questions

1. What do you think Dub is searching for?
2. What would it be like to work with Dub as his counselor?
3. What could you offer Dub that would be encouraging?

OVERVIEW

When clients are discouraged, they are experiencing a crisis of meaning. While human beings all live in the physical world, we also live in a world of meaning. It is often more important to be well adjusted in the meaningful world than in the physical world. Meaning is not encoded in facts or data, nor is it expressed in logic. It is organized as a life story. What our lives have been, according to this life story, tends to predict what our lives will be. Clients come to counselors with stories that are outdated, tragic, and rigidified. As a result, these clients experience their lives as repetitive, negative, and unchangeable. Your task as a counselor is to help the client construct a new and therapeutic narrative.

While clients may bear little responsibility for the story as written so far, they are responsible for rewriting the narrative so that they can break out of the "stuckness" in which they find themselves. Taking this position frees both the client and the counselor from the endless cycle of looking for causes. Instead, using such techniques as "externalizing the problem" can help turn the client's concern into an "external influence" that attempts to lure the client into unproductive thoughts, emotions, and behaviors. The counselor then can ask for "news of a difference"—times during which the client has succeeded in not listening, or not being lured into trouble.

The technique of "externalization" seeks news of past successes, while the use of "hypotheticals" encourages a client to create the image of a success in the future. The "miracle question" technique is a way of inviting the client to construct a detailed scene in which he or she has resolved the major concerns of his or her life. The counselor then asks a series of questions designed to further develop that image.

In this chapter, you will be instructed on how to "encourage" rather than praise or reinforce client behaviors. The use of the "encouragement triad" (energy, imagery, agency) helps clients focus on success, develop a clearer picture of what they desire, accept that they are responsible for past successes, and believe that they can—and will!—be successful again.

IDEAS

The Problem of Meaning

As stated in Chapter 5, Polkinghorne (1988) considered the most neglected subject matter of psychology to be the study of personal meaning. He asserted, "Human existence consists of a stratified system of differently organized realms of reality—the material realm, the organic realm, and functions to organize elements of awareness into meaningful episodes" (p. 1). In other words, what something means to you will determine its status in the material and organic realms. Think, for example, of your most prized material object. Is it a photograph, a stuffed animal, a piece of jewelry, or something else of value to you? Whatever it is, it is more than merely a thing existing in the material world. It is special because you have conferred meaning upon it. For someone else, your prized object is just a thing.

Now, at the organic level, think of someone you love. In a reductionist reality, this person is merely a human organism. But because you love that person, he or she possesses a meaning for you that other human organisms do not. You may hardly notice the person who asks, "Do you want fries with that?" at a fast-food restaurant, but if that person were your loved one, then your attention would be suddenly heightened. To sum up, anything that exists at the material or organic level will attract your interest only if it is meaningful to you. Otherwise, it might as well not exist at all. Therefore, the world is always a world "for us" in the constructivist sense.

When you attempt to understand a client's world, you are seeking the organization of the personal meanings that things and people have for your client. Polkinghorne (1988) suggests four intriguing features concerning the elusive nature of personal meaning.

First, personal meaning exists in a form different form the existence of natural objects—it obviously cannot be picked up and held or measured. Personal meaning cannot be observed in the way that objects can, nor can it be precisely replicated at another time, because it is a bit like the reality that we see as a reflection in a mirror. Personal meaning "presents itself in our consciousness as a fleeting trace or indication; it appears as a wisp . . . continuously being reconstituted as the rudimentary perceptions of consciousness change" (Polkinghorne, 1988, p. 7). Meaning, therefore, is not the same as behavior. You can grasp your client's meaning in the moment only by truly encountering your client and carefully listening to his or her story.

Another important feature of personal meaning is that humans have direct access only to one meaning system—their own. Meaning must be approached through self-reflective recall or introspection. Moreover, our meaning-making process operates largely outside our own awareness and all we can know of it are its products. This dynamic suggests that, as clients tell you their stories—put words to their experience—they will likely discover more about their own meaning system.

Third, human beings express themselves in language—not data or numbers. Language is equivocal—a single word can have a number of meanings. Korzybsky (1933) said that words themselves do not have meanings; people have meanings. The translation of an experience into a word is always a reduction, and words are never the same as the experience itself. For example, think of a time when you were in love. Do you remember how futile words seemed as you attempted to communicate your feelings to your loved one?

Finally, statistical analysis can never reveal the nature of personal meaning. Statisticians deal with the behavior of people in groups. Very little can be known about the individual person this way. Generalizations must be drawn with the greatest caution, and the recognition that the individual is always lost in statistics must be kept in mind. If you and your client come from similar cultural backgrounds, some of your meanings will overlap, but you must always check with the client to verify your understanding of his or her meaning.

Your main focus as you are doing counseling is your client's organization of meanings. The elusive nature of personal meaning suggests that you should be very cautious about interpreting the meanings of your clients. Don't assume you know the meaning merely because you know the definitions of the client's words. Nevertheless, you are constantly seeking to understand what the client means by truly engaging and listening to everything the client says or does.

Two Kinds of Knowing

Jerome Bruner (1986) proposed that there are two modes of cognitive functioning—the "paradigmatic" and the "narrative." The former mode is characterized by a well-formed argument, the latter by a good story. "Arguments convince one of their truth, stories of their lifelikeness" (p. 11). Bruner stated that paradigmatic logic has a "heartless" quality. It is a sterile and formal way to think. It possesses none of the flesh-and-blood quality of the narrative. When used imaginatively, the narrative mode can create "gripping drama, [and] believable (though not necessarily "true") historical accounts. . . . It strives to put its timeless miracles into the particulars of experience, and to locate the experience in time and place" (p. 13).

Most human meaning is produced as narrative—in the stories of people's lives. We are all constantly engaged in the process Nelson Goodman (1978) called "world making." A personal world is not made up of a litany of facts within a database, but rather of episodes within a plot. It may seem to you that to think of clients' concerns in terms of a story would be to trivialize what they are telling you. Most people have been trained in the scientific tradition to seek facts and their relations. As a result of this training, facts might then be seen as the "hard stuff" of client talk, while stories may seem "soft" in comparison. Stories are, after all, fiction.

The distinction between fact and narrative might be exemplified in the following way. You may remember that in 1066, the Battle of Hastings was fought in England. Along with 1492, 1776, and 1941, the date of the Hastings battle exists as an isolated fact for many people. In 1066, William the Conqueror landed on the shores of England and, after a battle, became the new king of England. These are the facts. But had you heard that, during the desperate struggle, King Harold, who was opposing William, was shot through the eye by an arrow? Do you now have a picture of this and a feeling to go with it? If you do, you can immediately grasp the experiential difference between a fact and a story. (To make this example even more intriguing, the fact of whether King Harold was really shot through the eye is disputed by some historians.)

People's life stories are always set against a plot structure that involves what Karl Popper (1965) called a "world hypothesis-conjecture" about how the world works and how events are likely to turn out. People live in the midst of their life stories. Their lives have not turned out yet. Some portion of the story is still to unfold.

Once a child begins to learn story structure, he or she will begin to store experiences in the organized, meaningful plot of a life narrative. "Narrative competence appears at about the age of three, when we are able to recognize narratives and to judge how well formed they are" (Polkinghorne, 1988, p. 160). It is interesting to note that computers are quite good at formal, paradigmatic logic, but they come off worse than the average 3-year-old in their ability to generate and "understand" stories.

Our previous discussion of the difference between the "rational" and "developmental-constructivist" forms of counseling (Mahoney, 1988) contrasted the way someone might work in the rational–emotive/cognitive–behavioral modes with the constructivist approach. The rational model favors the more paradigmatic mode of knowing, while the developmental–constructivist belief fits well with the narrative way of knowing. From the standpoint of narrative knowing, events must be organized into meaningful stories in order to be fully understood. Through building a story around a plot, the narrative form constitutes human reality into wholes, manifests human values, and bestows meaning on life. "[N]arrative meaning consists of more than the events alone; it consists also of the significance these events have for the narrator in relation to a particular theme" (pp. 159–160).

We can remember an old TV police drama called "Dragnet," in which the detective would ask people to tell their stories, but would then interrupt and say, "Just the facts." As a counselor, you are not a fact-seeking detective. Instead, you are a change agent, and your search is for how people make meaning. When you are listening to client's stories, remember to keep your own thinking in the narrative—not the paradigmatic—mode.

Outdated, Rigidified, and Tragic Stories

When people seek counseling, we presume that this is because the story they are living has colored or restricted their experience to the point at which they are suffering under its weight. The story may be *outdated*—the person is repeating the same story over and over, even though the context in which the story was originally constructed vanished long ago. The characters in the story may have changed to the point they are no longer recognizable and do not fit their roles in the old story. For example, parents will sometimes treat their adolescent children as they did when the child was much younger. As a result, there is friction in the family because the adolescent will not accept his or her role in the outdated story. The parent, in this case, may have "frozen" a story in time that portrays the child as much younger and in need of a great deal of instruction and protection. When children reject the ideas of their parents and resent the control of "overprotective" adults, they are viewed as rebellious, incorrigible, or perhaps even insane by the parents. The child's behavior, which in another context would be seen as a normal adolescent stage, cannot be accepted as such in the outdated story of his or her family. Similarly, married clients whose stories fail to take into account that their spouses are continually growing and changing, can sometimes be heard to say accusingly, "You're not the person I married!"

Rigidified stories are the result of adopting beliefs about how things are supposed to be, and failing to take into account that life rarely fits well into ideal categories. A typical example of a rigidified story that does not fit the experiences of some people is the "pursuit-of-happiness" myth. People somehow get the idea that if one works hard, saves money, and obeys the laws of the land, happiness will be an inevitable outcome. But many find that the harder they pursue happiness, the more empty they feel. We have all heard about the proverbial CEO of a Fortune 500 company, never stopping "to smell the roses," who ends up disenchanted and disappointed. Buddha taught that people make themselves miserable by doggedly focusing on the attainment of their desired goals, and failing to recognize the importance of the journey. So long as a person remains aware that life is teleonomic, and not fully teleological, then one can change a life story as experience dictates.

Many people suffer *tragic* stories. When they construct stories in which they are unhappy protagonists who face ruinous outcomes, they tend to incorporate all new experiences into this plot. In your work with clients, you may find such tragic stories to be the most difficult. There is often a "heroic" quality to the role of the protagonist in tragedy, and clients are often reluctant to give up their roles.

To be "long-suffering," for example, is to view oneself as bearing up under circumstances over which one has no control. Like Job in the Bible, events cannot be changed by the protagonist, but the heroic behavior of enduring the suffering may be seen by that person, as well as others, as an admirable quality.

Similarly, to grieve and mourn the loss of a loved one for an inordinate period of time may sometimes be viewed as overt testimony to the strength of a person's love. For the hero to refuse to go on with his or her tragic life story might be seen as an act of disloyalty to the lost loved one, since it would involve rewriting the story in a happier way.

Sometimes, clients may even find meaning in their roles as the victims of other people's insensitivity, callousness, or violence. The reasons for this can be quite complicated, but suffice it to say that while they do not enjoy being victimized, they may find it difficult to give up the role. Keep in mind, however, that this tragic story is much more complex than the simple idea of "secondary gain." Making meaning from suffering is far more crucial than merely gaining attention. Somehow, the role of "tragic hero" will have to be displaced by an equally powerful role before clients can change their stories.

As you attempt to influence a change in people's stories or narrative life plots, you should keep in mind what you are asking them to give up. If they give up an outdated narrative, they may grieve the lost time . If they give up a rigidified narrative, they must relinquish a sense of certainty or an ideal outcome for their life. Finally, if they give up the position of the heroic, but tragic, protagonist, they must find an alternative meaning for their role that, although no longer tragic, is equally heroic and just as romantic.

Narrative Therapy

Narrative therapy is most closely tied to the work of Michael White and David Epston (1990), two psychotherapists from "Down Under." Epston is from New Zealand and White from Australia. Epston started out as an anthropologist, which he said gave him an "intellectual poaching license" and a "disrespect for 'disciplinary boundaries' " (White & Epston, 1990, p. xvi). White traced his own interest in psychotherapy to the writings of Gregory Bateson, himself a poaching anthropologist. Epston and White have emphasized the importance and the power of written communication in therapy. They often use letters, proclamations, and certificates, for example, in their work with clients.

The core of narrative therapy is the constructivist view that all "knowing" is an act of interpretation. This belief was first emphasized in 1933 by Korzybski, when he stated that "the map is not the territory"; this was later reinforced by Bateson's notion that all information is news of difference, as explained in Chapter 5. In order to change one's narrative, he or she must receive news of a difference. In other words, the client must incorporate new information into the narrative, resulting in an alteration of the plot. This dynamic is not unlike Piaget's (1926) notion that when we perceive something for which we have existing schema or representations, we merely take in the event and store it in its assigned place—this is *assimilation*. But when we perceive something for which we have no adequate category or representation, then we have "information"—the news of a difference. In order to receive news of a difference, we must change our schema or representation—we must *accommodate* the information by changing our mind.

A narrative is a metaphorical map, never the territory. If our map is a reasonable fiction for navigating the territory of our lives—if it fits the lock—then our map is usually adequate. However, it must always be subject to revision. Have you ever seen one of those old maps that showed what the country looked like before it had been completely explored? Imagine trying to find your way across the country with one of those maps! Furthermore, try finding the interstate highways on a map that was published in 1950! These highways did not exist at that time. Even the road map that you used on your last vacation probably has errors and omissions. Moreover, a map that you can hold in your hand is quite small compared to the territory it represents. When you are actually driving from Salt Lake City to Yellowstone Park, you quickly realize that the distance is a good deal more than the few inches shown on the map, and those mountains on US 89 looked awfully flat on that cartographic paper. Now consider how much easier the mapping of physical territory is than the mapping of psychologically meaningful territory. Mountains and highways change slowly compared to the events of people's lives. People's meaning systems can sometimes change in an instant when news of a difference is received.

When you ask clients for their story, you are asking them to put themselves into the role of the story's protagonist and to "perform" the story as if you were the theater-goer and the client were giving a one-person show. In this process, the story must not only be retold, it must be reexperienced. This is the moment your opportunity arises to promote change in the client. Each time a person retells a life story, the story is reauthored. "The evolution of lives is akin to the process of reauthoring, the process of persons entering into stories, taking them over and making them their own" (White & Epston, 1990, p. 13).

Life stories always have a beginning (a past), a present, and a future (how the story will likely turn out). The present is the time in which the story is being told, and the future is predicted by how the story is going now. For example, people who are deeply depressed have a difficult time imagining that their lives could ever be different. In addition, the story performer finds it difficult to remember when he or she was not depressed. The current rendition of the story tends to push such incompatible recollections into the background. Part of your job as a counselor is to bring memories of happiness and well-being to the foreground. You can accomplish this by hearing and mishearing the client's story. "Those aspects of lived experience that fall outside of the dominant story provide a rich and fertile source for the generation, or re-generation, of alternative stories" (White & Epston, 1990, p. 15).

You must create a situation in which new and enduring stories are generated, by serving as the audience for the performance of the usually unarticulated dominant story. Remember that you and the client are engaged in mutual feedback that changes the client's story. Your first act is *witnessing*—you become the audience and set the stage for change. Secondly, the client as performer of the story "reads" your reactions as the audience and makes adjustments according to how the performance is being received. In this audience role, you can serve as an *encouraging critic* of the story line. From the performer's standpoint, and since the client is also the author of the piece, things that seem to "go over well" may be kept in, while the "clunkers" may be marked for a rewrite. It has been pointed out that even Carl Rogers tended to reinforce—to smile and nod affirmatively when the client was talking of things Rogers thought were important. Furthermore, since the client–counselor relationship is much more intimate and interactive than that of performer and audience, you can *question or creatively misunderstand* aspects of the story in an attempt to deconstruct its certainty. Finally, you may even make subtle *suggestions* for improving the story. If the timing is right, these suggestions might be incorporated into a newer version of the client's narrative. Experienced counselors know that this last intervention is the most difficult. Novice counselors always want to jump to the suggestion phase long before they have qualified as a good audience.

Experiencing This Idea

Think of a poem or piece of prose that you wrote at some time in your life under the influence of some inspiring muse and you will see immediately why that last step above must be taken with great caution. Remember the ecstasy (which is Greek for "crazy") you felt when you had finished it? Remember also how compelled you felt to find an audience? And remember how crushed you were if they seemed only to "wait-to-talk," rather than to really listen as you read your work to them?

Who Is Responsible?

Alfred Adler (in Kleinke, 1994) stated that, because of their discouragement, clients will come to counseling stating that they are unable to resolve their situation because of their symptoms. The client "expects from the others the solution of his [or her] problems, or the excuse from all demands, or, at least, the granting of 'extenuating circumstances' " (p. 31). Clients experience themselves as unable to change, and they would like to find some reason, other than their own responsibility, for their current predicament. Clients often wish for you to collude with them in their feelings of discouragement and helplessness. They do not want to experience the guilt that comes with taking the responsibility for the creation of their "problem," and because they feel helpless to solve it, they also feel the shame of inadequacy.

What is your personal theory—your world hypothesis—concerning responsibility? If your clients say (about their current situation) that they "can't help it," and hope you can solve it for them, what is your response as a counselor? It is important for you to explore your implicit beliefs about responsibility. For example, are you likely to see the client as a hapless victim of circumstance who is clueless as to how to go about resolving his or her situation? If you do, you may feel pity for your client. This condition may inspire your missionary zeal and rescue fantasy. On the other hand, do you see the client as being "in denial" and abdicating his or her responsibility for the current troubles? This view may instigate in you a feeling of challenge, and you may want to confront the client until he or she confesses. If you see the client as ill and looking for the right "medicine," you may adopt the role of healer and protector. Or do you see the client as philosophically ignorant and in need of instruction about how to live life? This last view might cause you to want to appear as the all-knowing sage or guru to your client.

The role that you adopt with your client, and the tone you set for the counselor–client relationship, will depend on how you have come to think of the client's responsibility in the process. Brickman, Zevon, and Karuza (1982) developed a matrix containing four possible ways of viewing the client who comes for counseling. Kleinke (1994) discussed these four beliefs, or models, about responsibility in terms of "problems" and "solutions." One of these four may reflect your current belief about the client's responsibility for his or her problems and solutions.

The *moral model* assumes that the client has a high level of responsibility both for causing the problem and solving it. In its most stringent form, this is the "you got yourself into this, now you get yourself out of it" belief about responsibility. Usually, in this model, the client must acknowledge that his or her negligent or harmful behaviors have created the problem situation and that he or she is required to take action to remedy the situation.

The *enlightenment model* holds the client responsible for causing the problematic situation, but the job of solving is not his or her responsibility. This belief could be characterized as one in which the client repents his or her past transgressions and the counselor shows the client the proper path. Kleinke (1994) suggested that, while this model encourages the client to take advantage of professional assistance, it can also "instill guilt and self-blame as well as limit feelings of self-esteem and internal control" (p. 29).

The *compensatory model* takes the stance that clients do not cause their problems, but that they are responsible for solving them. An example of this belief would be an athlete who has sustained a knee injury in a game. While surgery will repair the torn ligament, it is only the hard work of rehabilitation on the weight machines, for example, that will return him or her to playing condition. "The compensatory model has the advantage of encouraging mastery and internal control while avoiding guilt and self-blame" (Kleinke, 1994, p. 29).

The *medical model* is one in which the client is neither responsible for causing the situation, nor responsible for solving it. This approach is based on the disease or disorder assumption. The client has not contributed to having the disease or disorder, and neither could he or she be held responsible for the cure. Obviously, the medical model is the root metaphor of many of the helping professions. It certainly has it merits and seems to work generally well in the medical professions. In such a model, if the client (usually referred to as a "patient") follows "doctor's orders," then it is likely that he or she will get better.

As you consider these models of responsibility, perhaps you recognize one of them as closest to your assumptions. We would like to suggest, however, that if you do not have an affinity for the compensatory model, you might nevertheless adopt this view as a heuristic, or useful procedural basis, for the *externalization technique* that we will discuss in the "Tools" section of this chapter. The compensatory model has the advantage of avoiding recrimination and guilt on the part of the client and opens the door for the possibility that the client may be able to master the situation, despite the fact that he or she is currently feeling helpless. The externalization technique helps clients realize that they have already overcome the problem at times, and therefore, already possess the resources needed to generalize this skill.

Implications of These Ideas for the Counselor

The ideas of meaning making and narrative can have significant consequences for your work as a counselor:

- Counselors who are behaviorists prefer to work with behavior because it is overt, measurable, and relatively easy to manipulate. However, it is *meaning*—a far more ethereal and private phenomenon—that is the locus of change in clients.
- Paradigmatic knowing is the stuff of science, dealing with facts and their relations. Narrative knowing is metaphoric and constructed. People organize their meaning into narrative life stories that are not "true" in the logical sense, but are the stuff of the way we develop our world hypotheses. There is more power in a story than in a fact.
- As a counselor, you can help clients alter the outdated, rigidified, and tragic plots of their lives in two important ways. You can serve as the audience for their retelling of the story and then you can take advantage of any gaps or omissions you find in the narrative.
- Finally, the method of counseling we are advocating in this book works best when you adopt the compensatory model of responsibility. In other words, you take the general position that the client is not to blame for his or her current dilemma, but is responsible for its resolution.

Tools

Externalization

There are two meanings of the term *externalization*. The first describes the defensive style of a client who takes no responsibility for the problem situation and who blames everyone else. The second meaning—the one emphasized here—is that the counselor helps separate the problem from the self-image of the client. This technique, developed by Michael White (1988) is meant to keep the client from identifying with the problem. The motto is, "The person is never the problem—the problem is the problem."

There are several advantages to adopting this attitude regarding the difference between the client and the problem. First, the client usually comes to counseling already trying to externalize the problem, so this technique fits with the client's portrayal of the story. Second, the client may feel powerless to control the problem, even if it is seen by others as something he or she does "voluntarily." Third, by characterizing the problem as external, the counselor can enter into a "conspiracy" with the client against the problem, inviting more cooperation. Finally, the client can achieve a sense of agency as he or she battles the external problem. This action evades the defeating diagnostic merging of client and problem—"I am a Conduct Disorder, this is what I do"—which robs the client of a sense of personal agency.

Based on O'Hanlon's (1995) suggestions, the procedure for externalizing the problem involves several simple steps.

- Begin by speaking of the problem, even naming it, as if it were an *entity* that is plaguing the client. For example, you can personify the problem or characterize it as having a mind of its own—"Mr. Jealousy" or "Ms. Inferiority," for example. You will find that clients often come having coined their own names. In this case, use the clients' term.
- Then, characterize the problem as having *malevolent* motives. In other words, the problem "desires" the downfall of the client by trying to get him or her to think or do certain things.
- Third, continue the externalizing procedure by asking the client about the *ways* in which the external entity attempts to fool, influence, trick, or seduce the client into these thoughts or behaviors. For example, you might ask, "What does The Failure Trapper say to get you to try to get you to drop the ball on a project?" As you carry out this process, be sure *not* give the problem the power to cause the client's behavior—only to suggest or influence it.
- Fourth, ask presumptively about the times when the problem has attempted to influence the client, but the client has *ignored* the problem. For example, you might ask a child who has problems with anger, "When have you told the Temper Tantrum Monster to take a hike?"
- Finally, once the client has identified an exception, ask, *"How did you get yourself to do that?"* You can also explore details of a future in which the client is dealing successfully with this externalized problem. You might ask a client, "Which one of your friends would be the first to notice these changes? What would this person say to you about these changes?"

Externalizing the problem can be a very powerful tool in your attempts to influence the client to tell his or her story in a different way. Even if you do not you subscribe to the compensatory model of responsibility (described above), we strongly advise you to act as if you do. Kleinke (1994) pointed out that we are attempting, as counselors, to increase the client's sense of efficacy in the face of a situation he or she has defined as a problem, and in which a sense of helplessness has formerly prevailed. Kleinke stated that no matter what school of therapy you subscribe to, or what your personal biases may be, your primary aim is to help clients toward a sense of freedom. You want to help the client realize a sense of "I can" (p. 34). When you seek exceptions through the use of the externalization technique, you help clients to realize that the problem is not them—not "I *am.*" Furthermore, not only might they come to believe "I *can,*" but they might also realize that, once they have rediscovered their past successes, "I *already have.*" Clients overcome their problems often. There are many times when problems are *not* happening. It is your job to help clients remember these times and to get back in touch with the strategies they were using to not let the problem influence them.

Listening in on a Session

Review the story at the beginning of the chapter. A resolution-focused counselor might work to externalize Dub's concerns in the following way.

William: *(After the counselor introduces himself, William explains that his nickname has been Dub all his life, but that he would like for the counselor to call him William. When the counselor invites William to talk about what he would like to get out of counseling, William tilts his head slightly and gazes out the window.)* To tell you the truth, I don't even know exactly why I made this appointment. That's one of my problems, I guess. I just don't think I know *anything* anymore. I didn't even know how to introduce myself to you. I'm sick of being called Dub, but people give me such crap when I've asked them to call me William. They act like I'm putting on airs and trying to act superior or grown-up. Some are nice about it and call me William once or twice, but then they slip back into Dub. I feel guilty about bugging them, so I just say to myself, "Aw, to hell with it. Why should I make such a big deal over this. I mean, what do I know?" *(He shrugs his shoulders dismissively.)*

What's totally weird about this is that I used to be kind of a smart-ass, know-it-all guy when I was in college. I really got off on showing people how much I knew about motorcycles or NASCAR or music—even sports trivia. But now, I don't know crap. I don't know why I'm here, I don't know who I am, and I sure as hell don't know where I'm going with my life.

Counselor: So, lately, your life has been feeling like a real mystery to you and you've decided that it's finally time to look for some answers.

William: *(He nods his head slightly and smiles wryly.)* Yeah, it's like I'm searching for something, but I have no idea what it is, or where it is, or even if I'll recognize it when I find it.

(He pauses and waves off that idea.) Wait a second, that's not exactly it, either. It's like for my whole life, y'know, I've been riding along this highway. Don't get me wrong, it's been a pretty fun ride, but now I'm wondering if this is the highway I'm really meant to be on. I don't even know where this highway's taking me. Maybe I want to turn on a different road for a change.

Counselor: So it's like there's a traffic cop that keeps directing you on down that old, familiar highway. He doesn't care about where *you* really want to go—he just wants to keep traffic moving down that highway and he even wants you to keep your old name on your driver's license. What's this traffic cop been telling you to keep you traveling down that same highway?

William: Oh, he'll say that my friends will wonder, "Who the hell does Dub think he is?" or he'll say something like, "Dub, why don't you come along with your friends?"

Counselor: Tell me about the times that you've been able to follow your own road and not listen to this traffic cop.

William: Well, I guess that instead of tinkering with my Harley or partying, which is what I always used to do in my spare time, I've been keeping to myself more and tinkering with my mind lately. I try to put all this crap I'm going through into my music.

Reflecting Questions

1. How has William shaped his story?
2. How has the counselor used externalization?
3. How might you respond to William's last statement?

Using This Tool

Divide into groups of three. One of you volunteers to share some present concern. Another volunteers to listen, understand, validate, and, when appropriate, help the client externalize the problem. Finally, the third person serves as the recorder, who observes the activity and leads the feedback discussion.

Fantasy and the Hypothetical

Two paths toward constructing solutions identified by Walter and Peller (1992) are the "goal statement and hypothetical solution" and the "problem statement and hypothetical solution." If clients persist in the belief that the goal is never happening or do not state a goal in positive terms, you can use the hypothetical solution frame to explore details leading to a goal. When clients enter a hypothetical solution frame, they will likely offer details that allow you to focus on exceptions and to identify the times when they are already accomplishing the goal to some extent.

The use of the hypothetical frame temporarily relieves the client of the responsibility of changing immediately and tends to imbue the solution with a hopeful, yet tentative quality through the use of fantasy. "Fantasy is an expansive force in a person's life—it reaches and stretches beyond the immediate people, environment or event which may otherwise contain him [sic]" (Polster & Polster, 1973, p. 255). Fantasy is a vicarious form of enactment. If people have become discouraged and stuck with regard to their desires and goals, then as Minkowski (in Ellenberger, 1958) pointed out, their future becomes an impossibility; they foreclose on tomorrow and live in a "dammed-up" present.

In this condition, instead of liberating fantasies, they experience discouraging ruminations while their daydreams become ungrounded and extravagant. When liberating fantasies emerge in counseling, the client's energy increases and gives the client a new sense of self.

Basic to the fantasy process is the function of exploring the unknown as a way of orienting oneself to the complexities of life to prepare for future action and to sharpen one's sensibilities. It is an emotionally energizing experience similar to art. The creative thinking that produces art is not merely a playful musing—it is the process that enlivens our existence and causes us to notice relationships in fresh and novel ways. "The mind sinks into apathy unless its hungry roots are continuously searching the dark sustenance of the unknown, its sensitive foliage continuously stretching towards unimaginable light" (Read, 1965; in Polster & Polster, 1973, pp. 260–261).

As true art always implies both innovation and craft, so too are you attempting to engage your clients in the art of illuminating the unknown by creating a better future image for themselves. First, they must be able to imagine this possibility in fresh detail, which will energize their longing to complete the project, and second, they must go about crafting the image so that it can become real. Sometimes the fresh perspective—the change of *viewing*—will be sufficient to alter the crafting—the *doing*. Usually referred to as a reframe, this experience is what you hope to bring about in your clients. Once something is truly reframed, it can never again be seen the same way. In the Necker cube exercise in Chapter 2, recall how suddenly the picture changed and how you were then no longer able to imagine a single view. Change can sometimes come about suddenly, and no rational explanation can be offered for it. Old business gets finished, and even the client cannot say how. The world suddenly seems more welcoming and the future hopeful, though nothing has really changed in the client's circumstances. And the bittersweet longing returns to propel the client toward possibilities that did not seem to have been there before.

Pretending Miracles

When you ask your clients to enter the hypothetical frame, you are offering the opportunity for them to artistically create a future that will contain both a solution path and a resolution of their former difficulties. You ask for the "best-case scenario"—one in which they suddenly realize in fantasy that their problems are gone. One of the best techniques for accomplishing this is the famous "miracle question" developed by de Shazer (1985) and his associates. The client is asked to imagine that while he or she is asleep, a miracle happened that resolves the client's issues. You then ask for a detailed description of what the client—who was asleep at the time and did not know the miracle had happened—would notice that is different. The miracle question is used when clients are unable to identify any exceptions in their problem pattern. Once the client responds, you can help make the image as clear and concrete as possible. Cade and O'Hanlon (1993) suggested phrases such as the following:

> If you were in a restaurant and people were watching the two of you having a meal together, how will they know that you are getting on well?" (p. 102).

Walter and Peller (1992) sometimes used the notion of pretending with clients who are more "practical-minded" and are having trouble taking the miracle question seriously:

If . . . you were walking out of here with the problem solved, or you were at least on track to solving it, what would you be doing differently? (p. 80).

O'Hanlon (1995) suggested that children sometimes respond better to the notion of the therapist using a "magic wand" or a "magic pill" to solve the problem. Erickson (1954) employed the hypothetical as a "crystal ball technique." While clients were in a trance, Erickson would ask them to look into the crystal ball and see a future in which their problems had been eliminated. Then, he would have them peer back to the present from their place in the future and identify how they had been able to accomplish this change.

In any case, the idea is to follow up the hypothetical solution with inquiry about how the person will be different when the problem is solved. Whatever the client says about the difference, it will serve as a road sign on the path to a well-formed goal statement and, ultimately, toward resolution of his or her current difficulties.

Listening in on a Session

Review the story at the beginning of the chapter and the dialogue between William and his counselor in the previous section. A resolution-focused counselor might use the miracle question with William in the following way.

> **Counselor:** *(leans forward and prefaces the miracle question by briefly asking for permission, and taking care to call the client by his preferred name)* Let me ask you something, William. What if you went home after this session, spent a typical evening of maybe having something to eat, making some music for awhile, and then going to bed. Suppose that, while you were sound asleep in bed, a miracle happened that resolved your situation so you are living the life that you desire and have found the answers that you seek. However, since you were sound asleep, you didn't even know that this miracle had taken place. What would be the first thing that you would notice when you woke up in the morning that would show you that this miracle had happened?
>
> **William:** *(pauses, appears pensive)* Well, I guess that I would have more confidence in myself. It wouldn't bother me so much that I didn't know exactly where I was going. It would just be cool that I had decided to try going this way. I think that I'd be OK about reminding people that I now like to be called William. Maybe I'd feel proud for trying something different and I wouldn't be so hard on myself when I make mistakes.

Reflecting Questions

1. How has William envisioned his miracle?
2. How has the counselor used the miracle question?
3. How might you respond to William's last statement?

Using This Tool

Divide into groups of three. One of you volunteers to share some aspect of your life that you would like to change. Another volunteers to listen, understand, validate, and, when appropriate, pose the "miracle question." Finally, the third person serves as the recorder, who observes the activity and leads the feedback discussion.

The Interpersonal Perspective

Perhaps you have had the experience of having someone remark that you look as though you have lost weight, or that you are looking younger, or that you are appearing happier in recent days. Often such casual remarks can cause you to reassess your self-image and may even elevate your mood. Such mundane events are examples of the more profound changes in self-perception you can achieve in the counseling situation.

Counselors can capitalize on the human desire to "see ourselves as others see us"— to bring our self-perceptions into alignment with the perception others have of us. Therefore, as you elaborate on the client's image of success, whether as an exception or a hypothetical, you might wish to bring their significant others into the equation so that the client can also imagine being seen in more positive terms by these important people.

When your clients report exceptions, goals, or hypotheticals that suggest success or resolution, you will want to ask them how others will see them differently. The idea here is similar to the notion of "circular questioning" employed by the Milan family therapy group. In this case, clients were asked to take the interpersonal stance, and view themselves as others might. Using this device, the client is more able to take a different perspective and to describe in greater detail the behaviors that would be displayed. Walter and Peller (1992) used three levels of questioning for elaborating the hypothetical solution. They called these the *Self, Other*, and *Detached* views. The Other and Detached views give the client a perspective different from his or her own. From these views we see ourselves as others see us. An example of Self questions would be, "When things are better for you, how will your behavior be different?" and "What will your partner be doing that's different?" Then, seeking another level of perception, you could ask the Other question, "What would your partner say you will be doing that's different?" Finally, from the Detached point of view, you might ask, "As a fly on the wall, what will I see you (your spouse, both of you) doing differently?" (p. 176).

O'Hanlon (1995) asked the client to "video-talk" the scene, as if someone were following the client around with a camcorder to catch all behaviors and conversations in exquisite detail. Obviously, the more the client focuses on behaviors occurring after the problem has been (hypothetically) solved, the greater the focus on resolution. All problems exist in an interpersonal context. Sometimes people are primarily motivated to change so that others will see them differently. How we appear to others (or how we think we appear to others) exerts a powerful pressure on us to be viewed as OK.

Using This Tool

Divide into groups of three. One of you volunteers to share some hypothetical solution that you would like to achieve. Another volunteers to invite the client to describe the desired behaviors from self, other, and detached perspectives. Finally, the third person serves as the recorder, who observes the activity and leads the feedback discussion.

Encouragement Versus Praise

Jerome Frank (1985) said that many people who seek counseling are demoralized. He described demoralization as a state characterized by one or more of the following: "subjective incompetence, loss of self-esteem, alienation, hopelessness (feeling no one can help), or helplessness (feeling that other people could help but will not)" (p. 56). According to this view, clients seek not only to alleviate problems and symptoms but to decrease feelings of discouragement (Young, 1992). Resolution counseling focuses on solving problems, but also expects that people will become more encouraged by the process. Actually, this process is more important than solving problems. The ostensible problem solution activity is merely the vehicle for encouraging the client.

In addition to the concomitant encouragement that naturally comes with the resolution process, you can deliberately use statements designed to encourage people. Encouraging statements are different from praise, gratuitous compliments, or pep talks. They are designed to reflect an internal positive state existing within the client. Witmer (1986) stated that encouragement is used to inspire, hearten, and instill confidence, while praise is designed to maintain the strength of a specific behavior. Encouragement is designed to increase a sense of personal agency, while praise is designed for external control.

If, for example, a child displays a desired behavior, the praise response might be, "Great job!" or "I'm really proud of you!" or "You get an 'A' for that one!" On the other hand, the encouragement response might be, "I noticed you were really trying hard on that, and you did it!" or "How in the world were you able to do such a difficult thing!" or "Wow! Tell me how you did that!" In the latter responses, the evaluation is more in the form of an observation and the agency remains with the child. There is certainly nothing wrong with praising, complimenting, or cheering when someone does well. It is just that these behaviors are not as effective in building autonomy, an internal locus of evaluation, and a sense of personal power in the client. Remember, you are a significant other for the client, and the way in which you respond will affect the way the client sees himself or herself. If you wish to improve the client's self-concept, then encouragement is superior to praise or reinforcement.

If you appear too interested in the client's problem-saturated talk and self-deprecating statements, the client will likely imagine that you are invested in having his or her self-concept remain negative. Someone has said that when your clients are in a discouraged state, they always imagine that you secretly despise them. Just as you must "watch your language" with clients, you must also watch your reactions to their language. It is only when clients are reporting success—actual or hypothetical—that you should appear enthusiastic and intensely interested.

Compliments, Praise, and Encouragement

Ideally, you should motivate clients in a particular direction—from being discouraged to being encouraged. Walter and Peller (1992) correctly contended that you must "observe for positives." By this declaration they meant that feedback given to the client should focus on the things the client is doing well, rather than on the problem behaviors. They referred to this tactic as "complimenting" the client. It is important to note, however, that most of their compliments are in the form of encouraging statements, rather than praise. The difference between encouragement and praise is in the goal of such interventions.

If one wishes to strengthen the behavior under consideration, then praise is appropriate. The operant-conditioning behavioral literature has stressed this strategy. On the other hand, if your goal is to increase a client's self-esteem, you should use encouraging statements. Witmer (1986) discussed the sometimes subtle distinction between praise and encouragement. He suggested that in most situations in which you are attempting to develop a sense of agency and competence in the client, encouragement is a preferable technique. Encouragement motivates, inspires, heartens, and instills confidence in a client. However, praise or reinforcement is useful in maintaining or strengthening a specific behavior. Encouragement focuses on the client's inner direction, internal control, and effort. On the other hand, praise emphasizes your evaluation of the adequacy of a client's performance. Encouragement is more likely to promote the client's feeling of competence and independence, but praise or reinforcement may "develop a strong association, perhaps dependence, between a specific reinforcer and a behavior, [and may be] less likely to generalize to other life situations" (p. 142).

Using This Tool

Divide into groups of three. One of you volunteers to share some successful experience. Another volunteers to offer encouragement (rather than reinforcement) in the listen, understand, and validate process. Finally, the third person serves as the recorder, who observes the activity and leads the feedback discussion.

When a Client Focuses Positively (The Encouragement Triad)

Any time the client moves from problem-saturated talk to a positive focus, you will want to attempt to increase the vividness of the focus. If the client makes a goal statement, states an exception, or reports a success, you must try to—as they say—"make hay while the sun shines." Ask the client to elaborate the scenario, using the "fly on the wall" or "video-talk" techniques or any type of request for detailed information that fits your style.

Then, attempt to insert as many of the "encouragement triad" responses as you can into your reaction to the client (Figure 6-1). The three points of the triangle will serve to remind you of how you can get the most out your client's positive focus. First, get excited, and do everything you can to communicate your enthusiasm for the client's content. In other words, display *energy*. This message of excitement over what is being discussed has the effect of "reverse empathy" (to be explained further in Chapter 7). Clients also have empathic responses to the counselor, and your enthusiasm about their success can be contagious.

Secondly, pump the client for all the details. Make sure that you get a complete picture of what the client is talking about in all its concrete minutia. For example, if you

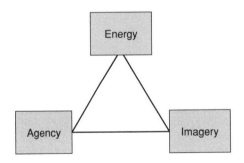

FIGURE 6.1   The encouragement triad

are exploring exceptions, you might ask. What did you say?" "What did other people say?" "What was different?" "What did the other people notice that was not there before?" "Where is the event taking place?" "What does it feel like?" In other words, you want to strive to have the client give as complete an account of the *imagery* (visual, kinesthetic, and acoustical) as possible. Make the scene as real for the client as you can by persistently asking for a complete description. In addition, make every attempt to use presumptive statements that assign *agency* to the client. In what way is the client responsible for the change or the positive turn of the situation? Try to reflect each external locus of responsibility statement back on the client, so that you communicate your belief that the client was, or will be in control, rather than being the passive recipient of fortune or someone else's good deed.

Using These Tools

Divide into groups of three. One of you volunteers to share a recent success experience. Another volunteers to engage the client in elaborating on the success by being enthusiastic, encouraging imagery, and promoting agency. Finally, the third person serves as the recorder, who observes the activity and leads the feedback discussion.

Finding the Pony

There is an old joke—author unknown—that dramatically illustrates the following technique, which is usually referred to as the "coping question" (DeJong & Berg, 1998). We believe this story serves to create a more powerful mnemonic in the mind of the counselor, rather the use of the bland term: *coping question*. The tale goes as follows:

> When the twin boys were born, it was immediately obvious to their parents that they had widely differing personalities. One seemed to be constantly fearful and cried easily, while the other cooed and smiled and seemed content with most any situation. While the latter was initially considered to be a good trait, when the smiling infant became a toddler, he displayed an undiscerning trust in everyone, and his parents worried that he might go to any stranger who beckoned, and, in this way, be kidnaped. The fearful child displayed no such tendencies: always clinging to his mother for support and bursting into tears at the mere sight of any stranger. The parents were concerned for both boys. But the pediatrician said what pediatricians usually say: "They'll grow out of it."
>
> They did not grow out of it, however. By the time the boys were 8 years old, the parents decided that both boys were in need of psychotherapy. The parents' goal for the therapy was that the "pessimistic" one would become more trusting and hopeful; while the "optimistic" one would be less gullible and more wary. The therapist designed a treatment plan for each boy based on the parents' goals. The overly pessimistic boy was to be placed in a room with an enormous quantity of wonderful toys and games and told he could do with them whatever he liked, while the optimistic boy was given a shovel and told that he was to spend the day cleaning out horse stalls. The therapy was to last from early morning until late afternoon.
>
> Toward the end of the day, the parents looked in on the pessimistic boy to find him sobbing in a corner of the room with all the toys still in their packages. When he was asked what was wrong, he explained that the toys were so marvelous that he was sure that if he played with any of them, he would destroy them all and never be able have them again. On the other hand, when the parents went down to the horse barn, they found the optimistic boy whistling with a broad grin on his face. The boy had finished cleaning several stalls, and had just opened the door to the next one, which was filled nearly to the ceiling with horse manure. When asked why he seemed to be so happy and optimistic in the face of such a task, he replied: "With all this horseshit, there's got to be a pony in here somewhere!"

When clients are feeling overwhelmed and can see nothing but doom and gloom in their lives, it is difficult for them to state well-formed goals or to notice exceptions to their woes. You will find that they often return to problem-saturated talk almost immediately after being asked for optimistic statements. They just cannot imagine anything being better in their lives. They are "complainants" of the first order. When you meet such clients, it will be necessary for you to pull out of their problem-saturated story something hopeful—however small—that they had failed to notice. Like the optimistic little boy, you are seeking to find a pony in all the crap.

When attempting to find the pony, always begin with an acknowledgment of the client's complaint:

"My god! First your mother died, and then you got the diagnosis of your breast cancer, and a notice that the IRS is auditing your tax return . . . all in the same week! How in the world are you even able to get yourself out of bed in the morning and do your job?!"

Never overlook the fact that your client is present in the room with you:

"With all that has happened, and as vulnerable as you say you have felt, I'm amazed that you were able to summon the courage to be here, with me, working on this issue! How did you get yourself to do that?"

Here is a useful variant on the old "things could be worse" adage: "With things seemingly going down the tubes the way that they have, how have you been able to keep the situation from becoming much worse than it is?"

When clients present themselves as a long-suffering martyrs, you can ask: "How in heaven's name have you been able to cope with this situation for such a long time?! Most people would not have been as (tolerant, resilient, strong, etc.) with all that wearing on them!"

When the client complains about someone else's behavior, you can say something like: "Yes, he really does sound like he would try the patience of Job! But you have hung in there and haven't let his behavior make you do something crazy. How on earth do you keep control when he says things like that?"

All these prototype responses for finding the pony should be offered as exclamations, to indicate that you should display amazement, wonderment, and enthusiasm when offering this intervention. Such a display of excitement serves to heighten the client's emotional arousal associated with his or her coping explanation. [We will discuss the management of emotional arousal in Chapter 7]. By increasing the client's energy and enthusiasm associated with positive behaviors, you will be highlighting the heroism, persistence, tolerance, understanding of others, and patience that are evident in the client's resilience. You are hopeful that the client will focus on personal resources and coping abilities for a while and become somewhat aroused to change. Even if the client says, "I don't know," you have planted a seed by introducing an aspect of the situation that the client did not previously have in focus. As a result, your client may have taken a small step toward finding the pony.

Listening in on a Session

Review the story at the beginning of the chapter and the two previous dialogues between William and his counselor. At this point in the session, a resolution-focused counselor might highlight William's resilience in the following way:

William: (*sighing*) I never had any delusions that I was going to be making a living from my music. That's really OK with me. I was just hoping that I might make some sense out of my life through my music, that I could be honest and real with it, and that I could maybe find something out about who I am. But my music's turned into a total waste — just like my whole life. It's all been really depressing. I mean, what's the point? At least before, when I was in college, I was heading somewhere, but now I'm just stuck and going nowhere fast.

Counselor: With all these feelings that your music's been wasted and that you're stuck in a life that seems pointless, how in the world did you get yourself to make the decision to come in here and search for some answers?

William: I really don't know for sure. Maybe it had something to do with how I feel when I do hang in there long enough to come up with at least a chord or phrase that seems to ring true for me. There's something in here [*tapping his chest*] that tells me I've got to keep on keepin' on. I told myself that talking with a counselor might be another way of coming up with something else that rings true.

Reflecting Questions

1. What's the pony here?
2. How has the counselor encouraged William in finding it?
3. How might you respond to William's last statement?

Using This Tool

Divide into groups of three. One of you volunteers to share some aspect of your life that you would like to change. Instead of presenting it as you usually might, however, be pessimistic about both the problem and yourself. For example, as you share your complaints, frame them in problem-saturated talk by focusing on the negatives, emphasizing your sense of helplessness, and portraying yourself as feeling overwhelmed by having tried everything to deal with this pervasive problem. Another volunteers to listen, understand, validate, and, when appropriate, find the exception or "the pony." Finally, the third person serves as the recorder, who observes the activity and leads the feedback discussion.

SEGUE TO CHAPTER 7

Think about the scariest movie you ever saw. Now think of the most boring lecture you ever attended. If someone were to videotape your reactions at those times, what could be seen of your emotional expression?

CHAPTER 7

Managing the Client's Emotional Arousal: Hot-Wiring

"Lovers and madmen have such seething brains
Such shaping fantasies, that apprehend
More than cool reason ever comprehends."
Shakespeare

CHAPTER GOALS

Reading about and experiencing the ideas in this chapter will help you to understand the following concept:

- Emotions must be appropriately engaged in order for clients to fully experience their successes.

Reading about and practicing the tools in this chapter will help you learn to:

- Manage the client's emotional arousal in the session to promote therapeutic change.

STORY OF CARLA

Although it had only been 6 months since her sudden and painful separation from Sandy, the only truly emotional expression that Carla would allow herself was a small, hesitant gesture. On those rare occasions when she came across one of her ex-partner's photographs, Carla found that she couldn't help touching it. It was only then that her eyes might glisten and she would exhale a hesitant, guttural sigh. A camera buff, Carla had once read how the light that imprinted someone's image on film had actually touched the person first. Somehow, that thought gave a tactile, almost intimate, quality to any of Sandy's pictures—from grainy, unfocused snapshots to the one well-crafted, professional studio portrait she had coaxed Sandy into having done.

Whenever Carla encountered a photo among the belongings that now cluttered the efficiency apartment, her hand would be drawn almost magnetically to Sandy's face, where she would tentatively stroke the image of her former lover's cheek. The gesture was a miniature imitation of one she had used on Sandy. Too late (that was the story of

121

her life!), Carla realized that the stroke had been one of the few affectionate gestures that she would use to express her feelings toward her partner. It was the only clear and consistent barometer of her mood. When she was playful, Carla had followed the stroke with a gentle pat or two. When she was feeling sensuous, her hand had lingered to caress Sandy's jawline and neck. Carla couldn't remember when her partner had stopped responding to the gesture, but it must have been months before their separation. Sandy's failure to react to that gesture was only one of the many warning signs that Carla had missed during that time.

For the past 6 months, Carla has felt stuck, her life put on hold, her existence frozen like the image of her expartner in one of her photos. At work, she has tried to jump-start herself, psych herself up, and become once again the energetic and confident person she used to be. Instead, she has found herself procrastinating, making excuses for missed deadlines, and avoiding her supervisors. Although this behavior has been unlike her, Carla has been even more surprised by her uncharacteristic attitudes of indifference and passivity regarding her poor performance. At one time, she had thrived on accepting challenging tasks and other demanding commitments, but now nothing seems to be worth the effort.

As bad as the work situation has become, Carla's social life has been worse. She has spent nearly all her free time alone in her apartment. Just as she has often gone to the office with resolutions to finish long-overdue projects, Carla has arrived home with the intention of calling an old friend, going out with an acquaintance, or joining a club. However, each evening she has sat curled up on an old sofa, listening to music, listlessly paging through magazines, thumbing through old photographs, and delaying taking any action until it was too late.

Last week, Carla's supervisor sat her down and shared her concerns regarding her poor work performance. Carla acknowledged that these problems were serious and admitted that she had been fooling herself by dismissing them as only a temporary setback from the separation. Reluctantly, she accepted the recommendation that she make an appointment with a counselor to deal with these concerns. Carla now enters the counseling room with a quiet, uncertain, and restrained manner.

STORY OF BOB

Bob was referred to the community counseling center by his minister, who decided that Bob was not having a "crisis of faith," but perhaps needed to work with a counselor on some "lifespan issues."

Fifty-five-year-old Bob began the session by announcing that he did not know what the hell a lifespan issue was. "It's probably just another new age BS term that was invented by some damn yuppie shrink to create a new insurance category to bilk the public out of more money."

The counselor began to acknowledge Bob's upset feelings but was interrupted by a torrential outpouring of red-faced, blustering anger.

"I don't know how you're going to be able to help me. Hell, I'm old enough to be your father. Just don't talk loud. Young people think because somebody wears a hearing aid that we are deaf and stupid. I was in a store last week and the clerk asked me in a placating voice if I wanted to buy the product I laid on the counter. I felt like telling her that I wouldn't have brought it to the damn cash register if I hadn't wanted to buy it. Things like that happen all the time."

Bob paused and shook his head disgustedly, then continued.

"I trained a kid 10 or 12 years ago who was no great shakes, but now he's my damn boss. . . . No, that's not true. . . . It's worse than that. He's my boss's boss! I feel like the world has passed me by. Last month at the office Christmas party, people huddled around in groups talking about the latest TV sitcoms, movies, or the internet. I'm sure people got tired of my asking who somebody was. Whatever happened to interesting conversation? Doesn't anyone read any more?"

Bob's voice trails off and he seems to shrink down into his chair.

"Herbie—I guess I should call him Mr. Parker—made me feel like such a dumb-ass when he suggested that I needed to get up to speed. Everybody got a big kick out of that."

Bob stiffens, sits up straighter and all but shouts, "Up to speed, my ass! Herbie wouldn't have lasted through his probationary period if it hadn't been for me wiping his nose for him when he first came to work here. The hell with him and with the rest of them. Who cares!"

REFLECTING QUESTIONS

1. What were your own reactions to these stories?
2. Which client is more similar to you?
3. With which client would you rather work?

CHAPTER OVERVIEW

All emotions are impulses to act. The very root of the word *emotion* is *motere,* the Latin verb "to move." When you encounter your clients, they have often moved away from fearful and painful circumstances and are usually feeling discouraged (Young, 1992). However, it is not moving-away behavior that you wish to have them practice. Instead, you want them to move toward a more productive way of thinking about their concerns and more effective coping behaviors.

A common misconception is that emotions are messy contaminants to effective problem-solving and good mental health. In fact, new discoveries in neuroscience are revealing that emotions are essential to good thinking. This chapter offers a discussion of new ideas taken from recent research into how emotions work and how they contribute to good social judgment. For example, in the brain, there are centers, such as the hippocampus, that encode and process cognitive memories. The amygdala, however, appears to be an older and more efficient processing location for helping human beings to respond to emotionally "hot" situations. When thought and emotion are working harmoniously, human information processing is complete.

In this chapter, you will learn the techniques for stimulating empathy in your clients, getting them to respond emotionally to positive images, and managing emotional arousal during sessions so that clients benefit from the optimal cognitive–emotional connection. The Yerkes–Dodson law—the inverted-U hypothesis—suggests that people are most productive when they are emotionally aroused to some extent, but their efficiency of thought declines after a certain point. Because too little or too much emotional arousal is counterproductive, your work as a counselor is to maintain your clients' arousal in the optimal zone.

IDEAS

Emotions and Thought

The philosopher René Descartes said, "Cogito ergo sum." ("I think, therefore I am.") With this statement, Descartes placed thought at the pinnacle of human existence. To think is to be, and to be is to think. Since Descartes's time, most people in Western society have accepted the notion that cognition ranks above emotion in importance. It is much better to use your head than to follow your heart. As a result, proponents of the many varieties of cognitive or rational therapies insist, as their main assumption, that once one's thinking is straightened out, one's emotions will automatically be brought into line. Emotions have taken a back seat to rational thought in many modern therapies. The belief that emotions only serve to contaminate good thinking has much currency in today's therapeutic market. Dispassionate thinking has come to be regarded as the highest accomplishment of our species.

Antonio Damasio (1994), a neuroscientist at the University of Iowa, argued that Descartes's omission of emotions in the enterprise of good thinking was an error. From his research, Damasio concludes that there is an intuitive–emotional side to knowledge, which, if missing, will impede or impair the reasoning process. In other words, emotions must be present in cognition for someone to make good decisions and to understand how to behave in social situations.

A New View of Emotions

As one peruses the indexes of books on solution-focused and solution oriented therapies, a striking omission becomes clear. In nearly all these books, there is very little mention of affect, feelings, or emotions. O'Connell (1998) acknowledged that feelings are often ignored during actual counseling sessions and that the amount of time spent on exploring feelings in solution-focused therapy is less than in other approaches. "Clients do not have to wait until they feel better before they begin to change things in their lives" (p. 109).

In their book, Cade and O'Hanlon (1993) devoted a scant six pages to the subject of emotions, contending that although it may be therapeutic to acknowledge strong feelings, counselors should not encourage clients to express emotions. Catharsis can sometimes be helpful, but the "ultimate modification of the constructs" (p. 45), according to Cade and O'Hanlon, is the truly essential condition for therapeutic change.

Although some writers have suggested that acknowledging a client's feelings is a valuable part of brief counseling, most consider a counselor's empathic response to the client's emotions to be useful only as a "hook" to entice the client into doing the real therapeutic work. This view is consistent with the cognitive stance in therapy, which we described in Chapter 5. It has as its basic premise the notion that if a client "thinks straight" the emotions will no longer be problematic.

Neuroscientific findings have cast some doubt on this assumption. In his book *Emotional Intelligence*, Daniel Goleman (1995) cited LeDoux's work on the function of the amygdala in the human brain. The amygdala (from the Greek work for *almond*) is an almond-shaped cluster of neuronal structures located just above the brainstem, deep within the temporal lobes, in an area sometimes called the "nose brain." It is so called because the olfactory sense sends messages to this area, and it is from this location that the more recent brain sections, such as the neocortex, evolved. The hippocampus and the amygdala are the key structures of the nose brain.

Typically, our senses transmit signals through the thalamus to the cortex, which assigns meaning to the sensed objects. For example, if the sensed object is a poisonous snake, the cortex assigns the meaning of danger, and sends a message to the limbic area that activates the emotional centers, and initiates action—in the form of running away. However, LeDoux identified a "smaller and shorter pathway—something like a neural back alley" (p. 17) of neurons that makes it possible for the amygdala to receive threatening data directly from the senses and to trigger an immediate emotional reaction before the cortex itself is activated.

Goleman suggested that the amygdala emotionally "hijacks" the stimulus before we can even make cognitive and conscious sense of what it is (Figure 7-1). Because emotions and reason seem to travel different paths, we can react emotionally without knowing the cause. In one study, LeDoux destroyed the auditory cortex of rats, and then paired the sound of a tone with an electric shock. The rats came to display a fear response in the presence of only the tone, despite the fact that their neocortex couldn't

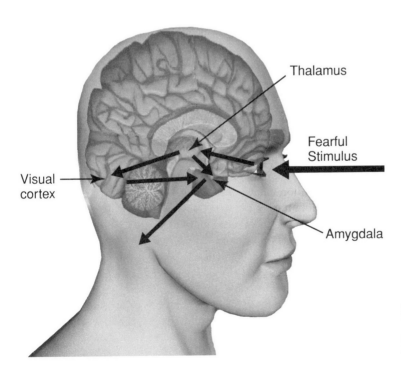

FIGURE 7-1 How the amygdala "hijacks" the stimulus for a short-circuited emotional response. (After Goleman, 1995.)

"hear" it. "The amygdala perceived, remembered, and orchestrated their fear indepen-dently" (p. 18).

According to Kosslyn and Koenig (1995), emotions prime people for action. How-ever, the emotions themselves can develop through two different processes. The "bottom-up" process takes place when an external stimulus or a change in one's bodily state prompts an emotion. The "top-down" process occurs when the creation of an emotion is the result of one's thoughts or memories. Therefore, cognitive therapies, which are based on the idea that thoughts create feelings, may be effective with top-down emotions, but not with bottom-up emotions, which are triggered without much cognition involved.

Recall a time when you suddenly felt an intense emotion and acted immediately. You may have even said or done things at the time that, on reflection, you would not nor-mally say or do. In such situations, emotions can have a sudden and powerful impact on what we are thinking and how we are acting. Goleman (1995) offers a fine example to demonstrate how a crisis is a bottom-up, rather than top-down, experience. Imagine, for example, that while hiking alone in an isolated area of Yellowstone Park you suddenly come face-to-face with a ferocious grizzly bear. At that precise moment, you are not com-posing a grocery list, balancing your checking account, or reflecting on the problems of grizzlies as an endangered species—you are only concentrating on this particular bear, scanning quickly for avenues of escape in this specific situation, and focusing all your thoughts on surviving. Like the Necker cube in Chapter 2, strong emotions bring cer-tain thoughts to the foreground of our attention and cause all other thoughts to recede. Our emotional system is older and operates more rapidly than our thinking system. As a result, when intense emotions arise, our ability to exercise cortical control over them is not equal to the task.

The Case of H.M.

Among the classic cases in the lore of psychology is that of Henry Mnemonic (H.M.—not his real name). In 1953, H.M. underwent a surgical procedure to control an in-tractable seizure disorder. Since it was assumed at the time that memory functions were distributed over the whole of the brain, the surgeons thought nothing of removing large sections of H.M.'s interior temporal lobes, especially the hippocampus. As a result, H.M. lost his ability to form explicit and conscious long-term memories (LeDoux, 1996). He could, for example, read the morning paper and then, a few hours later, read it again as though it were brand new information. He could hold on to information for only a few seconds. According to LeDoux, it was damage to the hippocampus that was mostly re-sponsible for H.M.'s memory difficulties.

Since that time, the role of the amygdala in memory formation has become clearer. There are two areas within the inner temporal lobes of the brain that are responsible for memory formation. The hippocampus appears to encode "explicit memories," while the amygdala creates "implicit emotional memory" (LeDoux, 1996, p. 202). In a stressful situation, the amygdala primes us for action and registers an emotional memory of the event, while the hippocampus lays down a conscious memory of the situation. These two areas respond simultaneously to the stressor, developing for us an emotional mem-ory (which captures our experiential reactions) and a memory of the circumstances (which captures our conscious recollections). While memories are not actually stored in these two areas of the brain, damage to either will result in long-term memory impairment. Damage to the amygdala can result in someone not knowing how to feel about intense events (Damasio, 1994).

Stress can also damage the hippocampus (LeDoux, 1996). When people are exposed to stressful situations, their adrenal gland releases hormones into the bloodstream, while the pituitary gland releases a hormone called ACTH. These are known as stress hormones. They flow to the amygdala, the hippocampus, and other areas of the brain. The hippocampus tends to produce a calming effect, because it sends signals to slow down the secretion of stress hormones. LeDoux (1996) pointed out that when someone is in a chronic state of emotional arousal, the amygdala and the hippocampus are at war with each other. The amygdala is stimulating the production of stress hormones throughout the body and brain, while the hippocampus is attempting to slow down this production. Engaged in such a conflict, the hippocampus may be unable to carry out its usual functions that support memory. In fact, there is some evidence that the continued flooding of the hippocampus with stress hormones eventually even kills neurons in the hippocampus. Studies of people who have suffered prolonged stress show a marked degeneration of the hippocampus. Although mild levels of stress can enhance memory, LeDoux (1996) suggested that the effects of intense stress on the hippocampus may account for the poor memory that often accompanies clinical depression and the memory losses people often experience in traumas.

Shapiro (1994) suggested that posttraumatic stress disorder may be the result of a separation of the functions of the hippocampus and the amygdala, so that emotional memories become independent of explicit memories. Hence, people can experience flashbacks of emotional terror in the absence of any real danger. In addition, any attempt to think "reasonably" about such events is largely ineffective. In spite of these attempts to exert cortical control, the amygdala continues to fire and signal danger, the stress hormones fill the brain, and the hippocampus fails to fulfill its function of calming the organism. Moreover, stress seems to enhance the function of the amygdala. As a result, it is possible for someone to consciously remember very little about a trauma, but the person may, at the same time, form strong "implicit, unconscious emotional memories through amygdala-mediated fear conditioning. . . . [T]hese potent unconscious fears can become very resistant to extinction. They can, in other words, become unconscious sources of intense anxiety" (p. 245).

These neuroscientific discoveries regarding memory formation have left us with some compelling speculations as to the formation of anxiety, depression, and posttraumatic stress disorder. Because experiences can actually change a person's brain functioning, you must remember that when you are counseling a person, you are also counseling a brain.

Attaching Emotions to Success

In contrast to the impression that you may gain from reading much of the literature, emotions can play a vital role in brief counseling work. However, your approach is dramatically different from the traditional counseling technique of encouraging clients to express their negative feelings as a means of catharsis. Instead, you are helping them to experience emotions connected with success—not stress. In terms of Goleman's example above, once your clients have escaped from a bear, you don't invite them to dwell on the fear response that motivated their actions. Those emotions already have served a purpose in stirring your clients to react quickly. In the counseling session following such incidents, your job is to help your clients turn their attention to how they orchestrated their escapes. In essence, you are attempting to transfer their emotional arousal from a negative image to a positive one.

This approach may sound preposterous, but studies have demonstrated that how people interpret their emotions depends on the context in which they experienced this arousal. These studies involved the injection of adrenaline into the bloodstream, which increased emotional arousal (Bruner, 1986). When the experimental circumstances promoted negative expectations, the participants who had been administered adrenaline reported feeling greater negative emotions, such as anger and sadness. However, when the situation suggested positive expectations, the participants, who received the same dosage of adrenaline, interpreted their arousal as heightened elation and other positive emotions. Therefore, if you ask emotionally aroused clients to dwell on images and memories of threats, then you may be escalating their experience of fear and vulnerability. On the other hand, if you invite your clients to describe how they successfully escaped, they are more likely to feel an elevated sense of satisfaction, relief, confidence, and pride.

We humans have a difficult time exerting our will over our emotions. One reason is that the connections in the brain that run from the frontal cortex to the amygdala are much weaker than those running from the amygdala to the cortex. Because our neurological dice are loaded in this way, emotions can often take over our thinking—and our thoughts have trouble inhibiting our feelings (Hampden-Turner, 1981; LeDoux, 1996). This human brain design is evolutionarily quite old and has served our species well. When you are confronted by Goleman's bear, it is better to let your emotional appraisal system make sense of the situation and immediately get you moving. If you allow your analytical cortex to ponder the situation, you are not likely to escape. Our brain is an amazingly efficient system, but this arrangement has its costs when emotions get the better of us. In the case of negative emotions, such as fear or anger, we find we are not open to reason. In the case of positive emotions, such as love, we are no more reasonable—that's why "fools rush in where angels fear to tread."

Experiencing This Idea

Join with four or five colleagues. One of you volunteers to share a time when the amygdala hijacked your reason. While telling the story, use a sculpting activity with two colleagues. Shape your colleagues into statues whose postures, gestures, and expressions indicate the depth of your affect. Then ask them to freeze for a few seconds as you explain the sculpture to the group. Then reshape the statues to illustrate the strategies that you used to manage your feelings. As time permits, continue with other volunteer sculptors.

Positive and Negative Affect

When people reflect on the impact of emotions on their thoughts and behaviors, they usually think first of negative emotions such as anger, fear, or sorrow as intruding into thoughts and interrupting behavior (Isen, 1984). "They almost never think of positive affect—joy, elation, contentment, relaxation, or a sense of well-being—as influencing behavior" (p. 187). The irony of this position, according to Isen, is that research suggests that positive affect exerts a powerful influence on thought and behavior. Perhaps it is because negative affect intrudes more often into consciousness that we tend to explain most of our thoughts and behaviors in terms of problems that cause discomfort or needs that require satisfaction.

Lazarus (1991) characterized negative feelings as "goal incongruent" emotions. When people encounter a situation that is blocking their path to a desired goal, they react with negative emotions, such as frustration, anger, or depression. On the other hand, if they come to a situation that may enhance their well-being, people have primary emotions, such as hope, enthusiasm, or even ecstasy. Your work as a counselor is to help clients discover the possibilities for successfully achieving their goals and to experience the energizing emotions associated with this process.

Scans of the brain reveal that when people are experiencing positive emotions, there is more activation in their left frontal lobes, while negative emotions are accompanied by more activation in the right frontal area (Davidson, 1993). Furthermore, positive emotional states have been found to inhibit the amygdala (Kosslyn & Koenig, 1995). When you are successfully counseling someone who is emotionally distressed, you are reducing the activation of the right frontal lobe, inhibiting the amygdala, and decreasing the chance that your client's emotions will be hijacked. By focusing on stories of survival, you are also activating the left frontal lobes and encouraging positive emotions. You also facilitate these changes in brain functioning by expressing more emotion yourself when clients speak of survival, thereby, entraining their emotions in a "reverse empathy."

Reverse Empathy

Perhaps no one did more to legitimize the place of empathy in the counseling process than Carl Rogers. *Empathy* comes from the Greek *empatheia*, which means to perceive the subjective experience of another. Early on in his career, Rogers insisted on what he called the "necessary and sufficient" conditions for a therapeutic relationship. Included in these conditions was the notion that the counselor must experience "an empathic understanding of the client's frame of reference and . . . communicate this experience to the client" (Corey, 1991, p. 212). This "accurate empathic understanding" takes place when the counselor senses clients' feelings as if they were his or her own, without becoming lost in those feelings. By moving freely in the world as experienced by clients, the counselor "can not only communicate to them an understanding of what is already known to them but can also voice meanings of experience of which they are only dimly aware" (p. 214).

While we agree with Rogers, we believe his idea to be an incomplete understanding of empathy. In his model, the counselor is the one who possesses a high level of empathic ability, while any consideration of empathy on the part of the client is totally ignored. However, accurate empathy, in which the counselor attempts to understand and to communicate this understanding to the client, is only one side of the story—clients have empathy, too. Appreciating the empathy that clients bring to counseling offers you another therapeutic opportunity. By creating an empathic resonance in the client, you can elevate emotional arousal and set the stage for a reframe or a shift in focus. Before considering the techniques involved, let's take a closer look at empathy and its neurological substrate.

The roots of empathy can be traced to infancy (Goleman, 1995). Shortly after birth, infants display sympathetic crying when they hear one of their nursery-mates cry. This reaction is the precursor to empathy. By their first birthday, children seem to understand that another crying child's distress is not their own, but they still express concern and an urgent confusion as to what to do. Later, a more mature empathy begins to form. Some people appear to be highly sensitized to other people in this way, while others are less so. For example, patients with brain injuries—with lesions between the amygdala and the association area of the visual cortex—appear to be unable to understand the emotional aspects of messages from others. "A sarcastic 'Thanks,' a grateful 'Thanks,' and an angry 'Thanks' all had the same neutral meaning for them" (Goleman, 1995, p. 102). By contrast, Goleman pointed to a study by Robert Levenson on empathy between married partners. The couples were videotaped, and their physiological responses monitored, while discussing a distressing aspect of their marriage. Each person then reviewed the videotape separately and reported what he or she was feeling at each moment. Finally, still hooked up to biofeedback equipment, the participants viewed the videotape once more to describe their partners' moment-to-moment feelings. Remarkably, as they focused on their spouses, the most empathically accurate persons displayed physiological reactions that mimicked those of their partners. The biofeedback patterns of the least empathic persons merely repeated their own original reactions during the discussion. "Only when their bodies were in synch was there empathy" (p. 104).

Empathy, then, is the ability to become emotionally aroused and resonate with the person you are encountering. Goleman called it "emotional contagion" (p. 114), in which people transmit and catch moods from each other. Furthermore, it seems that when two people are in contact, the more expressive person is the one who sets the emotional tone of the encounter. "The person who has the more forceful expressivity—or the most *power*—is typically the one whose emotions entrain the other" (p. 117, emphasis added).

If all this talk of power and dominance in the counseling relationship is bothersome to you, you are likely responding to the notion that empathy is to be possessed only by the counselor, who is to be entrained or driven by the client. However, when you are working briefly with clients you must be deliberate, strategic, and attempt to influence the client. In this case, you lead clients by your emotional expressiveness and attempt to stimulate their empathy. In doing so, you may be able to change the focus of their discussion from "problem-saturated talk" to resolution talk.

Emotional Arousal and the Yerkes–Dodson Law

Sometimes stress can help in the formation of explicit memories, making them stronger (LeDoux, 1996). Memory is likely to be enhanced under conditions of mild stress due to the facilitative effects of adrenaline, but too much adrenaline will block memory formation. In addition, mild stress will increase attention, while intense stress may fragment awareness. How can stress both help and hinder cognitive functioning? This paradox is sometimes called the Yerkes–Dodson effect.

Because the "shortcut" from the thalamus to the amygdala bypasses the neocortex, the amygdala can be a repository for emotional impressions and memories of which the person has never been fully aware (Goleman, 1995). It seems intuitively obvious that merely talking with a client will give little access to "shortcut" or "hijacked" emotions. What must happen is that you somehow arouse the client so that the door to these emotions is opened. What then? Do you encourage the expression of these emotions, or seek to displace them with new emotions that inhibit them? According to LeDoux (1996), "emotional experience is not really a problem about emotion. It is, instead, a problem about how conscious experiences occur" (p. 268). Emotional processing goes on at a level beneath our awareness. It is only when emotions become conscious that they can be dealt with.

Since you are attempting to work briefly, your hope is to acknowledge and encourage conscious emotional expression to the point at which the client is aroused, and then you will seek to "drag and drop" that arousal from problem-saturated talk to resolution talk. Since all memories are constructed memories, your aim in counseling is to deconstruct current memories, along with their emotional attachments, and to co-construct with clients new memories, with new emotional connections. But, as you attempt to arouse the client, you must be careful not to overarouse. As LeDoux (1996) advised, "You need to have just the right level of activation to perform optimally" (p. 289).

There exists a curvilinear (inverted-U) relationship between the level of emotional arousal and the efficiency of performance (Martindale, 1981). The Yerkes–Dodson law, first articulated in 1908, reflects this relationship. Simply put, the quality of performance on any task—physical or mental—is a function of the level of emotional arousal. Very low levels of arousal produce little in the way of efficient performance, while extremely high levels produce scattered and inefficient performance. Optimal performance occurs when emotional arousal is sufficient to motivate, but not so high as to fragment production. Our counseling students have dubbed this optimal area "the zone" (Figure 7-2).

Imagine that emotional arousal proceeds from left to right in Figure 7-2. Someone who is at the extreme left would be comatose, while someone at the extreme right would be on the verge of a breakdown. When your clients merely talk about emotions, or describe seeming emotion-producing situations in a flat narrative style, then they are operating closer to the left end of arousal. They are not sufficiently aroused to do produc-

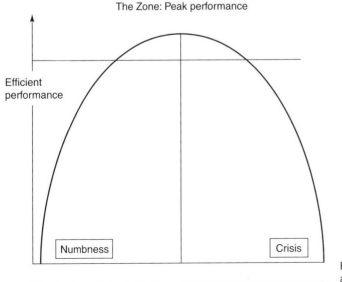

FIGURE 7-2 The "Zone."

tive work with their concerns. Because such clients have defensively withdrawn any emotional awareness from their narratives, any change brought about at this level will be sterile and intellectual.

On the other hand, when your clients are so overwhelmed as to not be able to "think straight," then they are in a state of crisis and closer to the far right. At this level of emotional arousal, your counseling work is not likely to be successful because your clients' amygdala has "hijacked" their emotions.

As a counselor, your job is to help clients to find their "zone," their ideal state of arousal. At this optimal midpoint of the Yerkes–Dodson curve, your clients' different brain structures are working together successfully.

An interesting aside regarding the Yerkes–Dodson law is that while Yerkes and Dodson did investigate the relationship between the strength of a stimulus (a shock delivered to a mouse) and task performance, they did not speak of "emotional arousal." Arousal was not a construct until the 1940s. Even though we should probably not refer to this relationship as the Yerkes–Dodson law, it is characterized as such by most psychology textbooks. One possible label is the "inverted-U hypothesis," but whatever its name, there is considerable support in the literature for the idea.

Implications of These Ideas for the Counselor

Ideas and research regarding emotions have significant implications for our work as counselors.

- Remember that emotions are motivating—having emotions means that the client is poised to act. Your job is to help the client find and capture that motivation.
- In order for clients to make good decisions in social situations, their emotions *must* be involved. Therefore, you need to notice when your client is displaying emotions in the session.
- When people experience high levels of stress, their amygdala "hijacks" their emotions, causing them to act without thinking.
- Counseling can be thought of as "knitting together" the top-down emotions stored in memory with the bottom-up emotions occurring moment-to-moment in the session.
- People who have experienced chronic stress have a difficult time with emotional memories. You must be careful to manage the amount of emotion that is aroused in the session as they talk of "problem-saturated" issues.
- People are prone to talk about negative emotions in counseling. Your job is to attempt to tap the positive emotions of clients and to help them associate these emotions with images of success and possibility.
- The person who displays the more intense emotion in a conversation is likely to "entrain" or influence the emotional arousal of the other. You should attempt to be the former when the client is talking about exceptions and images of success.
- You should observe where your client is in terms of emotional arousal in the session. Your goal is to keep him or her in "the zone." If the client is too far to the left on the Yerkes–Dodson curve, then perturb; if too far to the right, soothe.

TOOLS

Managing Emotional Arousal

Jerome Frank (1985) considered the arousing of emotions to be a curative factor in counseling and therapy. He and his colleagues found that when people were emotionally stimulated with ether and adrenaline, they were more susceptible to changes in attitude. It is also well known that clients are more motivated to seek counseling when they are suffering greatly or enduring tremendous psychological pain (Young, 1992). However, many people also come to counseling in a "dampened" condition. That is, they are employing some manner of defense that keeps them from being fully in touch with their emotions. In such cases, it is useful for you to arouse their emotions and increase their awareness of how they are feeling about their situation. Experiencing such an emotional arousal can set the stage for an attitude change.

Like Carl Rogers, who said that the client's experience of vulnerability was a core condition for successful therapy, Frank (1985) said that emotions of suffering supply the basic motivation for clients to seek change. Kurt Lewin (in Young, 1992) considered therapeutic change to be an "unfreezing and refreezing" process. By this metaphor, he meant that the client's old viewpoints, which are fixed and frozen, must be heated up by emotional arousal before they become softened enough to be remolded. Such arousal allows a new insight, discovery, or lesson to leave a deeper impression and have a more lasting impact on the client. After having the corrective emotional experience, the client can then "refreeze" to maintain the new perspectives and attitudes gained in counseling.

When clients are feeling emotionally overwrought about their current circumstances or are reacting to a recent traumatic event, your approach will be to soothe them. Their emotions are running too high for them to do productive work in the counseling session. Until their emotions are calmed to the point of being back in "the zone," it is best to offer emotional support. In the case of dampened or numbed clients, you will work to increase their emotional responses by challenging or perturbing them in some way. The goal in either case is to move the client into "the zone" by managing emotional arousal.

In addition to working to influence the overall emotional arousal of a client, you also will be responding to the emotional content of your client's narrative. Although you will acknowledge "problem-saturated" content so that you communicate your understanding of the client's pain, you do not wish to unduly heighten the emotional awareness of pain by probing or reinforcing it. The ideal you seek in counseling is that clients will become aroused, emotionally involved, and inspired when talking about their longings, their hopes, and their successes. By directing their attention to talking about these longings, hopes, and successes, and by asking for detailed concrete elaborations of the "viewing and doing" (O'Hanlon & Beadle, 1994) associated with these images, you are bringing clients into a more productive emotional zone.

A Reminder about Acknowledging Feelings

When a client expresses a feeling, it is very important for you to acknowledge it. While it may be useful to sometimes either exaggerate or minimize a feeling, most of the time, clients feel understood if you reflect back the feeling that they have expressed. If you simply restate the feeling, using the same word that the client used, little movement takes place in the client's thinking about the event. Usually, the best response is to use a different word that essentially matches the client's level of intensity. This way, the client is forced to perform a cognitive matching task of comparing one description with another. This process leads to three productive consequences. First, it compels the client to think about what he or she is saying. Second, if you have chosen a word or phrase that matches the client's level of feeling, the client feels that you understand. And finally, matching the client's feeling with a similar word or phrase tends to increase the emotional arousal connected with that word.

Lowering Emotional Arousal

If you are seeing someone who has recently experienced a major crisis, or if you are talking with a client who appears to be quite stressed or agitated, then you will have to employ some "quieting" techniques with your client (Young, 1998). Most quieting methods are "safe and quickly lead to positive experiences by clients" (p. 221). In your counseling work, you are likely to see many clients who would profit from quieting techniques. Virtually every article and book on stress has argued that contemporary conditions and lifestyles have increased our stress levels. To make matters even worse, our physiological and emotional reactions, although useful in helping us survive threats in more primitive settings, are rarely effective in helping us deal with today's threats and, in fact, can make us vulnerable to disease.

It is somewhat easier to stimulate increased emotional arousal than it is to decrease it. Arousal always seems to last longer than it is needed. People with posttraumatic stress disorder, for example, can remain in a hyperaroused and hypervigilant state for years after their traumatic experience.

For the above reasons, it is crucial that you intervene as soon as possible with people who are in crisis. As Yerkes and Dodson found years ago, a little stress is a good thing, but too much shatters one's ability to perform well cognitively or behaviorally.

Assessing the Client's Level of Arousal

You will have to make an assessment of your client's level of emotional arousal as you speak with him or her to determine whether he or she is too aroused to be in "the zone." If this is the case, you will want to comfort your client. Obviously, the first step is to communicate to your client by word and behavior that he or she is *safe* in this relationship with you. All of the suggestions for establishing the relationship with your client that were discussed in Chapter 3 apply here. You must not behave in any way that suggests that you disagree or want to contest your client's point of view.

Speak in *soothing* tones and work slowly. Your voice should be slightly less loud than your client's, though your decibel level should rise and fall with theirs, so as to match their fluctuations of emotional expressiveness.

You must determine how *physically close* to your client you should be in order to maintain comfort. Some clients want you to be quite near to them, while others will "need more space" and may see closeness as a threat.

The same goes for how much *eye contact* you maintain while talking with the client. Some clients may want a lot of eye contact to confirm that you are paying close attention. Others may not want you to look at them, because they believe that they "look a mess" or that you will easily detect their shame or guilt.

Above all, you need to convey to the client that you are interested in being useful in whatever way they will find helpful during this crisis. Until they are soothed enough to be entering "the zone," you should not use any influencing techniques.

Initially, use only attending skills and wait to be invited to help. As clients tell their story, if they see you as listening, understanding, and validating, they tend to feel less overwhelmed, and will often afterward report that a "weight has been lifted off their shoulders."

Listening in on a Session

Review Bob's story at the beginning of the chapter. A resolution-focused counselor might work to reduce the client's arousal in the following way. We pick up the dialogue with Bob's final comment.

Bob: The hell with him and with the rest of them. Who cares!

Counselor: (*While the client has been telling his story, the counselor has been look- ing Bob in the eyes, leaning forward, shaking his head, and reacting with empathic grimaces to the accounts of upsetting events, and nodding to the client's complaints. The counselor speaks and gestures with some energy and expressiveness, but more slowly and softly than Bob.*) You've really been feeling pissed off and fed up with the way people've been treating you.

Bob: (*This time, he allows the counselor to finish his comment.*) You're damn right! And I hate the way that they look at me like I'm some useless relic who's just tak- ing up space and the way they make me the butt of their snide comments. Of course, they say that they're just joking and that they don't really mean anything they're saying, but I'm not the doddering idiot that they take me for. I'm still sharp enough to notice when somebody's not treating me right. In fact, I didn't like it when Reverend Cummings told me I should come here. I'm not senile and I'm not "going postal," either.

Counselor: (*At the start, his voice has an edge that emphasizes "sick" and "tired" to convey the intensity of Bob's emotions.*) You're sick and tired of being typecast as "the bitter old man." Now you'd like to find a way to help people realize how hard you've had to work and how valuable your contributions have been over the years.

Bob: Bingo! But how the heck can I do that? Every time I think about how I'm treated, I get worked up and my good intentions go out the window. I'm sure that sometimes I do sound like some cranky old buzzard.

Counselor: (*Smiles at the "Bingo!" comment. He earnestly leans forward and looks directly at Bob for a moment.*) Bob, before we talk about how you're going to find a way to do that, I'd like to thank you for being so open and up front with me, even though I'm probably about the same age as these people at work. How did you get yourself to take that risk with somebody who's young enough to be your son?

Bob: (*He chuckles.*) It's not that hard because you're paid to be nice to me.

Reflecting Questions

1. Where was Bob on the inverted U when he entered the session?
2. What did the counselor do to influence Bob's emotional arousal?
3. How might you respond to Bob's last statement?

Using This Tool

Form a small group with two colleagues. One of you volunteers to role-play, with emotional intensity, a character similar to Bob. Another volunteers to listen, understand, and validate, while also using the above techniques to lower emotional arousal. Keep in mind that although your words are important here, your body language and tone of voice are essential influencing factors. Finally, the third person serves as the recorder, who observes the activity and leads the feedback discussion.

Stress-Reduction Techniques

Some authors (Thompson, 1996; Young, 1998) suggest certain deliberate techniques for reducing stress within the client. While we think these can be useful, they are not necessarily effective in the early stages of the relationship. Only after you have gained your client's trust and the reduction of stress or chronic anxiety has been established as your client's goal, should you suggest these as task assignments. The details of each of these intervention tactics are beyond the scope of this writing. We offer here a short list of the suggestions of the above-named authors. Interested readers should consult these and other sources to learn how to implement these techniques.

Relaxation Training.   This is a step-by-step technique for helping your client to learn to relax in the presence of emotionally arousing stimuli (Young, 1998). The procedure is based on the behavioral principle that one cannot be tense and relaxed at the same time.

Meditation.   This technique involves the practice of focusing one's thoughts in order to reduce the "chattering of the mind" effect that accompanies chronic emotional arousal (Young, 1998).

Writing.   Talking about an anxiety-producing situation is often more stressful than writing about it. Writing seems to make the events seem more distant, giving the writer more control over how the story is depicted; it also demands a more formal presentation (Thompson, 1996). In addition, turning the experience into creative writing, such as producing a poem about the situation, is an opportunity for the client to give voice to these emotions. Keeping a log of controlled reactions—times when the situation came to mind and the client did not feel overwhelmed by the emotions associated with the experience—would be a technique consistent with the search for resolution.

Favorite Quiet Place.   This is a kind of suggested imagery that has as its goal the reduction of unwanted anxious thoughts and images that come unbidden and interfere with progress. You ask the client to tell about a place where he or she has felt safe and calm, and to elaborate on that image so that it is vivid and the feelings associated with it are calming. Allowing the client to take a break and go to that imagined place when the conversation gets tense will reduce the escalating effect of thinking about the "problem."

Raising Emotional Arousal

The standard attitude toward increasing emotional arousal seems to involve getting the client "in touch with feelings"—the client should experience fully the pain of his or her situation before it can be worked through. This approach often involves recalling as vividly as possible a situation that has been "repressed" or from which the client has developed emotional distance. The theory behind this dates back to Aristotle, who noticed that when people attended a tragic play and had a "good cry," they felt a lot better. This notion of "catharsis" as the emotional release that cures tends to direct the client's attention to problem-saturated content.

Since it is our aim to move to resolution-saturated talk as soon as possible, we will not attempt to engage in "onion-peeling," meaning that we will not be probing for deeper levels of painful material. We will attempt to manage the amount of emotional arousal associated with the client's painful material. We will acknowledge that the client has been suffering under the situation we are discussing, but we will not display undue interest in knowing more about the client's suffering. We will acknowledge the pain and attempt to move on. If we have not acknowledged enough, the client will let us know by returning to problem-saturated talk; in which case we must acknowledge some more before once again attempting to move toward resolution-focused talk.

When clients are engaged in problem-saturated talk, we attempt to manage the associated emotional arousal by keeping it on the left side of the zone of the Yerkes–Dodson curve. When clients are engaged in resolution-talk, we attempt to increase emotional arousal so that clients' feelings will be in the zone.

Young (1998) enumerated the benefits of increasing emotional arousal and expression as stimulants for change. Some of his assertions are applicable here: Emotional arousal and expression tend to promote greater self-understanding, emotional arousal makes what would otherwise be merely an intellectual experience more real, it is "a confirmation, by direct knowledge, of the power of the helping relationship" (p. 230). Arousal can "melt down old attitudes . . . therapeutic change being an 'unfreezing and refreezing' process, meaning that the client's world view can be catalyzed by emotional arousal" (p. 231).

Memory of an Emotion Versus Emotional Memory

LeDoux (1996) stated that there are two different ways in which we remember emotions: one is by way of the explicit (conscious) memory of an emotion, while the other is through the implicit (unconscious) emotional memory. The hippocampus helps us to have a memory of an emotion. If we have had a traumatic experience, such as a bad car accident or a rape, we usually can remember the facts of the situation to some degree, but our memories of the emotions are just that—facts. Memory of an emotional experience is stored in the cognitive declarative memory and can be talked about without necessarily arousing any feelings. When clients are talking about emotion-provoking experiences, but are doing so with seeming detachment, they might be said to be merely tapping their cognitive memory of the emotions. Our client is giving us only "head talk." Emotional memories, on the other hand, involve the whole body: there is "muscle tension (a vestige of freezing), changes in blood pressure and heart rate, increased perspiration, and so on" (p. 201). In order to have an "emotional memory, complete with the bodily experiences that come with an emotion, you have to activate the emotional memory system . . ." (p. 201).

LeDoux suggests that both the memories of emotion and emotional memory systems come together in the working memory so that one has an immediate conscious experience of both remembering the facts and experiencing the feelings. It is necessary to activate both these systems in the counseling relationship, so that you can bring about "a change of heart" as well as a change of mind. Without emotional arousal emerging into consciousness, every experience would seem emotionally flat. When past memories are connected to a present emotional arousal, a "seamlessly fused" experience is created. "This unified experience of the past memory and the arousal can then potentially get converted into a new long-term memory" (pp. 201–202).

Our aim is an ambitious one: We hope to bring the level of emotional arousal in our client to the point that the implicit memory of an emotion is in the zone, and then work to change the associations with that negative emotion by changing the focus to a more positive emotional state, so that events are remembered with a different emotional tone.

In order to accomplish this feat, we must make sure that the client's emotional memory system is aroused in working memory (immediate awareness) to a level at which it will be sufficiently joined with his or her cognitive memories of the emotions. We will then work for a change of heart that matches the change of mind.

Inherent Arousal in the Counseling Situation

If you are a school counselor, you know well the scenario of a child sent to you for counseling because he or she is chronically "acting out." The teacher or principal or someone wishes for you to "fix" this child. This is the type of disorder that the DSM refers to as an "Oppositional Defiant" or a "Conduct Disorder." So, as you attempt to establish a relationship with the kid, he or she sits rigidly, with arms crossed on his or her chest, eyes rolling each time you speak. The child sighs heavily to let you see how boring it is to be in the counselor's office and to send the message that nothing you could do or say would make him or her warm up to you. In spite of the child's best efforts to inform you that he or she is "cool" in this situation, you know that the child's heart is probably beating like that of a captive bird. His or her best efforts to show no emotional arousal have failed to convince you.

The very experience of coming to a counselor's office for the first time brings with it an emotional arousal for child and adult alike. The situation is novel and cues as to how to behave are not clear. The client is in some sort of trouble. The client is not sure whether you will be friendly or punitive or whether you can be trusted at all. Furthermore, if you are doing your job correctly, you have placed the onus on the client to account for what has brought him or her to counseling, and it is not clear just what you want to know. He or she wonders whether you will decide that he or she is bad or crazy, and what sort of power you will have to cause harm to him or her. Merely coming to counseling is emotionally arousing!

Other aspects of the counseling situation, such as an unaccustomed amount of silence between verbal utterances, more eye contact than your client is used to, and being the person who is the focus of the entire conversation, can also serve to increase the stress level. For these and other reasons, it is not difficult to raise the level of emotional arousal in the first session with the client. The initial task, then, is to reassure the client to the point that arousal does not zoom past the zone and become crippling anxiety. You can merely let the context of counseling, with its inherent emotional arousal, take care of getting your client to the zone.

Evocations and Explications

An evocation happens when we do or say something that evokes or elicits emotional arousal in the client. An explication, on the other hand, is when we make something obvious, or explicit, to the client that was before only dimly known. Let us first consider the explication.

Whenever something that is implicitly known, but not explicitly thought about, is forced into our consciousness, it may be experienced as repugnant. "Yuck!" is often our immediate response. We have not integrated this knowledge—it is not really part of us—until we are fully conscious of it. Perhaps this knowledge is kept out of awareness because of its inherent "yuckiness," but it is more likely that we have simply not paid attention to it in a way that makes it vivid for us. Consider two examples offered by Combs and Avila (1985). If you accidentally knick your finger, you might automatically stick it in your mouth. As a result, you might drink some of your own blood, but you probably did so without much awareness or concern. However, you would probably be revolted by the suggestion of licking any blood after bandaging your finger. The second example is one that occurs even more frequently. Throughout the day, you are regularly swallowing your own saliva without any reaction. However, if this saliva were collected in a glass for you to swallow, you probably would have a strong reaction!

Dennett (1991), in his typically outrageous way of using what he calls "intuition pumps," offered another perturbing example. As he pointed out, the vast majority of people throughout the world believe that human corpses do not have souls and no longer experience any suffering. However, it would be shocking to think of discarding our dead in the same way that we discard trash, which is similarly lifeless, lacks a soul, and cannot suffer any indignity.

Did you feel anything as you read the above examples? If you did, the emotion you felt would have been, according to Damasio (1994), a secondary emotion. This process begins when you conjure up an image that does not fit with your conscious value system (drinking spit out of a glass or putting a dead person in a trash bag), but nevertheless is a compelling vision. At a nonconscious level, networks in your brain are reacting automatically to images that have been paired with particular emotions. Simply put, your disgust with saliva in a glass and your reaction to corpses in garbage bags are probably learned, rather than innate.

You may be wondering what these reactions to saliva and cadavers have to do with counseling. Actually, a great deal. In the counseling session, you occasionally will call attention to something that seems obvious, natural, and acceptable, but your comment strikes a nerve in the client. The idea was not previously apparent to the client, and now even considering the possibility of something that seems so unnatural and unacceptable is very distressing. As a result, the client reacts strongly and defensively. The client's emotional arousal may jump far to the right side of the zone in an instant. This intense reaction means that you should back off and soothe the client. But it also means that you might wish to come back at a later time when the client is seemingly more receptive to the content. Making implicit knowledge explicit is a powerful tool for raising emotional arousal, but it is not without risk.

Like explication techniques, evocation is a way to raise emotional arousal quickly. Evocation techniques range from the rather benign "clarification" of the client's statements, through the "reinterpretation" of client meanings, to the sometimes shocking "confrontation" of client discrepancies or distortions in the way they tell their story. We believe that confrontations can be so evocative that they should be used rarely. Just when is a good time to confront cannot be stated in a formula. Once you have developed a good working relationship and have established a sense of trust, you can effectively confront at times. When the client believes that you are not simply trying to make a fool of him or her, or to win some "putdown" game, the client will be more open to your feedback.

Evoking Emotional Arousal

According to Goleman (1995), a mildly elated, or energized, state is optimal for creative breakthroughs. When people are in a good mood, they can think more flexibly, are more capable of solving complex problems, and generally perceive the world more positively. As a counselor, if you can help your clients experience positive emotional arousal, you are actually helping them break out of rigid patterns of thinking. Many of the techniques you have already been practicing, such as looking for exceptions and conjuring images of success, have the added benefit of helping clients feel better. You can serve as a catalyst for a benign cycle by encouraging clients to focus on resolution, which in turn helps them to experience positive emotional arousal, and then leads to greater problem-solving abilities.

Young (1998) suggested other techniques, such as the use of media—music, videos, books—to evoke emotions. For example, he stated that a helper might suggest to a client from a military family the movie *The Great Santini,* and then follow up with a discussion of the emotions the client felt. Gladding (1992) advised inviting clients to participate in creative activities such as dancing, painting, writing poetry, drawing, sculpting, making collages, doing sandtray work, and using puppets and dolls. One example might be that the client could write a poem or paint a picture of some desired change in his or her life. Gladding also suggested a writing activity he called the "period log." In this activity, clients are asked to focus on a period in their lives during which change or personal growth was taking place. The clients are to write in a stream-of-consciousness manner, without censoring any thoughts or feelings. Many forms of psychotherapy involve physical actions that arouse emotions. Moreno (1958) developed the "psychodrama" technique in order to get clients to enact their concerns and to bring them to a satisfactory conclusion. Satir (1972) used family sculpting to help families resolve impasses. Someone in the family would place family members in physical positions that symbolize their roles and proximity to other members of the family. The sculptor would then redo the sculpture according to how he or she wanted the family to be. Gendlin (1982) designed a technique he called "focusing," in which people were led step-by-step through a process to get them in touch with their emotions. Perls, (1977) originated the "empty chair" technique, in which people were instructed to play parts of themselves talking to each other, or themselves talking to another person with whom they wished to resolve some issue. For example, clients, no longer having access to a parent because of a cut-off relationship or death, could carry on the conversation they wanted to have with the absent parent.

All of these techniques require additional study and practice, but we encourage you to become familiar with any of these methods you would like to try. They all are designed to arouse emotion and help clients resolve their issues or concerns. As we have seen from the neuroscience research of Damasio, LeDoux, and others, these techniques are correlated with events taking place in the brain.

Managing emotional arousal in your clients is very important to your eventual success with them. You may find it helpful to regularly imagine that you are viewing a client through a screen on which is located the Yerkes–Dodson curve, and that you are watching the needle that indicates where our client is emotionally from moment to moment. Assessing the client's emotional arousal is, of course, more art than science. But there is good science to indicate that when you are helping to manage the emotional arousal of your client, you actually are changing brain functioning (Vaughan, 1997).

Listening in on a Session

Review Carla's story at the beginning of the chapter. A resolution-focused counselor can work to increase her emotional arousal in the following way:

Carla: (*She glances occasionally at the counselor, gestures haltingly to emphasize a point, and speaks in a hesitant manner.*) To be frank with you, this . . . was not my idea. My supervisor at work strongly recommended that I make an appointment. Don't get me wrong—I don't blame her and I'm not here under protest. She's always been very caring and supportive . . . and I know she's been worried about me the past few months. Besides, things are such a . . . mess in my life right now that I agree with her that something has to be done.

Counselor: (*She speaks with a little more expressiveness than Carla and at a slightly quicker pace.*) So you have been unhappy with how things are going in your life and you're here now to do something about it.

Carla: (*She gives the counselor a quick, tight-lipped smile and raises her eyebrows.*) Yeah, but I've had plenty of good intentions and grand ideas before for turning my life around . . . and I'm still in this same mess. I'm reluctant to naively think that counseling is going to . . . magically change all that.

Counselor: (*She leans forward, continues to speak with more energy, and looks directly at Carla.*) Yes, but if you did turn your life around this time, how would it be different?

Carla: (*She tilts her head to one side and nods.*) I need to give that question some thought. Like I said, I've had some grand ideas these past few months, but that's where they've stayed—at the idea stage. It's been so rough with Sandy gone from my life that sometimes I wonder if I'll ever be able to turn it around. I've never been through such a painful time in my life.

Counselor: (*She maintains eye contact, pauses before speaking, and gestures to emphasize the feelings.*) You've been going through a time of *heartbreak* and *grief* that's been the worst that you've ever endured. How have you been able to hang in there through all this?

Carla: (*Her eyes glisten with tears.*) I have wondered about that myself.

Reflecting Questions

1. Where was Carla on the inverted U when she entered the session?
2. What did the counselor do to influence Carla's emotional arousal?
3. How might you respond to Carla's last statement?

Using This Tool

Form a group with two colleagues. One of you volunteers to role-play a character similar to Carla. In particular, try to duplicate her lack of emotional intensity. Another volunteers to listen, understand, and validate, while also using the above techniques to raise emotional arousal. Keep in mind that although your words are important here, your body language and tone of voice are essential influencing factors. Finally, the third person serves as the recorder, who observes the activity and leads the feedback discussion.

SEGUE TO CHAPTER 8

Think of those times in your life when you have "lost yourself" in something that completely involved you. What were you doing at the time? Did you find the experience rewarding? What changed in your way of viewing things as a result of this experience?

CHAPTER 8

Using Mystifying Techniques: Turning Stumbling Blocks into Stepping Stones

"The most protean aspect of comedy is its potentiality for transcending itself, for responding to the conditions of tragedy by laughing in the darkness."

Harry Levin

CHAPTER GOALS

Reading about and experiencing the ideas in this chapter will help you to understand the following concepts:

- Enchantment, trance, and mystification offer a variety of opportunities for influencing clients.
- You can use story-telling techniques to increase the impact on clients.

Reading about and practicing the tools in this chapter will help you to learn these valuable skills:

- Reframing to help clients alter the way they view their world.
- Using metaphors to employ the Zeigarnik effect of keeping clients wondering how things will turn out.
- Writing a follow-up letter to clients.
- Using a letter from an exotic audience.

STORY

Even though there were closer seats on the aisle, John spotted the one empty window seat near the back of the crowded bus and squeezed his husky frame into it. He sat by the window whenever possible because he liked to absent-mindedly gaze outside as the bus lumbered along. The muffled bits of conversation he overheard, the scenes of street life flashing by, and the rhythm of the bus made such a hypnotic combination that John typically relaxed to the point of falling asleep. But today there was too much on his mind for relaxing. Instead, he soon found himself entering a deep reverie.

On doctor's orders, John was on his way to his first appointment with a counselor. Since his heart attack 9 months ago, John has made regular follow-up appointments and endured countless medical tests to keep his truck-driving license. At his last check-up, his doctor was worried because John's health had deteriorated markedly. When the doctor questioned him, John admitted that he was no longer following the strict nutrition and exercise regimen that he had religiously observed for 6 months. John confided that it no longer seemed to be worth the effort since his third wife had left him. That's when the doctor laid down the law. Unless John agreed to attend a heart attack survivors support group, eat better, exercise regularly, and see a counselor, the doctor would not permit John to drive his rig.

Unlike any other truck driver he knew, John enjoyed riding public transportation. Letting someone else worry about driving felt so luxurious to him. But this day was different. John felt humiliated, ashamed, and outraged that he was being ordered to see a counselor. At one point, he was jolted by a sudden fantasy that he would be interrogated, judged, and found guilty by the counselor of ruining his marriages, abandoning friendships, and destroying his health. John's punishment would have to fit the crimes, so since he had lost everything else, he would surely lose his job. The only other time John had felt this scared, and had so much at stake, was over 40 years ago.

As the bus carried him to his current destination, that entire episode began to replay itself with the vivid detail of a videotape. It was the fall of 1956. General Dwight D. Eisenhower had just been reelected President and the Korean Conflict had ended, but the United States now found strife within its own society. For the first time in history, the "teenage" years were considered a distinct and troubled age—Rock and Roll was in its infancy, teens dressed in outrageous costumes, and *Rebel Without a Cause* was in the movie theaters.

Even though it was a school day, and a desolate November one at that, John had awakened chuckling to himself. He was celebrating a rare victory over his hypervigilant mother. Tonight he finally would be allowed to stay overnight at Leo's house. After two weeks of conniving, he had convinced his mother to accept two outrageous falsehoods. The first lie was that he and Leo were assigned to work together on a project in Mrs. Mc-Cormack's Latin class that was sure to take all of Friday night and most of Saturday to finish. The second untruth was that those rumors about Leo's wild adventures were largely unfounded. If the truth were told, Leo and John had secretly finished the project earlier in the week, and Leo was indeed the master of his unsupervised universe.

After school, the boys played pinball, drank cherry cokes at the drug store, shot three games of snooker at the bowling alley, and made themselves *personae non gratae*, as their Latin teacher would say, at cheerleader practice in the school gymnasium—all before 5 o'clock. On the way to Leo's house, they stopped at a playground and began an impromptu game of follow-the-leader on the jungle gym. As they tried to outdo each other with various gravity-defying contortions, a young slightly built 7th-grade girl brushed past them. Leo called after her in that taunting way that only 14-year-old boys can do justice to, "Hey, little girl, where are you going in such a hurry?" She seemed upset and wailed over her shoulder, "Just shut up, Leo!"

John defused the situation by chiding Leo for his unsophisticated way of dealing with the opposite sex and thought to himself that apparently his mother wasn't the only female in town who was not a big Leo fan. Just then a large man in an overcoat walked across the asphalt basketball court. Even though he passed within a few feet, he ignored Leo's wiseacre greeting and hastily moved past them.

Stung by the affront, Leo proposed, in a low voice, another contest to John. "I bet that I can throw a rock closer to that guy than you can, without actually hitting him." In spite of the alarm that sounded in John's head, he took the dare. After all, how could he turn down a dare from the number one daredevil in school? He'd never live it down. As he grabbed a hefty flat rock, John had an inspiration. If he were to aim to the right, he would be assured of a missing the mark, most likely losing the contest but definitely keeping his honor intact. By now the silhouetted figure of the man was at least 30 yards away, and John knew there was no way he could throw his rock that far.

John hurled the rock with all his might to the right of the stranger and followed its arc. He held his breath as he silently prayed for divine intervention. But the throw turned out to be magnificent, with the rock seeming to sail forever and then hooking to the left. The sharp flat edge of the missile caught the man right behind his ear with a sickening thud. Howling in rage, the man pressed his hand against his neck, blood spurting between his fingers, and reeled to charge the boys.

Leo and John had never run as fast as they did that day. They ran up the street, across back yards, and down alleys, finally hiding in the woods on the outskirts of town for what seemed to be hours. The rush of adrenaline had dissipated by the time they finally made it back to Leo's house and, after wolfing a couple of peanut butter and jelly sandwiches, they fell asleep in their sleeping bags in front of the television.

Leo and John decided it would be in their best interests to keep the incident to themselves. They vowed to tell no one, no matter what. On Monday, both boys were sitting in their Latin class when a student assistant knocked on the door and told the teacher that Leo and John were ordered to go immediately to the principal's office.

Both boys made their way down the hallway red-faced and sweating, with the catcalls of their classmates still ringing in their ears. At the office door, they were stiffly greeted by the principal, but their eyes were immediately drawn to the others seated in the room—two police officers, Sharon, (the seventh-grader from the playground) and her mother. The woman had her arm around Sharon, who looked about as scared as John and Leo. The principal asked Sharon if these were the two boys from the park. The girl's eyes quickly darted from Leo to John, then she nodded her head with a sense of urgency. For John, suddenly the room took on the stark, vivid stillness of an image that's been captured by a flash-camera.

Reflecting Questions

1. What is your reaction to the ending of the story?
2. What pictures came into your mind and what feelings did you experience as you read this story?
3. What emotions does John bring to his first counseling session?

OVERVIEW

This chapter offers ideas and tools for creating a "common everyday trance" in clients and for "mystifying" them into a different perspective. People who are discouraged have foreclosed on their dreams for the future. Nevertheless, their longing for a better life is always there, waiting to be brought out by the counselor. Your job involves tapping this longing and increasing the client's emotional arousal connected with the image of a better future. If you remember that the client's life is a narrative—a story—you can help your client to re-enchant the story. In order to do this, you will need to become sensitive to those times when the client is experiencing a "transderivational search." It is during these moments that the client is more open to co-creating metaphors, reframes, and new possibilities.

In this chapter you will learn to deliver the reframe, construct an enchanting metaphor, and write letters using an exotic audience to add impact to your attempts to influence the client. You will be offered some designs for constructing compelling metaphors with "dramatic hold" as you work with your client.

IDEAS

In this section, we discuss several ways in which you can help your clients to be more open to changing their perceptions of themselves and the world. If you understand the concepts of the transderivational search, common everyday trance, mystification, the Zeigarnik effect, and enchantment, you can appreciate their potential for influencing your clients. Clients come to you convinced that their way of viewing the world is the actual world itself. Part of your work involves encouraging them to experience some sense of confusion and enchantment, becoming open to the possibility of co-creating an alternative view.

The Transderivational Search

The amount of information coming to us, both from the outside world and from our inner experience, greatly exceeds our ability to process it consciously. As is well known to most psychology students, George Miller (1956) asserted that we can only hold seven (plus or minus two) bits of information in our short-term memory at any given moment. This is not to say, however, that everything else is sloughed off. In fact, we register a huge amount of information in long-term memory without ever consciously knowing it. In addition, most of those seven momentary bits of information are immediately sent to the purgatory of our memory without being adequately sorted and properly stored. Most of our memories are not stored in an orderly way, but are rather a kind of amalgam, a hodge-podge of stuff the significance of which remains unknown to us at a conscious level.

So long as we stay in "up time"—focused and deliberate in our thought processing—we do not allow unconsciously stored memories to be sorted out (Grinder, DeLozier, & Bandler, 1977). It is only when we allow our minds to wander that these memories arise. When working with clients, you should proceed slowly and allow sufficient time for them to stay with a thought or feeling to pull out of it a deeper, richer level of understanding. You are giving your client the chance to do a "transderivational search." This term was coined by Milton Erickson to indicate a process by which the client can experience "downtime" and "go inside" to organize his or her experience in a more coherent way.

The transderivational search is also used in Gestalt therapy. When the client seems to have trouble responding or pauses pensively, the Gestalt therapist might say something like, "I would like for you to stay with those feelings and even intensify them. Now allow yourself to think of some other time when you felt exactly the same feelings." A similar technique is employed in Gendlin's (1982) Focusing approach. The client is asked to focus on a "felt sense"—a vague and indistinct feeling that comes to the client from the periphery of experience.

The most important aspect of the transderivational search is that it allows your client time to access deeper sensations and ideas. Unless you offer this time, your clients will resort to an automatic way of describing or explaining themselves and will not learn anything new about their inner experience. Everyone develops a default way of characterizing experience that merely "skims off the top" and doesn't go very deeply into unprocessed thoughts and feelings. After a while, any default descriptions become a cliché, and we find ourselves feeling bored with a worn-out expression. Only when we give ourselves the time and opportunities to experience fresh sensations and new ideas do we become re-energized and invent new descriptions for our experiences.

The Common Everyday Trance

The transderivational search is a brief and mild form of the common everyday trance. When you read the word *trance,* you may automatically think of stage hypnosis. As a result, you may expect people under trance to be hapless victims who are forced to perform embarrassing acts, such as removing their clothing or quacking like a duck. Contrary to this popular misconception, someone in trance is not under the control of another person's will. In fact, the situation is quite the opposite—trance is an opportunity for people to discover their inner resources and exercise more fully their own personal power.

Another misconception is that trances are abnormal, bizarre, and unusual phenomena. In fact, if you pay attention to client behaviors, you will notice several times during a session when your clients are in a trance. For a brief time, your clients will unfocus their eyes, their breathing becomes deeper and slower, their tone of voice alters, and their facial expression flattens (Erickson & Rossi, 1979). This episode is the "common everyday trance" (Erickson, Rossi, & Rossi, 1976)—not the zombie condition created by Svengali-type characters in cheesy movies, but an intriguing experience that is familiar to all of us.

For example, recall a time when you may have been reaching up to put an item on a shelf, and you were suddenly distracted. You may have heard an old song that took you back to a special time in your life, or someone may have rushed in to tell you an intriguing story, or you may have been captivated by a news flash on television. Whatever the distraction, you were immediately engrossed in the song, story, or news. You were now reliving your past, caught up in some curious tale, or concerned about a late-breaking event. Of course, you had totally forgotten about your arm, which continued floating in the air, holding the item, and hovering there—no longer under your conscious control—as if it had a mind of its own. At that point, you were in a state of mild catalepsis, an everyday type of trance. A trance viewed in this way does not seem at all mysterious. You can recognize it as an often occurring experience.

Other common examples of everyday trances that you are likely to have experienced include traveling miles on the interstate highway system without recalling anything about major sections of the trip. Or you may have suddenly "awakened" when you realized you had absent-mindedly passed your exit because you were lost in your thoughts. In fact, a popular expression describing these experiences is "highway hypnosis." At home, you've probably had experiences in which you were so engrossed in a fantasy or reverie that you didn't even remember agreeing to perform an errand that your partner, friend, or housemate had asked you to do. If you have children of your own, you are likely to be all too familiar with "parent deafness" syndrome—in which important things you say to your children are never registered in their consciousness.

These examples are dissociative experiences—situations in which you are there, and yet not there at the same time. This is akin to daydreaming, and there is nothing particularly mysterious about it. When you notice this phenomenon in others, you can see that, during such a trance, they seem to disappear inside themselves. Their eyes lose the luster that indicates the "tuned in" appearance of perception. While they are still capable of operating in the world around them well enough to drive a car, carry on a conversation, or perform some other automated behavior, their thoughts are somewhere else. When your clients have these experiences in your counseling sessions, they are more open to possibilities because they have dropped their guards, set aside the censors that keep away any dissonant information, and embarked on transderivational searches.

Erickson advised that the client is, at such moments, engaged in an inner search of unconscious processes, and that you must be careful not to ruin this "precious" interlude. What you should do is stop talking for a while, and then perhaps say calmly, "That's right," or "Stay with that thought." You may even notice that your own rate of breathing begins to synchronize with your client's.

When your client returns from this trance, you will notice a change in demeanor. Your client reorients, as if on awakening, and looks expectantly at you. This is the creative moment—one in which "we can be more receptive to our own inner experience and unrealized potentials in ways that are most surprising" (Erickson, Rossi, & Rossi, 1976, p. 1). This moment is when your client is most open to engaging with you in co-creating a reframe, metaphor, or vision of new possibilities. If you can "catch the rhythm" of your client's reorientation to the present, you will know when the moment is right to inquire about trance experiences.

Experiencing This Idea

Think of a time when you recently experienced a memorable or productive everyday trance. It may have been when you were caught up in a captivating daydream or when you were "on automatic pilot" while driving. What metaphors come to mind when you describe your trance? As you reflect on that experience, what new ideas, realizations, or discoveries did you take from that everyday trance?

Mystification

A powerful way of changing clients' self-attributions is to "mystify" them (Laing, 1971). Mystification takes place when others suggest an idea that we eventually come to believe ourselves. Speculating that people's negative characterizations of themselves are the result of unconscious social influences, Laing wondered, "How much of who we are, is what we have been hypnotized to be?" (p. 79). He further offered an illustration as to how this may take place. For example, if a parent wishes to get a child to do something, one way would be to tell the child to do it. A better way would be to suggest to the child that he or she is feeling like doing it. The best way, according to Laing, is to tell a third party in front of the child that the child feels like doing it. The first strategy—telling someone to do a thing—is easily resisted. The second strategy of suggesting that someone feels like doing it, requires an internal search before it can be resisted. But the third technique, suggested by Laing, is mystifying to the degree that it is hard to resist.

Suppose, for example, you wish to change a client's self-label from "clinically depressed" to something more benign and less pathological, such as "discouraged." Instead of directly relabeling the client's attribution, you can indirectly accomplish this by commenting about your client to a third party. For example, you could bring a fellow counselor into the room while the client is present, and tell that person how your client now feels and label the client's feeling in a new way. If the third party is someone in authority, or is not well known to the client, this mystifying conversation will have extra impact. White and Epston (1990) called it employing an "exotic audience."

Another mystifying technique is to describe your view and reflections regarding the client in a letter to an exotic audience. For example, if you are a school counselor, you might write a letter to the principal or the director of guidance describing the progress your student has made, elaborating on his or her personal strengths, and labeling him or her in positive ways. If you are a counselor in a mental health setting, you might write to a colleague about your work with the client, describing his or her progress, and offering a label that is not pejorative and diagnostic. In both cases, be sure to give a copy of the letter to the student or client.

Finally, if resources permit, perhaps the best method of mystification is to use a reflecting team, either as consultants behind the one-way mirror who send feedback to the client through you, or by having the consulting team discuss, in front of you and the client, the client's progress and successes. We describe this technique in greater detail in Chapter 10.

In all these mystifying techniques, clients begin to set aside their hard-and-fast assumptions about themselves—even if those assumptions are highly critical—and catch a glimpse of a new way of regarding themselves positively.

The Zeigarnik Effect

Bluma Zeigarnik was a student of Kurt Lewin, the famous Gestalt psychologist. It was Lewin's custom to carry on lengthy discussions with his students in a cafe while drinking coffee and eating snacks (Hergenhahn, 1992). On one occasion, a number of students had been meeting with Lewin and each had placed an order with the waiter, who kept no written notes of their requests, but who had nevertheless delivered each order without error. When the bill was called for, the waiter tallied up in his head what each of them owed and the proper amount was paid. Later, Lewin called the waiter over and asked him if he would write out the check for them. To this, the waiter, who had displayed a fantastic memory for each order and its proper price, replied, "I don't know any longer what you people ordered. . . . You paid your bill" (p. 418). From this experience, Lewin hypothesized that before closure on a situation is reached, a tension system builds up, keeping items in people's memories, but once closure is achieved, the tension is discharged and the items forgotten. Zeigarnik tested Lewin's hypothesis by an experiment in which participants were permitted to finish some tasks but not others. She found that participants later remembered many more of the uncompleted tasks than the completed ones.

What the Zeigarnik effect means for counselors is that if you want your client to "chew" on an idea, rather than forget it immediately, you should introduce—but not complete—the idea. Have you ever had to leave a really good movie before it was over? Chances are you wanted to know how it turned out. If the movie was a suspenseful mystery, your need to know was increased and probably nagged at you. When the authors of this book were young, we often went to Saturday matinees at our local movie house. Besides the double-feature Westerns featuring Roy Rogers or Gene Autry, there was always a "serial." A serial was a short action feature in which the hero typically faced a life-threatening situation at the very end of the episode. Just as the hero was about to be eaten by alligators, crushed by a collapsing building, or hurled over a cliff in an automobile, the movie abruptly stopped, and an announcer exhorted us not to miss the next exciting episode. We were compelled to come back next Saturday to find out if our hero had escaped, only to be left with a new cliff-hanger at the end of that installment. Similarly, since no counseling session ever resolves all the issues your clients face, there is always some naturally "unfinished business." As the counselor, you can heighten the Zeigarnik effect by inviting your clients to continue working on particular issues outside of the session or call their attention to uncompleted tasks. If you allow your clients to leave appointments hanging on at least one suspenseful note, they are more likely to keep reflecting on what happened in their sessions to seek a meaningful closure.

A well-known television evangelist regularly left his congregation with these words, "Something good is going to happen to you today!" This prediction obviously left believers in a positive mood, wondering what he was talking about, and being on the alert for the good happening. In a similar way, we counselors want to leave our clients searching for positive events in their lives and for ways to escape the perils of their existence, just as our hero in the movie serial did every Saturday.

Experiencing This Idea

You may have experienced the Zeigarnik effect at the beginning of this chapter because John's story of his rock-throwing incident was cut off just before its resolution. Other examples include the film *Limbo* by John Sayles, the story *The Lady or the Tiger,* and most television soap operas. What episodes in your own life have been left unresolved? What have been your reactions at these times?

Longing as "Unfinished Business"

Sometimes clients come to counseling with unfinished business in their lives that takes the form of "set-aside" or foreclosed hopes and dreams. When people have tried and failed repeatedly to attain their goals, it becomes a very reasonable strategy to seek peace by setting aside those goals so that they are not continually agitated by the fact that their dreams have not been achieved. If, for example, one longs for a loving and secure relationship, but has never found it, one way of defending against the disappointment is to not expect or desire such a relationship. This response might be called the "sour grapes" defense—putting dreams and goals out of mind, convincing oneself that they were not important after all, and damping all the emotions associated with the longing for what's out of reach. We discussed this dynamic in Chapter 7, when we addressed the topic of emotional arousal. Here, we are making the additional point that although people may attempt to shut down their emotions, longing is always unfinished business. They long for a resolution of their desires and a completion of each vignette within their life story. Even if people have attempted to "turn into stone" so as not to experience their emotions, they are still agitated by an underlying tension.

In order to tap into their longings, the first thing you can do is invite your clients to talk about their goals, a process that immediately arouses your clients' dormant desires for something better. In effect, you are reopening the case on their thwarted and foreclosed dreams. It is amazing how reluctant clients are to do this. They seem to resist talking about what they wish for, and often report feeling childish or stupid for wanting it. Somehow, they have convinced themselves that wanting something that they have thus far failed to achieve is unrealistic.

Furthermore, clients may not want to stir up the associated feelings of pain, frustration, and helplessness that they have so neatly packed away. They often speak of their longing in a distant way—as if it belonged to someone else. But somewhere within clients, the longing is still alive as unfinished business. Like the Zeigarnik effect, the case truly remains open until closure can be reached. As their counselor, you can help your clients get back in touch with those feelings of longing and begin to entertain their hopes and dreams as possibilities once again. By reviving and rehearsing images of attaining their goals, your clients can become inspired to act in new and more likely ways of achieving these goals. Your job is to increase your clients' emotional arousal enough to activate this tension of longing for a better future. Once clients are back in touch with the feelings of wanting something better, these feelings become motivational.

One approach you can use is to explore the past as a way of envisioning a future direction for your work together. For example, you might say to your client:

> Let's go back to your wish for [the longed-for situation]. If you had possessed everything you needed back then to have that dream come true, what would have been different about the way things went? What would you have done differently?

This technique is sometimes referred to as "history change." It is similar to the miracle question described in Chapter 6, but the change is happening in the imagined past, rather than in the future. Once the client has described in detail how things would have been different, you might be able to capitalize on the resources your client identified as necessary for satisfactory closure:

> Now that you have more experience in dealing with situations like that, which of those resources do you now have more of that you didn't have enough of then? What part of [the longed-for situation] can you now attain with your newer resources?

However the story turns out, in the process of recovering this past situation, your client has been able to yearn and long for a better outcome, rather than to seal away the desire and use the sour-grapes defense. Whether the initial desired goal could still possibly be attained will depend on the situation. If, for example, a male client laments that he wishes he had possessed the courage to ask someone out on a date 15 years ago when they were both seniors in high school, you probably can't change that history. But what if, at the next high school reunion, he runs into her and finds she is divorced and seems interested in him? It could happen.

Enchantment and Moments of Inspiration

Without using any formal hypnotic induction techniques, you can encourage your clients to enter and use common everyday trances. Once they have entered such a state, you should not interrupt this important inner work. When your clients begin to reorient themselves from these reveries, they are especially open to engaging in creative encounters with you. These are the moments of inspiration—when the Muse speaks, lightning flashes, pieces of the puzzle come together, and the person has an "Aha!" experience. Lankton and Lankton (1986) referred to these moments as times when the client is ready to become "enchanted." They considered enchantment to be a concept in therapy as important as empathy. When clients are enchanted, they are intrigued—even enraptured—by the fascinating reframes, bewitching metaphors, and alluring images that emerge in their collaborative work with their counselor. What you need to keep in mind is that you are no magician, wizard, or witch with mysterious powers over clients. The trick is that there is no trick. You do not cast spells or recite incantations to enchant a client. Instead, you provide your client with a safe haven, develop a trusting relationship, communicate your faith in your client's inner resources, and carefully use several tools to invite, encourage, and help your client take full advantage of the enchantment process. The most important task you have is to help your clients accept, experience, and use mystification and enchantment. It is in these moments of artfulness that the counselor–client relationship shifts in some mysterious way so that your clients discover precisely what to do and no longer turn to you for advice.

"Sounds good to me!" you may be saying, "but how do I do it?" On closer inspection, you will find that you have already been doing it through the use of the deconstructing and influencing skills you have been learning. For example, your use of presuppositional questions and statements are a form of enchantment. When you say, for example, "*When* you have solved this problem, how *will* you know?" you are inviting the client to enter an enchanted place.

Another mystifying technique is reframing a situation so that the facts remain the same, but the interpretation is called into question. Consider the example below:

> **Parent:** He never listens to a word I say! He is willful, belligerent, and he ignores me like I don't have good sense. I tell him to get his homework done and then I go to his room an hour later and he hasn't even started. He's a lazy bum!
>
> **Counselor:** Yes. It must be really hard for you to have a son who is going through that "parent deafness" phase. All those raging hormones seem to plug up their ears at that age. I'll bet he's gotten pretty clumsy and forgetful, too. It also sounds like he may be so concerned about messing up on his homework assignments that it feels safer not to even get started.

By changing "willful belligerence" to a "parent deafness phase" and laziness into "concerned about messing up," the counselor preserves the facts of the situation, but offers a different interpretation. Rather than argue with the parent, the counselor simply sees it another way. This strategy stands a chance of subtly deconstructing the way the parent will tell the story.

Vital to the reframing approach is your acceptance and appreciation of the client's story. You utilize the undeniable facts of your client's current problem to lead to less constricting, more normal behavior. Dolan, (1985) stated that reframing involves altering the context. For example, if you put a green frame around a picture, it will bring out whatever green is in the picture. "The picture will look different than it did before the new frame was placed around it" (p. 91).

In fact, all the brief counseling tools discussed so far fall under the heading of enchantment if they are effective at the time of their use. Whether your client is enchanted, mystified, hypnotized, or otherwise influenced is more a matter of the quality of your relationship and the timing of your intervention. There are no compelling hexes or magic potions that can make this happen. It is always a function of your artfulness in engaging with your client in a co-creative therapeutic alliance. And how do you get to be artful? The same way that you get to Carnagie Hall—practice, practice, practice . . . and listening carefully to your clients for directions.

Implications of These Ideas for the Counselor

- When your clients appear to be in a transderivational search, do not intrude. When they reorient, you have an opportunity to find out where they have been.
- Be sensitive to those moments when your client enters a common everyday trance. These can be very productive times.
- To convince your client of a new way of seeing things, you can employ an "exotic audience." In front of the client, you can communicate to a third party your perception of how the client has changed.
- Keeping in mind the Zeigarnik effect, you want to leave things open, so the client can reach his or her own closure.
- All clients have longings that represent unfinished business. Your job is to help them rediscover their longings.
- Use whatever devices you can to "enchant" your client. Enchantment is simply an altered state, a sense of disorientation that is pleasantly fascinating and intriguing.

TOOLS

Delivering the Reframe

Suggesting a reframe to clients is not simply a matter of telling them how you see things or arguing against their point of view. *You* don't reframe a client's perspective, the client does. This point is often misunderstood by novice counselors. An example of this misunderstanding came from one of our trainees, who, in a supervision session proudly announced that he had used a reframe with his client. We asked for his account of the reframe, and he said, "Well, my client was complaining that he couldn't get to work that day because his car wouldn't start, and I said that he should be grateful that he even has a car." This "look on the bright side" form of counseling is not a reframe. Reframing results in your client making a second-order change, either a change of context or a change of rules. There must first be some confusion on the part of the client when his or her interpretations of events are not verified, but since there is no argument about the facts of the situation, the client cannot dismiss the new idea as simply wrong or crazy.

An example of a context change would be if in working with a couple, both members are telling war stories, attempting to explain how wrong or obnoxious the other is through the use of anecdotes. You might say to them:

> I'm afraid that just telling me about how you fight with each other is making it hard for me to understand what really goes on. And it sounds like you're not exactly sure how all this takes place either. How would it be if you two would just go ahead and argue as you normally do, and I can then interject comments as to what I understand you to be saying?

This technique not only places the argument in a different context—the counseling room instead of, say, the bedroom—but it also is experienced at first as confusing to the couple. They initially seem not to know where to start, and they often get faint smiles on their faces. If they comply with the request to recreate an argument in the office, they will not be able to carry it off in the usual way, and they will offer the counselor the opportunity to acknowledge and add reframes. The counselor can creatively misunderstand and help deconstruct the story they have automated about each other's motives and attitudes. Conversely, if they refuse to argue in the office, then their original contentious way of presenting has been defused for the time being. Either way, they will have to experience their arguing in a different way.

Another type of context change used with couples who are on the verge of divorce is said to have been developed by Carl Whitaker (1976). He called this technique "decourting." He would begin by acknowledging that it looked like divorce would be the best thing for the couple, but then he would ask how long they had "courted" before they married. The couple might, for example, tell him that they had dated for 8 months before marrying, and had been married for 10 years. Whitaker would then say something like:

> You have been with each other for 10 years and 8 months. Research suggests that in that length of time you have developed habits of living together that must be carefully separated. If you simply pull this marriage apart, it would be like tearing conjoint twins apart—there will be a lot of bleeding. Since you courted for 8 months, you need to take at least that length of time to decourt your marriage.

The couple is then instructed to act as if they are not married, but to live as though they are dating. They are to behave with each other in ways similar to their original dating period. In this context, some couples actually fall back in love. Even if other decourting couples do ultimately divorce, they generally have more "civilized" conclusions to their marriages.

A form of reframing that attempts to change the rules that connect words with behaviors is the relabeling technique. If clients are describing events, themselves, or others in pejorative terms, you can employ more innocuous words when you acknowledge their statements. Linda Metcalf (1995) offered a variety of helpful examples of relabeling. For example, if someone is labeled as "hyperactive," you can describe this person as "sometimes too energetic." If a parent labels a child as having "attention deficit disorder," you can depict the child as being "inattentive at times." Someone who is characterized as an "angry" person can be someone who "gets upset sometimes." A "rebellious" woman is "developing her own way" and a "shy" man "takes a little time to get to know people."

This small list of relabeling examples should be enough to give you the idea of how you would be changing the rules in such cases. You take the client's hard and fast diagnostic and damning labels and turn them into process terms that are descriptive and normalizing. Of course, this must be done gently, so subtly that the client hardly notices that you have changed the words being used. Relabeling is never a matter of debating with the client what a behavior is properly called.

Using This Tool

Form a small group with two colleagues. One of you volunteers to role-play a client whose self-labeling is sabotaging the potential for positive change. Another volunteers to listen, understand, and validate (LUV) while also turning those labels into descriptive process items. The third person serves as the recorder, who observes and leads the feedback discussion.

Constructing an Enchanting Metaphor

In Chapter 2, we discussed how metaphors are tools of the counselor—not just the poet and artist. We explained that metaphors offer you ways to understand how your clients perceive their world and to respond to your clients empathically. Now we return to metaphors to explore how they can be used for the purpose of enchantment.

Metaphors, more than any other therapeutic technique, characterized Milton Erickson's approach to therapy. He used metaphors "to motivate, to create new perceptions and behaviors, to overcome limitations, and as a teaching tool" (Dolan, 1985). Dolan pointed out that the most important ingredient in the design of a successful metaphor is the quality of the rapport between the counselor and client. You need to know your clients' metaphors, so that your design will be a good fit with their way of representing their world. As de Shazer (1982) put it, your communication with clients must be "isomorphic" with their world view. Two systems are said to be isomorphic when one can be mapped onto the other so that part of one system corresponds to part of the other. In other words, your story must match their story—except for the "news of difference" that you mean to communicate.

According to Dolan (1985), the first place to start is to make a list of the verbs and adverbs that your client uses to describe concerns. For example, the client whose wife has divorced him may say, "I just can't seem to let go of her. . . . I hang on to old memories of our relationship" (p. 113). You can use these phrases in a later metaphor in which "hanging on" might represent a problem and "letting go" might represent a goal. Perhaps the metaphor may be mountain-climbing. Obviously, hanging on is important when scaling a mountain, and letting go could be dangerous under certain circumstances, but is ultimately a necessary part of leaving the mountain to go on with one's life.

Metaphors with "Dramatic Hold"

Lankton and Lankton (1986) suggested that when you offer metaphors to clients, they will work best if you embed "dramatic hold" in your delivery. They have offered a structure for creating this dramatic hold in metaphors, and suggested that stories can be one of three types: Suspense, Mystery, or Surprise/Shock. The criteria that separate these forms is how—and to whom—the information is revealed. These forms are illustrated in Figure 8–1.

Good writers and film-makers use these dramatic hold devices all the time. If we think about it, we can realize the impact that these techniques have on us as the audience. Whenever we are emotionally affected by the tension in the plot, we are in the grip of dramatic hold.

A story that contains *suspense* is one in which the protagonist is about to experience an event that the audience knows about, but the protagonist does not. Of course, the advantage that movies have is that they can signal the impending event with musical sound tracks, which increase the viewer's tension level, but to which the person on the screen is oblivious. For example, the music begins to swell with a " 'da-dump, da-dump, da-dump, da-dump' and you know that Jaws is coming. The audience knows and the protagonist doesn't know so you are wondering how this is going to turn out" (Lankton & Lankton, 1986, p. 190).You are doing more than merely wondering. You might, in such cases of suspense, even be moved to yell "Look out!" to the person on the screen. You are enchanted and emotionally involved in the outcome of the situation.

Another type of plot is the *mystery*. In this format, the protagonist knows what is going on, but has not yet shared it with the audience. You know the story—the inspector gathers all the suspects, announces that he or she has examined all the clues, and knows the murderer's identity. But before the murderer is named, we are given several false leads, which point to people who turn out to be innocent. Finally, when we have completely been thrown off the track, the inspector reveals the true murderer, who obligingly confesses. Sherlock Holmes and Miss Marple always seem to end their investigations in this manner. Speaking of mystery, in Chapter 9, you will read a story that would qualify as a mystery because the title, "The Counselor Who Cured Childhood Psychosis with a Baseball," sets the reader to wondering how something so preposterous-sounding could happen, and the mystery is not revealed until near the end of the story.

TYPE OF STORY (the design)	CLIENT (the audience/listener)	PROTAGONIST (in the story)
Suspense	Knows	Doesn't know
Mystery	Doesn't know	Knows
Surprise/Shock	Doesn't know	Doesn't know

FIGURE 8-1   Dramatic hold metaphor guide. After Lankton and Lankton, 1986, p. 190.

The third type of dramatic hold—*surprise, shock, or humor*—involves a situation in which neither protagonist nor the audience is aware of what is going to happen. In the last scene of many horror movies, for example, everyone—rescuers, victims, and audience alike—are both relieved and exhausted by the ordeal of finally killing the monster. Suddenly, the not-quite-dead fiend, accompanied by very loud music and noise, reappears to start the struggle again. This surprise takes our breath away, because this new threat has caught us off guard and has suddenly changed our feelings from those of relief to those of terror.

An example of a scene in which surprise is coupled with humor is the one you may remember from the movie *Raiders of the Lost Ark*. Our anthropologist hero is confronted by a villain who draws a very large scimitar and proceeds to go through a posturing ritual that should strike fear into anyone. However, our hero, who appears rather bored, simply takes out his revolver and shoots the man. This was, by the way, a second-order change strategy on the part of the anthropologist, who must have read Gregory Bateson, because the expectation was that he would enter into the game the attacker had initiated. We all laughed when we realized that, of course, shooting the villain was a much more efficient solution, and that we had almost been drawn into the game ourselves.

The purpose of this discussion is not to convert you into novelists, playwrights, or movie makers—of course, the goal of counseling is not to entertain clients. Our point here is to encourage you to give yourself permission to add a touch of mystery, hint of suspense, sense of humor, and dramatic flair to your counseling style. Although listening to your client is certainly vital to the success of your counseling work, it is just as essential that the client is listening to you.

By using these techniques, you can capture the attention of clients when you are about to offer them a metaphor. You can use metaphors as indirect ways of suggesting changes in attitude or behavior to your clients. You must deliver the metaphor in a way that holds them until you end your offering. Of course, you are not Stephen King or Alfred Hitchcock, but as the Lanktons said, you are not attempting to win a Pulitzer Prize or Academy Award. You are merely trying to get your clients to open up to the possibilities contained in your message.

Listening in on a Session

If Zeigarnik is in effect for you, you probably don't need to review John's story at the beginning of the chapter. As you will see, a resolution-focused counselor can use common everyday trance, mystification, reframing, and metaphor in a number of ways.

John:　(*John arrived for his session and demonstrated his desire to be a "customer" of counseling by responding quickly when the counselor invited John to discuss his goals. With some facilitation and help from the counselor, John articulated that one of his major goals was to take better care of himself so that his cardiac health would improve significantly. He suddenly turns to discuss his apprehensions in coming to a counselor.*) You know, to be honest with you, I wouldn't be here if my doctor hadn't threatened to flunk my physical for my license. I think that you deserve to know that because I don't want to be BS-ing you here just to keep my license. In fact, I got really scared about you taking away my permit when you find out just how screwed up I am. I almost got off the bus to catch another one heading back home.

Counselor: (*He has found John to be an engaging client who has already taken a couple of risks in disclosing himself earlier in the session.*) John, with so much at stake now and feeling really scared, how did you work it out to go ahead and come in here to deal with all this stuff?

John: (*He turns his eyes to the ceiling, tilts his head, shrugs his shoulders in an exaggerated fashion, and lifts his hands, palms up.*) It's hard to say. . . . (*He pauses.*) Maybe it had something to do with what I was remembering on the bus. My high school buddy Leo and I were involved in this incident one Friday evening. We had made this stupid bet and I wound up accidentally hitting a man in the head with a rock I had thrown. God, there was blood gushing all over that guy.

Anyway, we were able to escape from him that night, but the next Monday we were called into the principal's office. Man, we were so scared! There were even a couple of cops at the meeting and we thought we were dead meat. Then we heard one of the cops tell the principal that if it weren't for our quick thinking, this girl might not have been able to escape a stalker who had tried to molest her. Her mom reported him to the police and a cruiser picked up this guy who was running around the neighborhood, mad as hell, and holding a bloody handkerchief to his head. Leo and I thought they were hauling our asses off to jail, but then they called us "heroes."

Leo and I kidded each other about that for years. . . . (*John laughs, shaking his head ruefully, then stops, sighs, gazes out the office window and is silent.*)

Counselor: (*After 5 or 10 seconds of silence, the counselor offers an acknowledgement in a soft, affirming tone of voice.*) Yeah, there's sure a lot there to sort through.

John: (*He pauses for a few more seconds, then squints his eyes as if there had been a sudden glare on the window. John looks toward the counselor, blinks rapidly several times, and begins to chew his gum again.*) Yeah. . . . Leo and I kinda drifted apart the past few years, but somehow he heard about my heart attack and called me at the hospital. The first thing he said to me was, "Hey, how's your throwing arm?" (*John smiles and pauses again, staring vacantly at the pattern on the parquet wood floor, and rubbing his right arm like a pitcher preparing to toss a few warm-up pitches. After a few seconds of silence, he raises his head to face the counselor and continues.*) God, it felt so good to hear his voice then. When I had my heart attack, I felt like some big thug had come up, stomped me in the chest, and shook me like I was a rag doll. Even later in the hospital, I was feeling pretty frantic and wondering if this was the end. But when Leo called, I began to think that maybe I was actually going to make it.

Counselor: (*The counselor winces as he listens to John's account of his heart attack.*) Whew! I'm struck by how powerfully you just put that—your heart attack was like being physically attacked by a thug. Whether it was a sex stalker when you were in high school or a death stalker a few months ago, you've somehow managed to survive . . . and you had Leo around both times.

John: You know, I need to call Leo . . . and another guy from the Army, Randy. He called me, too, in the hospital. On my bus rides, I've been thinking a lot more about my life now that I almost lost it and I realized that I don't have time to waste anymore. If I don't do something today, I may not get the chance tomorrow.

Reflecting Questions

1. What was your reaction to hearing the resolution of John's earlier story?
2. How do you deal with silence in a counseling session?
3. How might you respond to John's last statement?

Get It in Writing

It was Bertha Pappenheim, Freud's "Anna O," who coined the phrase, "the talking cure" (Schultz & Schultz, 1996). Now, more than one hundred years later, we counselors are still talking to our clients and asking them to talk to us. But instead of listening for the hidden symbolic meaning in your clients' verbal utterances, as was done in the Freudian tradition, you can take their talk at face value and try to understand the stories of their lives.

The client tells stories and you enter into these stories. For clients, just being able to tell their story to someone who is truly an interested listener is a rare and wonderful event. How often do people get this opportunity? But even beyond this oral communication, there is something that may be even more powerful—the written word. The idea that written language may be more powerful than spoken language might, at first blush, seem strange to counselors. But consider this—once a verbal utterance is aired, it vanishes. While our oral tradition would have us trust language when we "hear it from the horse's mouth," our tradition of writing makes it official only when it is "in black and white." In a literate culture, a verbal contract has a much shakier credibility in a court of law than one that has been written, witnessed, and signed by all parties.

What can be read and reread obviously lasts longer than what can be heard. Written documents have the capability of enduring. Even in a technological age, when sound recordings are possible as a way to archive information, it is the visual event that makes the more lasting impression. White and Epston (1990) suggested that this is because of our "ocularcentrism." People who exhibit a vast amount of knowledge are often called "insightful," "perceptive," and "farsighted," while those who lack this quality are considered to be "blind" or "shortsighted." "And those ideas that are most likely to be embraced are those judged to be 'illuminating,' 'enlightening,' and 'visionary' " (p. 34). As a counselor in our ocularcentrist culture, you should consider "getting it in writing," as well as in talking. For example, you might consider getting a written contract with clients regarding the nature of your work together. Especially with young clients, there appears to be enchantment in this ritual.

White and Epston (1990) also made extensive use of awards and certificates. Presenting an award for an accomplishment is a long-standing tradition. Perhaps you are displaying on your wall some certificate or written proclamation of your own accomplishments. School counselors know that the impact of an award is increased if it is presented by a person who is known only by reputation to the people receiving them. The principal of the school, dean of the college, president of the company are all people who are known, but students or employees do not regularly consort with them. These people, and those who hold similar positions, constitute what White and Epston (1990) called the "exotic audience."

The counselor, too, is an exotic audience for the client. So long as counselors remain somewhat mysterious, there is a desire on the client's part to know what is in the counselor's mind, and for the counselor to approve of him or her. It is one thing to get such an approbation in the session, but quite another thing to get the same validation in a written message. A letter, whether it is sent by the postal service or email, can be a powerful tool you can use to support your client's discoveries, decisions, and changes. Of course, people enjoy receiving correspondence—both old-fashioned and electronic versions. "You've got mail!" is the favorite greeting our computer can offer us. Words in the written form, even if on the computer screen, offer us a tangible record of someone's thoughts, observations, and reflections. However, counseling clients especially appreciate receiving correspondence because they are going through times of both distress and change. They can return to electronic or hard-copy letters whenever necessary. As Friedman (1997) points out, "Letter writing makes concrete the ideas discussed with clients, further amplifies and highlights exceptions, and opens the door to action possibilities" (pp. 86–87).

A study conducted by Nyland and Thomas (1994) indicated that the impact of a letter written to a client was equivalent to more than three face-to-face sessions. Some of the participants in the study claimed that one letter was worth 10 sessions, and 50 of those surveyed responded that the letter alone was responsible for their major gains in therapy. Similarly, David Epston (in White, 1995) claimed that one letter was equal to 4.5 sessions of therapy. Especially now that email has resurrected written correspondance as a popular form of communication, writing to your clients is a counseling strategy that should be part of your therapeutic tool kit.

Using This Tool

Gather a small group of your colleagues to participate in this activity. Each of you anonymously composes a note to every other member of the group. Start your note with "The thing I like best about you is . . ." and complete the phrase. Then tell about a particular time when this person showed this trait. Exchange the notes with one another. Each person then reads his or her notes aloud and then shares his or her reactions.

A Protocol for a Follow-up Letter

In the protocol below, we offer suggestions for what you might wish to include in a letter that you would send to your client after a productive first session. You will want to modify your letter according to the needs of your client. Take the following only as an example:

1. *Thank* the client for coming, and indicate your pleasure in working together.
2. Restate your pledge of *confidentiality.*
3. Reacknowledge your client's *main concerns* and suggest how the client is coping in spite of these challenges—in other words, find the pony.
4. *Externalize* the problem as an outside force that is attempting to influence or trick the client, and point out *exceptions*—times when the client has resisted or not been influenced.

5. *Compliment* your client on the strengths, resources, and insights that you noticed. As much as possible, use the client's own descriptions and metaphors.

6. Offer a *bridge*. Restate the goal that your client stated in the session and begin your suggestion with ". . . and since what you wanted to work on . . . ," or "since what you were hoping for . . . ," etc.

7. Before making a suggestion, determine whether your client–counselor relationship was a *customer, complainant, visitor,* or *involuntary* one.

8. Based on the above estimate, *offer* something you think might encourage the client to think about the concern in a different way. Be careful about suggesting behavioral change.

9. Suggest that you know the client is working hard toward improvement and that he or she is pleased with the way in which he or she has been able to, in spite of occasional setbacks, continue to get better. Offer *encouragement,* not praise.

10. *Close* your message in a friendly, collaborative manner, rather than sounding like a distant expert.

Listening in on a Session

Review John's story at the beginning of the chapter and the exerpt from his counseling session. Here is the counselor's follow-up letter to John:

> Dear John,
>
> I first want to thank you for your willingness to come in, work intensely, and make the most of our session together. Most people who see me on doctor's orders don't take the risks that you did during our first meeting, so I was both surprised and glad to see you being so open and involved. I thoroughly enjoyed working with you in such a productive meeting.
>
> Before I offer you some of my thoughts and impressions, let me just remind you once again that everything that you have shared with me is confidential. The only exceptions are if you give me your permission to share information with certain people, or if you are presenting an imminent danger to yourself or to others. You have my personal guarantee that I will carefully follow both the law and my professional ethics in protecting your confidentiality.
>
> You came to me for counseling because you wanted to make a good recovery from your heart attack, deal with your separation from your wife, get closer to people again, handle stress better, and get back to a healthier lifestyle. You've already taken positive steps toward these goals by going to your check-up appointment, letting your doctor know about your situation, following his recommendation to see a counselor, and then openly talking with me in our session together.
>
> This "Death Stalker" has been trying not just to rob your life, but to fool you into being his accomplice. He's trying to get you to do his dirty work by convincing you that you shouldn't even give at least as much effort to the care and maintainance of yourself as you do of your truck. He's not satisfied with taking your life, though. The "Death Stalker" is out to steal all the satisfactions of life, too—friendship, love, and peace of mind.
>
> John, you have battled stalkers a couple of times in your life—once when you were a teenager and didn't even realize it! In our session, you told me how you had kept up an impressive regimen of good nutrition and exercise for 6 months. You also shared how you had recently rediscovered two long-lost friends—Leo from your high school days and Randy from your time in the service—who called when they heard about your heart attack. You also described how at least the first couple years of your marriages were generally happy and intimate. You're now wanting to keep that special love alive in the future. Over the years as a long-distance truck driver, you have coped with all the stresses of trucking, including gas crises, long hours, loneliness, fatigue, and dangers.

You've come through many tough times, including a life-threatening heart attack, with a strong appreciation for life and a commitment to make the most of it. You've been able to use your stubborn streak to "keep on truckin'"—as we used to say in the 1960s. During our session, I don't know how you were able to hang in there, even when the words didn't come easily for you. When you were patient and continued to explore yourself, you shared reflections and recollections that had both richness and depth. You seem to realize now that you have much to offer and lots of living to do yet.

Since your dream is to live both a long AND satisfying life, it seems to me that you already have most of the pieces of this puzzle—taking good care of yourself, being more open with others, keeping love alive in your life, savoring all that life has to offer, and making peace with yourself. As you find out how these pieces fit together in your new life, I wonder what new joys you'll find and what old ones you'll rediscover in your reveries—on the bus and other places, too.

Thanks again, John, for getting our work together off to such a fine start. I'm looking forward to hearing how you plan to continue this positive momentum!

Sincerely,

Elias McCoy, LPC

Using This Tool

Write a follow-up letter to the colleague who shared concerns with you in the exercise from the previous chapter. Follow the protocol above in writing it. Reconvene your group and exchange letters. Discuss your reactions to what your colleague wrote about you.

A Letter from an Exotic Audience

Freeman and Lobovits (1993) wrote of the case of Yoshi, a boy of 8 from a family of divorced parents. Yoshi was brought to the counselor by his mother, Mariko, who complained that there was constant fighting and tension between them. Mariko stated that because of this, her patience with Yoshi had "shrunk 200%," that she didn't like him anymore, and was ready for him to go live with his father. In the counseling sessions, Yoshi refused to talk. Instead he would growl and mutter. The counselor, Jenny, decided to ask him if they could find another way to communicate. She discovered that she could ask questions, and Yoshi would nod his head if he agreed or "growl menacingly" if he disagreed. Later, he would reply by writing "yes" or "no" on a piece of paper. Finally, he would write brief answers, draw pictures, and use the sandtray or puppets in response to her questions. The importance of this procedure was that Yoshi was able to cooperate with the counselor on his own terms.

Yoshi was, of course, having problems in school as well. One of his drawings portrayed him hiding behind a file cabinet outside the teacher's lounge at school and laughing as a bomb-blast destroyed the place. He was pictured with a balloon over his head which said, "Die! Die!"

His problems were externalized as "misery" and "temper" and work was done to get him to identify those times when he was able to master those problems. He was asked about his willingness to change his relationship with temper and misery. Jenny told Yoshi that there was a Temper Tamer's Club of Australia and New Zealand, and she thought they might consider him for membership if he continued to do so.

Yoshi came to the next session saying that he wanted to have temper and misery quit ruling his life. He said that he wished to choose a "life free of misery." Instead of getting into trouble all the time, Yoshi just wanted to play and have fun. Sometime later, Jenny and Yoshi composed a letter of application to David Epston and the Temper Tamer's Club. This activity was to establish an "exotic audience" for Yoshi's success and to enchant him into continuing with the progress he had already established. Epston wrote back in a brilliant letter which reinforced the counseling that had been done with Yoshi:

> Dear Yoshi,
>
> Jenny told me that you might be a candidate for the Temper Tamers' Club of Australia and New Zealand. If you were to be successful, I guess you could set up a branch office in Berkeley and be our American agent. The next board meeting is in a month's time. So far, from what Jenny told me, you are looking good.
>
> However, I need to ask you for some further information. I have some questions for you. . . .
>
> 1. Is it true that your temper didn't want you to come to therapy and work . . . to get rid of it in the first place and that you refused to go along with your temper?
> 2. Is it true that you freed yourself from its grip and are now more able to talk for yourself and to turn around some things in your life . . . ? . . . Are you finding it easier the more you do it?
> 3. I was excited to hear that you and your mom came up with some interesting peace ideas to stop the temper and fighting that were coming between you. Could you let the people in Australia and New Zealand know what your favorite ideas were and which worked out the best?
> 4. Do you think your temper is in favor of your decision to choose happiness instead of misery in your life? . . .
>
> I am looking forward very much to hearing from you through Jenny. Once I have, I will give this information to the board and inform you about their decision. From what I have heard so far, I am confident on your behalf.
> Yours sincerely,
> David Epston (Freeman & Lobovits, 1993, p. 207).

As you read the above letter, perhaps you could realize the power that receiving a letter from an exotic audience such as David Epston, or any stranger who lives "down under," might have on the client. Sports figures, rock stars, or actors would, of course, constitute more powerful exotic audiences for children, but you can find other "exotic" people who might cooperate with you in the letter writing. Once you have found someone, you can write the letter yourself and give it to that person on a computer disk so that he or she can print it on letterhead stationery and sign it. This action on your part would reduce the burden on the exotic audience and increase the likelihood that you could use the person again.

Segue to Chapter 9

The movies *Back to the Future*, *Sliding Doors*, and *Run, Lola, Run* are based on the idea that dramatically different outcomes can evolve from a seemingly insignificant event. Think of an event in your own life that seemed small at the time, but cascaded into something large. For example, what led you to graduate school? What might have happened if that event had not taken place? Write a summary of what was and what could have been.

CHAPTER 9

Chaos and Complexity in Counseling: Butterflies and Loaded Dice

"The reverse side also has a reverse side."
Japanese Proverb

CHAPTER GOALS

Reading about and experiencing the ideas in this chapter will help you to understand the following concepts:

- Small perturbations can lead to dramatic change in complex systems, a phenomenon known as the Butterfly Effect.
- Instead of falling apart, complex adaptive systems come together to reorganize themselves.

Reading about and practicing the tools in this chapter will help you to learn these valuable skills:

- Confusion techniques that perturb and help people to reorganize their thinking.
- Paradox, a technique that, in some situations, can be a powerful counseling tool.

STORY

The Counselor Who Cured Childhood Psychosis with a Baseball

His name was Mike and he was 7 years old. He had an unusual gait, and he giggled inappropriately as the social worker introduced him to the counselor. His eyes were fixed on the ceiling as they shook hands, and he wobbled his head back and forth, like one of those floppy dog figurines you see peering out of the back of some cars. He was clearly one of those kids that the physicians often cryptically refer to as "FLK" in their charts. When the doctors aren't sure what is wrong with a child, they will sometimes write, "This seven-year-old, white, FLK . . ." (funny-looking kid).

"This is Dr. Jordan," said the social worker. "He's going to be your friend." Jordan always hated it when they told the kids whom they brought to the mental health center for counseling that he was there to be their "friend." It just didn't seem honest. What

Jordan was really going to be was someone who would try to change Mike in certain ways, and someone who would report on his progress to the Department of Social Services.

Jordan had already read the file on Mike. It was pretty thick for such a little guy, but Mike had really been through the mill! Child Protective Services people had found him, at age 4, half-starved and chained to a bed while his mother was whoring in a local bar. The mother explained that she could not afford a baby sitter, so she had kept him chained for his own protection every time she went out—which was often. As it turned out, Mike had also been physically and sexually abused by one of his mother's former lovers.

Since that time, Mike had been expelled from a series of foster homes for one reason or another. The reason most often given was that Mike was "crazy." But no one held it against him. They said, "Who wouldn't be crazy after a life like that?" The social worker said pretty much the same thing, and a consulting psychiatrist had declared that Mike was suffering from a Childhood Psychosis NOS. NOS (not otherwise specified) is that catch-all category at the end of each diagnostic group in the DSM. It really means, "This behavior doesn't fit anything we know." The school psychologist who tested Mike said that he was "Emotionally Disturbed" and that he should be in a self-contained classroom. The worker who brought Mike to see Jordan said that she would pick him up in an hour . . . then she left.

Jordan stood there in the waiting room, looking at Mike. Mike was still looking at the ceiling with an absent grin on his face. "What the hell am I going to do with this kid?" The counselor wondered to himself as he reached out his hand. Mike grabbed on to it tightly and they walked together to the playroom. Jordan knew very little about play therapy, but his mental health center had a very fine playroom, and play was the expected treatment method for children in that center. And so he watched Mike play, while he attempted to make all those "tracking" statements and reflective comments that authors like Axeline and Landreth would be proud of. He was not sure, however, how this was going to cure Mike's Childhood Psychosis NOS.

Reflecting Questions

1. What are your reactions to Mike?
2. If you were the counselor, how would you work with Mike?
3. What is the impact of Mike's diagnostic label on others?

OVERVIEW

This chapter introduces some of the more controversial approaches to counseling—the use of "confusion techniques" and "paradox." Because they are relatively new, the ideas that support these tools are generally not well understood.

Chaos Theory suggests that complex systems can be highly unstable and that small perturbations, known as butterfly effects, can throw such systems off course. People are complex systems. They organize their experiences within complex representational schemes. Part of our work as counselors is designed to perturb these schemes and to throw them into chaos.

The other side of Chaos Theory is a new science known as Complexity. The central idea in this theory is that living systems are adaptive and self-organizing. Instead of falling apart, complex adaptive systems reorganize themselves and grow. When they are perturbed, they put themselves back together in a new way. This principle is called emergence—something new emerges from something old, but we cannot explain this process by referring to what existed before. Therefore, searching for causes to problems is a useless pursuit.

In this chapter, we discuss ways of using confusion and paradox in counseling relationships. We also offer a caveat—use paradox only at certain times and with certain clients.

IDEAS

Chaos and Order in Counseling

Anyone who has seen the movie *Jurassic Park* has heard of Chaos. The character played by Jeff Goldblum was a mathematician who was interested in nonlinear equations. In one scene, he pedantically explains Chaos Theory to Laura Dern, as they sit in a sport utility vehicle, waiting for those huge Jurassic creatures to make themselves known. Goldblum's character explains that Chaos is the savage unpredictability of the universe, but that "nature always finds a way." In that scene, Chaos had an ominous ring to it, because we all knew that nature was about to show its capricious strength, and that someone would be devoured by a dinosaur.

Chaos Theory and its conjoint twin, Complexity Theory, are very important new scientific ideas about how change and order come about in the universe. These theories not only form the explanations that underlie human thought, but also provide strategies for changing minds. O'Hanlon and Weiner-Davis (1989) suggested this in their book on solution-oriented therapy. Despite the fact that things are constantly changing in the universe of the human mind, the seeming chaos turns out to be quite orderly. When complex systems such as human minds are perturbed, they respond by rearranging their patterns.

Small perturbations can have a profound effect on complex systems such as the weather or the stock market, but what do the behaviors of cyclonic storms and Dow Jones averages have to do with brief counseling? The answer is that all complex systems display a common dynamic, which, if recognized by counselors, makes human behavior more understandable.

Human beings exist within a dialectical tension of mind. On the one hand, we seek growth, change, and novelty. On the other hand, we desire certainty, stability, and order. Our minds are constantly attempting to adapt to new information, a process that initially throws our thoughts into chaos, until we can achieve order out of the chaos. It is what Piaget (1926) called "assimilation by accommodation." This tension between chaos and order is the essence of learning. If, however, people experience more chaos than they can accommodate, they are in crisis. Conversely, if humans do not experience enough change and diversity in their lives, they feel bored. They consider their lives to be stale and barren. When clients come to you in crisis, they are already in chaos and are seeking some way to reorganize their thoughts and resolve the chaos. However, if clients are experiencing the anhedonia of depression, the hopelessness of discouragement, or the emptiness of an "existential vacuum," you must first perturb them before they can begin to find a new pattern or resolution to their situation.

In the Chaos/Complexity Theory, the nature of change has three principles that are important in counseling. The first principle is that large changes can result from small perturbations—the "Butterfly Effect." The second is that change begins suddenly and resolves rapidly—it is, in a word, "brief." The third relevant principle of Chaos/Complexity Theory is that change is a complete reordering of the client's experience—something unexpected and new will emerge, and nothing is ever the same afterward.

Chaos and Complexity

Since Chaos and Complexity theories may be new to you, we will offer a brief explanation of these important twin scientific theories. From Chaos Theory, we learn that infinitesimal changes within a system can have profound effects on the behavior of that system (Gleick, 1987). The notion of the "Butterfly Effect" gives us a vivid and poetic image of a new cause-and-effect relationship in the universe. If a butterfly flaps its wings over Bejing today, the weather will, sometime later, be altered over New York as a result. Some have suggested that Chaos Theory means that nature has a mind of her own, and that the old cause-and-effect relationship—the mechanistic clockwork universe—so central to the classical scientific enterprise, must be abandoned when dealing with complex systems. As Gleick put it, "Where chaos begins, classical science stops" (1987, p. 3). Only recently have physicists become aware of the importance of disorder in nature.

The predictable clockwork universe of 17th-century science just does not keep time the way we thought it did. Its periodicity, thought to be so regular when astronomers could predict that the Halley Comet would return in exactly 76 years, seems now to be only part of the story. Bossomaier and Green (1998) suggested that at least four different patterns can be detected in nature. The first behavioral pattern is a frozen state. Objects that seem to be fixed and immutable—rocks, houses, tables, and chairs—are examples of this pattern.

The second pattern is one of cyclical behavior. Early astronomers, who noticed that planets periodically returned to their former positions even though they were in constant motion, adopted this model. Consequently, these astronomers thought the universe was like a giant clock and that humans were different versions of clocks. We have called this the "dead rock" theory, because its prototypes are dead planets orbiting the sun.

A third pattern is more complex—"chaotic, aperiodic behavior in which the system never settles down to a constant pattern" (Bossomaier & Green, 1998, p. 55). In the medical model, most mental "disorders" are viewed as chaotic systems, on which professionals must intervene to stabilize and restore order.

Beyond the pattern of chaos, but connected to it, is the behavior of complex adaptive systems. Complex adaptive systems are inherently unstable and "exhibit the most interesting behaviors" (p. 57). They exist at the edge of chaos, and with the slightest perturbation, can sometimes go into chaotic fluctuation. But because they are self-organizing systems, they will restore order to themselves. This is not, however, the cyclical order of the less complex periodic pattern. When order is restored, this type of system is not in the same place—it is somewhere else. People are complex adaptive systems. Moreover, the human mind is a complex adaptive system. This means that our minds are always at the edge, ready to change. If perturbed, people experience mental confusion or chaos, but then they will accommodate, and make sense of what has happened by restoring order. The important thing to remember about complex systems is that they never return to their former states. However, because most change is uncomfortable for us, we are reluctant to accept it. And when we are under threat, we become rigid in our thinking and tend to suffer from "hardening of the categories."

A Little More Chaos

It all started when Edward Lorenz, a meteorologist from New England, tried to model weather on his computer. Gleick (1987) provided a brief account of this seminal event. Lorenz was using a primitive computer to boil all aspects of weather—winds, temperature, pressure, etc.—down to its "barest skeleton." All these aspects "matched his cherished intuition about the weather, his sense that it repeated itself, displaying familiar patterns over time, pressure rising and falling, airstream swinging north and south" (p. 15). So, it seemed that even unruly phenomena such as weather were nothing but cyclical activities that could be turned into standard mathematics and modeled successfully on a computer. And it appeared that changes in complex systems were finally going to reveal themselves as predictable cycles whose laws could be mapped in probability theory.

To make the patterns plain to see, Lorenz created a primitive kind of graphics program. Instead of just printing out the usual lines of digits, he would have the machine print a certain number of blank spaces followed by the letter *a*. He would pick one variable—perhaps the direction of the airstream, and follow the behavior of that variable. Gradually, the *a*'s marched down the roll of paper, swinging back and forth in a wavy line, making a long series of hills and valleys that represented the way the west wind would swing north and south across the continent. The orderliness of it, the recognizable cycles coming around again but never twice the same way, had a hypnotic fascination. The system seemed slowly to be revealing its secrets to the forecaster's eye. But one day in 1961, Lorenz took a shortcut. Instead of starting the whole run over, he started midway through. To give the machine its initial conditions, he typed the numbers straight from the earlier printout, and left the machine to do its work. When he returned an hour later, something unexpected had happened, something that would lay the foundation for a new science.

What should have happened is that the new run would exactly duplicate the old one. Nothing of the input had really been altered; the program was the same and Lorenz had typed the numbers in himself. What he found, however, was that his printout portrayed a totally new weather pattern that within a short time lacked any resemblance to the former pattern. They were so different that he might have chosen the two randomly out of a hat. A glitch in the computer, you say? Well, that was Lorenz's first thought. After all, it was 1961, and it was a pretty crude computer by today's standards. The glitch turned out to be in the way Lorenz had entered the numbers. The original number, carried out to six decimal places was .506127. To save space, he had rounded off to .506, assuming that such a small difference was inconsequential. "It has long been thought that small variations within large systems were inconsequential. . . . Yet in Lorenz's particular system of equations, small errors proved catastrophic" (Gleick, 1987, pp. 16–17). Contrary to the scientific notion that small causal differences "wash out" and make little or no difference in the effect, it now seemed that even minute variations of input can cause the whole system to change dramatically—hence, the Butterfly Effect. Lorenz realized that a physical system that behaved nonperiodically would be unpredictable.

Humans seem to live in a world of periodic cycles. There are circadian cycles, menstrual cycles, seasonal cycles, business cycles, to name only a few. Therefore, it has always seemed reasonable to apply the pattern of cycles to human behavior. But science has always found humans to be somewhat unpredictable. Perhaps this is because we are sensitive to small perturbations that render us nonperiodic, and therefore outside the realm of prediction. The Butterfly Effect appears to apply to human systems as well as weather systems.

Complex Adaptive Systems

The science of complexity is the investigation into the nature of change. Results revealed by this area of study have suggested that when things get complex, simple cause-and-effect notions go out the window. There is a difference between a complex system and a merely complicated one (Cilliers, 1998). An internal combustion engine, for example, is complicated, but it is not complex. A complex system consists of a very large number of elements that interact dynamically with each other and are constantly changing.

Any element in the system influences—and is influenced by—others in the system. The interactions among elements are nonlinear—a small change can make a big change. Complex systems are self-organizing, and consequently are not subject to entropy. The concept of entropy, or the second law of thermodynamics, predicts that everything runs down or falls apart. Negentropic systems grow. As you may know, your own body is constantly acting as if it were about to fall apart through catabolic processes, while anabolic processes are continually renewing it. Finally, it is not possible to precisely predict the outcomes of a complex system, or to reduce the functioning of the system to its elements.

The relatively new field of Complexity Theory explores how such change happens and how to engineer desired change. To date, the theory offers a global explanation, but not a detailed one. Nevertheless, a new view of change is taking place. What the behaviors of complex systems have in common is that they are probably the result of "spontaneous self-organization" in which pattern shifts result from perturbations within the complex system. Waldrop (1992) offered some examples from nature. Birds in flight "adapt to the actions of their neighbors, unconsciously organizing themselves into a flock. Organisms constantly adapt to each other through evolution, thereby organizing themselves into an exquisitely tuned ecosystem" (p. 11). The development of new patterns is not random—it is adaptive. Everything is in a constant process of dissolving and resolving so long as the system exists.

The Emergence of Something New

If you look closely at a photograph in your morning newspaper, you will see that it is really just an assembly of dots. Look again from a greater distance, and a recognizable image appears. So it was with the paintings of Seurat, who painted with dabs and dots that formed an image. How is this possible? The Gestalt psychologists had a phrase: "The whole is greater than the sum of the parts." The concept of emergence describes a situation in which, among other things, a picture emerges from dots, and a mind emerges from neurons. Knowing about the dots or the neurons tells us nothing about the picture or the mind. It is only the pattern of the whole array of dots that makes the picture. The pattern that is created is the emergent property of the components, but totally different from the components themselves.

At this point you may be wondering if this is still a book about counseling. Yes, it is! As you use these new ideas about complex systems, you will gain fresh insight into your clients. Since humans are complex adaptive systems, until the moment our lives end, we are living within the struggle between chaos and organization, between entropy and emergence. The really good news is that no matter how chaotic our lives and our minds may become, we are capable of creating new patterns from that seeming chaos. We will not fall into entropy, but are capable of rising like the phoenix from the ashes of our seeming destruction. We are never broken and in need of repair—we are simply re-organizing and attempting to adapt.

Given this view, dignified by the new science, you can have faith that your clients have the built-in capability to change. If your clients are in crisis, then they have already begun the process of change. If your clients come to you in a "stuck" place, you can use influencing interventions to perturb their system of thinking so that it will be thrown into some creative level of chaos. Your aim is to create the conditions that will foster the emergence of a new and more productive pattern of thought. Remember—you can't have an emergence without first having an emergency!

Implications of These Ideas for the Counselor

The ideas of Chaos Theory and Complexity Theory can have significant consequences on our work as counselors.

- The idea of the Butterfly Effect, translated into counseling parlance, suggests that you do not have to summon heroic interventions to overcome your client's stuckness. A small change can bring about a large result.
- Because the shift from chaos to self-organization often occurs quite rapidly, clients can often change long-standing concerns in a very short time.
- "Dead rock theory," which is the root metaphor for many traditional counseling approaches, is insufficient to capture the complexity of humans.
- People are complex adaptive systems. We cannot know them by reducing them to personality types, disorders, brains, neurons, molecules, or atoms. Instead, we must attempt to understand their changing patterns.
- When clients are confused, they are in chaos, but they are not falling apart. Instead, they are on their way to coming together—achieving a new organization of mind.
- Any time people are in the process of self-organizing, something new will emerge. A stuck client is like a planet held prisoner by the sun's gravity. Your use of confusion techniques and other perturbations can help your client move off a cyclical pattern and toward a new self-organization.

TOOLS

Techniques for "Butterfly" Perturbations

One really nice thing about the Butterfly Effect metaphor for counseling is that it suggests you use a small, gentle, and subtle perturbation of the client's current cognitions, rather than the "disputation," "countering," and annihilation of client thinking recommended by Ellis (1982) and other rational therapists. Resolution counseling is a "kinder, gentler" form of perturbation. You are not out to do violence to your client's thought organization; you hope to gently stir it up so that the client can reorganize his or her thinking.

We have already considered the deconstruction of client stories through creative misunderstanding and adding possibilities to our acknowledgments. Both of these techniques are subtle ways of perturbing the client's rendition of the facts, of throwing the "facts" into chaos. All the tools we have suggested so far are designed to "unfreeze" client thinking and to open the way for new organization. In the following sections, we will discuss some techniques that are not quite as subtle as the ones we have thus far offered. These techniques are designed to perturb the client's representational system. You use them in the way that road builders might plant small explosive charges to clear a path. You are not necessarily able to predict their precise effects, but armed with the knowledge that complex adaptive systems will reorganize themselves in the most desirable manner, you can use them with an attitude of cautious optimism. These Butterfly perturbations fall under the general headings of *confusion* and *paradox*.

Confusion

When you try to change a client's mind, what is it exactly you are attempting to do? Some counselors hope to persuade their clients into seeing the world as the counselors see it—in other words, "more realistically." Other counselors attempt to teach clients a new system of logic through which to extrude their experiences, so as to reconsider their "irrational thinking." Still others try to argue the faulty inferences of their clients into submission. All these forms of counseling have had some success.

Each of the above approaches has as its aim the clarification of clients' thinking and the removal of all the cognitive fuzziness that has confused and vexed them. Milton Erickson (1967), on the other hand, believed it could be good to confuse clients. What is the benefit, you may be wondering, of confusing your clients? Aren't clients already confused enough? The short answer is that clients are often not confused at all, but rather, confounded. As you learned in Chapter 2, such clients have "hardening of the categories." Their thinking has become so automatic that no new information can alter their categories of thought.

In the book *Through the Looking Glass* (Carroll, 1896/1991), when Alice read the poem about the Jabberwock, she was confused. The poem begins with the following lines:

> 'Twas brillig, and the slithy toves
> Did gyre and gimble in the wabe. . . . (p. 141)

Despite the fact that she found herself vexed by these words, Alice was nevertheless intrigued.

> "It seems very pretty," she said when she had finished it. "But it's *rather* hard to understand!
> . . . Somehow it seems to fill my head with ideas—only I don't know exactly what they
> are." (pp. 141–142)

The point is that when people are faced with confusing circumstances, they work very hard to make sense of them. When thrown into chaos, they will reorganize and adapt. In a manner similar to the Zeigarnik Effect, discussed in Chapter 8, the human mind always struggles to clarify uncertainty. As Aristotle said, "Nature abhors a vacuum." Presenting clients with ideas that are not clear perturbs their thinking and forces them to reorganize.

In summary, when people are confused, their thoughts are chaotic. On the other hand, when they are confounded, they are perplexed about how to solve a problem, but they experience themselves as thinking straight. They are confounded because they have tried a number of reasonable approaches that have failed. However, because these are the only strategies people know, they try them again. You will recall that Freud called this "repetition compulsion"—the need to keep trying the same failed strategy, hoping that it will finally turn out differently.

Clients often come to counseling saying that they are at their wit's end. When situations they have defined as problems arise, they implement "more of the same" strategies to try to solve them. Some brief and strategic therapists have even suggested that it is not the problem that is the problem, but rather, the failed solutions that are the culprits (Watzlawick, Weakland, & Fisch, 1974).

Deautomatization and Reorganization

Clients' reactions to their problems have usually become automated—their "viewing and doing" responses occur almost without their awareness. Like flying on automatic pilot, their thinking can become automated when they place things or events into categories. These categories later "harden," or become so rigid that it is impossible to see these things or events in more flexible ways. Such a process, Watzlawick, Weakland, and Fisch (1974) warned, can trap clients into seeing the categories themselves as the "reality." Confusion techniques deautomatize clients' thinking by perturbing the categories and throwing them into chaos. This deautomatization can help clients escape the cognitive trap, reprocess their experiences, and achieve a reorganization of thought processes.

Gill and Brennen (1959) developed the concept of deautomization to characterize a temporarily chaotic and disorganized state that can lead to a more advanced level of organization. Following on this idea, Deikman (1973) suggested that when deautomatization takes place in someone's thinking, the person becomes attentive, focused, and mindful. In deautomatization, one also abandons the abstract and intellectual by regressing to the sensual and perceptual level of experience. This different level of experiencing involves "perceiving a new brilliance to the world, of seeing everything as if for the first time, of noticing beauty" (p. 223). This activity has been compared to the religious conversion phenomenon of "seeing the light." The poet William Blake called it the cleansing of the doors of perception.

Milton Erickson (Erickson, Rossi, & Rossi, 1976) pointed out that there is a powerful human need to resolve confusion. It is almost as if our automated thought processes, once disrupted and thrown into chaos, seek not only to reorganize but to reautomate themselves. When people are confused, they are desperately seeking further information that will help reorganize their confused experience into an orderly new frame of reference. This state of confusion can set the stage for second-order change. Like the fly seeking a way out of the fly-bottle that we described in Chapter 1, clients may first need to be confused and disoriented in order to free themselves from their traps.

Experiencing the Following Idea

Imagine that your counselor has directed you to go to the local bowling alley, rent a pair of freshly sprayed shoes, and select a bowling ball. You have also been instructed not to keep score, but instead to enjoy the total experience of bowling—swinging the ball, watching it roll down the lane, and hearing the pins drop. What might you discover about yourself from this odd experience?

Ambiguous Function Assignments

Most of the interventions we will be discussing are best employed after the consulting break, which we will describe in Chapter 10. However, as the opportunity arises in any part of the session, and the timing seems right, you may wish to interject some of these "stronger" influencing techniques. There is no hard and fast rule that tells you when to employ these methods. Knowing when and how to intervene is, of course, the art of counseling, and you must bring your artistic sensibilities to the session.

The ambiguous function assignment is called a "directive" because you are suggesting that your client do something definite. However, there are two elements about the directive that make your client experience the assignment as unusual and ambiguous. First, the assignment seems paradoxical or absurd in light of the goal for the task, and, second, you don't give reasons for the assignment. Your client must try to make sense of it on his or her own.

You know the old joke in which the patient comes to the doctor, lifts his arm, and complains, "It hurts when I do this." The doctor advises, "Well, don't do that." In this scenario, the doctor has offered a straightforward and logical solution to the problem of the client's pain. This is often how people go about solving their problems at the first-order change level. In other words, "It hurts when I do this, so I'm just not going to do this . . . but I can't help it." Persistently attempting to apply the logical, but failed, solution eventually produces a sense of helplessness. Not only do people still have the pain, but they feel incapable of changing the situation. They believe that even more heroic measures, such as psychoanalysis, medication, hospitalization, or surgery, must be taken to solve their problem.

Ambiguous function assignments can throw the problem definition into chaos, leading to a reorganization in which the problem is no longer seen as a problem. Lankton and Lankton (1986) proposed that ambiguous function assignments disrupt habitual thought patterns, cause the client to think more deeply, increase emotional arousal, stimulate the client's search for alternative solutions, and make the process more personally meaningful.

You can offer an ambiguous function assignment by first stimulating your client's interest. Introduce the assignment with a metaphor or cryptic introductory statement. Your voice tone and expression will convey the seriousness of the task, so that the client will want to listen with "compelling expectancy," rather than take it as a joke. The client might occasionally ask, "Are you serious?" and you honestly indicate that you are.

Cade and O'Hanlon (1993) have offered some examples of ambiguous function assignments that were taken from the work of Milton Erickson. In one case, a couple who continually fell to arguing, even though they made conscious attempts not to, were told that, as soon as they began to argue, they were to go to the bathroom, where the husband would remove his clothing and the wife was to sit, fully clothed, on the toilet. They could then go ahead with the argument. Apparently, they complied and reduced the frequency of their arguing.

Another example of an ambiguous function assignment involved telling a child who was a thumb-sucker to perform the behavior better. The therapist coached the child on how to make thumb-sucking even more disgusting to the parents, while the parents had, in the meantime, agreed to say nothing to the child about thumb-sucking for several weeks. The result was a reduction in thumb-sucking.

Cade and O'Hanlon (1993) also described the case of a 13-year-old girl, whose elderly parents were constantly checking on her because they saw her as untrustworthy, aggressive, lazy, uncooperative, and unhelpful. Initially, the girl expressed little interest in the family counseling sessions until the therapist asked if she were interested in trying to trick her parents. She was directed to do several things during the next couple of weeks that she knew would please her parents, but she was to do these behaviors in such a way that the parents could not detect that she was doing them. If asked, she was also not to confess to her parents that she had done these things. The parents were given the task of finding out each time that she had engaged in one of these "parent pleasing" behaviors and to keep a log of each discovered behavior. They could discuss their findings with each other, but not with their daughter. When the girl was seen alone at the beginning of the next session, she reported that the family atmosphere had greatly improved, but acknowledged that she had not carried out any secret tricks. However, the parents brought in a long list of "parent pleasing" behaviors they believed that they had detected.

Listening in on Several Sessions

Let's return to the story from the beginning of this chapter. You may need to review it before reading the conclusion below. As you read on, notice not only how the client changes, but also how the therapist's thinking is affected when they embark on an ambiguous and paradoxical experience together.

As the weeks of play therapy went on, Jordan became convinced that Mike did not have Childhood Psychosis NOS, whatever that was, at all. Mike certainly was a strange and daffy little guy, and from the way he giggled and failed to make eye contact, Jordan could see how he didn't fit anyone's idea of a normal kid. But Mike's thought processes seemed to be intact; he was quite compliant and orderly in his play. Mike never attempted to cut off the heads of the toy animals or to try any funny stuff with the anatomically correct dolls. He told Jordan that he liked to watch baseball on television, and he knew all the names, and most of the batting averages, of the players on the Atlanta Braves. Jordan asked Mike if he had played baseball, and he said that no one would play with him. So, Jordan and Mike dug into some boxes in the back of the playroom and pulled out two baseball gloves, a bat, and a baseball.

Jordan said that this change of treatment method was as much a relief for him as it was for Mike. After weeks in the playroom, Jordan could hardly stand to hear himself saying things like, "And now I see you are interested in playing with the BoBo doll" or "You'd really like to knock all those blocks down." Let's face it . . . Jordan was as clueless as Mike was. But baseball! There was something Jordan knew something about. So they sneaked out the back door of the mental health center like two kids playing hooky, and walked into the warmth of the Georgia afternoon. They could smell the newly cut grass and feel the humid air sticking to their skin as a whisper of a breeze went by. It was definitely baseball weather! They took their positions. Jordan threw the ball gently to Mike. As the ball aired its way toward him, Mike giggled, gazed up at the heavens, covered his torso with his arms, and crossed his legs like someone who really had to go to the bathroom. The ball fell with a dull thud at his feet. The kid needed work.

Jordon is not sure exactly when it dawned on him. It seemed to come on slowly, imperceptibly. He began to understand, as he and this little boy played catch in the back yard of the mental health center, that everyone on Mike's case had been looking in the wrong direction. Instead of seeing him as a damaged, psychotic child, Jordan began to view him as merely "uncivilized." Mike just didn't seem to know that you are supposed to look other people in the eye when you are with them, or that you don't giggle when they want to have a serious conversation with you. Mike hadn't learned any of the ways of being with people that we expect all children to pick up automatically. Suddenly, Jordan felt confident that if Mike could learn some of these behaviors, he wouldn't be "crazy" anymore.

Baseball is a game of rules. So Jordan told Mike what their rules would be. First, Jordan wouldn't throw him the ball unless Mike looked Jordan in the eyes and asked him to throw the ball. Second, because baseball is a serious game, Mike would not giggle. Third, they would not move on to batting practice until Mike got good at the rules for catching the ball. So they began.

The results were amazing! In a few weeks, the social worker began to comment on Mike's improvement, and she told Jordan that the new foster parents were growing quite fond of Mike and had requested that he stay with them permanently. Indeed, Mike was beginning to act like a normal kid. After a couple of months, the Department of Social Services suggested that he didn't need to return to the mental health center anymore. A mild wave of disappointment swept over Jordan. It was then that he realized that he had kept Mike in what they referred to as "therapy" much longer than necessary, and that this was obviously because he had enjoyed their baseball experience so much. "Countertransference" is what therapists call this phenomenon.

During the next school year, Mike was reevaluated by the school psychologist and placed in a regular classroom, where he did well academically. He also made some friends, and was invited to play in games because of his newfound physical skills and coordination. Jordan imagines that, today, Mike is living a happy, normal life and that he might even occasionally get down to Atlanta to see a Braves game.

So that's how the counselor cured childhood psychosis with a baseball. It just goes to show you that if you label a kid something bad and look for the behaviors that go with it, you just may find them. On the other hand, if you see a kid as normal and help him toward better solutions for his problems, he might turn into someone who is mentally healthy . . . and maybe even a pretty good baseball player.

Reflecting Questions

1. If you were to make up a moral for this story, what would it be?
2. What did Jordon do with this child that was therapeutic?
3. How did Jordon "break the rules" so that Mike could learn them?

Paradox as Confusion

Paradoxes have intrigued philosophers, mathematicians, and poets since the beginnings of humanity. Thousands of years ago, Lao Tse wrote, "A wise man, having given away all he had, is rich indeed." In one of his sonnets, Shakespeare proclaimed, "Death once dead, there's no more dying then." Frankl even commented on American history to point out another paradox of life, "Though the Declaration of Independence declares that we all have the right to pursue happiness, happiness cannot be attained by pursuit, it ensues" (Frankl, 1969).

Even if you don't intentionally use paradox in your work, when you look carefully, you will notice that paradoxes abound in counseling. One fundamental paradox is that clients come to you seeking your counsel, but you rarely offer them advice. Another example is that the harder your clients may try to force themselves to relax, the more tense they become. In couples counseling, the more one partner nags, the less likely is the other to comply. Paradoxes can vex, confuse, and annoy us, while, at the same time, capture our attention like an itch we can't scratch. According to Watzlawick, Beavin, and Jackson (1967):

> [T]here is something in the nature of paradox that is of immediate pragmatic and even existential import for all of us; paradox not only can invade interaction and affect our behavior and our sanity but it also challenges our belief in the consistency, and therefore the ultimate soundness of our universe. (p. 18)

On the other hand, people often greet the problem caused by a paradox with amusement and delight. Semantical paradoxes (called antinomies), such as "I am lying," appear at first glance to present no problem. But if people claim to be lying, then they are telling the truth *only* if they are lying. And if they are indeed lying, then you cannot believe the truth of what they are saying—that they are lying. As you read the previous sentences, you may have experienced a momentary confusion, and you may have smiled (or frowned!) as you found yourself on, as they say, "the horns of a dilemma." Getting into a paradox is a bit like falling into an endless loop. Usually, the only way out is to break the implicit rule that compels you to stick with the problem until it is solved. A paradox is insoluble in the conventional manner.

Don't read this sentence! You see?—in order to comply with the previous sentence, you had to violate its injunction. That is, you had to read it. It would appear there is no escape. Carl Rogers (in May, 1983) had the following to say about one of the paradoxes of human experience:

> It is my conviction that a part of modern living is to face the paradox that, viewed from one perspective, man is a complex machine. . . . On the other hand, in another dimension of his existence, man is subjectively free; his personal choice and responsibility account for his own life; he is in fact the architect of himself. . . . If in response to this you say, "But these views cannot both be true," my answer is, "This is a deep paradox with which we must learn to live." (p. 19)

Therapeutic Paradox

The use of paradox has been a controversial topic in the therapeutic literature. Strategic therapists tend to use it frequently and blatantly. On the other hand, most brief therapists are much more conservative and subtle in their use of paradoxical techniques. Interventions with paradoxical techniques have a long and colorful history, yet today some counselors are either unaware of them, or are suspicious of their use. We believe that paradox can be a valuable tool when it is timely, intended only for the benefit of the client, and the counselor has established strong credibility with the client to warrant offering a paradoxical intervention.

Alfred Adler, in 1914, was the first person in Western civilization to write about the therapeutic use of paradox (Mozdzierz, Macchitelli, & Lisiecki, 1976). Adler believed that counselors should take care to avoid power struggles with clients, and should instead side with client resistances—preceding by decades Erickson's notion of utilization. Adler would often prescribe the symptom, encouraging the client to practice doing the symptom better, rather than attempting to eliminate it. Dunlap (1928) employed this technique with clients, calling it "negative practice." This technique is paradoxical in that the apparently reasonable response to a symptom is to fight it and try to stop it. Adler found that, if he gave the client permission not only to have a symptom, but to embellish and refine it, the symptom came under the client's control and grew weaker.

When a client has a perceived problem, he or she has two concerns. The first, of course, is the problem itself. The second, and perhaps more frustrating, is that the client has tried everything he or she can think of that, logically, should eliminate the problem. Every attempted solution has failed, each time confirming not only that the problem is serious, but also that the client is helpless in the face of it. This is what the theorists at the Brief Therapy Center (BTC) meant when they stated that the many attempts at solution are usually part of the problem. Therefore, abandoning solutions and practicing the problem may actually serve to bring the problem back under the control of the client. Of course, on the face of it, this solution makes no logical sense. That is why it is called paradoxical.

Adler would also sometimes predict a relapse, stating that although the client might be experiencing improvement, he or she would inevitably backslide. Students of behaviorism know that when we are attempting to extinguish a behavior, at some point the behavior will "spontaneously recover." Clients will, therefore, often report that the treatment has failed because the symptomatic behavior has returned. Predicting a relapse is based on our knowledge of the spontaneous recovery, and makes good sense as a way of preventing client disappointment. Predicting a relapse makes the counselor appear to be a good prognosticator of behavior. Instead of a relapse weakening the counselor's credibility in the eyes of the client, predicting the relapse tends to increase the counselor's credibility.

A variant of the "liar paradox" above is when the counselor says to the client, "You can't believe anything that I say" (Hayes & Melancon, 1989). This statement seems, on the face of it, to weaken the credibility of the counselor. But a logical analysis of this declaration indicates that it is self-contradictory and means, "Believe me when I tell you not to believe me." However, at a fundamental level and from a phenomenological perspective, it is also a true statement, because whatever the counselor says about the client's world will have to be at least slightly off the mark. Only the client can correctly say anything about his or her unique and personal world.

Another paradoxical device sometimes used by counselors is to declare helplessness. The paradox is that the client comes for help, and the counselor is saying, "I can't help you." Clients are not, as a rule, enthusiastic about the idea that they will have to somehow change in order to resolve their situation. If your clients do not wish to change, if you attempt to change them you only develop a power struggle, and the net result is that they will not change. Furthermore, even if your clients wish to change, your answers, which are not those of your clients, ultimately will not work. Declaring help-lessness places the responsibility on your clients for both the motivation and the strat-egy for change. What you are really saying is, "I can't help you, but I can help you help yourself." Openly declaring this paradox decreases the possibility of a power struggle and assigns agency to your clients.

Bornstein, Krueger, and Cogswell (1989) discussed the technique of cautioning the client against changing. This is known as restraining. Although a client may feel de-moralized by the apparent unalterability of a problem, this sense of permanence is not without its advantages—predictability, security and certainty do have their attractions. Change, however, can be threatening because it involves the unknown and offers no guarantee that the future will be any better. If your clients experience themselves as changing, they are giving up the cozy sense of familiarity that they currently have for the uncertain prospect of a positive resolution. The technique of restraining addresses your client's ambivalent feelings about change and it may also serve as a good reminder to yourself that you should not be working harder than your clients.

The restraining paradox is one of the techniques that has come from Milton Erickson's notion of utilizing the reluctance of the client (Watzlawick, Weakland, & Fisch, 1974). Some clients come ready to play the game of "Why don't you. . . . Yes, but . . ." with the counselor. This game was originally described by Eric Berne (1964), but everyone knows it well. It begins when someone complains to you of a problem or concern, and implies that he or she is asking your advice. You may believe that you see a way out of the situation, and, in order to be helpful, you offer your solution. The com-plaining person then responds by telling you that he or she has already tried that, or gives several contextual reasons why your solution would not work. Consequently, you then work even harder to come up with a better idea than had originally occurred to you. But instead of reaching a resolution, the process merely becomes a first-order change merry-go-round that all helpers, at one time or another, have found themselves riding. Sound familiar? No matter how many good ideas you come up with, the complainant can always add new information about the situation, proving that each of your solutions will fail. The end result of this game is that the complainant always wins, and goes off seeking a wiser person than you, or decides to quit counseling. Meanwhile, you are left feeling incompetent or angry, or both. The second-order change option for this game is to "ask the (only apparently absurd) question, 'Why should you change?' " (p. 134).

We should note that viewing this type of interaction as a game is simply a way of making it clear. The complainant does not know that he or she is playing a game. In fact, what he or she is actually experiencing is intense discouragement, because everything has been tried and no one can come up with a solution that will work.

In restraining the client, you suggest that a drastic change in the client will bring about a jarring, and perhaps disastrous, effect on the client's world. The ripple effect of such a change will affect all the client's relationships, his or her values will change so that things now prized may no longer be important, and a general dissatisfaction with the status quo will result. The client is advised that, if he or she still intends to go ahead and change, the change should be undertaken very slowly. This "go slow" admonition could also be coupled with a "giving in" suggestion. Giving in to the symptoms that the client is trying to avoid sometimes eliminates the catastrophic fantasies associated with them, such as, "If I don't quit this pretty soon, then everything is doomed."

Prescribing the Symptom

We have previously pointed out that there are two levels of difficulty that clients experience when they come for counseling. This principle is important enough to warrant restating it here. At the first level of concern, clients are troubled by whatever they have defined as the problem. At the second level, clients are vexed by the fact that they have attempted several logical or common-sense solutions that have not worked, leaving them feeling helpless. Simply put, not only do they have a problem, but they can't help having the problem. The clients then feel defeated and discouraged. As Haley (1973) put it, "When a person has a symptom, by definition, he is indicating that he cannot help himself. His behavior is involuntary" (p. 24). All attempts to solve the problem have only served to teach clients that they are indeed helpless to change the situation, so why try? This is the essence of Seligman's (1994) concept of "learned helplessness." Furthermore, your clients now live in dread that the problem will happen and bring all those negative feelings—at both levels—with it. This adds the element of anticipatory anxiety.

In order to deal with such situations, Victor Frankl, as early as 1925, began to experiment with therapeutic paradox, eventually developing a technique he called the "paradoxical intention" (Ascher, 1989).

> [H]e suggested that individuals actively court the very behavior of which they wished to rid themselves. Accordingly, a person who remained at home fearing a possible heart attack would be encouraged to travel far from home, to increase cardiac rate, and to "provoke a heart attack." [Provided, of course, a medical examination has ruled out a cardiac condition!] . . . When an individual is able to employ the procedure in the recommended fashion, anticipatory anxiety is reduced, as are its deleterious effects on behavior. (p. 4)

The paradoxical intention involves prescribing the symptom. You ask your client to have the symptom or to create the problem at will. If your client can do the problem deliberately, then the problem may come under the client's control. If so, then the client's level-two feelings may be reduced. He or she is no longer helpless in the face of the problem, and sitting around anticipating its occurrence is no longer necessary. The client may, as a result, begin to feel a sense of control of the level-one problem.

As you learned in Chapter 1, Gregory Bateson's original Palo Alto group came up with the theory of the "double-bind" as an explanation of mental illness (Bateson, Jackson, Haley, & Weakland, 1956). This is the "damned if you do; damned if you don't" theory of how we sometimes experience our options. Later, the MRI group began to use the double-bind theory in helpful ways. They designed the therapeutic double-bind, in which the client is given a paradoxical prescription or directive that, if the client complies he or she may get better, and if the client resists, he or she may get better. Such situations are often referred to as "win–win." This description fits Milton Erickson's notion of utilization: if you suspect that clients will resist your directive, give them permission to resist: set the situation up so that they can resist—and if they do, they may benefit. The important thing to remember about the use of all confusion and paradoxical techniques is that you are not trying to get clients to see the error of their ways. In addition, you are not trying to provide the client with "an insight." Haley (1973) characterized insight interpretations as "absurdly reductionistic, like summarizing a Shakespearian play in a sentence" (p. 29).

Dolan (1985) used what she called a "Paradoxical Attendance Contract" with clients who request and apparently need counseling help, but who persistently fail to show up for sessions. The common-sense approach to this resistance might be to ask the client why he or she misses appointments, to instruct the client on the importance of keeping appointments, or to threaten to terminate with the client if he or she fails to show up again. Dolan takes an entirely different tack. She offers a paradoxical "Therapy Attendance Contract." In this contract, she cautions the client not to schedule more appointments than the client feels are needed. She further insists that the client must listen to his or her own needs. Therefore, if the client misses a scheduled appointment, the client is asked to wait a certain number of days before attending the next appointment. She ends the contract with the following rationale: "This will ensure that you do not inadvertently attend appointments more frequently than you feel you should" (p. 186). The number of days the client is asked to wait before attending another session is based on the average amount of days the client is usually absent after missing an appointment.

If the client "resists" coming to sessions, then this behavior is framed as taking care of himself or herself. If the client does not wish to have to wait the allotted time between sessions, then the client will come regularly. Either way, the guilt and anticipatory anxiety of having to face the counselor and coming up with a plausible excuse is eliminated and the rapport between counselor and client is increased.

Using This Tool

Divide into groups of three. One of you volunteers to share some concern that you would like to change, but have been unable to. Another volunteers to listen, understand, and validate (LUV), while also using one of the paradoxical suggestions. The third person serves as the recorder, who observes the activity and leads the feedback discussion.

A Caveat on the Use of Paradox

Paradoxical techniques seem to work best with clients who are reluctant or who have defined their problems as being out of their control. Keep in mind, however, that the use of paradox is often a shocking experience for clients, and you may run the risk of losing your client's trust. On the face of it, paradox seems deceptive. If clients think that you are trying to "pull a fast one" or "get over on" them, you may find that they will be more wary of you than before.

In our opinion, counselor-designed paradoxes should be used sparingly and only as a last resort. Living paradoxes, such as "the more important a good performance is to you, the more likely you are to mess it up," will occur spontaneously in conversation with clients and can be most effective. In such cases, the paradox will fit the client's content at the time it is being produced. On the other hand, when people are in crisis, they do not respond well to paradox or ironic observations of their situation. You should avoid such techniques with someone in the throes of a personal disaster. Timing is everything!

Many authors offer lists of situations in which the use of paradox is contraindicated (Duncan, 1989). "Usually such lists include crisis situations, situational violence, grief, suicide, and psychosis, to mention a few" (p. 340). Duncan, however, does not believe that paradox should be approached as cautiously as we believe it should:

> Paradox is not something a therapist does to manipulate or trick people out of their problem. It is exactly the view that paradox is a thing to do to "resistant" clients that results in such contraindication lists. It is also this view of paradox that can lead to arrogances of power and control. (p. 341)

You may initially find yourself feeling that the use of paradox is above your skill level. Our advice is to listen for living paradoxes in your conversations with clients, and when you are reflecting on your intervention plan between sessions, try to think of a counselor-constructed paradoxical technique that could be used with that client—whether you would actually use it or not. On the other hand, if you find that you are quite good at coming up with paradoxical ideas, be careful that you do not employ them with clients for the thrill of doing so. Paradox can be such a powerful technique that it sometimes leads to gaming with clients and getting "one up" on them. Any use of paradox should always be approached consciously and attempted only for the benefit of the client. If you find that you love using paradox and are exhilarated when your paradox "traps" the client, then you must consider that you may have a countertransference problem.

Using this Tool

Form a small group with three colleagues. One of you volunteers to read the part of Emma and another person reads the part of Hector in the case presented below.

Imagine how they might act in the circumstances portrayed, and try to capture the intensity of their emotions as you read their parts. One of the remaining volunteers serves as the counselor and the other will observe, record, and time the role-play. Then the counselor should try at least one and perhaps more of the "butterfly perturbations" in this chapter. Lastly the group would discuss and give feedback to the counselors.

STORY

Maryanne, a counselor in a community mental health clinic, is meeting with a couple for the first time. From intake information and referral files from other agencies, she has learned that they have a history of involvement with various community service organizations. Hector and Emma had been together for about 3 years and had been previously court-referred to a pastoral counselor and then to a family therapist. Their latest attempt at staying together was to enroll in a community marriage enrichment program.

Maryanne introduces herself and begins her brief first-session orientation remarks when she is interrupted by Emma.

Emma: Here we go again. (*to Hector, her voice dripping with sarcasm*) Well, hotshot, why don't you tell the lady why we're here.

Hector: (*mumbles*) Who cares?

Emma: (*her voice rising in anger*) Tell her what a loser you are, go ahead. Look (*to Maryanne*), I don't know what good you can do, we've been to social workers, counselors, and then to that dumb couples group. You're looking at the problem right there (*points to Hector*).

Hector: (*sighs, says nothing and looks forlornly out the window*)

Counselor: (*looking and sounding confused*) Wow, something really awful must have happened between you two since last . . . let's see (*glancing through some papers in a manila folder*) Wednesday. Yes, Wednesday was when you went to the marriage enrichment group, right?

Emma: What do you mean? (*sounding slightly confused herself*)

Counselor: It says here that the group leaders couldn't understand the reason for your dropping out since you two were doing extremely well in the group. I wonder what the mix-up is.

Emma: Oh, that. All the couples did this stupid communications exercise, and I guess we were the best. But, it didn't mean anything 'cause in the real world, that don't mean squat.

Counselor: Oh, I see, you would like to find a way for the communication exercise, or something like it, to work for you and Hector in your day-to-day lives.

Hector: (*coming alive for the first time*) She "communicates" pretty good already—in fact all the time. What we really need is a "shut-up" exercise instead.

Emma: (*looking surprised*) Well what do you know, it can talk!

Hector: Hell, yes I can talk when I get a chance.

Counselor: (*Emma scoots forward in her chair, gets an agitated look on her face and seems ready to cut loose, but before she can, the counselor interrupts.*) Yes, yes, I think I see what you're both saying. (*Pausing, leaning forward, and looking like she's really concentrating, trying hard to understand, she talks very slowly and with a dramatic effect.*) Hector, you think Emma is a good communicator—talker as you say. Emma, you think Hector is a good listener and I guess both of you would like to find a way to get your spouse to help you get better at what you are already good at.

From what I've read in your file, you two have tried lots of things to try to stay together. What a hassle that must be. Trying to get strangers to understand your relationship. I don't know how you can keep doing it. I wish more couples I work with were as committed to each other as you are. You must really love each other a lot! (*Hector and Emma both look stunned. They look at each other and grin sheepishly.*)

Hector: (*slumps back in his chair, his posture and manner conveying defensiveness*) I don't know about that, lady, you sure you are not blowing smoke? We fight all the time, or haven't you noticed?

Counselor: Yes, I see what you are saying, I think. You find it hard to believe that someone, such as myself, could look beyond the times that you used to argue and see the deep caring you have for each other. I don't know for sure, but the way you look at each other reminds me a lot of people who love each other. (*pauses as Hector and Emma give each other a quick glance*) Maybe you are like a lot of young couples who would like to get better at arguing, you know, do it better.

Emma: (*to Hector smiling and shaking her head*) Baby, I think you are right, she might be blowing smoke. (*The counselor smiles and Hector and Emma seem gen-*

uinely amused as they both laugh long and loud. Finally, Emma looks at the counselor and asks a question in a much softer voice.) Are you serious, you think that there's a good way to argue?

Counselor: (*She nods her head.*) I sure am!

Emma: This I have to hear.

Hector: Yeah, me too.

SEGUE TO CHAPTER 10

Think about a time when you had a concern and needed to talk about it. You asked someone to listen, but instead of listening, the person seemed to be waiting for you to stop talking, so that he or she could offer you advice. Did you find yourself resisting the advice, even if it made sense?

CHAPTER 10

The Reflecting Team, Consulting Break, and Offering Suggestions

"Find out what they want to do and advise them to do it."
Harry Truman

"Advice is seldom welcome, and those who need it the most, like it the least."
Lord Chesterfield

Chapter Goals

Reading about and experiencing the ideas in this chapter will help you to understand the following concepts:

- A reflecting team can add a powerful feedback experience to your counseling session.
- The consulting break can serve several useful functions.
- Suggestions are different from advice because they are more subtle and tailored to the client.

Reading about and practicing the tools in this chapter will help you to learn these valuable skills:

- Being an effective reflecting team member.
- Using a consulting break well.
- Designing successful suggestions.

Story

As she ground her way home through the grid-locked Friday afternoon traffic, Judy tried to have pleasant thoughts about the upcoming weekend. She was still feeling the afterglow from the regional meeting she had attended. Everyone liked her ideas on the new project and afterward she received high praise from her boss and co-workers.

If only she were as successful at other things. It was as if she lived in two completely different worlds. Hardworking, capable, creative, and a wonderful manager at work but, according to her teenaged daughter Susan, a cruel, nagging witch at home. Maybe she and Susan would be able to work out their problems soon and there wouldn't be any more scenes over money, clothes, boyfriends, curfew, homework, grades, meals, bedtime, visitors—the list was endless. Judy and her own mother had disagreed over similar issues 25 years ago, but there had been no screaming, swearing, or running away back then.

Two weeks ago tonight, Judy had muttered the hoary ultimatum, "As long as you are living in this house, young lady, you'll obey my rules." A 20-minute shouting match ensued, followed by a 2-hour search through the neighborhood for her daughter. Things had been quieter but chilly between them ever since.

As Judy pulled off the interstate and drew closer to her neighborhood, a numbing resignation began creeping over her like fog through a mountain hollow. Things would only get worse. She had tried everything she could think of and had spent hours talking on the telephone about these problems with her friends, co-workers, mother, and sister. If Susan were only like her older brother Mark, Judy told her confidantes, things would be fine. He's the perfect child. He never complains about what other families have. He reads all the time and makes good grades, does his chores—and sometimes Susan's, too—and only gets mad when Susan teases him about being "the golden child."

Judy had wondered many times what things would be like between her and her 13-year-old daughter if Ken had not left them. Her eyes began to moisten, and she missed her turn. She swore angrily and, for an instant, was tempted to get back on the interstate and hit a couple of "happy hours" out by the airport. But she sighed and felt her shoulders slump forward as they once again took on the heavy weight of responsibility. Judy arrived home to an empty house. According to a hastily scribbled note on the refrigerator, Susan had made plans for an overnight stay at her best friend's house, and Mark was away on a weekend camping trip with the Boy Scouts. She began to worry if she should have given her permission for Mark to go since the weather was turning cold. She also wondered how she could check up on Susan without starting World War III.

Someone had left the television on and Oprah was just giving a recap of that day's show. Apparently, the program had been about the conflict between teenage daughters and their mothers. With a little time to kill before the end of the program, Oprah gazed at the audience and asked them how many of them filled their own cavities at home without bothering to go to the dentist. Two or three hands went up and everyone else laughed and shook their heads. "Anybody overhaul your own automobile transmissions when they go out?" A similar reaction from the audience. Then in a slow deliberate voice, she looked into the camera and asked everyone in the studio audience and the millions of television viewers how many of them knew their families were in need of some professional help but had tried the "do-it-yourself" approach instead? She concluded with a quiet thought, "Think about it."

As the audience clapped its approval and the credits rolled, Judy realized that it wasn't just Susan who needed help—they all did. Within a few days, Judy, Mark, and Susan were referred to a family counselor by her pastor. Judy did most of the talking—and crying—during the first half of the session as she described her concerns and frustrations. Susan sulked, but grudgingly answered the questions that the counselor asked her directly. Mark often stared at his shoes and regularly insisted that things weren't all that bad and besides, his mother and sister never have gotten along anyway and they probably never will. After they had met for about 35 minutes, the counselor invited the family to take a break and to observe a reflecting team discuss their observations of the session so far.

Reflecting Questions

1. What are your impressions of these three clients?
2. What are your recommendations regarding intervention?
3. How might you describe the session?

OVERVIEW

This chapter offers ideas and tools for dealing with the latter portion of the counseling session. First, we discuss the reflecting team—a strategy for involving other counselors in your work to increase its impact. We urge you to set up such a team and to observe for yourself the benefits that can result. If you are working alone, you may wish to employ the consulting break. This technique involves leaving the room for a few minutes to either consult with an available colleague or to reflect on your own. During this break, you can decide on a therapeutic suggestion to offer your client.

Suggestions are not the same as advice. Advice is when you "just tell 'em." Suggestions are more subtle and tailored to your client's style. We discuss this important difference and present guidelines for offering successful suggestions.

IDEAS

The Reflecting Team

If you are lucky, you will be working in a setting where colleagues are available for consultation on your counseling cases. Or if you are even luckier, your colleagues can be watching behind a one-way mirror, able to consult on an immediate basis. No counselor should ever attempt to work completely alone, even if this means simply consulting with a colleague after the session. Not only do you miss many cues and dynamics that are immediately happening with your clients, but you are also unable to maintain a reflective stance when you are absorbed in the moment-to-moment counseling relationship. You have probably already noticed that being there with the client is quite different from watching the session on videotape. Later, you see things you were unaware of before, you can make sense of things that had you stuck or baffled in the session, and you are better able to formulate a plan once you have the luxury of a bit of psychological distance from the event.

Think back to a time when you went to see a movie and found yourself totally absorbed—living it as though you were the protagonist, losing all sense of your surroundings, and being emotionally overwhelmed by the experience. For you, that was a truly effective movie. It did what all movies should—it involved you totally. However, when friends asked, "How did you like the movie?" you found it hard to find words to convey the depth of your experience to them. It was one of those "you had to be there" experiences. But maybe you decided to go to see the movie a second time because you hoped to recapture the experience that you originally had. It didn't quite work, did it? Somehow, the second viewing seemed to have lost some of its power to involve you. You may have felt disappointed and may have mourned the loss of that first-time experience. Unfortunately, that's the way it is with all "first times."

The good news, however, is that the second time you see a movie, you see it from more of a distance—with some perspective. This change makes it possible to observe things you could not see the first time. You may, for example, notice how well the dialogue is written, how well the characters are developed in the script, the special devices or techniques used by the director to make the experience real for the viewers; or you might begin to grasp a subtext or symbolism in the story that completely eluded you the first time around.

Both these levels of experience are important in counseling. Being fully involved with your client will help you make that vital connection between the client's world and your own. You will intuitively understand and gracefully convey your empathy. Unencumbered by self-consciousness and doubts, you will find yourself really listening—rather than merely waiting to talk. But at this level your ability to analyze what is dynamically important in your relationship with your client is lost. Fully engaged, you cannot reflect on where you should be going next, and what strategy might be the most beneficial for your client's growth. Of course, as you develop as a counselor, you will find yourself better able to move back and forth between these levels as the counseling session is unfolding. But this switching of levels is like the Necker cube you saw in Chapter 2—you can never see both faces of the event at the same time, so it is likely that you will miss something from the other level at any given moment. If you are analyzing, you are not empathizing. When you are totally involved, you are not understanding fully what is happening.

As you practice the techniques in this book, they will become second nature to you, and you will not have to think as much about how and when to use them. The awkwardness you may now feel in the use of new techniques will eventually fade. This emerging comfort will allow you to really "be with" your client. But you will also find that, even if you possess the most amazing set of skills, there are times—many times!—when you experience yourself as stuck, confused, and uncertain what to do next with your clients. At such times, you may be able to grab a colleague in the hall for quick discussion, present your case at a staff meeting, go back to the books and study, or find a quiet spot and simply reflect. All these are useful options, but Friedman (1997) suggested that the most helpful and, paradoxically, even the most cost-effective option would be to enlist colleagues as members of a reflecting team.

The purpose of a reflecting team is to supply new information, from another perspective, to the client and the counselor. As an adjunct to therapy, the team may watch through the one-way mirror and phone in to the counseling room when they see something the counselor misses, or they may be available for immediate consultation when the counselor feels stuck. In the latter case, the counselor takes a break, leaves the room, speaks with the team for a few minutes, and then returns to the counseling session. This technique is often crucial when the counselor is working with a family, a situation in which so many dynamics are at work that it would be impossible for any one person to attend to all of them. The session may also be designed so that a break is scheduled, whereupon the counselor and client(s) leave the room and take up a position behind the one-way mirror, while the team sits in the counseling room, discussing their observations of the session they have been watching.

Berlyne (1960), Fiske & Maddi (1961), Hebb (1946), and Hunt (1965) suggested that when people are confronted with large amounts of novel or unexpected information, they become overwhelmed and distressed. However, when given information that is neither too novel nor discrepant with their experience and expectations, these same people will be receptive to altering their points of view. As we discussed in Chapter 4, such "news of difference" (Bateson, 1972) inspires people to expand their views, consider novel or previously denied information, and soften up old rigid categories. Tom Anderson (1987), who first wrote of the use of a reflecting team in therapy, designed the reflecting team's intervention as a way to unstick "stuck systems."

In this approach, a team of counselors observes the session from behind a one-way mirror until a predetermined time—usually about 30 minutes into the interview. Then, the team exchanges places with the client and counselor who were in the session. From behind the one-way mirror, the counselor and client now become the observers, while the team discusses what they observed. Of course, the team members, being savvy in the ways of brief counseling, focus on the client's strengths and resources as they talk about the case. The format also contributes to the power of this technique in several crucial ways. First, exchanging places allows the client to gain some perspective by observing the reflecting team from a distance. Second, the reflecting team serves the function of an "exotic audience" (White & Epston, 1990) that we described in Chapter 8. Finally, no longer being required to participate in the interaction, the client can quietly focus on "hearing in new ways and being 'captured' by new information" (Friedman, 1997, p. 97).

Reflecting teams are a powerful brief counseling intervention technique. In fact, Michael White (1995) claimed that one reflecting team session was worth about five sessions of regular counseling. Many clients have reported to us later that observing their reflecting teams after a break was the single most potent event in their counseling sessions.

The Consulting Break

For most counselors who have been traditionally trained, the idea of taking a break toward the end of the session may seem awkward and disruptive. It did to us also, until we came to realize the powerful benefits that such a break can provide. If you are working alone—without a reflecting team—some of the benefits can still be captured by employing the consulting break. Most solution-focused theorists offer little in the way of a rationale for the break, but we have found at least three ways in which the break itself can positively affect the counseling session.

First, the break affords you the opportunity to get your thoughts together. When you are in the midst of the session, it is often difficult to reflect on the significance of what your client is saying because you are so involved in the process. Carl Rogers (1965), on his famous "Gloria" videotape, stated that he remembered very little of what had happened during the counseling session after it was over, and only later was he able to recall more of it. The interruption of the session brought about by the break allows you to perform a quick recall or to study notes you took during the session. From this, you can form a plan for the post-break intervention. You then reenter the session in a different state of mind, with your thoughts clarified, and having a clearer sense of what to do.

For your clients, the break offers respite from what can sometimes be an intense experience—a chance to get their feet back under them. It is also a time for the client to consider what has been said. The break can hold the client where he or she is, and keep from "breaking the spell." Clients may leave a typical counseling session and immediately face the distracting demands of the day, which can rob them of the opportunity to reflect on their counseling experience. When the time is up, the client must compose a social face and reenter the everyday world in a more decorous and superficial manner.

Studies of memory have suggested that the formation of new long-term memories takes some time. "Retroactive inhibition"—a new experience eclipsing an older memory—can cause new learnings to vanish before they become part of the client's repertoire. Furthermore, we all know that we must go over something several times before we can "know it by heart." So taking a break, and sitting in silence with one's thoughts, can be a very useful learning event for the client.

Finally, just imagine the power of the dynamics that are set up by the consulting break! Remember the last time you visited your physician with a nonspecific complaint that worried you? You told the doctor your symptoms, which he or she wrote down, and maybe you had a urine analysis and some blood-work performed, or perhaps, an x-ray. Then the doctor leaves the room and you languish in silence, staring at the walls, for what seems an eternity. You begin to perspire as you sit there, semi-nude, with your legs dangling off the examination table. You go over again the pointed questions that the doctor asked during the interview, and you wonder what he or she might have been getting at . . . what diagnosis was being sought. You note that the doctor is taking an unusually long time to return. It must be really bad news, and he or she is trying to think of a way to tell you so that you won't cause a scene in the office. It's just as you suspected—you have only a short time to live! But then, the doctor returns with a big smile, looking over your chart, and says, "Well, everything looks OK."

This dynamic of expectation set up by such a consulting break brings about an emotional arousal and focused attention. The client is eager to hear the news. As a brief counselor, you will deliver news of positive differences and offer a suggestion as to how the client might proceed from this point in time. Because of the way the conditions have been set by the consulting break, there is an increased likelihood that the client will be open to your suggestion.

The Suggestion

A suggestion takes place when someone is influenced by another in what Lozanov (1978) called a "paraconscious" way, meaning that the influence takes place largely out of the awareness of the person being influenced. A direction, on the other hand, is much more explicit and much more easily defied. If people do not wish to follow a direction, they can argue with its feasibility or they can subvert it in ways that they might not even understand. A well-placed suggestion, on the other hand, "sticks" in a person's experience at a level where it cannot be argued and where it may not even be noticed.

When a client comes to you with a concern, he or she will attempt to explain the complaint in reasonable terms. Not to do so would be to complain in an illogical and crazy way—and people do not want to present themselves as "crazy." If you, as the counselor, respond to your clients only at the level of reason and logic, you are missing the level where most of the action takes place. Freud (1900) called it the "primary process" level of thinking. Suggestions, therefore, should be "embedded" rather than detailed explicitly. One way to do this is to wonder aloud about possibilities. Another way is to leave the suggestion open enough so that the client can fill in the gaps. Either way, the technique of suggesting becomes like a Rorschach ink blot onto which the client can project an experience.

Experiencing This Idea

Read the following correspondence between a son and his father. See how embedded messages adds an entirely new dimension of communication between the correspondents.

> Dear Dad,
> $chool i$ really great. I am making lot$ of friend$ and $tudying very hard. With all my $tuff, I $imply can't think of anything I need, $o if you would like, you can ju$t $end me a card, a$ I would love to hear from you.
> Love,
> Your $on
>
> Dear Son,
> I kNOw that astroNOmy, ecoNOmics, and oceaNOgraphy are eNOugh to keep even an hoNOr student busy. Do NOt forget that the pursuit of kNOwledge is a NOble task and that you can never study eNOugh.
> Love,
> Dad

Symptom Substitution?

For decades a dispute has raged between psychoanalysts and behaviorally oriented therapists. Behaviorists say that the client's symptom is the problem, and, therefore its elimination is the goal of therapy. The psychoanalytic therapists believe that merely eliminating symptoms is a superficial approach that fails to get at the "root" of the problem. It's kind of like getting dandelions out of your lawn. If you pull up the part of the plant that is above the surface, you have not solved the problem. The root remains and another blossom will surface. Problems, viewed in this way, are considered to be "deep-seated." This controversy as to whether symptom substitution will occur continues today between the "depth" psychologists and the behavioral psychologists. Shapiro (1994) claimed there is no evidence that supports the notion of symptom substitution. If the symptom or problem is eliminated, then nothing new will take its place. But, unlike the behaviorists, Shapiro also stated that symptom elimination should not be the goal of therapy. "A psychotherapist is not a dentist extracting parts of a personality that are no longer useful as if they were rotted teeth" (p. 6).

Haley (1976) considered all negative symptoms to be patterns of behaviors that maintain the particular ways that people relate to each other. From this perspective, the counselor is not concerned with what has caused the problem—its root—but, rather, what maintains it—its recycling pattern. Change some small aspect of the pattern, and the problem—with its negative consequences—disappears. This creates "the difference that makes a difference." It is the Butterfly Effect and can be applied to any complex system. If you perturb the system, it will change.

The notion of "negentropy" also suggests that living systems are less likely to fall apart when you perturb them than they are to reorganize themselves. In other words, instead of going to pieces, such systems create themselves anew. In humanistic terms, this stance is a belief in growth and health. If a defeating pattern is changed in some small way, then people, families, and organizations will be freed up to function at a healthier level. With some guidance from the counselor, this process will happen automatically. Earlier therapeutic notions of "breakdown" were based on entropy—the idea that everything falls apart and that perturbing it accelerates the process. In complex systems theory, you may not be able to predict how the system will change once it reorganizes, but you can count on something new emerging. If the context for positive change has been established in the counseling relationship, then that "something new" is likely to be positive.

Advice Versus Suggestions

Most of you have been trained, early on, not to give advice as counselors. It's much better, you were instructed, to have your client arrive at his or her own insights, solutions, or conclusions. But on the other hand, if you didn't wish to influence people toward more productive thoughts, more peaceful emotions, and more effective behaviors, you probably wouldn't be in the counseling business. You are not simply an empathic listener. You want to have on impact on your clients, so that they can live happier lives.

The question is how best to make an impact. The most efficient method would be to offer sage advice on how to live life, and then have the client follow your advice to the letter. The problem, of course, is that this approach rarely works. Even if clients do follow your advice, you have robbed them of their own initiative and may have recapitulated old relationship patterns that keep them dependent (Teyber, 2000). Furthermore, hardly anyone qualifies as a sage, and absolutely none of us can be expert enough on someone else's life to offer advice that is completely relevant and helpful.

Orlinsky and Howard (1986) conducted an extensive review of the use of advice and concluded that "advice does not appear to be an aid in psychotherapy" (p. 328). Kleinke (1994) concurred and pointed out the obvious: "Clients can get all the advice they want from acquaintances, friends, and family members. They hardly need to pay a therapist to tell them what to do" (p. 9). Clients will often come to counselors because they believe you will offer superior advice to that of others. If you respond to their request for advice, you will usually find yourself in that "why don't you"–"yes, but" game.

Harry Stack Sullivan (1970), an early contributor to the psychoanalytic literature, decried the therapist whose missionary zeal prompts him or her to impose a personal value system on the client. Sullivan said that there were few things he could think of that were "so harrowing as the occasional psychiatrist who knows a great deal about right and wrong, how things should be done, what is good taste . . ." (p. 214).

Perhaps you have heard the therapist on "talk radio" who calls herself "Dr. Laura." She knows everything about how life should be lived and she freely dispenses gratuitous advice, after hearing about callers' situations for less than a minute or two. These callers seem to fall into two categories: sycophants and combatants. The combatants ask for her advice and then argue with her. She usually dismisses them if they don't accede to her analysis and directives after a couple of iterations. The sycophants lavishly thank her and are treated by her as if they were ignorant children. Either way, while it may make for entertaining talk radio, Dr. Laura is likely to be recapitulating old, established problematic relationship patterns in the lives of these callers, driving yet another nail into their problem-saturated boxes.

We are not saying that you should *never* offer advice to the client. Sometimes a piece of advice at just the right moment can be helpful. But these "just right moments" are rare, and you are much more likely to miss than to be on target. Even well-meant advice is then, for the client, often a bit like getting a pink, fuzzy set of rabbit pajamas (including a sleeping cap with ears and a puffy tail on the trap door behind) for your 13th birthday from your Aunt Martha. (Did you see the movie *A Christmas Story*?) What can you possibly say to Aunt Martha, who has just watched approvingly as you unwrapped this monstrosity? "Just what I always wanted"? When you offer your warm and fuzzy advice, you may place the client in the position of having to be concerned about not hurting your feelings.

Donald Meichenbaum (1990) commented on his own experience with the nature of advice in therapy. He opined that he was at his very best at those times when clients were just one step ahead of him; offering themselves the advice that Meichenbaum would otherwise have given. "And the artfulness of therapy is how to provide the conditions whereby they come up with it" (quoted in Kleinke, 1994, p. 8).

It is this "artfulness" that is, at once, most effective and most difficult to capture in a textbook on counseling. It comes as one of those "you have to be there" moments. However, we will attempt to describe this art as the use of "suggestion" rather than advice. Suggestion is more subtle and generally more effective than advice. Suggestion may be the quintessence of all the counseling skills. When delivered well, it is hypnotic and becomes embedded in the client's schema. Even when a suggestion is delivered without skill, it is more likely to be successful than advice because it is a more gentle and less intrusive way to work with clients.

Implications of These Ideas for the Counselor

The idea of a reflecting team can have significant consequences on your work as a counselor.

- Always seek consultation on your counseling cases. Not only will this action help prevent burnout, it will also clarify your thinking regarding what is taking place in your sessions.
- A reflecting team can offer observations and comments so as to extend and elaborate the therapeutic power of your counseling.
- Since you are not likely to have colleagues available for a reflecting team during every session, you will find it helpful to schedule a break in order to collect your thoughts and to design an after-the-break response.
- Clients will also use the break to reflect on what they have said and to anticipate what your response might be. When you come back into the room with "good news," your clients are primed to hear it.
- When you offer something to the client after the break, it usually should take the form of a suggestion rather than a directive. You usually do not want to place the client in the position of having to either rebel or comply with your direction.

Tools

Successful Reflecting

When you are a member of a reflecting team, your job is to offer a highly concentrated version of brief counseling techniques. Within the space of a few minutes, you acknowledge the client's concerns, identify exceptions, emphasize strengths and resources, use the client's metaphors, and work to deconstruct the client's stagnant portrayals. You can increase your effectiveness as a reflecting-team member by following a few simple guidelines (Friedman, 1997).

First, keep in mind that a client is more likely to hear news of difference when your reflecting team first acknowledges the client's complaints, difficulties, and issues. Like the counselor, as a member of the reflecting team, you must demonstrate that you have listened, understood, and validated the client's concerns. The observing client must see that you and the other members of the reflecting team have an empathic feel for the client's pain and concerns.

Second, you should state your observations in a positive manner. To increase your impact as a reflecting team member, be sure to discuss the client's strengths, resources, and successes. Avoid "hollow compliments" and hackneyed generalizations by basing your comments only on the client's specific actions that you observed during the session, as well as particular information that the client has shared.

Third, state your remarks concerning the client in a tentative manner, rather than authoritatively. Avoid making definite and certain claims regarding the client's personality traits. Instead, begin your remarks with such phrases as "I'm wondering if . . ." or "It may be that . . ." or "Perhaps. . . ."

Fourth, as a member of a reflecting team, you can increase your therapeutic impact by highlighting the exceptions to problem-saturated talk that you noticed. You want to emphasize the times the client was successful, either completely or partially, in coping with the presenting problems. When you do acknowledge the client's concerns, you can add follow-up statements of "finding the pony." For example, during the discussion, you might ask, "How in the world has the client been able to come this far, given the fact that the concern was so much a part of her life?"

Fifth, feel free to talk in the form of metaphors, images, fantasies, and wonderments, rather than assertions of "reality." Whenever possible, you want to expand on the metaphors that the client already used during the session. If these were "problem" metaphors, you can conjecture about an unexpected twist or a positive outcome to the metaphor. You want to use terms, images, themes, or cues that have personal meaning to the client.

Finally, you are most productive when you use your own voice, rather than attempting to speak as an objective observer. "Situate your questions/comments in your own life experience. Be transparent; use ordinary language rather than psychiatric jargon" (Friedman, 1997, p. 100).

As a member of a reflecting team, you perform several vital functions. By speaking metaphorically, you generate images that can intrigue and alter the client's understanding of the situation. By pointing out strengths and resources, you are offering the client a more productive view of self and others. By creating alternative stories, you are opening space for fresh perspectives. And by highlighting the changes you've already observed in the client, you are authenticating the transformation process.

Listening in on a Session

Review the story at the beginning of the chapter. The two members of the reflecting team that observed this family's session now convene to discuss their impressions while the counselor and family members watch and listen.

> **Reflector 1:** I'd like to begin with something that struck me right at the start of the session. There seems to be a lot of stress in this family, especially over the past few months. It looks to me like each family member may be facing different challenges and coping differently with this tension, but it appears that there's plenty of strain and pressure to go around here.

> **Reflector 2:** Yeah, there especially seemed to be some tension and apprehension in the session at the start, as if everyone had a sense of what was at stake here. It looked like even deciding where each of them was going to sit was an important consideration.

> **Reflector 1:** They seemed to take some care to stake out their territory, but it didn't have the feel of a "land rush," where people were competing for the prime acreage. It had more of a feel of a tentative minuet. Did you notice that Mark seemed to be acting the gentleman, allowing the women to enter the room first? Then the daughter and mother had this awkward moment when Susan sat in the middle of this sofa and Judy sat next to her. Susan then gave a little sigh—maybe of exasperation—and then moved over to give herself more space. I would guess that Judy noticed her daughter's reaction, but she let it pass. It was neat to see Susan carving out her own area and to see Judy wisely allowing her daughter to have more space.

> **Reflector 2:** They all probably felt apprehensive about what was going to happen in this session, but the three of them settled in here with a couple of gestures that suggested that they were at this session to deal with some important issues, however irritated they may be with somebody or awkward they may feel as they work out new ways of relating to each other. The fact that they all came together is evidence that they would like things to be better in their family.

> **Reflector 1:** I was impressed by how Susan and Mark dealt with Judy's tears. It was pretty apparent that their mom was upset, but neither of them rushed in to rescue her. I guess they must know that Judy's crying has been an indication of how much she cares about them. I sensed that Susan is committed to becoming who she's meant to be. As she sorts that out, Susan may be making sure that she has the space to do it. And Mark seems to have his emotional antennae up, and he thoughtfully decides not to jump in when his mom and sister are dealing with their issues.

> **Reflector 2:** What you're saying relates to two questions I have. How did Judy manage to get two teenage kids to come with her to counseling? And where do all three of these people get their determination to cope with the loss of a father and

husband, be successful in school and at work, face these arguments with one another, and still forge ahead with their own lives? It's really intriguing to me since we don't often see that kind of determination around here.

Reflector 1:　Yeah, I wonder what answers they will have to your question. You know, at one point, Judy said that she lives in two completely different worlds. In the work world, she feels successful, talented, and confident. It will be really exciting to see how she's going to apply her creativity and managerial skills to deal with these challenges that she now faces in her home world.

Reflecting Questions

1. What metaphors did the reflectors use here?
2. How might you respond to Reflector 1's final statement?
3. If you were the counselor, how might you use this material with the family?

Using This Tool

Meet with three other colleagues to experience the impact of a reflecting team. One of you volunteers to share a personal goal you would like to achieve. Another volunteers to be the counselor. The other two serve as the reflecting team. If you do not have access to a room with a one-way mirror, the reflecting team can sit off to the side to observe the interaction. After the client and therapist have interacted for about 15 or 20 minutes, they switch seats with the reflecting team. The therapist and client then observe as the team members discuss the client they have been watching. The reflecting team should acknowledge the client's concerns, offer positive comments, give observations tentatively, present exceptions, and offer metaphors. Afterward, discuss your reactions to this process from your perspectives as client, therapist, or observer.

Task Assignment

Following the break, you will have to decide whether to simply leave the client with a vague suggestion, or to offer a task that the client might try between this and the next session. Tasks given to clients should maintain the therapeutic momentum of the session and to "carry the work of the therapy session into the client's real life" (Butler & Powers, 1996, p. 238). The best times to offer these tasks are usually after the consulting break and at the end of the session. Successfully assigning a task involves several steps. You should begin by acknowledging how the client has struggled. Next, you should compliment the client's strengths, perseverance, successes, and resilience. After both acknowledging the struggle and complimenting the client, suggest a task and provide a rationale.

Perhaps the most successful task assignment that the BFTC team hit upon was what they called the "Formula First Session Task" (de Shazer in O'Hanlon & Weiner-Davis, 1989). You can suggest this task by saying, for example, "Between now and the next time we meet, I would like you to observe what happens that you would want to have continue to happen."

In a follow-up survey, 50 of 56 clients returned having noticed things that they wished to continue in their lives, and 46 of the 50 described at least one of those things as something new. After giving the "Formula First Session Task," it is crucial that you not ask at the next session, "Did you notice anything?" You should always approach the follow-up interview with presumptive language by saying, "What was one thing you noticed?"

Studies on the formula first session task assignment conducted by Adams, Piercy, and Jurich (1991) found that 60 percent of clients given this task at the end of the first meeting reported that their situation had improved. However, this same study revealed that tasks tailored to the stated problem were equally successful. In another study of the formula first session task assignment, Jordan and Quinn (1994) found that clients generally reported that their situations had improved, their optimism that these concerns would be resolved had increased, and they saw their first session as having been a positive experience.

Delivering Suggestions

So that suggestions do not sound as if you are implying that what is offered will absolutely solve a problem, it is often a better strategy to disclaim them. For example, you can say:

- "This is going to sound strange, but I just had the image of you . . . [the behavior that might bring about the resolution to the problem in graphic detail]." or
- "You know, last night I dreamed that you were . . . [same as above]." or
- "You know, when you were talking about [the concern], I zoned out and I thought you had said . . . [something about the resolution]."

If you are attempting to mystify the client, then you might say something like:

- "It is clear from what you say about . . . [elaborate what the client has said] . . . that what you really want is. . . ."
- "Since you decided to come for counseling, that must also mean that you. . . ."
- "As you continue to talk about this issue, it is obvious that you are searching for the thing you want most to change."

The artfully delivered suggestion is subtle. If it results in a change in clients' viewing or doing, they should think it was their own idea, or they should be encouraged to come up with their own interpretation of what you suggested in the session. For example, the client may say, "You know last week when you said [xxxxx]? I figured out what you were up to. You really wanted me to. . . ." If the client's interpretation sounds like good advice, you show your surprise and say that you had not thought of it exactly that way. It is likely that you hadn't.

The bottom line is that all good suggestions should end up as the client's idea. If you offer them softly, tentatively, and skillfully, they won't be remembered as yours. Your clients will feel certain that it was their own insight that created the new idea, attitude, or behavior.

The metaphor for an effective suggestion is Milton Erickson's "utilization" story of how he got a stubborn cow into the barn. Instead of pulling it forward or pushing it from behind, he grabbed hold of its tail. The cow attempted to get away, and as it did, Erickson steered it in the direction of the barn. Seen this way, it was the cow's will to resist that gave the cow the idea that it wanted to go to the barn (Lankton & Lankton, 1986).

Your suggestions can take many forms. Suggestions can be offered as metaphors, speculations, paradoxes, fantasies and dreams, anecdotes, confusion techniques, oxymorons, and, only occasionally, as direct advice (Lankton & Lankton, 1986). You can offer suggestions in a soft tone of voice, with a shift of emphasis on the part that you wish to punctuate. Be sure that your suggestions are tentative, nonauthoritarian, and fit the "facts," as told by the client. Finally, when you give a suggestion, consider using the Zeigarnik effect, which we described in Chapter 8, by leaving the idea without closure.

The TFA Matrix

As you are deciding what type of suggestion you will be making to your client, you must first determine whether your client is a customer, complainant, visitor, or involuntary. Second, you should consider your client's processing style. Hutchins (1979) created the TFA matrix system for characterizing client styles (Figure 10-1). In this system, the T stands for thinking, the F for feeling, and the A for acting. According to Hutchins, a client has one of four major styles, and knowing your client's processing style can help you design a suggestion. The four styles are: acting–thinking, thinking–feeling, feeling–acting, and balanced style.

Someone with the acting–thinking [A-1, T-2, F-3] dominant style is characterized by Hutchins and Cole (1992) as a person who can see things that need to be done and acts decisively, carrying out plans and completing tasks. This person is characterized as a "can do" individual. Someone with a style similar to this would probably be likely to carry out a behavioral task—if he or she is a customer—and could be asked to do it on his or her own.

A person with the thinking–feeling [T-1, F-2, A-3] style would be concerned with what other people think and is stimulated by ideas and the consequences of events. This person may not be able to sustain the energy to carry out the actions, even though he or she is excited by the idea of doing so. In such a case, perhaps you would not want to offer this person an action plan, but rather, a task of observing and thinking about what to do.

The style of feeling–acting [F-1, A-2, T-3] is portrayed by Hutchins and Cole (1992) as someone who will let the situation at hand dictate action. This person might be considered as impulsive at times, but they may tend to be "open and affectionate. They trust others and enjoy social interaction" (p. 24).

The TFA matrix can be a useful tool, something to keep in mind as an aid for designing suggestions. However, do not use the TFA as a hard-and-fast diagnostic instrument. Even though two decades of research by Hutchins has validated these four styles, logic suggests that there may be others. For example, an F-1, T-2, A-3 style might be different in some ways from either the thinking–feeling or feeling–acting styles.

One way in which the TFA matrix might prove useful to you would be as a reminder that you do not want to try "one size fits all" suggestions with clients. You must get to know your client so that you can anticipate which sort of task—a thinking, feeling, or acting one—might be most effective. When you are contemplating using a suggestion, take a moment to reflect on whether you consider your client's processing style to be primarily thinking, feeling, or acting. This information may help you avoid offering an idea that will not be seen as helpful.

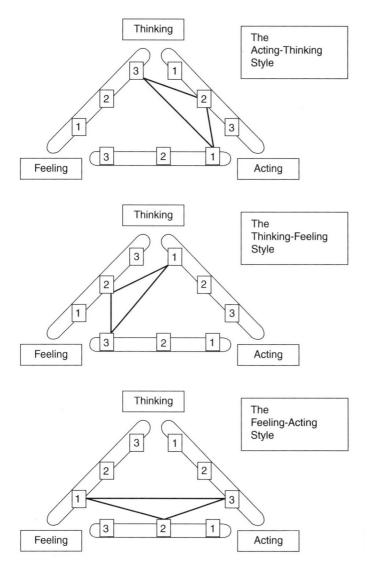

FIGURE 10-1 The TFA matrix system. After Hutchins (1979).

Many tasks in counseling are geared to stimulate clients' thinking and acting — to changing either their "viewing" or their "doing" (Friedman, 1997, p. 77). Feeling tasks, on the other hand, are aimed at changing your client's mood or attitude. For example, asking a family to rent the movie *Ordinary People*, and then return with a list of the emotions they experienced during the film, obviously has its "viewing" and "doing" aspects, but the main focus would be on the emotional.

The consideration of the TFA matrix may help you to tailor your suggestion to the style of your client. It is an ingredient, rather than a rule, for your creation of an effective task for your client. Perhaps the following checklist will be helpful as you design this suggestive feedback. Ask yourself these questions:

1. Do I truly feel invited to suggest something to my client?
2. Has my client already come up with a possible task? If this idea is "more of the same"—a first-order change—is there a way I can modify it?
3. Is our relationship at the level of customer, complainant, visitor, or involuntary?
4. Is my client's dominant processing style thinking, feeling, or acting?
5. What has my client already tried?
6. How has my client responded to other suggestions?
7. How can I incorporate my client's own words into the framing of this suggestion?
8. How can I offer my suggestion in a way that will bridge from the client's goal?
9. How can I offer my suggestion in a tentative and helpful tone?

Delivering the Suggestion—A Protocol

When you return to your client after the break, begin by asking whether there is anything that occurred to him or her that is important to tell you. You might say, "While I was out of the room thinking about our conversation together, what else did you remember that you wanted to say? What possible ways out of your situation occurred to you that we haven't talked about?"

If the client has come up with a way of resolving the situation while you were out, capitalize on this idea. Marvel—out loud—at the proposed solution, using the "encouragement triad." Sometimes, however, the client will begin by going back to "problem-saturated" talk. Of course, if this happens, it will be your signal that you must acknowledge these concerns. In general, you may begin the post-break interaction by following the protocol below:

1. *Reacknowledge* your client's stated concerns, but also continue to relabel and deconstruct as you had before. Use your client's metaphors that were descriptions of the concerns. At this point, you are speaking in a sympathetic, but not energetic, tone of voice.
2. *Compliment* your client on having coped with these concerns, restate the exceptions to the problem, and point out your client's strengths and resources. Now you are speaking enthusiastically to entrain your client's emotional arousal.
3. Determine whether the client is in a *"yes set."* Usually, at this point your client is nodding affirmatively to your acknowledgments and compliments.

    If your client does not appear to be affirming your compliments, you may wish to use an immediacy designed to create a yes set. For example, you could say, "As I am saying these things, I notice that you are looking down, shaking your head, and frowning. I guess that there is something I have said that doesn't ring quite true to you." In this situation, you also can use scaling by saying, "I guess you think I'm a little more optimistic right now than you are. On a scale of 1 to 10, with 1 being that you are reluctant to believe that things will get better, and 10 being that you are absolutely convinced, where are you now?"
4. If the client is in a yes set after your compliments, you can *bridge* from the client's goal to your task suggestion. For example, you might say, "And because you said that what you would like to work on in the future was to be more assertive, I thought you could. . . ."

Obviously, this after-the-break protocol is more a rough sketch of the process than a script. Because you can never anticipate exactly how your clients will respond, you should regard this protocol as only a guide.

Listening in on a Session

Review the story at the beginning of the chapter and the previous session excerpt. The family and counselor return to the room and sit in the same places to continue the session. Near the close, the counselor turns to Judy.

> **Counselor:** (*Looks at Judy and begins speaking with a sympathetic tone of voice. As the counselor discusses Judy's goal, the tone of voice becomes more energized.*) These past few months have been an especially stressful time for you, Judy. On your own, you've had to navigate through two very challenging worlds—the one at work and the one at home. As you continue to work on these very different tasks, it's obvious that you are searching for how to feel successful and enjoy the world of your family just as much as you do the world of your work. This may sound a little strange, but as you were talking just now I had an image flash through my mind that you would be the best person to do something for me. I've been looking for someone with good analytical skills to give me an opinion on this book, *Parenting for Success,* that I've received. The image was one of you reading a little paperback that had just arrived in my mail this morning and then giving me your opinion of it. I'm interested in finding out its informational and entertainment value as a reading for a parenting class.
>
> **Judy:** Gee, I don't know. You realize, of course, that it's advertising—and not counseling—that's my area of expertise. And I know as much about good parenting as I do about nuclear physics, which is nothing.
>
> **Counselor:** (*Smiles, nods reassuringly, and hands her the book.*) It's your opinion as an expert in influencing and managing people, not as a professional counselor, that matters to me here.
>
> **Judy:** Well, I can't promise that I can read all this any time soon. Things are awfully busy at work right now, but I can certainly try to find time to read it and let you know what I think—if that's what you really want.

Reflecting Questions

1. What metaphor did the counselor use in shaping the suggestion?
2. In what ways did this suggestion differ from advice?
3. How would you respond to the client's final statement?

How to Select Suggestions after the Break

It might be helpful to you to think of the after-the-break procedure as specific to your client's level of motivation. Your responses and suggestions will be tailored according to whether you see your client as a customer, a visitor, a complainant, or an involuntary. Below, we offer some ideas based on these categories of relationship.

Clearly, if your client–counselor relationship is the customer type, your job is going to be easier. You have been able to establish the proper conditions for the client to be ready to move toward a positive change. So your first response on returning from the break would be to acknowledge using "Carl Rogers with a twist" (O'Hanlon & Beadle, 1994) while remaining sensitive to whether the client is in a yes set.

If the client has a clear "miracle picture" but has not named exceptions, you might use the "as if" suggestion (DeJong & Berg, 1998). For example, you could say to your client, "I wonder if you would be willing to choose one particular day next week and pretend that this miracle has happened. You can just go ahead and live out that day just the way you described it here to me."

When you are dealing with a client who is motivated, but has not stated any clear goals or identified any exceptions, you could suggest a different response to the problem. Following de Shazer's (1985) suggestion, you could respond, "Wow! This has certainly been a stubborn situation for you. What do you think would happen if, when that comes up again, you would just do something completely different—even if it seems totally weird or off-the-wall to you?"

In addition, you can emphasize your client's goal-seeking behaviors if the client has clear goals and self-caused exceptions. In this situation, you might say, "It is amazing to me that you remain so clear as to how you want things to turn out! And in spite of some setbacks, you have continued to hang in there, and you describe so clearly how these behaviors are getting you closer to your goal. Between now and the next time we meet, it seems like you would want to continue to do those things that are working and even see what else you can try that will get you even closer."

If you determine that your counselor–client relationship is a visitor type, as described in Chapter 4, then you must honor the person's reluctance to invest in a change. When you go into a retail store and the sales clerk asks if he or she can help, and you say, "I'm just looking," you are probably annoyed if the clerk stalks you and keeps asking to help. Similarly, the visitor wishes to "peruse the merchandise" before making a commitment to become fully involved. Acknowledge the client's reluctance to become involved or the stated objections to being present. You might say, for example, "You're meeting with me for this counseling session, even though it's not your idea. You could have taken the easy way out by not coming at all."

You will want to reframe the behavior of remaining aloof in a family session as positive, by saying something like, "It's clear that you don't want to make things worse by adding your problems to an already difficult situation and that you are the type of person who can work things out on your own." Rather than trying to get the visitor more involved, you can use a bridge and invite him or her back. You could say, "So, we should work together to get you out of this situation as soon as possible. What would you say to meeting next week and working toward that goal?"

If you judge your counselor–client relationship to be a complainant type, then your client is likely viewing the counseling session as a place to come and vent his or her troubles and emotions, but is not yet seeking change. You must, of course, acknowledge the client's complaints by including the words (metaphors) that he or she has used to describe the stated problems. Display your concern, but do not emphasize the negative affect. For example, you might reflect, "It sure sounds like it has been one damned thing after another for you lately. It's been hard for you to get your feet under you and find a way to finally climb out of this pit you were in."

When your client names no exceptions or goals, or a poorly formed goal, you can use the first session formula task (de Shazer, 1985). You could suggest, "Between now and the next time we meet, I'm wondering if you would be willing to notice—so that you can describe it to me next time—something that happens in your life that you'd like to see happen more often."

On the other hand, if your client names exceptions, you will be a step ahead and you can capitalize on them. Following the recommendation of DeJong and Berg (1998), you might encourage your client by saying, "Pay special attention to those times when things are going well. Notice what's different about those times and what you did to encourage them."

When your clients name other people as the reasons for exceptions, encourage them to focus on themselves. For example, you could say, "Be especially interested in finding out what *you* are doing to help these people make a positive difference in this situation."

If your counselor–client relationship came about as the result of the client being coerced by a third party into seeing you, then it is likely that you have begun as an involuntary alliance. It is important to acknowledge the client's reluctance and possible resentment at being ordered to come. State your interest in hearing his or her side of the story by saying, "I guess if I were in your shoes, I wouldn't have been too happy at being sentenced to counseling either, and I'd have a hard time seeing what good it will do. I've heard from the people who referred you why they thought you should be here, but I'd like to hear your side."

If possible, attempt to refocus your client from being forced to be here to having chosen to be. You can take your client's presence as prima facie evidence that he or she is avoiding a worse consequence by showing up for counseling. You could say, for example, "While coming for counseling would not have been your first choice, the fact that you are here means that you have chosen this over something else. What purpose will coming here serve for you?"

If your client does not name a purpose, ask what the referring party wishes for the client to do differently. If the client can name something that the third party wishes to see changed, you might seek to shift the focus to the client. In this situation, you might say, "So Ms. Thompson thinks you should be doing your homework and staying out of trouble in school. What part of what she wants is something you want, too?" If, for example, the client were to reply, "I just want her to get off my case!" then you might respond, "How would things be different for you if she got off your case?" When your client names a difference, this is your opportunity to say, "So, maybe you and I could work together on getting this to happen."

When your client cannot say what the referring party wishes, then you can send the client to the referring party to ask. On return, find out if this change is something the client also wishes. If not, then you can explore with your client the consequences of not coming to sessions and then terminate. If your client does find a goal for counseling, then you can state your conditions for further work together. For example, you might state, "since you have been required to come for eight sessions (that's 8 times 50 minutes), and I am required to report on our work together, as long as you are working to change in the session, I will count those minutes toward the total 400 minutes that are required."

Obviously, we want all our relationships with clients to be customer types. Unfortunately, it is rare for a client to enter counseling as a full-fledged customer. Your job is to search for something that clients might be a customer for, while at the same time honoring the position they have adopted. When people feel that you have listened, understood, and validated their point of view (LUV), they often move toward the customer relationship. If, on the other hand, you challenge them or try to overcome their resistance, they will "circle the wagons" and try to protect themselves from your assaults. Promoting such a siege mentality will only make your work more difficult.

A Task Construction Paradigm

Friedman (1997) did not use the Hutchins TFA classifications, but he did organize tasks into either behavioral—doing something—or nonbehavioral—thinking about something. He also set up a matrix based on whether a task would be offered directly or indirectly. This "Task Construction Paradigm," as he called it, would then yield the four different types of tasks described below.

Direct-Behavioral.   These tasks involve obliquely suggesting what the client might do. For example, you might say, "[What if you were to] do one good thing for yourself each day" (p. 78), or "How do you think your wife would react if you were to surprise her by doing something unexpected that she would like?"

Direct-Nonbehavioral.   These are tasks that involve suggesting a focus for the client's thinking. "How about thinking of something you could do that would be totally different from your usual way of approaching your husband about his drinking, yet might help you worry less" or "*Notice* when you wife is acting in ways you would like" (p. 78, emphasis added).

Indirect-Behavioral.   These tasks are suggestions regarding possible actions the client could do. "I wonder if you visited your father's grave and got his advice about this problem, what he might say" (p. 78).

Indirect-Nonbehavioral.   [A metaphor delivered to a woman who had lost her house after 50 years.] "Losing your house is like a turtle losing its shell. You're all vulnerable and exposed. I wonder how a turtle goes about growing a new shell" (p. 78).

Friedman's task construction ideas might be helpful to you as you attempt your own designs. We found it especially illuminating to distinguish between direct and indirect tasks. Direct tasks may seem to border on advice, but are usually offered tentatively and without the assertion that they will solve the situation.

Listening in on a Session

Review the story at the beginning of the chapter and the earlier session excerpts. The second session began much differently, as both teenagers sat closer to their mother and to each other. They were all chatting away like old friends at a reunion when the therapist walked into the room.

> **Counselor:**   Hello, everyone, I'm glad to see you back. What would you like to accomplish today with the time we have together.

Judy: Well, we had a pretty good week.

Counselor: (*Glances around the circle to see that everyone is smiling and looking expectantly at the counselor.*) From the smiles on your faces, it looks like you must have had a *very* good week. Gosh, when you left here last week I really didn't know what to expect. I'd really like to learn how the family got together in such a short period of time.

Judy: (*Long pause, as the three of them exchange glances and giggle a little bit. Judy holds back until both children urge her to "go ahead and start." The counselor notes that their interaction is quite different from last week's session.*) OK, I'll start. Nobody talked much in the car on the way home and I forgot about the book you gave me to review until I finally did find some time when a customer stood me up for lunch. As I skimmed through the book I became interested in a case study about how a family turned their lives around by essentially learning to be positive with each other. There were some tricky parts that I wasn't sure of, but in spite of my misgivings, I decided to tell these two about it. All right, somebody else talk for awhile. I don't want to hog the spotlight.

Susan: (*trying to sound annoyed but not being very convincing*) Well, I don't know if Mom drank a magic potion or what, but all of a sudden she wasn't getting on my ass about everything. It was pretty cool.

Mark: Yeah, Mom fixed this great breakfast for us and. . . .

Susan: (*Interrupts*) You better not count on that every morning, Dorko (*pauses*) . . . I mean Mark.

Mark: (*Bows slightly towards his sister and continues without mentioning the interruption.*) Anyway Mom goes, "Hey you two, I was reading that book Dr. Miller gave me to read last weekend. There was this one part about this family that was a lot like us, you know—divorce, and everything—they even had a teenage girl who everybody blamed for the trouble."

Counselor: (*He grimaces slightly as if anticipating something very unpleasant.*) Wow! Then what happened?

Mark: Susan freaked, what did you expect? (*Mark continued his explanation by delivering a fair rendition of Susan's reaction to her mother. He demonstrated how Susan's hands flew to her ears and how she warned her mother not to deliver another lecture.*)

Counselor: Well, I have to tell you that I'm really stumped. I mean, no offense, but I haven't heard anything yet that would get you to come together like you have today.

Judy: I don't know what happened to me, but all of a sudden when I read about that family I realized I was so angry at my husband and his drinking that I had been taking it out on the kids. Of course, they were both doing really dumb things, but I didn't understand what was going on until I read that book. (*looking at Susan and Mark*) I realized that you two were trying to keep the family together the only way you knew how. You thought if somehow you could divert all the negative attention to yourselves—kind of like lightning rods—that your dad would quit drinking, we wouldn't get knocked around, he and I wouldn't fight and the family would stay together. (*turning to the counselor*) They were heroes, I'm so proud. (*Judy pulls out a tissue and begins to cry. Both children move closer to her and put their hands on her shoulders.*)

Mark: It's OK, Mom. We'll be fine.

Reflecting Questions

1. Point out the ways that the counselor influenced the clients.
2. Identify the client strengths that are emerging.
3. How would you respond to the clients at the end of this segment?

Using These Tools

Meet again with the three other colleagues who had experienced the reflecting session. Continue with the helping sessions that you had started earlier. This time, the counselor offers suggestions and, with the help of the two observers, assigns a task at the end of the helping session. Then discuss your observations, reflections, and reactions.

SEGUE TO CHAPTER 11

In order to help you synthesize the ideas and tools in the next chapter, we would like you to think of a time when you had been practicing a series of specific and separate skills that were components of a complex skill that you finally mastered. This process may have involved studying the grammatical elements of a foreign language, practicing the particular steps in a gymnastics routine, learning to drive a car, or learning to play a musical instrument. Whatever the skill, think about how you were able to integrate all these parts into a unified whole. Reflect on how you accomplished that feat of gracefully, naturally, and effortlessly juggling all those individual skills.

CHAPTER 11

The "Brief Attitudes," the Second Session, and Beyond

"Life is either a daring adventure or nothing. To keep our faces toward change and behave like free spirits in the presence of fate is strength undefeatable."

Helen Keller

CHAPTER GOALS

Reading about and experiencing the ideas in this chapter will help you to understand the following concept:

- Brief counseling is not just a set of techniques—it is an attitude about "reality," people's resilience, the process of change, and the importance of every therapy session.

Reading about and practicing the tools in this chapter will help you to learn these valuable skills:

- Encouraging and consolidating the process of change.
- Recognizing that your client's responses are clues to change.
- Using termination as an opportunity for reflecting on lessons learned and resources discovered.

STORY

Let's go back to Edra's story in Chapter 3. As you may recall, she decided to seek the counselor's help after a series of events left her believing that her "whole life was screwed up." Before continuing with Edra's story here, you may want to review both her first story and the two "Listening in on a Session" segments of the first session in Chapter 3. Toward the end of the first session, the counselor made a suggestion that some things in Edra's life might change over the next week and it would be good if she kept track of them.

Reflecting Questions

1. What changes did you notice in Edra?
2. How could you use these changes?
3. How might you begin your next session with Edra?

OVERVIEW

In this chapter, we offer a review of the fundamental ideas that form the "brief attitude." Brief therapy is not just a set of techniques to be applied to a "problem." It is a way of regarding the world and what clients need in order to move from a stuck position to one of creative possibilities.

In the "Tools" section of this chapter, we focus on working with your client in the second session and beyond. Now that you have completed the first session with your client, you want to keep that positive momentum. At the start of your second encounter, ask for a report on what has improved. Be presumptive, and look for exceptions, however small. You also want to learn what effect your suggestion at the end of the first session had on your client. If the suggestion seemed to the client not to be effective, then you take the blame. If your client has done something positive, assign agency to the client. The manner in which your client responded to the last suggestion should give clues as to how you want to offer another suggestion.

Finally, we discuss techniques for deciding when to terminate with clients, as well as rituals for consolidating changes that the client has made. Clients sometimes have misgivings at the termination of counseling, so we suggest some ways of dealing with these misgivings.

IDEAS

Brief Ideas and the "Brief Attitude"

Back in Chapter 1, we explained to you that we had designed this book's format to parallel the process of brief therapy. Because the therapeutic process is goal-oriented, we began each chapter with a statement of goals. Since the narrative perspective is central to brief therapy, we offered in each chapter a story to give life to the concepts and techniques. And to be consistent with our belief that theory and practice are intertwined, we included both concepts and techniques in all chapters. Now that you are nearing the end of this book, we invite you to engage in another process that parallels the work of your clients as they near termination—to consolidate the lessons learned, the discoveries made, and the perspectives developed.

Brief counseling is an attitude that you embrace, and not just a series of influencing tactics that you employ during the session. The brief attitude comes from both the experience of using the tools described in this volume, and also from adopting the beliefs—or ideas—that support the tools. Remember that Immanuel Kant said that "intuitions without concepts are blind." And a colleague of ours asserts that a "technical eclectic" is someone with both feet firmly planted in midair. That is why the concepts, or ideas, are actually tools to which you can return when things get foggy in your work with clients.

You do not perform brief therapy by simply trotting out an intervention technique without knowing why you are doing it. What follows is a collection of briefly stated ideas that make up the brief attitude. They are culled from the concepts and theories we have described earlier. We offer them as a list for you to contemplate as you near the completion of this book.

Change is Inevitable

You do not have to motivate people to change—they are already in the process. Your job is to help your client channel this change process toward the desired end.

Small Change Leads to Big Change

Contrary to one of the popular myths in counseling, the amount of time it takes to reach a resolution does not have to equal the amount of time involved in acquiring the problem in the first place. Neither does the strength of your intervention have to surpass the strength of the problem. A gentle nudge may be all that's necessary.

Clients Don't "Resist"

What counselors have traditionally called "resistance"—and have believed to reside within the client's "bag of skin"—is actually a quality that exists in the relationship between counselor and client. The "resistant" client is telling you that he or she cannot cooperate with your current tactics, but could cooperate in some other way.

Clients Have All They Need to Resolve Concerns

Clients are the experts on their own lives. Their concerns are usually not the result of ignorance, stupidity, or illness. Given the opportunity, they can resolve their own concerns. Your job is to help them believe in themselves.

Meaning is Co-constructed

Lives are stories that we have constructed. They are made up of meanings. When you work together with your client, you are deconstructing the old life story and co-constructing a new one.

Actions and Descriptions Are Recursive

Nothing in the world has a label that we haven't given it. We also define what a problem is. Our reactions to labels and "problems" then validate the labels and problematic nature of the things to which we are reacting. This expectation becomes a vicious cycle. Once we begin to see things as the labels we give them, and problems as we have defined them, then we can change the way we react to these phenomena.

If It Works, Don't Fix It

Even if you would not do it the way your client does, if it isn't a problem for the client, it isn't a problem. Do not seek underlying or deep-seated issues that the client does not see. Remember that different people have different values. It is not your job to sell your values to your client.

Stuck? Do Something Different

Do not simplistically adopt the attitude of "if at first you don't succeed, try, try again." If at first you don't succeed, don't try harder, try something else.

Keep it Simple

Since small perturbations can produce large changes in the system, you really don't have to come up with grandiose strategies for change. Most of the time, something simple will do. Furthermore, clients would rather try something simple that seems easy than to try to implement a heroic plan.

Approach Each Session As If It Were the Last

Since studies show that most counseling is single-session, your first meeting with your client is likely to be your last. Make hay while the sun shines.

There Is No Failure, Only Feedback

So-called failure is merely a message that what you have tried isn't working. As it is with cybernetic "smart missiles," negative feedback will give clues to the location of the target.

Don't Go "Sightseeing"

As early as possible, you should help clients determine their goals for counseling and then relentlessly help them pursue these goals. Stay away from side issues and lines of inquiry that have stimulated your curiosity, but have nothing to do with the therapeutic goals.

Your Client Determines the Goal

Don't unilaterally decide that the client should be working on something else, rather than what you two have agreed on. But if the client seems to have little energy for the stated goal, you might ask if the goal has changed.

Slow Pitching

It is sometimes tempting to become excited by an idea and attempt to sell it to the client. You should offer such "sales pitches" both rarely and gingerly. Be ready to immediately stop your pitching and return to attending if your client does not seem receptive.

Label Jars, Not People

Accepting diagnostic labels or pejorative terms as if they are reality only serves to reinforce your client's negative story. You are working to deconstruct such stories, so describe your client in terms that suggest emergence, competence, and uniqueness.

Listen for Client Intrigue

Pay particular attention when your client becomes intrigued or enthused by an idea. Sometimes differences that will produce change emerge in the midst of problem-saturated talk. It takes a sensitive ear to pluck them out of the noise.

Custom Design Interventions

General strategies never apply to an individual—each person is different. Even though we have offered you techniques that can be helpful, you need to tailor all these counseling interventions to fit your individual client. Don't assume you know anything about the client—ask.

Teleology, Not Etiology

Figuring out why the client has the problem rarely helps. You don't need to know very much about the problem to be helpful in resolving it. Don't waste your time—and your client's—worrying over how the client got into this fix. Just look for the way out.

Use What Is Already Being Done

People are always solving problems—your job is to find out how they do it. Clients are more amenable to doing something that fits their style than trying something that seems foreign to them. Keep reminding yourself that it is better to channel a river than to dam it.

Work with the Client's World

Work with the world the client created—not the world "out there." It is not your job to align the client's thinking with "reality." Neither is it your job to straighten up your client's "crooked thinking."

Watch Your Language

The way you talk about your client's situation helps to make it "true." If you conspire with the client to use language that implies pathology, absoluteness, and hopelessness, then that is the world you and your client will create together. On the other hand, if you use words that make client behaviors legitimate, that open "problem" descriptions to new interpretations, and that indicate that change is inevitable, then a different world will be created. Use presumptive language to make exceptions definite.

Go for the Goal

If you don't know where you are going, how will you know if you get there? The well-formed goal is focused on change in the client's viewing and doing, in the presence—rather than the absence—of something. Make sure that you and the client are always revisiting the goal. Find out how much of the goal must be accomplished in order to be "good enough." Keep going until you get there—then stop.

Major Life Concerns Are Never Solved

If you can't decide whether to serve red or white wine at your dinner party, you have a problem. The problem will have a solution, probably based on what food you are serving. However, problems and their solutions are trivial compared to the major life concerns that people bring to counseling. People do not "solve" life concerns. Instead, they achieve some form of resolution by transforming themselves, transcending the issues, or translating chaos into meaning. Rather than being merely solved, life concerns are *dis*-solved, *ab*solved, or *re*solved.

Communication Is in Context

A behavior takes its meaning from the situation in which it is behaved. For example, wearing a swimsuit at Daytona Beach conveys a quite different meaning than wearing the same swimsuit in Saint Paul's Cathedral. Once you understand the psychological and social context of your client's concerns, you have a better chance of helping your client find a resolution. Sometimes, all it takes is for your client to move to a psychological or physical place that offers a different context.

Systems Have Rules

Every interchange can evolve into a rule. Once behaved, a transaction may come to be expected as "the way we are supposed to behave with each other." After a time, we may not even be able to say what our rules for behaving with each other are, although we may feel slighted if the rules are not observed. As a brief counselor, part of your job is to deconstruct these rules so that clients can discover that rules need not be so tyrannical in their lives.

People Punctuate Reality

She says, "I nag you because you drink." He says, "I drink because you nag me." Both believe they have the better grasp on reality. In the cybernetic perspective, the way in which we punctuate, or emphasize, aspects of our experience is purely arbitrary. Any event can be punctuated another way. This offers the opportunity for you to look elsewhere for explanations.

"Problems" Are Maintained

As a counselor, you are more likely to be successful if you look for how "problems" are maintained, rather than how they are caused. Once the rules and roles are established in a relationship, and behaviors come to be seen as problems, then rule-governed reactions to the problems are established. Though these reactions are meant to solve the problems, they often serve to maintain them. People try to solve problems by doing what seems to be intuitively obvious. They attempt to overcome them. This only adds another level of concern—helplessness in the face of the "problem." If you can help the client interrupt the loop that maintains the problem situation, then change is possible.

Like Painting, Brief Counseling Requires Detail Work

By encouraging your clients to be detailed and specific in describing their current circumstances and future goals, you are helping to set the stage for therapeutic change. When clients state their concerns in behavioral terms and depict their circumstances with attention to the particulars, they are making it more possible for you to relabel, addressing the facts of the situation. And when clients describe their goals in such detail, they are creating a vision that offers vividness, power, and hope for a better future.

Client's Metaphors Are Bridges

What is not literal and concrete in your client's portrayal of the concern is metaphorical. For example, the client may report feeling "down," "dumped on," "slammed," or "blown-off." If you employ these terms in your acknowledgments, the client will feel understood—that you have bridged a connection.

Clients Have Tried Solving Their Concerns

It is important to know what has been attempted so that you do not suggest something that has already been seen by the client as a failed solution. Furthermore, the client may be repeatedly trying solutions that maintain the problem. Your client may say, for example, "When my son acts belligerently toward me, I make a lot of threats, but end up not doing anything."

All Client Behaviors Make Sense

Before you can communicate respect for the client's position, you must believe that people do the best they can, and are making reasonable decisions, given the way they view the situation they are in. If they saw the situation differently, they would do something different.

All Counseling Is Collaborative

You must have a relationship with the client in order to do effective work. You must be invited by the client before you can be helpful. This will not happen if you are argumentative, demeaning, or adversarial. The client's world view is the client's reality, and the client's "resistances" make very good sense, given this reality. Contributing your part of a "binocular" view of the situation will influence your client to begin to alter his or her view only if you can offer your perspective in a respectful, collaborative, and genuine manner.

Create a Difference That Makes a Difference

Effective binocular views that make a difference are neither too small to be noticed nor too big to disorganize the system. Instead, they both match—to some degree—the client's perceptions and serve as perturbations that deconstruct the old view. They are intriguing and offered in an atmosphere of safety. Re-view, reframe, and relabel problems so that they will be easier to resolve.

Be Positive, Resolution-Focused, and Future-Oriented

Remember that you're not a dentist—you don't need to probe where it hurts. Instead of focusing on your client's painful recollections, you can move the dialogue to a discussion of goals, and emphasize past successes that will be helpful in working toward change. With this approach, you and your client are moving nearer to the future horizon rather than doing archeology on the past.

Exceptions Are Clues

The times when the problem is not happening involve the behaviors and thoughts that can lead the client to the goal. You will have to probe for exceptions, because they usually go unnoticed by the client. The problem is not *always* happening—exceptions are clues to resolution. Get the client to do more of what is already working.

Experiencing These Ideas

Form a small group with two or three colleagues. Address the fact that you will soon be terminating this training experience you have shared. Even though you may continue to see these colleagues regularly, you will be ending this particular shared experience. Recall your first meeting together. What have you learned? How have you changed? Help one another to consolidate these learning experiences and changes.

Reflecting Questions

1. What were some of the common themes in the lessons you learned?
2. How did you help one another to consolidate these learning experiences and changes?

Implications of These Ideas for Counselors

The ideas regarding the brief attitudes have important implications for how to work with clients in the second session and beyond.

- Since you have demonstrated these attitudes in the first counseling session, you can keep the changes going.
- Continue to look for small exceptions in your client's report regarding the past week.
- Build on reports of success by gathering more details.
- Find out what the client considers to be "good enough" success. This information will give you a clue as to when to suggest termination.
- Don't just terminate—make the last meeting a ritual in which you take inventory of the client's new learnings and freshly discovered resources.

TOOLS

What Next?

Your client returns for a second session. You have used most of the influencing techniques that have been described thus far in this book. So, what do you do now? The answer is that you continue to do most of what you have already done with the client, but with a slightly different emphasis.

You and your client have created a history together, and it's likely that your client now trusts you more than he or she did during the first visit. If this is the case, you will not have to reinvent the wheel—a relationship is already present, so it is not necessary to begin at the beginning. Another difference is that your client has already learned "the drill"—he or she has more accurate expectations about how the counseling session will go. Therefore, you both can hit the ground running. Begin by asking presumptively, "What did you notice that got better since last time?" This question starts the session with the desired emphasis on the positive.

No matter what your client's motivation is for returning, you can assume that you now have some sort of leverage. The leverage may be that your client trusts you, believes that counseling will be helpful, or is simply submitting to the coercion of a referring party. You should regard your client's presence as an opportunity to help him or her move closer to a goal. Furthermore, you probably left your client with a suggestion at the end of the previous session. The client's response to this suggestion should give you some clues as to how to proceed. However, rather than asking at the beginning of this session whether the client did what you suggested, ask a question that is more oblique. For example, you might say, "Since our last meeting, what have you found yourself doing that is *different* than usual?"

Of course, at some point, you will want to know whether your suggestion was helpful to your client, but it is better to wait and let your client spontaneously mention it. If this does not happen, you can wait until the end of the current session to decide whether to offer something else. You might say something like, "The last time we met, I gave a suggestion at the end of our session. How useful was that for you?"

Another way to discuss the outcome of the previous session's suggestion is to introduce the subject through scaling, a technique we described in Chapter 4. For example, you could ask, "On a scale of 1 to 10, with 1 being that my suggestion was a total flop, and 10 being that it greatly improved your situation this week, what number would you give it?" As we discussed earlier, scaling can invite your client to focus on the process of progressing toward a goal. For example, if the client responds with a "3," you can then ask, "So, if something could have been added to my suggestion that would have made it a '4,' what would it have been?" Answering this follow-up query, your client is tailoring the suggestion to best fit his or her needs, and is focusing on improvement, rather than the failure of the suggestion.

Our review of the literature suggests that task assignment does not occupy the same central role in brief counseling that it once did. The emphasis has moved to supporting tasks that the client has designed. Ambiguous assignments leave the client free to make of them what he or she will, and indirect suggestions and metaphors will likely be useful in this regard. However, some clients will want explicit suggestions in the form of homework. You have to determine your client's expectations. Sometimes you cannot do this accurately until you learn the results of the suggestion you made in the previous session. "Textbook" clients do not exist, so you must custom design your interventions to fit each unique client.

How your clients respond to the first session will vary tremendously. Some will experience sudden and dramatic change, while others will proceed more slowly. You must be careful to guard against displaying impatience with your client's progress. If your client reports change for the better, rejoice and attempt to consolidate the change. If your client returns to problem-saturated talk, then you must return to acknowledging (the LUV triangle), because that is your signal that the client is not sure you fully understand the intensity of the situation.

Consolidating Change

Very few clients will experience sudden breakthroughs that bring them to an epiphany. Most of the time, you must be satisfied with less dramatic, but steady, progress. Because improvement is often a "two steps forward and one step back" process, you continue to encourage your client throughout counseling. Clients can become discouraged easily, and tend to focus on the "one step back," taking it as a sign that change is impossible.

It is not unusual for a client to return for the second session saying, "I tried what you suggested, but it didn't work." If you gave the formula first session task, the client may report not seeing anything that was happening that would be worth pursuing. If you gave a more direct suggestion, the client may report trying what you suggested with no results, or not trying it at all. Looking disappointed at this point will only communicate your acceptance of the client's discouraging view. Instead, you look for exceptions to the client's report—you once again deconstruct the story without disconfirming it. You might respond with one of the following examples:

- "So things are pretty much the same. Well, what were you doing to keep things from getting even worse?"
- "That sounds pretty tough. So, how did you manage to maintain your belief that things can be better?"
- "Even with all that, you came back, so I take that to be a strong statement about your determination."

Obviously, if the client is unwilling to accept your assumption that he or she has continued to cope or is still hopeful, the conversation will be reverting to problem-saturated talk. In this case, you are nearly back to square one—don't forget that you have developed a relationship—and you should repeat the first session's LUV triangle work to set the stage for positive change.

It is vital that your client feel comfortable reporting failures as well as successes. Clients sometimes try to please their counselors by making only positive reports, but it would be counterproductive for you to evoke or reinforce only the stories of successes. There is also a dynamic tension between your client's experience of your unconditional positive regard and your expectation that he or she will carry out a between-session task. You must continue to walk a tightrope between communicating acceptance of the client's position while, at the same time, pushing for change. So long as the client believes that you are working for—rather than against—him or her, your client will continue to experience the therapeutic relationship as a collaboration.

Notice Small Changes

As you listen to the details of your client's report, you will often find clues that a change, however slight, is taking place in his or her viewing, doing, or feeling. The Butterfly Effect has begun, even though neither you nor your client can know just what will result. If you find that you are feeling frustrated that the client has not realized that a change has indeed happened, then you are too far ahead of the client. Insight on the client's part may not be necessary for the consolidation of change. You must be careful not to invalidate the client's story by arguing that a change has happened, even though he or she has not noticed.

In order to reassure the client that important changes often are small and imperceptible, you must believe it yourself. If it is crucial to you that the client achieve the kind of change that you think should be taking place, you are likely to find yourself dissatisfied with the way things are going, and you will communicate your disappointment to the client on some level. It's a bit like the mother who reports that she finally got her adolescent son to take out the garbage, but she is still not happy because he won't smile when he does it. Your goal is not for your client to gain a cataclysmic insight or undergo a sudden metamorphosis. You seek only to perturb some small change in a representational system that has become discouraging for your client.

Many clients will report progress following the first session. The progress may be due to a variety of reasons. In fact, simply seeking help can sometimes restore a feeling of agency to a person. As we described in Chapter 3, merely experiencing an authentic and supportive relationship can also be a catalyst for change. Perhaps the progress is due to the relief of having shared a burden or secrets with another human being who has not met this confession with a negative judgment. Whatever the reason, if your client reports progress or success, you respond to this report with the encouragement triad. Show your enthusiasm, imply agency on the part of the client, and ask for a complete picture of the events. You might say something like any of the responses below:

"Wow, that couldn't have been easy to do!"
"How did you get yourself to do that?"
"I'm not sure I would have thought to say that."

When the client returns and you ask, expectantly and presumptively, "What's better this week?," whatever the client reports will be grist for your mill. If the client says that things are better, you may find that the improvement had little or nothing to do with the suggestion you offered in the previous session. The client has either found a new way to a resolution, drastically revised your suggestion, or developed a new perspective on the situation. In any case, you follow the client's positive report with that solid-gold question, "How did you get yourself to [do, see, believe] that?"

If the client reports that things are the same or worse, then you should accept the responsibility for the suggestion that was not useful to the client. "Well, I guess that idea that I offered you was a dud!" So long as you do not express disappointment with the client, or annoyance when you learn that the client did not really implement the suggestion, you avoid a relationship in which the client feels he or she has failed you. You should be guided by a principle first articulated by William Glasser (1965), in which he said that the client never fails, it is only the plan that fails. Furthermore, the plan was not a failure in that you now know more about what not to do. Remember the cybernetic foundations of the work you are doing. A missile that is on target receives little or no feedback, but one that has strayed receives feedback that will correct its course. This is why counselors who work briefly say, "There is no failure—there is only feedback."

Listening in on a Session

Review Edra's story in Chapter 3. Here, the counselor is beginning the second session with Edra.

Counselor: (*smiling and speaking with energy*) Edra, tell me what you've found yourself doing that's different since our first meeting.

Edra: (*exhaling heavily as she shakes her head, arching her eyebrows, and shrugging her shoulders in exasperation*) Well, everything in my life is still kind of a mess.

Counselor: So it sounds like there are still some things you want to work on. I'm glad to see that you've decided to come back. With all those things continuing to be in kind of a mess, how were you able to make it through in spite of that?

Edra: I don't know, I guess it helped that I didn't get into as much trouble this week. (*quickly adds*) Probably because I was out sick for 2 days.

Counselor: Oh, I'm sorry to hear that you were sick. It looks like you've recovered well from whatever you had. And somehow to me you seem a little different this week—maybe more relaxed—I'm not sure. What do you think?

Edra: (*looking thoughtful and a little more interested*) Hmm, I don't know, I don't feel much different. Nobody else has told me that.

Counselor: If you looked in that mirror over there, I wonder if you would be able to see something that's different about you this week.

Edra: (*looking in the mirror, and fusses with her hair and collar*) Oh God, I look awful, look at that zit. (*Turns quickly away and giggles.*) I don't think that was there last week.

Counselor: (*smiling slightly after a brief pause*) I guess that's a nice way of telling me that my suggestion wasn't very helpful. Darn, I guess I messed that one up. What could we change about the suggestion that might make it work better?

Edra: Oh, I don't think it was your fault exactly. It's just that I have so much to do that I didn't have time to think of whether things were good or bad or whatever. I don't know, maybe I chilled out a little more when things started going wrong and maybe they didn't seem like the end of the world.

Counselor: (*leaning forward slightly more and speaking slowly*) So the keeping track wasn't important, but you got yourself to chill out when things started getting tough. I wish I would have thought of that—it sounds like a good strategy. I'd really be interested in hearing what you said to yourself when you decided not to let things bother you so much.

Reflecting Questions

1. If you were the counselor, how would you respond to Edra?
2. What does Edra want from you?
3. How is she portraying herself in the session?

Using Client Feedback as Clues

When your client returns and replies to your inquiry as to how things have gone, you will often find that the suggestion that you had painstakingly crafted during the previous week's consulting break has been subverted by the client. If you take this information as feedback and nondefensively explore the details, you will obtain clues as to how to best proceed with your client.

Steve de Shazer (1982) devised a scheme for identifying client responses to suggestions. What the client did with your last suggestion offers a clue for designing successful follow-up suggestions. When the client has followed the suggestion in a straightforward manner, then you may end the current session with a direct suggestion. If your client's response indicates that the task you suggested was modified in some way, then you should offer indirect or modifiable tasks. This task could be in the form of a metaphor or wonderment. You might speculate, for example, by saying, "I wonder what would happen if you were to. . . ." When your client has done the opposite of what you suggested, then you can offer paradoxical tasks that have the potential for being opposed in ways that can benefit the client. Finally, if your client's report is so vague that it is unclear just what the client did, then you can offer tasks in a similarly vague manner. This can include stories or ambiguous statements. For example, you might say, "I wonder what part of what you are already doing or thinking will turn out to be the key to the resolution of your problem." These words are evocative of Erickson's "confusion technique."

Although this scheme for designing tasks appears to be quite systematic, de Shazer (1982) included this caveat:

> Of course, this flow chart or decision tree is only a guide to assist the therapist in determining what category of task to design. . . . What is important to recognize here is that the [client's] response report shows the [counselor] how best to continue cooperating with the [client's] manner of cooperating. (p. 59)

de Shazer also offered a metaphor that you may find useful. Client feedback is like a red light on the dashboard of your car. It tells you what action needs to be taken in order to get everything running smoothly and optimally again.

When Should You Stop?

Since the research shows that the modal number of sessions for any type of therapy is one, there simply may not be a "next time." Obviously, if you are doing crisis work, or if you are a school counselor who may see hundreds of students in an academic year, the probability that you will have only one session with a client is quite high. Whatever the setting in which you see clients, you should always treat each session as though it is your last. Even if you do see clients for multiple sessions, your most significant impact will likely take place in the first few meetings. Koss, Butcher, and Strupp (1986) conducted research that suggested that the maximum benefit in counseling sessions takes place within the first six to eight meetings. The most important criterion that would indicate when it is time to stop is that the client has made sufficient progress to carry on without meeting on a regular basis.

If you are uncertain as to whether the client has arrived at such a state, use the scaling technique. You can invite your client to reflect on progress since the first session by saying, "When we first met, you said that your problem was at a '3.' Where would you say you are now, and what number will we have to get to that will let you know you can carry on without counseling?" Another approach is to focus on the present by asking, "On a scale of 1 to 10, with 10 being that you are confident that you can keep these changes going yourself, and 1 being that you are not at all confident, where are you right now?" You can then follow up on your client's answer by asking, "Where will you have to be for your work here in counseling to be a success?"

If your client is reporting being close to the desired level of progress or change, then you might ask, "How many more times do you think we will have to meet in order for you to get to this number?" By responding to this question, your client is predicting success. This prediction can then become a self-fulfilling prophesy.

Termination and "Flight into Health"

In the conventional view, termination comes only after a cure has been achieved by a doctor with the patient. At such a point, the patient is dismissed. Budman (1990) suggested that this model of ending psychotherapy was promulgated by Sigmund Freud, who saw the therapist as the surgeon who excised malignant issues from the patient's consciousness. If the patient would ever have to seek help after termination, this would indicate that either the therapy had been a failure, the patient had a new illness, or that the individual would have experienced a "flight into health," causing a premature termination of the therapy.

A flight into health is seen as a rather sudden—but false—experience of improvement. The conventional wisdom suggests that when such a flight into health occurs, the counselor should persuade the client that the time is not yet right to end the therapy. In fact, some therapists would predict doom for these clients, leaving the impression that there was a ticking bomb in their psyche that would eventually bring them back to therapy. Conversely, counselors who do brief work expect to terminate with clients as soon as possible. When they suspect that their clients are experiencing a flight into health, they suggest that the treatment of choice is to "keep 'em flying."

In mental health settings, 70% of all clients come for six or fewer sessions (Taube, Goldman, Burns, & Kessler, 1988). And as we stated previously, the most common number of sessions for all types of counseling is one. Budman (1990) suggested that the conventional notion of termination—taking place only after a cure has been achieved—does just not fit the facts of the situation. In several follow-up studies he reviewed, nearly 60% of terminated clients later returned for additional counseling, even though they often felt the original sessions had been successful. Budman stated that it would be arrogance on the part of therapists to think that we can "prophylactically cure" our clients. From time to time, clients may return for more work with us, and this should be regarded as an indication of our good relationship with them, rather than as our failure to fix the problem in the first place. We should remember "that returning in this way is unrelated to the quality of the original therapy or its benefits to the patient" (p. 217). Termination, then, is simply the occasion when you and your client will no longer have regular appointments. It is the session in which you attempt to "take inventory" and consolidate the work that you have done together so that the client can carry on without counseling.

Dealing with Client Misgivings

You can end your counseling relationship in a way that ensures that the changes your client has made will continue. Of course, termination of counseling should be a cause for celebration. After all, your client has successfully achieved his or her goals for counseling. However, when you and your client have had several sessions together, your relationship has likely deepened to the point that termination will present some possible problems. For example, when your client has felt helped by you, there may be some question in his or her mind as to whether he or she can go it alone. In addition, your client could have feelings of abandonment—of being set adrift in a sea of trouble. Also, it may not be clear to your client that the time is right to quit seeing you. Endings often can be ambiguous (Teyber, 2000), and you should anticipate and clarify this ambiguity. Finally, the client will often feel unfinished. He or she may believe that all concerns must be addressed and resolved before stopping counseling.

The best way to clarify when to terminate counseling is to regularly communicate, right from the start, the expectation that your work together will end when your client achieves the counseling goals. For example, early on you can ask, "How much of this situation that is so troubling to you would have to clear up to let us know that it is time to stop our work together?" Since no life concerns are ever fully resolved, you are consistently suggesting, from the time your client sets the counseling goals to the times you review your progress, that termination will be taking place once the client feels confident about continuing to address these concerns on his or her own. Remember—it is your job as a brief counselor to work yourself out of a job as soon as possible!

Sometimes clients will have anxious feelings about stopping their counseling, and they may even feel angry or disappointed when talk of termination becomes the focus. They may, however, keep silent because of their fear that they are not being a "good client" and that you might be disappointed in them for having misgivings. They may believe you think they are stronger than they actually are. Remember that whenever your client experiences feelings of anguish, you must acknowledge them. You might open the subject by saying,

> When people have accomplished the goals that they have set for themselves and it is time to stop counseling, even though they feel confident and able to carry on, they might also, at the same time, have some negative feelings about stopping. I wonder if there is any of that going on with you.

With such a statement, you can validate these concerns and invite your client to bring them to the table. Of course, the length of time you and your client have been working together will determine the strength of some of these negative feelings. One of the benefits of working briefly with people is that deep feelings of transference and dependency typically do not develop, so the stress of termination is eased for the client.

If your original goal-setting with the client included the presence of something that was doable in a brief setting, then it should be clear to both parties when that goal has been approximated. Also, you will have communicated to the client early on that, on a scale of 1 to 10, nobody ever reaches a 10.

Keeping Changes Going

Michele Weiner-Davis (1993) suggested that when positive changes have taken place in people's lives, they are reluctant to "look a gift horse in the mouth" (p. 206). By this, she meant that people worry that analyzing success might cause it to vanish. Somehow, you must help your clients overcome this reluctance and talk about these positive changes in analytic detail. You want your clients to tell you how the changes have affected other areas of their lives. How have these changes affected the way the client feels about himself or herself? What would significant others say are the changes they would want to see continue? What else is needed to keep these changes going? What challenges are still present that may threaten these changes, and what plans does the client have for dealing with these challenges? Weiner-Davis also suggests that clients need to understand that change happens in small steps, and that occasional backsliding is not failure. Clients should not expect too much too soon. Clients must also understand that change must be evaluated in terms of "good enough," rather than expecting a perfect 10.

Sometimes people do not trust their own success. Despite tentative hopefulness, they may still secretly suspect that everything will eventually collapse, and that they will be thrown back into the same situation that brought them to counseling in the first place. Weiner-Davis (1993) suggested that it may be possible to inoculate clients against such obsessive thoughts by suggesting these misgivings represent sound reasoning on their part. Predicting a relapse is occasionally a good way to normalize events that might otherwise signal catastrophe to the client. Weiner-Davis suggested that we should encourage clients to ask themselves several questions. First, they should attempt to recall how long the good periods have usually lasted in the past. Second, they should note how long things have been better currently. Then, they should be able to ask themselves how much longer things will have to continue to be better for them to say, "Something different is going on here. This isn't just another false start. It looks like things are really beginning to change" (p. 215). Finally, Weiner-Davis stated that clients must be careful not to take change for granted. The reason that change is taking place is because the client is responding differently to his or her situation and has new ways of doing and viewing. In order to keep the changes going, clients must continue to practice these new ways of acting and to maintain the new perspective they have gained.

You will have to watch for client notions that might undermine the work that has been done. If misgivings come up in the conversation, you can deal with them directly. In addition, you could say, "Well, you scale your confidence level that these changes will continue to happen at an 8. I assume that means you still have a few worries. Let's talk about these so we can plan how to handle them when they come up." The trick, of course, is to help clients deal with misgivings at a time when they are also feeling confident enough to continue on their own. You do not want to throw cold water on their hopefulness. Unfortunately, we do not have a specific suggestion as to how to do this. We trust that you are enough of an artist in your counseling work to be able to deal gently with client worries without dashing client hopes.

You may also wish to offer your clients an appointment in 6 months (or some reasonable period of time) for a check-up. This will communicate to them that you are available for support and they will not have to continue these changes "cold turkey." The notion of a check-up is usually seen by clients as an opportunity to report further success, and to make minor course adjustments. This plan also keeps some leverage on clients—if they plan to see you in 6 months, they will likely feel the desire to report success, and as a result, be successful.

Making Saying Goodbye Work

Based on the goal that was established early on, or perhaps renegotiated as you went along, the criteria for knowing when you have done enough should be reasonably clear. When you and the client agree that you are nearing termination, it is time to plan for making saying goodbye work.

Epston and White (1995) pointed out that termination is often considered as loss. When clients leave therapy, they lose the hand-holding of the therapeutic relationship and must then face the world alone. The most productive scenario at termination would be for clients to feel more confident and fully aware of their abilities. You need to do everything you can to promote the notion of termination as an anticipated rite of passage. Epston and White believed that certain therapeutic rituals at termination can help secure the gains your client has made in counseling. They conclude their counseling relationships by inviting clients to attend a special meeting so that what they have learned from the counseling can be documented. Clients will have learned more about themselves, others, and relationships and will have developed new strategies for achieving their goals. However, they may have not been fully aware of just how far they have traveled in their short time with you, and will need to be reminded.

In this special meeting, the centerpiece for interviewing clients regarding their successes is the question of "presumptive agency." That is, the counselor always asks "How did you get yourself to do that?" No successful event is addressed as though it might have happened by accident, or was due to the behaviors of someone else, or some fortuitous alignment of the planets. The purpose of this termination interview is to make clear the client's successful steps toward solutions, calling attention to the resources possessed by the client, and attempting to give the client a third-person view of progress during the sessions by asking how he or she would advise others. This process confirms that the client has made valuable discoveries that could be shared with others. For example, the client might be asked to imagine meeting with another person or family experiencing a concern similar to the one the client has been working on. The client would then be asked what advice might be helpful to these other people. The counselor might also ask, "If at any time in the future you needed to take a 'leaf out of your own book,' what advice would be written on it?" (p. 347). Epston and White also ask what they call "unique account questions." Instead of accepting general or vague descriptions of the client's success, they bore in for the details. "So what led up to this breakthrough? Tell me about your preparation for this. What advice were you giving to yourself?" (p. 348).

"Unique redescription questions" are another category of inquiry during the termination ritual. These questions are designed to encourage clients to reflect on what they now know about themselves, others, and their relationships. Clients are asked to imagine observing themselves changing for the better by altering their viewing or doing. They are then asked what new conclusions they have reached about themselves and their relationships—"conclusions . . . that were not available to you before? What do you now know about yourself as a person that you would not have known otherwise?" (p. 349). "Unique possibility questions" encourage clients to speculate about options and possibilities that are now within their grasp. They are asked to imagine themselves in the future, having reached some important destination, and looking back on the present. They are then asked, "With the benefit of hindsight, what stand out as the most significant steps that you are taking at the moment, and where did those steps lead to next?" (p. 350).

Finally, the "circulation questions" used by Epston and White are designed to get the client to go public with his or her new realizations: "Now that you have reached this point . . . who else should know about it? What difference do you think it would make in their attitude toward you if they had this news?" (p. 351).

Epston and White (1995) have made major contributions to our understanding of the use of the termination ritual in counseling. The careful selection of the words and phrases that they use with clients points out how important it is to choose language for its impact. We must strategically design our interventions, right up to the last session, in order to maximize the lasting efficacy of our work. When clients terminate their collaboration with us, we wish for them to carry with them the seeds of future work that they can perform on their own. If we have done our job well, "saying goodbye" can have great therapeutic value beyond our time with the client.

SEGUE TO CHAPTER 12

Think of a time that you were required to meet with someone against your will. Perhaps the meeting was a requirement that you considered to be unreasonable, was a punishment for something you had done, or was seen by others to be "for your own good." What were some of your feelings as you began that meeting? How were you behaving?

CHAPTER 12

Dealing with Involuntaries and Revisiting the First Session

"To make ideas effective, we must be able to fire them off. We must put them into action."
Virginia Woolf

CHAPTER GOALS

The goals of this chapter are to help you to understand these ideas and to use these tools:

- Some ways of dealing effectively with involuntary clients and their referring third parties.
- Skills that are used throughout the first session of brief therapy.

STORY

Act I

He sat in the counselor's office slumped in a chair with his arms and legs crossed and a look of studied indifference on his face. The vice-principal had escorted him, holding his arm tightly, and had shoved him through the open door. Exclaiming in a loud voice that betrayed intense frustration, the vice-principal had said, "Here's Caleb. You'd better convince him to clean up his act, or he's outta here for good!"

The counselor had seen Caleb many times before because of his antics in class, his acts of minor vandalism, and his generally surly attitude, which his teachers found intolerable. This time, however, it seemed that Caleb had added the "straw that broke the camel's back." He would need to show some dramatic change in behavior or he would be expelled from school.

The counselor believed that Caleb was basically good at heart, but had developed a rebellious style as a self-protective facade. "Well," said the counselor, "It looks like we need to work together to find a way out of this scrape. Want to tell me about it?"

"I don't give a damn!" said Caleb, trying to look nonchalant and attempting to hide the fact that his eyes were moist. "They can all take a flying leap as far as I'm concerned!"

Reflecting Questions

1. How would you be feeling if you were the counselor in this situation?
2. What strengths can you imagine finding behind Caleb's facade?
3. How would you attempt to convince both Caleb and the vice-principal to give it another try?

OVERVIEW

In this chapter, we discuss in greater depth the challenges presented by the involuntary client. We offer hints on helping this person to become a customer and suggestions for dealing with the referring third party. Finally, we present an overview of the process of the first therapy session and summarize the tools that you can use to succeed as a brief counselor. This overview is simply a guide and not a script. If you find yourself confused or stuck in your session, this guide can help steer you back to the resolution path.

The tools are organized according to the "Flow of the First Session" shown in Figure 12-1 in the "Tools" section, and are divided into five parts. First, and most important, is the section on acknowledging—using the LUV triangle—and deconstructing the client's story. After the client has invited you to help, you can move to the second section by inviting the client to establish a well-formed goal for counseling. The third section contains a number of influencing tools that have been found in the literature on solution-focused therapies, narrative therapies, and other approaches to brief counseling. You can use these tools as needed in order to help your client envision a sharper image of success and realize latent or ignored resources. The fourth section covers the break, during which you normally leave the room to plan a concentrated intervention for the client. Several schemes are offered in this section to help you analyze your counselor–client relationship and design a task assignment to bring back to the client. Finally, in the fifth section, we suggest procedures for rejoining your client. You may wish to photocopy this section of the chapter and keep it as a quick reminder of the possible uses of the tools you have already practiced in the previous chapters of this book.

IDEAS

Who's the Client?

The resolution approach to counseling is a consumer-oriented model that espouses a philosophy of "The customer is always right." But those who come to counseling because they are mandated or coerced by others are often very reluctant consumers. In fact, they are not customers at all. This situation brings up the old "Who's the client?" problem that counselors often face. The person who sits with you in the first session, looking annoyed, indifferent, or frightened, is your primary client. However, in the involuntary scenario, there is a referring agent who is also a client. This person may be a parent, teacher, principal, social worker, judge, probation officer, or someone else who possesses coercive power over your primary client.

Whether you are a counselor in a school, an agency, or private practice, you will regularly find yourself in the situation of having a primary client mandated by the referring client. Each of these people appears to have a different agenda. For example, a teacher may perceive a student as having a "bad attitude" due to a "poor self-concept" and refer this student to you, expecting you to fix this problem. The primary client, the student, may interpret the situation as "the teacher doesn't like me" and only expresses to you the wish for this teacher to "get off my case." You are caught in the middle of these conflicting views.

Can both of these clients be satisfied? Your counseling work in these situations will feel very much like a high-wire balancing act. You may believe that you will be required to side with one or the other of the clients because neither person is a customer for the stated goal of the other. At best, they are both complainants, believing that their problems would be solved if the other party simply changed his or her behavior. The real art involved in dealing with any involuntary situation is to discover how each party might become a customer. Everyone is a customer for something. If you can help them find a goal that is congruent with the desires of both parties, then it may be possible to have a "win–win" situation. In order to achieve this outcome, you must find a way to cooperate with both parties (Tohn & Oshlag, 1995, 1996).

Walter and Peller (1992) suggested that there are four roles that may be attributed to you when dealing with involuntaries. These roles include the investigator, reporter, and manager. However, you are usually most interested in playing the fourth role—the helping person.

The "investigator" is someone who tries to find out what is going on in the world of the involuntary client that may be harmful. For example, the referring agent may suspect a child is a victim of sexual abuse and wishes for you to confirm this suspicion. In another case, the referring agent may suspect that the client is a perpetrator who is physically abusive to his wife or is driving while intoxicated. Your investigation is expected to take the form of interviewing collaterals, testing and interviewing the involuntary, or bringing in others who may even exacerbate the problem. Obviously, the involuntary client would be wary in this situation.

The "reporter" is the person who communicates to someone in authority about some wrongdoing. The most obvious example would be if you were to learn that the involuntary client, who is a child, has been abused or neglected in some way. In such a case, you are required by law to report this knowledge. The reporter role can seriously reduce the candor with which the involuntary client responds in the session.

The "manager" serves as observer of the behaviors of the involuntary client and often sets the requirements that will constitute the achievement of the referring agent's goals. In cases of court referral, the manager checks up or attempts to prevent a recurrence of problematic behavior. In this role, you will find the referring agent expecting you to bring the involuntary into compliance with the rules of the system.

The "helping person" is the role in which the counselor attempts to facilitate change in the client that the primary client desires. By our definition, this role is the one you will be playing as you follow the procedures outlined in this book, working for the benefit of the primary client.

Performing the roles of reporter, investigator, or manager can seriously compromise your ability to perform the role of helper. If the other roles are necessary, then someone else should perform them. Keeping these roles separate and clear allows you to focus on the challenge of converting an involuntary client into a customer. Walter and Peller warned that if you attempt to behave as both the therapist and the manager, then the involuntary clients "can have a harder time separating your role as social control agent who may take away their children or put them in jail from your role as the solution-focused therapist" (p. 245).

Cooperating with Both Primary and Referring Clients

Tohn and Oshlag (1996) suggested that there are six essential components to working in an involuntary, or mandated, situation. These steps include honoring your client's world view, establishing well-formed counseling goals, using the referral source to further establish these goals, using the referral source to sustain progress, identifying and using the client–therapist–goal relationship, and helping clients move toward their goals.

Little needs to be said here about the first two steps because these have already been covered in this book. We should point out, however, that it is sometimes easy to slip into the assumption that the involuntary client may, or at least should, have the same world view and goals as the referring agent. Taking this idea for granted is guaranteed to result in a muddle.

Most referring agents are credible people who are sincerely interested in improving the situation for the involuntary client. Since they are often people in authority, it is easy to believe that their version of reality is accurate and can be taken as a good starting point for the counseling work. However, this assumption can lead to a situation in which you believe you must convince the involuntary client that he or she has a problem.

If you perceive your clients to be "in denial" in such situations, they may wonder if you have truly listened, understood, and validated their world view. Of course, any attempts to convince your clients to change will strengthen your alliance with the referral source—the spouse, probation officer, or supervisor. However, in doing so, you have failed to establish rapport with the most important person—your primary client.

Involuntary clients often come to counseling believing that you and the referring agents are working together in a conspiracy to make them change against their will. You will have to be careful not to engage in behaviors that strengthen this suspicion. You must always start with a clean slate. with involuntary clients, even though you may already possess a great deal of referral information.

Opening the Session.   There are a number of openings you can use with involuntary clients (Walter & Peller, 1992). For example, after introducing yourself, you might simply inquire, "Whose idea was it that you come to counseling?" Once you have this information, you can ask several important follow-up questions. First, you can determine the goals of the referring agent by asking, "What does this person want to see happen as the result of counseling." Your next step is to check if this goal matches with your primary client's goal. You might say, "How about you? How much of [the referring agent's] goal do you want to see happen?" If your client responds that the referring agent's goal is also his or hers, then you can proceed as you would with a voluntary client. If not, you can ask:

> "Well, now that you are here, let's see how we can work together to make this situation better for you. We know what [referring agent] wants, what do you want?"

Walter and Peller's procedure appears a bit optimistic for those of us who have had many involuntary clients. For example, they suggest that if the client claims not to know what the referring agent wants, then you should send the client to that person to ask for specifics. Our belief is that this task is better done in a conjoint meeting in which the goals of all parties can be clarified. Those attending such a meeting would be, at least, the referring agent, the involuntary client, and you. Another possibility would be to ask the referring agent to fill out a Desired Behaviors Form (Chapter 4), indicating which behaviors the complainant wishes to see increased and which behaviors the client already exhibits.

What Does an Involuntary Client Want?

If you ask your involuntary clients what they really want, they will likely tell you that they would wish not to participate in counseling. They would rather be just about anywhere but here. This may be a reasonable goal, but it does not fit the criteria for a well-formed goal. So, you can take this opportunity to ask them, "If you didn't have to come here anymore, what would you be doing instead?"

Remember that old "instead" question you can ask to turn the desire for the absence of something into the presence of something. If your client says he or she would rather be home, at work, or even at a baseball game, then you can help the client elaborate on this hint of a goal statement. You might consider, at this point, that your client could be a customer for being there, rather than here. Then, once your client has clearly created an image of this goal-state, you could ask, for example,

> "What do you think it would take to convince the people who referred you that you don't need to come here anymore, so that you could be somewhere else instead?"

The client may be able to state some behaviors that the referring person would wish to see in order to be convinced that your client no longer needed counseling. If this is the case, then you might ask, "What part of what this person wants do you want, too?"

The "Client–Therapist–Goal Relationship"

Building on the ideas of de Shazer (1988) and Berg and Miller (1992), Tohn and Oshlag (1996) have characterized several "triadic" relationship styles that can be operating at any given time in the interaction between you and your client. They see identifying and using these relationships as crucial in successful counseling. They suggest that the counseling relationship will change depending on your client's relationship to the particular goal under discussion. "It is important to remember that these relationships are goal-specific. One client can have multiple goals and different relationships to each goal" (p. 165). In each of the triadic relationship styles discussed below, you will be cast in the middle role, e.g., "seller," "listener," "host," or "jailer."

The "customer–seller–goal" relationship is operating when the client—the customer—knows a lot about the problem situation, is clear about what to do to change it, and is willing to do something. You should not expect mandated clients to arrive ready to establish this type of relationship. They may be more likely to come seeking a "complainant–listener–goal" relationship. In this relationship, the client knows a lot about the problem situation, but claims that something in the environment, usually the behavior of another person, is blocking the attainment of the goal. Many mandated clients have this relationship triad connected to at least one goal. Statements about the problem are often couched in the "everything would be all right if . . ." mode. For example, they might say, "Everything would be all right if we had a little more money, . . . if we didn't live so close to his mother, . . . if they would just get off my back, . . . if he would just stop drinking, . . . if they would show me a little respect." The "visitor–host–goal" relationship is one in which the client claims to see no problem. If no problem exists, then obviously nothing needs to be done. The client will likely shrug his or her shoulders and wonder aloud, "Why are we talking about this?"

As previously mentioned, we believe that the "involuntary" client relationship goes beyond that of the visitor. In fact, the client views the involuntary relationship as an adversarial one. Using Tohn and Oshlag's scheme, we could characterize this relationship as "involuntary–jailer–goal." The involuntary client will often see you as an agent of the establishment. In the client's view, you are simply there to complete the punishment by forcing him or her to engage in counseling. In everyday conversation, you can often hear people say that someone has "undergone" counseling, as though it were a surgical procedure or a brainwashing technique. The term *shrink*, which refers to counselors and other psychological helping professionals, implies that one will be somehow diminished after having been counseled. In the "involuntary–jailer–goal" relationship, the client will seek to escape before some great harm comes to him or her. Obviously, this is where your skill at relationship-building comes into play. You must "enchant" the client into believing that, despite the fact that the referring agent is also your client, you are not there to carry out some punishment dictated by the referral.

Using the referral source to sustain treatment progress is another important strategy with involuntary clients (Tohn & Oshlag, 1996). You should routinely "check in" with the referral person and other involved parties to discuss any progress they have noticed. By checking in frequently, the message you are communicating to referral sources is that they should expect to notice positive change. Sometimes the referring agents are so angry and discouraged that they are not likely to notice any changes or to acknowledge the clients' efforts. Acknowledging their feelings is a great way for you to gently shift them toward anticipating and noting progress.

Remember that the referring persons are your clients, too. If you do not acknowledge their frustrations and concerns, they will be uncertain as to whether you really understand the seriousness of the problem, and so they might have to continue to notice more problems until you are convinced. Furthermore, when the primary client, the involuntary, does show improvement and the referring person fails to notice, the primary client might figure, "What's the use?" Then you will have two discouraged and hopeless clients on your hands.

By keeping in touch with the referring person, you stand a better chance of being able to influence both clients at the same time. For example, Tohn and Oshlag (1996) show how you can work both ends of the referral at the same time. After your involuntary client has moved to a "customer–seller–goal" relationship and has agreed to try something different with the referring person, you may say to the referral source something on the order of:

> I have asked your employee to work on some issues between now and the next time we meet, and I would like you to notice what he is doing differently in the next week that you would like to see more of. (p. 177)

Even if your primary client does nothing different in the next week, but the employer notices something different, you are on your way to the iatrogenic resolution of the problem. A good deal of improvement comes about because the counselor is a powerful exotic audience for both the client and the referring agent.

What If the Involuntary Client Remains Involuntary?

As you read the past few sections on dealing with the involuntary client and the referral source, you may have found yourself feeling skeptical. You may have had involuntary clients before and found them to be "impossible." In many instances, so have we.

Sometimes, regardless of your best efforts to enchant an involuntary client, not much happens. At some point, you must consider whether to continue with a client in the "involuntary–jailer–goal" relationship. As you reflect on your sessions with the client, you may notice that you have been working much harder than the client. Your work together just doesn't seem to go anywhere. You may even feel burned out. Walter and Peller (1992) are quite explicit about how to handle the involuntary if he or she continues in this sort of relationship with you. They suggest that if the client refuses to adopt any aspect of the referring person's goal, you should compliment the client and then:

1. say goodbye or
2. state conditions for further sessions if continued sessions are required by the court or agency policy (p. 248).

Of course, it is not necessary for your client to completely adopt the referring person's goal, but your counseling relationship must move beyond that of "involuntary–jailer–goal." You need to be able to establish together a well-formed goal that will be generally consonant with the referring person's desired outcome.

O'Hanlon (1995) suggested that you can use your role of manager as leverage by telling the client that you will keep track of the time in each session during which he or she is actually working toward a solution. Only the time spent in the work will count toward completion of the "sentence." For example, a court may have ordered the client to participate in eight 50-minute sessions of counseling. However, if the client spends only 10 minutes per session actually working, it will take 40 visits for the client to work off the sentence. You can dramatize this strategy by using a large stopwatch to indicate when the client is working. This method may solve the problem of a client merely marking time to fulfill the referral. Of course, if the client is really good at holding out, you may find yourself turning into an involuntary therapist as a result of this plan!

It may be a faint hope, but you can always choose to believe that the client does have a goal that can be fulfilled by being with you, or else he or she would have chosen some other alternative. The remedy is to find that goal and help the client work toward it.

Listening in on a Session

Review Caleb's story at the beginning of this chapter. The counselor asks Caleb if he could wait a few minutes while she makes some preparations to meet with him. Caleb mutters his acceptance and the counselor heads for the vice-principal's office. Vice-Principal John Von Sant is a young (late 20s), action-oriented, and energetic man who is sometimes uncomfortable in his position around older teachers and staff members.

Act II

Counselor: John, I wanted to chat a few minutes before I begin my meeting with Caleb. Can you spare some time now?

Vice-Principal: (*Calmer than earlier and apologetic.*) Yes, sure, come in. I'm sorry about barging in on you like that, but that kid drives me crazy.

Counselor: (*Opens a small notebook and begins writing.*) John, I could tell it was an emergency because otherwise you would have scheduled an appointment. Now, I wanted to get a few things down to get me up to speed before I see Caleb. OK if I take a few notes off the record?

Vice-Principal: No problem, what do you want to know?

Counselor: Whatever you want to tell me that I might not be able to find in his file. You know, maybe what you would like to see happen with Caleb.

Vice-Principal: (*He telephones the secretary in the main office and asks for the in-school suspension and the after-school detention files. He checks both files for a few minutes.*) Well, it turns out that Mrs. Tingle is Caleb's homeroom teacher and his 10th-grade English teacher. All the in-school suspensions and after school detentions were initiated at her request. I'd say those two don't. . . . (*He stops himself.*) Anyway, Caleb has got to learn to get along with everyone, including Mrs. Tingle. I mean, I know his folks from church and they've had some problems but that's no excuse. (*He speaks louder and with intensity.*) He's such a hothead, he'll get right up in your face if you push him.

Counselor: You gave me an idea, John. I like to check with referring teachers anyway, so if you don't mind, I'd like to chat with Mrs. Tingle before I see Caleb tomorrow.

Act III

The counselor returns to her office, where Caleb is moodily staring out the window.

Counselor: Caleb, I'm awfully sorry, I'm not going to be able to talk to you very long today other than to set up another time we could meet. (*Caleb remains silent and detached with no eye contact.*) I'll bet it seems to you that you've been sentenced to counseling, huh?

Caleb: (*He smiles slightly in spite of himself.*) What are you going to do—analyze me? If anybody needs analyzing around here, it's Tingle.

Counselor: I'll try not to do too much analyzing. If I do, you call me on it, OK?

Act IV

Counselor: Thanks for agreeing to see me on such short notice, Mrs. Tingle. I understand that you have referred Caleb to us and I thought I'd check with you first and see what you would like to see Caleb accomplish.

Mrs. Tingle: (*Has a condescending attitude toward anything "modern," such as counselors, self-help movements, MTV, and the internet.*) First of all, I did not refer anyone to guidance or counseling or whatever you people call yourselves. I was teaching high school before there was such a thing as "counselors" and we seemed to get along fine.

Counselor: *(with intense interest)* Mrs. Tingle, I wasn't aware that you began teaching when teachers pretty much had to "do it all." I can't imagine the energy it must have taken.

Mrs. Tingle: No one does. Why, I can't tell you how many girls I helped who had "gotten in trouble." In 1957 alone, I. . . . *(She takes about 5 minutes to replay her 1957 and she becomes quite enthusiastic toward the end).*

Counselor: With all the work you had to do, you still found time to help these young people. I imagine it felt good to help those kids that everyone else had given up on. I guess, in a way they were kind of like a lot of kids today. . . ." *(She trails off.)*

Mrs. Tingle: Well, not exactly, those girls adored me, they didn't wear those stupid baseball hats, sass me, or make fun of me the way that Caleb does.

Counselor: *(Again, she pulls out her ever-handy small notebook.)* This has been helpful, Mrs Tingle. I want to get some of this down, off the record of course, so Caleb and I can begin working on some goals together, OK?

Mrs. Tingle: That would be fine, but what can I do? Kids are a lot different than they were even 10 years ago. Sometimes I don't even have a clue about what they are talking about and they laugh at me. I wouldn't know an MP3 if one came to my house for dinner.

Counselor: I was wondering how you could help me with Caleb. As I work with him, could you watch for signs that our efforts are successful. . . . Maybe jot down small positive changes in his attitude.

Mrs. Tingle: *(laughing)* With 32 students, I don't think I have time for a behavior-modification program." *(She pauses.)* If I happen to notice something, I'll let you know, but don't get your hopes up.

ACT V

Counselor: Thanks for coming back, Caleb. . . .

Caleb: *(Slumps in chair then interrupts.)* I thought I had to.

Counselor: Gosh, you had me worried a little bit there. I was afraid you were going to choose after-school detention instead.

Caleb: *(smiling)* Naw, I was just kidding. I'll stay here.

Counselor: Caleb, how would you like to use the time we have together today?

Caleb: I'd just like to get these people off my case and quit accusing me of having an attitude problem.

Counselor: Caleb, it sounds like you'd like to find a way to get others to see you the way you really are.

Reflecting Questions

1. In what ways did the counselor work with both the primary client and the referring agents?

2. How can the counselor build on this collaborative foundation?
3. Write a possible response to Caleb's last statement.

Implications of These Ideas for the Counselor

These ideas have significant implications for your work with involuntary clients.

- It is important to keep in mind that the person who sits before you is the primary client. However, the referring agent is also a client. You will need to balance the expectations of each client in order to be effective.
- Clients who have been sent by a third party often are reluctant to become involved in counseling. They begin their session as "involuntary" clients.
- It is unlikely that your involuntary client will become a customer if you begin the session by playing the role of "investigator," "reporter," or "monitor/manager."
- You will quickly be in a muddle if you assume that the involuntary client will see circumstances in the same way as the referring agent. Get the primary client's version of the situation.
- You must differentiate yourself from the referring agents, while not abdicating your responsibility to them.
- The involuntary client is always a customer for something. Your job is to find out what that is.
- The involuntary situation is a relationship. Your behaviors could reinforce the client's expectations that you are the jailer, or you can try to deconstruct them so that your relationship becomes more workable.
- Watch your language when speaking with the referring person. You can construct expectations of success by communicating that you are also expecting success. Help this person to look for exceptions and to notice small changes.
- Sometimes, despite your best efforts to establish another type of relationship, you will not be able to change your client's involuntary stance with you. At this point, you either say goodbye or apply leverage.

TOOLS: THE FLOW OF THE FIRST SESSION (FIGURE 12-1)

1. Starting Out

After introducing yourself, if you are going to employ a break, you might say:

> "I am going to talk with you for about 30 minutes about what you want to change in your situation. After that, I will take a break and leave the room for awhile to think over all you have said and come back with some reactions and ideas."

If you are going to take notes during the session, you can explain:

> "As we talk, I'll be taking notes so that I can remember what you say. This will help me later as I am thinking about your situation and putting the pieces of your story together in my mind."

Open with a positive question that invites your client to discuss possible goals for counseling. Several possible versions of this opening question are:

> "What is it you would like to change in your life?"

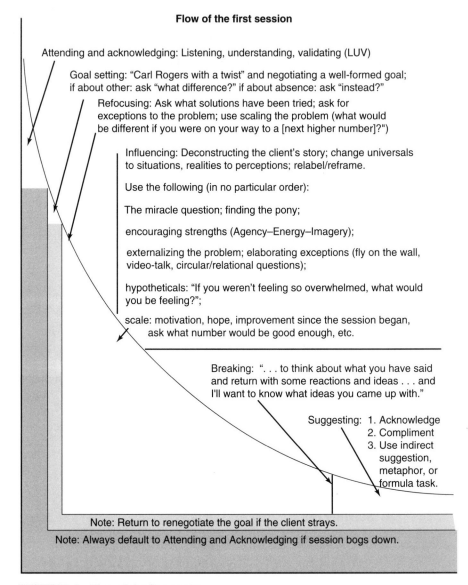

Flow of the first session

Attending and acknowledging: Listening, understanding, validating (LUV)

Goal setting: "Carl Rogers with a twist" and negotiating a well-formed goal; if about other: ask "what difference?" if about absence: ask "instead?"

Refocusing: Ask what solutions have been tried; ask for exceptions to the problem; use scaling the problem (what would be different if you were on your way to a [next higher number]?")

Influencing: Deconstructing the client's story; change universals to situations, realities to perceptions; relabel/reframe.

Use the following (in no particular order):

The miracle question; finding the pony;

encouraging strengths (Agency–Energy–Imagery);

externalizing the problem; elaborating exceptions (fly on the wall, video-talk, circular/relational questions);

hypotheticals: "If you weren't feeling so overwhelmed, what would you be feeling?";

scale: motivation, hope, improvement since the session began, ask what number would be good enough, etc.

Breaking: ". . . to think about what you have said and return with some reactions and ideas . . . and I'll want to know what ideas you came up with."

Suggesting: 1. Acknowledge
2. Compliment
3. Use indirect suggestion, metaphor, or formula task.

Note: Return to renegotiate the goal if the client strays.

Note: Always default to Attending and Acknowledging if session bogs down.

FIGURE 12–1 Flow of the first session.

"What do you want me to help you change?"
"What difference in your life do you want our work together to make?"
"What is your goal in coming here?"

Using This Tool

Join with a colleague to take turns being the counselor and client. As the counselor, practice starting up a session by using your own words to complete four tasks: introduce yourself, explain the break, brief your client regarding note-taking, and invite your client to discuss counseling goals. As the client, ask questions about the process.

2. Acknowledging

As your client discusses concerns, use the LUV triangle to communicate that you are listening, understanding, and validating the client's view.

- *Listen* so that your client recognizes that you are paying attention. Let your body convey interest, maintain good eye contact, be relatively relaxed, but remain intensely focused on the client.
- Communicate to your client that you *understand* what is being said. Repeat or paraphrase your client's statements, check your understanding by saying what you think the client means and asking for verification, nonverbally match your client's mood and the pace, and stay at the same level of abstraction. Match the feeling words and metaphors that your client uses in telling the story. Do not probe for additional feelings of pain or go much beyond the facts that are offered. Ask only enough to give yourself an idea of what the client is saying about the "problem." Ask for descriptions of behaviors and not emotions.
- *Validate* the client's perspective. Nod affirmatively as the client speaks, smile approvingly, and offer encouragers, such as "hmm," "I see," and "yes, go on." Indicate, in every way you can, your openness and willingness to believe what your client is telling you. Avoid asking questions that may indicate that you are forming a diagnosis of the client or an alternative interpretation of the facts.

Using This Tool

Together with a colleague, take turns being client and counselor. As the client, share a recent experience that involved some frustrations, difficulties, or disappointments. Your partner acknowledges your story using the LUV triangle. As the counselor responds to your story, when you feel especially understood and validated, give the "thumbs-up" sign. If your counselor drifts from the LUV triangle, rotate your thumb down. When you have finished, offer feedback and switch roles.

3. Offering Carl Rogers with a Twist (O'Hanlon, 1995)

This crucial turning point in the session is the first time that you are intentionally deconstructing your client's narrative. The technique involves three simple but elegant moves:

- Feed back the *meaning* of the client's complaint.
- Place that complaint in language of the *past* tense.
- Replace client language of "stuckness" or despair with language of *possibility*.

The language of possibility serves to deconstruct the client's complaint in subtle but powerful ways. When you are referring to the problem, you can use past-tense verbs, such as "was" or "has been." You can demonstrate your positive expectations by saying, for example, "*When* you change . . ." or "You haven't figured out *yet.* . . ." This presumptive language communicates your belief in the client's potential for progress and improvement. You can turn nouns or adjectives into verbs. For example, instead of accepting your client's self-characterization as a "loser," you can say that your client "has not been succeeding, and is seeking a more successful way of living." In other words, you change the labels into behaviors. Another example of the language of possibility is to relabel—"depressed" becomes "You just haven't been able to get up and go." Negative terms such as "bum," "screw-up," or "fool" can be relabeled as "the old you."

Using This Tool

Join with your colleague and once again take turns being counselor and client. In the role of the client, return to telling your recent experience of frustration and disappointment. Your counselor is to use the above strategy to move your complaints to the past tense, while stating your implied goal in the future tense and using the language of possibility. Continue your story until your counselor has made two "Rogers with a Twist" statements. Switch roles and repeat the process.

4. Deconstructing Complaints

Encourage the client to be specific, concrete, and detailed in describing the behaviors involved in the complaints. Acknowledge, but do not accept complaints such as, "I'm just not good at anything," or "She really doesn't care about me," or "Nothing ever turns out right." Ask for particular scenarios by asking, for example,

> "Give me an example of what has happened when you tried to do something well"
> "What has she done that convinced you that she didn't care about you?"
> "Tell me something that didn't turn out the way you wanted."

Keep your affect even and do not probe for more feeling from the client. There are excellent methods to deconstruct portrayals that sabotage change. For example, if the client . . .

- Speaks of the problem in *universals*—the problem is *always* happening—then speak of the problem as *episodes* or stages that the client is passing through.
- Characterizes the problem as *reality* or truth, then speak of the problem as a *perception*—the way the client sees it.
- Uses *pejorative labels* to describe the problem, then ask for a description of how and when the problem happens, then *relabel* it.
- Speaks of the problem as a *global* one—the problem happens everywhere—then ask the client to describe the context in which the problem is happening and ask for an *exception*—when the problem is not happening.
- Speaks in terms of *pathological* diagnoses, then normalize or *destigmatize*. For example, depression becomes "you've been feeling down and really lousy."
- Gives a *litany* of problems, then focus on the *most workable* of the problems on the list.
- Portrays himself or herself as the passive *victim* of the problem, then *externalize* the problem as trying to influence the client. Seek an exception by asking for a time when the problem attempted to influence the client and the client "didn't listen."
- Describes the problem in *vague* terms, then use the fly on the wall or ask the client to video-talk the situation to give it *vivid* detail. Creatively misunderstand aspects of the problem.

Using This Tool

With a colleague, take turns being counselor and client. The client is to complain using one of the classes of statements listed above. The counselor is to use suggestions that deconstruct the client's complaint.

5. Using Metaphors

You can use metaphors in several important ways:

- Identify the metaphors your client uses and employ them in feedback.
- Subtly alter the client's metaphor. This may be in the client's depiction of the situation, the client's feelings and attitudes, the client's description of the behavior of others, etc.
- Compare the client's situation and its resolution to some well-known situation. For example, the counselor might find something that greatly interests the client and build a metaphor on that topic. With an adolescent boy who follows football, you might say, "In the last minute of the AFC Championship Game, in which the winner would go to the 2000 Super Bowl, it looked like all was lost for the Tennessee Titans, until they pulled off the 'Music City Miracle.' "

Using This Tool

Pair up with a colleague to alternate being counselor and client. The client is to tell the story of his or her concerns to the counselor, while the counselor notes the metaphors used by the client to portray both the complaints and the desired outcomes. The counselor is to use the client's metaphors in acknowledging and deconstructing the client's story.

6. Waiting to Be Invited

Your client can invite you to participate in many ways, both direct and indirect. For example, your client may directly ask you for an expert opinion by simply saying, "What do you think?" or "Have you ever worked with someone like me?" or "What would you recommend in my situation?" More often, however, your client will invite you to help in less direct ways. For example, your client might simply become silent and look expectantly at you, or shift to the present and future tense in describing the situation (Miller, 1995).

Using This Tool

With a colleague, take turns being counselor and client. The client is to complain for a while, but then indicate in some subtle way that the counselor is being invited to help. As the counselor, see if you can recognize the invitation.

7. Seeking Goals

Find out what the client wants as a result of working with you. You must be careful to avoid accepting goals from the client that are not well formed or workable. Otherwise, you may find that you have contracted for something that is either impossible or unclear. Workable goals:

- Involve the presence, rather than the absence of something.
- Are concrete, specific, and behavioral.

- Are centered on change in the client.
- Are possible and within the client's control.

You can help your client establish workable goals by asking what the client expects that will be a positive outcome of the counseling. For example, you might inquire, "What will be the very first sign that things are starting to be on the right track?" Once the client provides an answer, you can ask, "What part of that is already happening?" You can gather even more details by wondering, "So if you were already on track to this goal, what would you be doing differently now?"

Using This Tool

With a colleague, take turns being counselor and client. The counselor is to ask for a goal. The client is to offer an ill-formed goal. The counselor is to then ask for an elaboration that will make the goal well-formed.

8. Using Hypotheticals

Whenever your clients say, "I don't know" to your request for a goal statement, you can ask them to guess. For example, you might repeat your request with the preface, "If you did know . . . ," "If you did have an idea . . . ," "If you could figure it out . . . ," "Your best guess. . . ." These possible leads encourage your client to set aside feelings of reluctance and to explore a hypothetical possibility that is much less threatening.

Walter and Peller (1992) sometimes use the notion of pretending with clients who are more "practical-minded." For example, you might ask, "Let's pretend that we are in our last session together, and our work has been successful. So if you were satisfied that your concerns were sufficiently resolved, what would you be doing that's different? What will you be saying to yourself and others that will show that difference?"

Using This Tool

With a colleague, take turns being counselor and client. The counselor is to ask the client to pretend or hypothesize an image of success—a situation in which the "problem" is no longer happening. As a co-narrator, the counselor is to help the client describe in greater detail and with more emotional intensity, the narration of hypothetical resolution.

9. Scaling

You can invite your client to scale the problem by first asking,

> "On a scale from 1 to 10, where 1 represents things at their worst, and 10 represents how things will be when these problems are resolved, where would you place yourself today?"

If, for example, your client answers with the number "4," you can follow up by inquiring,

> "What would be one thing that would be different to let you know that you were on your way to a 5?"

As Berg (1991) pointed out, you can also use scaling techniques to help your client explore virtually any personal attribute or situational characteristic that relates to positive change. For example, you can ask about the client's level of self-confidence, support from others, motivation, feelings of belonging, hope, closeness to friends, and personal satisfaction.

The scaling device is also helpful for addressing the decision to terminate (Walter & Peller, 1992). You can bring up the topic of termination whenever you do a progress check by asking, for example,

> "If 1 is how you were feeling when you first came here and 10 is how you'll be feeling when you end counseling, where do you put yourself right now?"

Using This Tool

Pair up with a colleague to practice this skill. When you are the client, talk about some concern you're currently facing. Your counselor is to scale your present level of difficulty and then ask what change would indicate that you were on your way to the next higher number. At another point, your counselor can offer another scaling opportunity by asking about your level of hope, support, or motivation. After you have discussed the experience, switch roles.

10. Looking for Exceptions

Ask for exceptions—the times when the concerns are not happening—then elaborate these exceptions in great detail. Presume agency on the part of the client for the existence of all exceptions. While you do not accept a contract with the client to work on the absence of something (e.g., not smoking, not drinking, not being depressed), you are always searching for absent and overlooked positive attitudes and behaviors behind the client's story. The exception, the time when the problem is not happening, is a solution that the client is already doing. This "exception talk" must be carried on while continuing to acknowledge the pain of the complaint; otherwise, it trivializes the client's concerns. Be presumptive. Instead of asking, "Has there been a time . . . ?" say, "Tell me about a time. . . ." Be sure to assign personal agency to the client as exceptions are named: "How did you get yourself to do that?" This teaches the client that behaviors thought to be accidental or fortuitous are actually within the client's control.

Using This Tool

With a colleague, take turns being counselor and client. The client is to complain while the counselor acknowledges the pain of the client. At some opportune moment, the counselor is to ask for an exception. The client is then to report to the counselor if he or she felt disconfirmed and unwilling to offer an exception, or rather that he or she felt sufficiently acknowledged and willing to search for an exception to the complaint.

11. Asking for Other Views

Besides getting the client to name exceptions about himself or herself, try to get an externalized view of the client's success: How did the client look, from a third-party perspective, when he or she was doing something different? O'Hanlon (1995) asks the client to "video-talk" the scene, as if someone were following the client around with a camcorder to catch all behaviors and conversations in exquisite detail. He also asks what the counselor or someone else would see when the complaint wasn't happening, from the perspective of a fly on the wall.

Using This Tool

With a colleague, take turns being counselor and client. The counselor asks for an exception (as above). The client is to speak of a time when the complaint was not happening. The counselor is then to ask for details from a third-party perspective and try to get the client to elaborate the exception in "exquisite detail."

12. Asking the "Miracle Question"

When you ask the "miracle question," you are attempting to get the client to envision a desired change in the presenting concern. An example of how this technique can be approached is as follows.

Ask the client to imagine that tonight, during the time when the client is sleeping, a miracle has happened that completely resolved the concerns that the client is working on. But, of course, since the client was asleep, he or she does not know that the miracle has happened. So you follow up this image by getting the client to describe the changes that would be noticeable on awakening. "How would you know? What would be different? What will you notice different the next morning that will tell you that there has been a miracle?" (de Shazer, 1991, p. 113).

In order to capitalize on the miracle image, you will also want to ask for third-party observations, such as:

"When the miracle has happened, who will be the first person to notice? What will he or she say is different about you?" or "If your mother were here and I were to ask her what had changed about you, what would she say?" or "When I talk to your teacher and she tells me that you are doing better, what exactly will she talk about?" or "What will your boss say you are doing more of than before?" or "What will it take to convince her that you are a changed person? What will she have to see to be convinced?"

Using This Tool

With a colleague, take turns being counselor and client. The counselor is to practice asking the miracle question. Try delivering the question in elaborate detail and match the pace of the delivery to the client's respiration. Most people go too fast when asking the miracle question and do not match the client's rhythm. After the client offers the miracle situation, try to keep the image going by asking for more detail and becoming excited by the descriptions of resolution (as above).

13. Externalizing the Problem

By characterizing the "problem" as external, you can enter into a conspiracy with the client against the concern. You are portraying yourself as an ally in your client's opposition to the concern. This strategy also curbs the defeating diagnostic fusing of person and problem, which can rob your client of a sense of agency—"I am a Conduct Disorder, this is what I do."

O'Hanlon (1995) suggested some steps for externalizing the problem. First, give the problem or concern a name, and treat it as though it were an external entity. Then, find out how the client has been influenced or tricked by this entity. ("What do you do when Mr. Angry sneaks up on you and tells you to turn red and yell?" "When does the shyness creature whisper in your ear and tell you to be embarrassed?") Ask about times when the client has been able to resist the influence of the external entity, or even make it go away. Finally, using presuppositional language, explore in detail what a successful future, when the client has achieved full control over the entity, will be like. ("How will your life be different when you finally lock Mr. Angry in a cage for life?")

Using This Tool

Join with a colleague and take turns being counselor and client in order to use this technique. As the client, tell about some recurring difficulty you've faced, exaggerating your sense of helplessness in dealing with it. Next, the counselor externalizes the problem by following the above steps. Give feedback and switch roles.

14. Finding the Pony

First, you acknowledge the misery that your client has endured, but you also ask for the positives that occur alongside it. For example, if your client describes a series of painful events, you may say, "That sounds as if those were awfully tough times for you!" Remember that you state the acknowledgment in the past tense and express it with somewhat less intensity than your client's level of emotional arousal. And then you might say, "Tell me how in the world you are able to cope with this lousy situation!" At this point, your emotional expression should send the message of wonder and awe. Then, as your client mentions a way of coping, express curiosity and ask for more details about this strategy. Keep your level of expression slightly more intense than your client's. You should display amazement, wonderment, and enthusiasm when using this intervention. This will serve to heighten the client's emotional arousal associated with his or her coping explanation. By trying to tap the client's energy through your attempts at emotional contagion, you are highlighting the client's heroism, persistence, tolerance, understanding of others, patience, etc.

Using This Tool

With a colleague, take turns being counselor and client. The client is to try to tell a story of awful happenings in which anyone might feel overwhelmed. The counselor is to try to "find the pony"—asking for ways in which the client has been able to cope in spite of such an immense crisis. Afterward, the client will report whether the counselor's questions felt well-timed.

15. Offering Encouragement

Anytime the client moves from problem-saturated talk to a positive focus, you will want to attempt to increase the vividness of the focus. If the client makes a goal statement, states an exception, or reports a success, then you must try to—as they say—"make hay while the sun shines." Ask the client to elaborate the scenario, using the "fly on the wall" or "video-talk" techniques or any type of request for detailed information that fits your style.

Next, attempt to insert as many of the "encouragement triad" responses as you can into your reaction Figure 12–2. The three points of the triangle will serve to remind you of how you can get the most out your client's positive focus. First, get excited and do everything you can to communicate your enthusiasm for the client's content. Display *energy*.

Second, pump the client for all the details. Make sure you get a complete picture of what the client is talking about in all its concrete minutia. For example, what was or will be the exact wording of the conversations involved? Who is there? Where is the event taking place? What does it feel like? What is different about it? Try to create complete *imagery*.

Finally, make every attempt to use presumptive statements that assign *agency* to your client. Ask, for example, "How did you get yourself to do that?" In what way is the client responsible for the change or the positive turn of the situation? Try to reflect each external locus of responsibility statement back to the client, so that you communicate your belief that the client was, or will be in control, rather than being the passive recipient of fortune or someone else's good deed.

Using This Tool

With a colleague, take turns being counselor and client. The client is to report a success or an exception to a concern. Using the encouragement triad, the counselor is to respond to the client's report. Afterward, discuss how it felt to be the client in the exercise.

16. Taking The Break

Take a break by saying, for example, "I'm going to leave the room for a few minutes to think about what we have said together, and I'll come back and give you my thoughts. I'll also want to hear what other ideas about solving your problem come to you while I'm out of the room." If you have a reflecting team, they will do the feedback.

Using This Tool

With a colleague, take turns being counselor and client. Each of you is to come up with your own version of what you will say when announcing a break during the counseling session.

17. Analyzing Your Relationship

Your relationship with your client, by break time, should be somewhat clear to you. Take a moment to reflect on the following types of relationships before deciding on an influencing strategy for after the break. Your relationship will likely fit roughly into one of the following four categories.

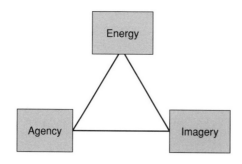

FIGURE 12-2 The encouragement triad.

A visitor (also called a "window shopper") is uncommitted (de Shazer, 1988). It may be clear to others that the visitor "has problems" but this client has little motivation to change. The best way to respond initially to the visitor is to listen respectfully, compliment and encourage when possible, but give no suggestions or tasks.

Complainants present problems, either specific or vague, about which they wish to talk at some length. Complainants may take the position that positive change is the responsibility of someone else, and that they are helpless. It is not initially clear whether you are being invited to give advice or to help them change someone else. Complainants should be treated initially as visitors.

A customer comes with a complaint, gives a reasonably clear description of it, and wishes to do something about it. The customer is fairly easily moved to a position of recognizing that change starts with the customer.

School counselors typically receive a referral from a teacher or parent who is a complainant, about a child who is a visitor, and the task is to turn both complainant and visitor into customers. Worse yet, the child is often presented as an involuntary by people in authority. The involuntary is counter-committed, meaning that to comply or cooperate would be an admission of guilt or weakness. Becoming a customer would be a capitulation for this client. Obviously, the counselor has the most difficult time establishing a contract with the involuntary.

Using This Tool

With a colleague, take turns being counselor and client. The client is to present himself or herself as a complainant, visitor, or involuntary. The counselor is to respond in a way that attempts to cooperate with the client's way of presenting. Afterward, talk about alternative ways of dealing with each of the above counselor–client relationship patterns.

18. Deciding on a Task Type

Consider how much influence you are likely to have earned during the session with your client. Also, try to determine your client's lead style (thinking, feeling, acting). Based on this information, you can decide among the following task types suggested by Friedman (1997):

1. Direct-Behavioral, such as: "Do one good thing for yourself each day" or "Surprise your wife by doing something unexpected that she would like."
2. Direct-Nonbehavioral: "Think about something you could do that would be totally different from your usual way of approaching your husband about his drinking, yet might help you worry less" or "Notice when you wife is acting in ways you would like."
3. Indirect-Behavioral: "I wonder if you visited your father's grave and got his advice about this problem, what he might say" (p. 78).
4. Indirect-Nonbehavioral: (a metaphor delivered to a woman who had lost her house after 50 years) "Losing your house is like a turtle losing its shell. You're all vulnerable and exposed. I wonder how a turtle goes about growing a new shell" (p. 78).

Friedman's task-construction ideas might be helpful to you as you attempt your own designs. It is especially illuminating in distinguishing between direct and indirect tasks. Direct tasks are usually reserved for customer relationships. Whether you are designing a direct-behavioral task or a direct-nonbehavioral one depends on what you make of the client's "lead style." If you see your "customer" client as exhibiting primarily an "acting" style (Hutchins, 1979; Hutchins & Cole, 1992), you may try a direct-behavioral task. If, on the other hand, your customer client is seen as primarily a "thinker" or "feeler", then a direct-nonbehavioral task is indicated. The so-called Formula First Session Task (de Shazer in O'Hanlon & Weiner-Davis, 1989), described in Chapter 10, is useful: "Between now and the next time we meet, I would like you to observe what happens that you would want to continue happening."

Using This Tool

With a colleague, take turns being counselor and client. The client is to behave in ways that would indicate a lead style from the above lists. (For example: thinking customer, feeling complainant, thinking visitor, acting involuntary, etc.). Based on the perceived client style, the counselor is to design a task for the client (e.g., direct-behavioral, indirect-nonbehavioral, etc.). Afterward, the client will reveal the style he or she was attempting to portray, and whether the task given by the counselor seemed to fit.

19. Doing a "Preflight" Test and Offering a Suggestion

After deciding on a task, you should review the following checklist. If you are able to answer "yes" to every question, rejoin your client and follow the protocol for continuing your session after a break.

1. Do I know what my client has already tried?
2. Am I certain that what I am suggesting is not simply "more of the same"—a first-order change strategy?
3. Do I have a suggestion that fits our relationship—customer, complainant, visitor, involuntary?
4. Have I taken my client's lead style into consideration in designing my suggestion—thinking, feeling, acting?
5. Have I incorporated some of my client's own words in the framing of this suggestion?
6. Am I prepared to offer the suggestion in a way that will bridge from the client's goal?
7. Am I prepared to offer the suggestion in a tentative and helpful tone, rather than a dogmatic, pedantic manner?

When you return to your client, you can begin by inviting your client to share any important information or solutions that may have occurred to him or her during the break. For example, you could say,

> "While I was out of the room thinking about our work together, perhaps you remembered something that you wanted to say. Maybe a way out of your situation occurred to you that we haven't discussed."

If the client has discovered a way of resolving the situation, then capitalize on this idea. Otherwise, begin the following protocol:

- *Reacknowledge* your client's stated concerns. Use the client's metaphors that were descriptions of the concerns. Speak empathically, but in a somewhat neutral voice.
- *Compliment* your client on having coped with the concerns thus far, restate any exceptions, and point out the strengths and resources that your client has demonstrated despite the situation. (Do this enthusiastically, so as to entrain the client's emotional arousal.)
- Determine whether the client is in a *"yes set."*
- If the client is in a "yes set," then *bridge* to the task delivery.

Using This Tool

With a colleague, take turns being counselor and client. The counselor is to follow the "after-the-break protocol" by acknowledging, complimenting, checking for a yes set, and then delivering a task assignment. The client is to suggest ways of improving the after-the-break delivery.

Continuing to Use These Tools

By regularly reviewing and practicing these techniques of the first session, you can consolidate your knowledge of brief counseling and increase your expertise in the use of these tools. Just as your clients benefit from focusing on their successes, you will discover that, with persistence, patience, and practice, you can master brief counseling. As we have said before, you can use these tools without slavishly following a manual. Once you have learned these techniques, you can fit them into your personal counseling style. What's more, you can easily incorporate counseling therapy techniques into other forms of counseling and therapy.

For now, use what feels comfortable to you, and put the rest of the tools on the shelf for future reference. Thomas Jefferson offered some good advice on handling tools. He said, "Always take hold of things by the smooth handle." Counseling is tough work, but using these techniques successfully can help your work go more smoothly. We believe that they all have merit, but that none of these tools can work without first establishing a good working relationship with your client. Of course, keep in mind that timing is everything. Remain sensitive to how your client is responding as you try to influence the process of the session. If you fit into the rhythm of your client's movement, and you have confidence in your use of these tools, you will find yourself enjoying greater success in your counseling work.

A Final Review

In Chapter 1, we offered you the guarantee that the more active you were in reading this book and participating in its activities, the more knowledge and skills you would gain. We invite you to take a few moments and review the book that you have co-created with us. What comments did you write in it? What material did you highlight? What observations and reflections did you have regarding the stories and exercises? What discoveries did you make? What skills did you develop? What ideas are you taking with you? What counseling tools have you added to your professional tool box?

Segue to Your Own Next Chapter

As we discussed in Chapter 11, brief counseling is fundamentally an attitude. You may recall a saying that was popularized in the movie, *Dead Poets Society*. The slogan was "carpe diem," or, literally, "seize the day." One of the important themes of this book has been to recognize that you must make the most of the limited time you have been allotted to work with a counseling client. Of course, you can apply this perspective to much more than counseling sessions. It's also a great way to view your training, career, and life. We encourage you to remain resolute in your commitment to not only "seize the day" but to seize your future as you continue your personal and professional journey.

REFERENCES

Chapter 1

Becvar, D. S., & Becvar, R. J. (1993). *Family therapy: A systemic integration* (2nd ed.). Boston: Allyn & Bacon.

Berg, I. K., & Miller, S. D. (1992). *Working with the problem drinker: A solution-focused approach.* New York: Norton.

Bloom, B. L. (1997). *Planned short-term psychotherapy: A clinical handbook* (2nd ed.). Boston: Allyn and Bacon.

DeJong, P., & Berg, I. K. (1998). *Interviewing for solutions.* Pacific Grove, CA: Brooks/Cole.

de Shazer, S. (1982). *Patterns of brief family therapy: An ecosystemic approach.* New York: The Guilford Press.

de Shazer, S. (1985). *Keys to solution in brief therapy.* New York: W. W. Norton.

de Shazer, S. (1988). *Clues: Investigating solutions in brief therapy.* New York: W. W. Norton.

de Shazer, S. (1991). *Putting difference to work.* New York: W. W. Norton.

Fisch, R. (1982). Erickson's impact on brief psychotherapy. In J. K. Zeig (Ed.), *Ericksonian approaches to hypnosis and psychotherapy* (pp. 155–162). New York: Brunner/Mazel.

Fisch, R., & Schlanger, K. (1999). *Brief therapy with intimidating cases: Changing the unchangeable.* San Francisco: Jossey-Bass.

Friedman, S. (1997). *Time-effective psychotherapy: Maximizing outcomes in an era of minimized resources.* Boston: Allyn & Bacon

Gilligan, S. (1997). Living in a post-Ericksonian world. In W. J. Matthews & J. H. Edgett (Eds.), *Current thinking and research in brief therapy: Solutions, strategies, narratives* (Vol. 1, pp. 1–23). New York: Brunner/Mazel.

Haley, J. (1973). *Uncommon therapy: The psychiatric techniques of Milton H. Erickson, M.D.* New York: W. W. Norton.

Haley, J., & Richeport, M. (1993). *Milton H. Erickson, M.D.: Explorer in hypnosis and therapy* [Videotape]. New York: Brunner/Mazel.

Hoyt, M. F. (1994). Characteristics of psychotherapy under managed care. *Behavioral Healthcare Tomorrow, 3,* 59–62.

Kolb, D. A. (1984). *Experiential learning: Experience as the source of learning and development.* Englewood Cliffs, NJ: Prentice-Hall.

Lipset, D. (1980). *Gregory Bateson: The legacy of a scientist.* Englewood Cliffs, NJ: Prentice-Hall.

Madanes, C. (1990). Strategies and metaphors of brief therapy. In J. K. Zeig & S. G. Gilligan (Eds.), *Brief therapy: Myths, methods, and metaphors* (pp. 18–35). New York: Brunner/Mazel.

Mahoney, M. J. (1995). The modern psychotherapist and the future of psychotherapy. In B. Bonger & L. E. Beutler (Eds.), *Comprehensive textbook of psychotherapy: Theory and practice* (pp. 474–488). New York: Oxford University Press.

Neimeyer, R. A., & Mahoney, M. J. (1995). *Constructivism in psychotherapy.* Washington, DC: American Psychological Association.

Nichols, M. P., & Schwartz, R. C. (1991). *Family therapy: Concepts and methods.* (2nd ed.). Boston: Allyn & Bacon.

O'Hanlon, W. H. (1995, May). *Brief solution-oriented therapy.* Printed material presented at workshop. Front Royal, VA: Garrison House Seminars.

O'Hanlon, W., & Beadle, S. (1994). *A field guide to possibility land: Possibility Therapy methods.* Omaha, NE: Possibility Press.

CHAPTER 2

Carroll, L. (1991). *The complete illustrated Lewis Carrol.* New York: Gallery Books. (Original work published 1865)

Caruth, E., & Ekstein, R. (1966). Interpretation within the metaphor. *Journal of the American Academy of Psychiatry, 5,* 35–45.

DeJong, P., & Berg, I. K. (1998). *Interviewing for solutions.* Pacific Grove, CA: Brooks/Cole.

Dolan, Y. M. (1985). *A path with a heart: Ericksonian utilization with resistant and chronic clients.* New York: Brunner/Mazel.

Efran, J. S., Lukens, R. J., & Lukens, M. D. (1988). Constructivism: What's in it for you? *Family Networker, 12*(5), 27–35.

Ehrenwald, J. (1986). *Anatomy of genius: Split brains and global minds.* New York: Human Sciences Press.

Erickson, M. H. (1975). The varieties of double bind. *American Journal of Clinical Hypnosis, 8,* 57–65. In E. L. Rossi (Ed.), *The collected papers of Milton H. Erickson* (Vol. 1). New York: Irvington, 1980.

Erickson, M. H., & Rossi, E. L. (1973). A taped dialogue. In E. L. Rossi (Ed.), *The collected papers of Milton H. Erickson* (Vol. 4). New York: Irvington, 1980.

Erickson, M. H., Rossi, E. L., & Rossi, S. (1976). *Hypnotic realities.* New York: Irvington.

Eron, J. B., & Lund, T. W. (1993). How problems evolve and dissolve: Integrating narrative and strategic concepts. *Family Process, 32,* 291–309.

Gaarder, J. (1994). *Sophie's world: A novel about the history of philosophy.* New York: Berkley.

Garfield, S. L. (1978). Research on client variables in psychotherapy. In S. L. Garfield & A. E. Bergin (Eds.), *Handbook of psychotherapy and behavior change.* New York: Wiley.

Haley, J. (1973). *Uncommon therapy: The psychiatric techniques of Milton H. Erickson, M.D.* New York: W. W. Norton.

Kopp, S. (1985). *Even a stone can be a teacher: Learning and growing from the experiences of everyday life.* Los Angeles: Jeremy P. Tarcher.

Lakoff, G. (1987). *Women, fire, and dangerous things: What categories reveal about the mind.* Chicago: University of Chicago Press.

Lambert, M. J., Shapiro, D. A., & Bergin, A. E. (1986).The effectiveness of psychotherapy. In S. L. Garfield & A. E. Bergin (Eds.), *Handbook of psychotherapy and behavior change* (3rd ed.). New York: Wiley.

MacCormac, E. R. (1985). *A cognitive theory of metaphor.* Cambridge, MA: The MIT Press.

Maruyama, M. (1963). The second cybernetics: Deviation-amplifying mutual causal processes. *American Scientist, 5,* 164–179.

O'Hanlon, W. H. (1995, May). *Brief solution-oriented therapy.* Printed material presented at workshop. Front Royal, VA: Garrison House Seminars.

O'Hanlon, W. H., & Weiner-Davis, M. (1989). *In search of solutions: A new direction in psychotherapy.* New York: W. W. Norton.

Prochaska, J. O., & Norcross, J. C. (1999). *Systems of psychotherapy: A transtheoretical analysis.* Pacific Grove, CA: Brooks/Cole.

Siegelman, E. Y. (1990). *Metaphor and meaning in psychotherapy.* New York: Guilford Press.

Talmon, M. (1990). *Single session therapy.* San Francisco: Jossey-Bass.

Watzlawick, P., Weakland, J. H., & Fisch, R. (1974). *Change: Principles of problem formation and problem resolution.* New York: W. W. Norton.

Wright, K. J. T. (1976). Metaphor and symptom: A study of integration and its failure. *International Review of Psychoanalysis, 3,* 97–109.

Young, M. E. (1998). *Learning the art of helping: Building blocks and techniques.* Upper Saddle River, NJ: Merrill.

CHAPTER 3

Becvar, R. J., Canfield, B. S., & Becvar, D. S. (1997). *Group work: Cybernetic, constructivist, and social constructionist perspectives.* Denver: Love Publishing Co.

DeJong, P., & Berg, I. K. (1998). *Interviewing for solutions.* Pacific Grove, CA: Brooks/Cole

Duncan, B. L., Hubble, M. A., & Miller, S. D. (1997, July/August). Stepping off the throne. *The Family Therapy Networker, 22*–33.

Egan, G. (1994). *The skilled helper* (5th ed.). Monterey, CA: Brooks/Cole.

Frank, J. D. (1985). Therapeutic components shared by all psychotherapies. In M. J. Mahoney & A. Freeman (Eds.), *Cognition and psychotherapy* (pp. 49–79). New York: Plenum Press.

Hobbs, N. (1962). Sources of gain in psychotherapy. *American Psychologist, 17,* 741–747.

Kahn, M. (1991). *Between therapist and client.* New York: W. H. Freeman.

Kleinke, C. L. (1994). *Common principles of psychotherapy.* Pacific Grove, CA: Brooks/Cole.

Luborsky, L., Singer, B., & Luborsky, L. (1975). Comparative studies of psychotherapies: Is it true that "Everybody has won and all must have prizes?" *Archives of General Psychiatry, 32,* 995–1008.

Marmor, J. (Speaker). (1985). *The nature of the therapeutic process.* (Cassette recording L330-19). Phoenix, AZ: Milton Erickson Foundation.

Miller, G. (1997). *Becoming miracle workers: Language and meaning in brief therapy.* New York: Aldine de Gruyter.

Miller, S. (1996). *Solution focused brief therapy*. Workshop given for the Virginia Counselors Association Convention, Williamsburg, VA.

Moore, R., & Gillette, D. (1990). *King Warrior Magician Lover: Rediscovering the archetypes of the mature masculine*. San Francisco: Harper Collins.

Norcross, J. C., & Newman, C. F. (1992). Psychotherapy integration: Setting the context. In J. C. Norcross & M. R. Goldfried (Eds.), *Handbook of psychotherapy integration* (pp. 3–45). New York: Basic Books.

O'Hanlon, W., & Beadle, S. (1994). *A field guide to possibility land: Possibility therapy methods*. Omaha, NE: Possibility Press.

Oltmanns, T. F., & Emery, R. E. (1998). *Abnormal psychology* (2nd ed.). Upper Saddle River, NJ: Prentice Hall.

Rogers, C. R. (1969). *Freedom to learn*. Columbus, OH: Charles E. Merrill.

Toulmin, S. (1982). *The return to cosmology: Postmodern science and the theology of nature*. Chicago: University of Chicago Press.

Walter, J. L., & Peller, J. E. (1992). *Becoming solution-focused in brief therapy*. New York: Brunner/Mazel.

Young, M. E. (1992). *Counseling methods and techniques: An eclectic method*. New York: Merrill.

CHAPTER 4

Berg, I. K. (1991). *Solution-focused approach to family based services*. Milwaukee: Brief Family Therapy Center.

Berg, I. K., & de Shazer, S. (1993). Making numbers talk: Language in therapy. In S. Friedman (Ed.), *The new language of change: Constructive collaboration in psychotherapy* (pp. 5–24). New York: The Guilford Press.

Cade, B., & O'Hanlon, W. H. (1993). *A brief guide to brief therapy*. New York: W. W. Norton.

DeJong, P., & Berg, I. K. (1998). *Interviewing for solutions*. Pacific Grove, CA: Brooks/Cole.

de Shazer, S. (1988). *Clues: Investigating solutions in brief therapy*. New York: Norton.

de Shazer, S. (1991). *Putting difference to work*. New York: W. W. Norton.

Furman, B., & Ahola, T. (1992). *Solution talk: Hosting therapeutic conversations*. New York: W. W. Norton.

Kral, R. (1986). Indirect therapy in the schools. In S. de Shazer & R. Kral (Eds.), *Indirect approaches in therapy: The family therapy collections* (Vol. 19). Rockville, MD: Aspen Press.

Mahoney, M. J. (1995). The modern psychotherapist and the future of psychotherapy. In B. Bonger & L. E. Beutler (Eds.), *Comprehensive textbook of psychotherapy: Theory and practice* (pp. 474–488). New York: Oxford University Press.

O'Hanlon, W. H., & Weiner-Davis, M. (1989). *In search of solutions: A new direction in psychotherapy*. New York: W. W. Norton.

Palmer, D. (1994). *Looking at philosophy: The unbearable heaviness of philosophy made lighter* (2nd ed.). Mountain View, CA: Mayfield Pub. Co.

Prochaska, J. O., & Norcross, J. C. (1994). *Systems of psychotherapy: A transtheoretical analysis*. Pacific Grove, CA: Brooks/Cole.

Rychlak, J. F. (1980). Concepts of free will in modern psychological science. *The Journal of Mind and Behavior, 1,* 9–32.

Schultz, D. P., & Schultz S. E. (1992). *A history of modern psychology* (5th ed.). San Diego: Harcourt Brace Jovanovich.

Seligman, M. E. P. (1974). *Helplessness: On depression, development and death*. San Francisco: W. H. Freeman.

Sklare, G. B. (1997). *Brief counseling that works: A solution-focused approach for school counselors*. Thousand Oaks, CA: Corwin Press, Inc.

Tohn, S. L., & Oshlag, J. A. (1996). Solution-focused therapy with mandated clients. In S. D. Miller, M. A. Hubble, & B. L. Duncan (Eds.), *Handbook of solution-focused brief therapy* (pp. 152–183). San Francisco: Jossey-Bass.

Walter, J. L., & Peller, J. E. (1992). *Becoming solution-focused in brief therapy*. New York: Brunner/Mazel.

Young, M. E. (1998). *Learning the art of helping: Building blocks and techniques*. Upper Saddle River, NJ: Merrill.

Young, M. E. (1992). *Counseling methods and techniques: An eclectic method*. New York: Merrill.

CHAPTER 5

Bateson, G. (1979). *Mind and nature: A necessary unity*. Toronto: Bantam Books.

Benjamin, A. (1987). *The helping interview: With case illustrations*. Boston: Houghton Mifflin.

Benson, A. J., & Presbury, J. H. (1989). The cognitive tradition in schools. In J. N. Hughes & R. J. Hall (Eds.), *Cognitive-behavioral psychology in the schools: A comprehensive handbook* (pp. 37–61). New York: The Guilford Press.

Berg, I. K. (1994). *Family-based services: A solution-focused approach*. New York: Norton.

Brammer, L. M. (1979). *The helping relationship: Process and skills* (2nd ed.). Englewood Cliffs, NJ: Prentice-Hall.

DeJong, P., & Berg, I. K. (1998). *Interviewing for solutions*. Pacific Grove, CA: Brooks/Cole.

de Shazer, S. (1985). *Keys to solution in brief therapy*. New York: W. W. Norton.

Egan, G. (1986). *The skilled helper* (3rd ed.). Monterey, CA: Brooks/Cole.

Ellis, A. (1982). Psychoneurosis and anxiety problems. In R. Grieger & I. Z. Grieger (Eds.), *Cognition and emotional disturbance* (pp. 17–45). New York: Human Sciences Press.

Eron, J. B., & Lund, T. W. (1993). How problems evolve and dissolve: Integrating narrative and strategic concepts. *Family Process, 32,* 291–309.

Goswami, A., Reed, R. E., & Goswami, M. (1993). *The self-aware universe: How consciousness creates the material world.* New York: Jeremy P. Tarcher/Putnam.

Grieger R., & Grieger, I. Z. (1982). Preface. In R. Grieger & I. Z. Grieger (Eds.), *Cognition and emotional disturbance* (pp. 11–16). New York: Human Sciences Press.

James, W. (1890). The principles of psychology. In B.W. Wiltshire (Ed.), *William James: The essential writings.* Albany, NY: SUNY Press.

Landreth, G. L. (1991). *Play therapy: The art of the relationship.* Denton, TX: Center for Play Therapy.

Lyddon, W. J. (1995). Forms and facets of constructivist psychology. In R. A. Neimeyer & M. J. Mahoney (Eds.), *Constructivism in psychotherapy* (pp. 69–92). Washington, DC: American Psychological Association.

Mahoney, M. J. (1988). Rationalism and constructivism in clinical judgment. In D. C. Turk & P. Salovey (Eds.), *Reasoning, inference, and judgment in clinical psychology* (pp. 155–181). New York: The Free Press.

Martindale, C. (1981). *Cognition and consciousness.* Homewood, IL: The Dorsey Press.

Miller, G. (1997). *Becoming miracle workers: Language and meaning in brief therapy.* New York: Aldine de Gruyter.

Moore, H. B., Presbury, J. H., Smith, L. W., & McKee, J. E. (1999). Person-centered approaches. In H. T. Prout & D. T. Brown (Eds.), *Counseling and psychotherapy with children and adolescents: Theory and practice for school and clinical settings* (3rd ed., pp. 155–202). New York: Wiley.

O'Hanlon, W. H. (1995, May). *Brief solution-oriented therapy.* Printed material presented at workshop. Front Royal, VA: Garrison House Seminars.

Penn, P. (1982). Circular questioning. *Family Process, 21,* 267–279.

Polkinghorne, D. E. (1988). *Narrative knowing and the human sciences.* Albany, NY: State University of New York Press.

Prochaska, J. O., & Norcross, J. C. (1994). *Systems of psychotherapy: A transtheoretical analysis.* Pacific Grove, CA: Brooks/Cole.

Purkey, W. W., & Schmidt, J. J. (1996). *Invitational counseling: A self-concept approach to professional practice.* Pacific Grove, CA: Brooks/Cole.

Schultz, D. P., & Schultz, S. E. (2000). *A history of modern psychology* (6th ed.). Fort Worth, TX: Harcourt Brace College Publishers.

Seligman, M. E. P. (1974). *Helplessness: On depression, development and death.* San Francisco: W. H. Freeman.

Seligman, M. E. P. (1994). *What you can change and what you can't: The complete guide to self-improvement.* New York: Simon & Schuster.

Sommers-Flanagan, J., & Sommers-Flanagan, R. (1993). *Foundations of therapeutic interviewing.* Boston: Allyn & Bacon.

Walter, J. L., & Peller, J. E. (1996). Rethinking our assumptions: Assuming anew in a postmodern world. In S. D. Miller, M. A. Hubble, & B. L. Duncan (Eds.), *Handbook of solution-focused brief therapy.* San Francisco: Jossey-Bass.

Watzlawick, P. (Ed.). (1984). *The invented reality: How do we know what we believe we know?: Contributions to constructivism.* New York: W. W. Norton.

Weiner-Davis, M. (1993). *Divorce busting: A revolutionary and rapid program for staying together.* New York: Summit.

White, M., & Epston, D. (1990). *Narrative means to therapeutic ends.* New York: W. W. Norton.

CHAPTER 6

Brickman, P., Zevon, M. A., & Karuza, J. (1982). Models of helping and coping. *American Psychologist, 37,* 368–384.

Bruner, J. (1973). *Beyond the information given: Studies in the psychology of knowing.* New York: W. W. Norton.

Cade, B., & O'Hanlon, W. H. (1993). *A brief guide to brief therapy.* New York: W. W. Norton.

De Jong, P., & Berg, I. K. (1998). *Interviewing for solutions.* Pacific Grove, CA: Brooks/Cole.

Ellenberger, H. F. (1958). A clinical introduction to psychiatric phenomenology and existential analysis. In R. May, E. Angel, & H. F. Ellenberger (Eds.), *Existence: A new dimension in psychiatry and psychology* (pp. 92–124). New York: Clarion Books.

Erickson, M. (1954). Pseudo-orientation in time as a hypnotic procedure. *Journal of Clinical and Experimental Hypnosis, 2,* 261–283.

Frank, J. D. (1985). Therapeutic components shared by all psychotherapies. In M. J. Mahoney & A. Freeman (Eds.), *Cognition and psychotherapy* (pp. 49–79). New York: Plenum Press.

Korzybski, A. (1933). *Science and sanity.* Lakeville, CT: International Non-Aristotelian Library.

Kleinke, C. L. (1994). *Common principles of psychotherapy.* Pacific Grove, CA: Brooks/Cole.

Mahoney, M. J. (1988). Rationalism and constructivism in clinical judgment. In D. C. Turk & P. Salovey (Eds.), *Reasoning, inference, and judgment in clinical psychology* (pp. 155–181). New York: The Free Press.

O'Hanlon, W. H. (1995, May). *Brief solution-oriented therapy.* Printed material presented at workshop. Front Royal, VA: Garrison House Seminars.

Polkinghorne, D. E. (1988). *Narrative knowing and the human sciences.* Albany, NY: State University of New York Press.

Polster, E., & Polster, M. (1973). *Gestalt therapy integrated: Contours of theory and practice.* New York: Vantage Books.

Read, H. (1965). *Icon and idea.* New York: Schocken Books.

Walter, J. L., & Peller, J.E. (1992). *Becoming solution-focused in brief therapy.* New York: Brunner/Mazel.

White, M., (1988). *The externalizing of the problem and the reauthoring of lives and relationships.* Dulwich Centre Newsletter, Summer, 3–21.

White, M., & Epston, D. (1990). *Narrative means to therapeutic ends.* New York: W. W. Norton.

Witmer, J. M. (1986). *Pathways to personal growth.* Muncie, IN: Accelerated Development.

Young, M. E. (1992). *Counseling methods and techniques: An eclectic method.* New York: Merrill.

Chapter 7

Bruner, J. (1973). *Beyond the information given: Studies in the psychology of knowing.* New York: W. W. Norton.

Cade, B., & O'Hanlon, W. H. (1993). *A brief guide to brief therapy.* New York: W. W. Norton.

Combs, A. W., & Avila, D. L. (1985). *Helping relationships: Basic concept for the helping professions* (3rd ed.). Boston: Allyn & Bacon.

Corey, G. (1991). Invited commentary on macrostrategies for delivery of mental health counseling services. *Journal of Mental Health Counseling, 13,* 51–57.

Damasio, A. (1994). *Descartes' error: Emotion, reason, and the human brain.* New York: G. P. Putnam's Sons.

Davidson, R. J. (1993). Parsing affective space: Perspectives from neuropsychology and psychophysiology. *Neuropsychology, 7,* 464–475.

Dennett, D. (1991). *Consciousness explained.* Boston: Little, Brown, & Co.

Frank, J. D. (1985). Therapeutic components shared by all psychotherapies. In M. J. Mahoney & A. Freeman (Eds.), *Cognition and psychotherapy* (pp. 49–79). New York: Plenum Press.

Gendlin, E. T. (1982). *Focusing.* New York: Bantam.

Gladding, S. T. (1992). *Counseling as an art: The creative arts in counseling.* Alexandria, VA: American Counseling Association.

Goleman, D. (1995). *Emotional intelligence.* New York: Bantam Books.

Isen, A. M. (1984). Toward understanding the role of affect in cognition. In R. S. Weyer, Jr. & T. K. Srull (Eds.), *Handbook of social cognition* (pp. 179–236). Hillsdale, NJ: Lawrence Erlbaum Associates.

Kosslyn, S. M., & Koenig, O. (1995). *Wet mind: The new cognitive neuroscience.* New York: The Free Press.

Lazarus, R. S. (1991). *Emotion and adaptation.* New York: Oxford University Press.

LeDoux, J. (1996). *The emotional brain: The mysterious underpinnings of emotional life.* New York: Simon & Schuster.

Martindale, C. (1981). *Cognition and consciousness.* Homewood, IL: The Dorsey Press.

Moreno, J. L. (1958). *Psychodrama.* (Vol. 2) New York: Beacon House.

O'Hanlon, B., & Beadle, S. (1994). *A field guide to possibility land: Possibility therapy methods.* Omaha, NB: Possibility Press.

Perls, F. S. (1977). *The Gestalt approach: An eye witness to therapy.* Palo Alto, CA: Science and Behavior Books.

Satir, V. (1972). *Peoplemaking.* Palo Alto, CA: Science and Behavior Books.

Shapiro, L. E. (1994). *Short-term therapy with children.* King of Prussia, PA: Center for Applied Psychology.

Thompson, R. A. (1996). *Counseling techniques: Improving relationships with others, ourselves, our families, and our environment.* Washington, DC: Accelerated Development.

Vaughan, S. C. (1997). *The talking cure.* New York: Henry Holt & Company.

Young, M. E. (1992). *Counseling methods and techniques: An eclectic method.* New York: Merrill.

Young, M. E. (1998). *Learning the art of helping: Building blocks and techniques.* Upper Saddle River, NJ: Merrill.

Chapter 8

de Shazer, S. (1982). *Patterns of brief family therapy: An ecosystemic approach.* New York: The Guilford Press.

Dolan, Y. M. (1985). *A path with a heart: Ericksonian utilization with resistant and chronic clients.* New York: Brunner/Mazel.

Erickson, M. H., & Rossi, E. L. (1979). *Hypnotherapy.* New York: Irvington.

Erickson, M. H., Rossi, E. L., & Rossi, S. I. (1976). *Hypnotic realities.* New York: John Wiley & Sons.

Freeman, J. C., & Lobovits, D. (1993). The turtle with wings. In S. Friedman (Ed.), *The new language of change: Constructive collaboration in psychotherapy* (pp. 188–225). New York: The Guilford Press.

Friedman, S. (1997). *Time-effective psychotherapy: Maximizing outcomes in an era of minimized resources.* Boston: Allyn & Bacon.

Gendlin, E. T. (1982). *Focusing.* New York: Bantam.

Grinder, J., DeLozier, J., & Bandler, R. (1977). *Patterns of the hypnotic techniques of Milton H. Erickson, M.D.* (Vol. 2). Cupertino, CA: Meta Publications.

Hergenhahn, B. R. (1992). *Introduction to the history of psychology.* Belmont, CA: Wadsworth.

Laing, R. D. (1971). *The politics of the family and other essays.* New York: Pantheon Books.

Lankton, S. R., & Lankton, C. H. (1986). *Enchantment and intervention in family therapy: Training in Ericksonian approaches.* New York: Brunner/Mazel.

Metcalf, L. (1995). *Counseling toward solutions: A practical solution-focused program for working with students, teachers, and parents.* West Nyak, NY: The Center for Applied Research in Education.

Miller, G. A. (1956).The magical number seven, plus or minus two: Some limits on our capacity for processing information. *Psychological Review, 63,* 81–87.

Nyland, D., & Thomas, J. (1994, Nov./Dec.). The economics of narrative. *The Family Therapy Networker,* 38–39.

Schultz, D. P., & Schultz, S. E. (1996). *A history of modern psychology* (6th ed.). Fort Worth, TX: Harcourt Brace College Publishers.

White, M., & Epston, D. (1990). *Narrative means to therapeutic ends.* New York: W. W. Norton.

White, M. (1995). *Re-authoring lives: Interviews and essays.* Adelaide, Australia: Dulwich Centre Publications.

CHAPTER 9

Ascher, L. M. (1989). Therapeutic paradox: A primer. In L. M. Ascher (Ed.), *Therapeutic paradox* (pp. 3–13). New York: The Guilford Press.

Bateson, G., Jackson, D. D., Haley, J., & Weakland, J. (1956). Toward a theory of schizophrenia. *Behavioral Science, 1,* 251–264.

Bornstein, P. H., Krueger, H. K., & Cogswell, K. (1989). Principles and techniques of couples paradoxical therapy. In L. M. Ascher (Ed.), *Therapeutic paradox* (pp. 289–309). New York: The Guilford Press.

Bossomaier, T., & Green, D. (1998). *Patterns in the sand: Computers, complexity and everyday life.* Reading, MA: Perseus Books.

Cade, B., & O'Hanlon, W. H. (1993). *A brief guide to brief therapy.* New York: W. W. Norton.

Cilliers, P. (1998). *Complexity and post-modernism: Understanding complex systems.* New York: Routledge.

Dolan, Y. M. (1985). *A path with a heart: Ericksonian utilization with resistant and chronic clients.* New York: Brunner/Mazel.

Deikman, A. F. (1973). Deautomatization and the mystic experience. In R. E. Ornstein (Ed.), *The nature of human consciousness: A book of readings* (pp. 216–233). New York: The Viking Press.

Duncan, B. L. (1989). Paradoxical procedures in family therapy. In L. M. Ascher (Ed.), *Therapeutic paradox* (pp. 310–348). New York: The Guilford Press.

Dunlap, K. (1928). A revision of the fundamental law of habit formation. *Science, 67,* 360–362.

Ellis, A. (1982). Psychoneurosis and anxiety problems. In R. Grieger & I. Z. Grieger (Eds.), *Cognition and emotional disturbance* (pp. 17–45). New York: Human Sciences Press.

Erickson, M. H. (1967). The confusion technique. In J. Haley (Ed.), *Advanced techniques of hypnosis and therapy.* New York: Grune and Stratton.

Erickson, M. H., Rossi, E. L., & Rossi, S. (1976). *Hypnotic realities.* New York: Irvington.

Gill, M., & Brennen, M. (1959). *Hypnosis and related states.* New York: International Universities Press.

Gleick, J. (1987). *Chaos: Making a new science.* New York: Viking Penguin Inc.

Hayes, S. C., & Melancon, S. M. (1989). Comprehensive distancing, paradox, and the treatment of emotional avoidance. In L. M. Ascher (Ed.), *Therapeutic paradox* (pp. 184–218). New York: The Guilford Press.

May, R. (1969). *Love and will.* New York: W. W. Norton.

Mozdzierz, F., Macchitelli, F., & Lisiecki, J. (1976). The paradox in psychotherapy: An Adlerian perspective. *Journal of Individual Psychology, 32,* 169–184.

O'Hanlon, W. H., & Weiner-Davis, M. (1989). *In search of solutions: A new direction in psychotherapy.* New York: W. W. Norton.

Seligman, M. E. P. (1994). *What you can change and what you can't: The complete guide to self-improvement.* New York: Simon & Schuster.

Watzlawick, P., Beavin, J. H., & Jackson, D. D. (1967). *Pragmatics of human communication: A study of interactional patterns, pathologies, and paradoxes.* New York: W. W. Norton.

Watzlawick, P., Weakland, J. H., & Fisch, R. (1974). *Change: Principles of problem formation and problem resolution.* New York: W. W. Norton.

CHAPTER 10

Adams, J. F., Piercy, F. P., & Jurich, J. A. (1991). Effects of solution focused therapy's "formula first session task" on compliance and outcome in family therapy. *Journal of Marital and Family Therapy, 17,* 277–290.

Anderson, T. (1987). The reflecting team: Dialogue and meta-dialogue in clinical work. *Family Process, 26,* 4, 415–428.

Bateson, G. (1972). *Steps to an ecology of mind.* New York: Ballantine Books.

Berg, I. K., & Miller, S. D. (1992). *Working with the problem drinker: A solution-focused approach.* New York: W. W. Norton.

Berlyne, D. E. (1960). *Conflict, arousal and curiosity.* New York: McGraw-Hill.

Butler, W. R., & Powers, K. V. (1996). Solution-focused grief therapy. In S. D. Miller, M. A. Hubble, & B. L. Duncan (Eds.). *Handbook of solution-focused brief therapy* (pp. 228–247). San Francisco: Jossey-Bass.

DeJong, P., & Berg, I. K. (1998). *Interviewing for solutions.* Pacific Grove, CA: Brooks/Cole.

de Shazer, S. (1985). *Keys to solution in brief therapy.* New York: W. W. Norton.

Fiske, D. W., & Maddi, S. R. (1961). *Functions of varied experience.* Homewood, IL: Dorsey Press.

Freud, S. (1958).The unconscious. In J. Strachey (Ed. and Trans.). *The standard edition of the complete psychological works of Sigmund Freud* (Vol. 14, pp. 159–215). London: Hogarth Press. (Original work published 1915)

CHAPTER 11

Budman, S. H. (1990). The myth of termination in brief therapy: Or, it ain't over till it's over. In J. K. Zeig & S. G. Gilligan (Eds.), *Brief therapy: Myths, methods and metaphors* (pp. 206–218). New York: Brunner/Mazel.

de Shazer, S. (1982). *Patterns of brief family therapy: An ecosystemic approach.* New York: The Guilford Press.

Epston, D., & White, M. (1995). Termination as a rite of passage: Questioning strategies for a therapy of inclusion. In R. A. Neimeyer & M. J. Mahoney (Eds.), *Constructivism in psychotherapy* (pp. 339–354). Washington, DC: American Psychological Association.

Glasser, W. (1965). *Reality therapy.* New York: Harper & Row.

Koss, M. P., Butcher, J. N., & Strupp, H. H. (1986). Psychotherapy methods in clinical research. *Journal of Consulting and Clinical Psychology, 54,* 60–67.

Taube, C. A., Goldman, H. H., Burns, B. J., & Kessler, L. G. (1988). High users of outpatient health service. I: Definition and characteristics. *American Journal of Psychiatry, 145,* 19–24.

Teyber, E. (2000). *Interpersonal process in psychotherapy: A relational approach* (4th ed.). Pacific Grove, CA: Brooks/Cole.

Weiner-Davis, M. (1993). *Divorce busting: A revolutionary and rapid program for staying together.* New York: Summit.

CHAPTER 12

Berg, I. K. (1991). *Solution-focused approach to family based services.* Milwaukee: Brief Family Therapy Center.

Berg, I. K., & Miller, S. D. (1992). *Working with the problem drinker: A solution-focused approach.* New York: W. W. Norton.

de Shazer, S. (1988). *Clues: Investigating solutions in brief therapy.* New York: Norton.

de Shazer, S. (1991). *Putting difference to work.* New York: W. W. Norton.

Friedman, S. (1997). *Time-effective psychotherapy: Maximizing outcomes in an era of minimized resources.* Boston: Allyn & Bacon.

Hutchins, D. E. (1979). Systematic counseling: The T-F-A model for counselor intervention. *Personnel and Guidance Journal, 57,* 10, 529–531.

Hutchins, D. E., & Cole, C. G. (1992). *Helping relationships and strategies.* (2nd ed.). Pacific Grove, CA: Brooks/Cole.

Miller, S. D. (1995). *Solution-focused brief therapy: Focusing on "what works" in clinical practice.* Chicago: Miller Publications.

O'Hanlon, W. H. (1995, May). *Brief solution-oriented therapy.* Printed material presented at workshop. Front Royal, VA: Garrison House Seminars.

O'Hanlon, W. H., & Weiner-Davis, M. (1989). *In search of solutions: A new direction in psychotherapy.* New York: W. W. Norton.

Tohn, S. L., & Oshlag, J. A. (1995). *Crossing the bridge: Integrating solution-focused therapy into clinical practice.* Natick, MA: Solutions Press.

Tohn, S. L., & Oshlag, J. A. (1996). Solution-focused therapy with mandated clients. In S. D. Miller, M.A. Hubble, & B. L. Duncan (Eds.), *Handbook of solution-focused brief therapy* (pp. 152–183). San Francisco: Jossey-Bass.

Walter, J. L., & Peller, J. E. (1992). *Becoming solution-focused in brief therapy.* New York: Brunner/Mazel.

INDEX

Acceptance, 215
Accommodation, 106
Acknowledging clients, 49, 133
Action goals, 67
Adler, Alfred, 63, 108, 177
Adrenaline, 127–28
Adversarial relationships, 229
Advice, 186, 191–92
After-the-break protocol, 245
Agency, 102, 117
Ambiguous function assignments, 173–74
American Society of Clinical Hypnosis, 10
Amygdala, 123, 125–26
Anticipatory anxiety, 179
Aristotle, 60–61
Arousal, emotional
assessing, 134–35
importance of, 133
lowering, 134–36
raising, 137
Assimilation, 106
Attending to clients, 49
Awards, 159

Bateson, Gregory, 5, 8–9, 15, 98
Beck, Aaron, 87
Behavior patterns, 167
Beneficence, 46–48
BFTC. See Brief Family Therapy Center
Blake, William, 172
Bodin, Arthur, 9
Brain centers, 123, 125
Breaks, counseling, 200–202
Breakthroughs, 140
Brief, interpretations of, 27

Brief attitude
actions and description, 208
change, 208
client intrigue, 209
collaboration, 212
context, 211
detail work, 211
failed solutions, 212
feedback, 209
focus, 209
goals, 209–10
importance of, 207
interventions, custom-designed, 210
labels, 209
language, 210
life concerns versus problems, 210
meaning, 208
metaphors, 211
reframing, 212
resistance, 208
rules, 211
simplicity, 209
single-session counseling, 209
teleology, 210
Brief constructivist model, 24–25
Brief Family Therapy Center (BFTC), 5, 12, 28
Brief Therapy Center (BTC), 11–12, 27, 177
Butterfly Effect, 169–70, 215

Carl Rogers with a Twist, 50–53, 67, 235–36
Carroll, Lewis, 25
Catharsis, 124
Certificates, 159
Change
brief attitude, 208
clients, helping to, 21

Change (cont.)
commitment to, 68–70
consolidating, 214–15
facilitating, 19
implications for counselors, 30–31
Necker cube example, 22
noticing, 215–16
Change agents
counselors and psychotherapists as, 3
cybernetics, 8
Chaos Theory, 165, 167–69
Childhood psychosis, 164–65
Circular questions, 98–99
Client categories, 69
Client intrigue, 209
Client models, 108–9
Clients, involuntary
acknowledging, 235
Carl Rogers with a Twist, 235–36
checklist, 244–45
client-therapist-goal relationship, 228–33
complaints, deconstructing, 236
encouragement triad, 241–42
exceptions, looking for, 239
finding the pony, 241
first session, 233–34
goals, 227–28, 237
helping person role, 226
hypotheticals, 238
impact on counselor, 225–26
investigator role, 226
invitations, waiting for, 237
manager role, 226
metaphors, 236
miracle question, 240
problems, externalizing, 240–41
relationships, analyzing, 242–43

Clients, involuntary (*cont.*)
  reporter role, 226
  scaling, 238–39
  session openings, 227–28
  task types, 243
  third-party perspective, 239–40
Clinical depression, memory loss
    and, 127
Co-construction, 92
Cognitive declarative memory, 137
Cognitive functioning, types of,
    103–4
Collaboration, 212
Commitment, 68–70
Common everyday trance, 147–48
Common factors, counseling
    therapies, 43
Common-sense therapy, 10
Communication, 8
Compensatory model, 109
Competency-Based Future-Oriented
    Therapy, 5
Complainant-listener-goal
    relationship, 228
Complainants, 69
Complaints, deconstructing,
    53–56, 236
Complex adaptive systems, 167–68
Complexity Theory, 166, 169
Compliments, 115–17, 199
Conduct disorder, 138
Confrontation, 29
Confusion techniques, 165,
    171–72, 176
Conscious memory, 137–38
Constructivism
  definition, 24, 83, 85
  existence, types of, 86–87
  implications for counselor, 91–92
  rationalist *versus* developmental
    perspectives, 87–88
  representation, 85–86
Constructivist Therapy, 5
Consulting breaks, 12–13, 188–89
Consumers, of mental health
    services, 3
Context, 211
Contract, 69
Cooperation, 28
Coping questions, 118–20
Cortex, 125
Counseling relationships
  centrality of, 48
  conducting *versus* reacting to, 24
  detached concern, 47
  new ways of viewing, 5
  strategic approach to, 22–24
  types, 201–2
Counselor roles, 226
Countertransference, 175
Creative activities, 140

Customers, 69
Customer-seller-goal relationship,
    228
Cybernetics, 7–8
Cyclical behavior, 167

Damasio, Antonia, 124
Daydreaming, 147–48
Dead rock theory, 167
Deautomization, 172
Deconstructing complaints, 53–56,
    236
Deconstruction, 92
Decourting, 154
Descartes, René, 124
de Shazer, Steve
  Brief Family Therapy Center, 12
  consulting break, 12–13
  solution-focused model, 13
Destigmatizing problems, 236
Detached concern, 47
Detached views, 115
Detail work, 211
Developmental view, of mental
    processes, 87–88
Difficulties, overcoming through
    ordeal, 10
Direct-behavioral tasks, 203
Directives, 10–11, 173
Direct-nonbehavioral tasks, 203
Discouragement, 214
Dissociative experiences, 148
Double-bind theory, schizophrenia, 9
Double description, 98
Dramatic hold, 155–56
Duhl, Fred, 44
Duncan, Barry, 44

Ellis, Albert, 87
Emergence, 166, 169–70
Emotional contagion, 130
Emotions
  acknowledging, 133
  arousal, 133–37
  attaching to success, 127–28
  catharsis, 124
  implications for the counselor, 132
  importance of, 123–24
  intervention and, 88–89
  inverted-U relationship, 131
  memory and, 137–38
  positive and negative affect,
    128–29
  rationalists *versus* constructivists,
    88
  recent findings regarding, 125–26
  thought, relationship to, 124
  top-down *versus* bottom-up, 126
Empathy, 46–48, 129–30
Empiricism, 83
Enactment, 112

Enchantment, 152–53, 155
Encouragement, compared to praise,
    115–17
Encouragement triad, 102, 117–18,
    241–42
Encouraging critic, 107
Energy, 102, 117
Enlightenment model, 108
Entropy, 169
Epistemology, 85
Epston, David, 106
Erickson, Milton
  confusion, 172
  Erickson's First Law, 11
  legacy, 15
  resistance, 29
  utilization, 29–30
Etiology, 9, 61–62
Evocations, 139–49
Exceptions, looking for, 74–76, 239
Existence, types of, 86–87
Exotic audiences, 149, 159, 162–63
Explications, 139–49
Explicit memory, 137–38
Externalization, 109–12, 240–41

Failed solutions, 212
Fantasy process, 112–13
Favorite quiet place, 136
Fears, unconscious, 127
Feedback, 209, 217–18
Felt sense, 147
Fictional finalism, 63
Finding the pony, 118–19, 241
First sessions, 218
Fisch, Richard, 9, 27
Flight into health, 218–19
Focus, 140, 147, 209
Follow-up contact, 221
Follow-up letters, 160–61
Formula First Session Task, 195
Frank, Jerome, 43, 115, 133
Freud, Sigmund, 21, 159, 189
Frozen state, 167

Gestalt therapy, 147, 149–50
Getting by questions, 95–96
Glasser, William, 216
Goal incongruent emotions, 129
Goals
  brief attitude, 209–10
  creating, 66–67
  exceptions, looking for, 74–76
  inviting clients to set, 64–65
  positive, 66
  presumptive *versus* subjunctive, 68
  simplicity, 68
  teleology, 60
  third-party, 71–72
  well-formed, 65–66, 70–71
  workable, 13

Goal statement, 112–13
Goleman, Daniel, 125

Haley, Jay, 9
Helping person role, 226
Helplessness, declaring, 177
Hippocampus, 123, 126–27
History, brief-resolution counseling
    movement, 7–8
History change, 151
Hobbs, Nicholas, 43
Hope, overcoming blocks to, 63
Hubble, Mark, 44
Humanistic movement, 24
Hypnotic therapeutic techniques, 8–9
Hypotheticals, 102, 238
Hypothetical solution, 112–13

Iatrogenic resolution, 229
Imagery, 102, 117
Immaculate perception, 83, 87
Immediacy, 29
Implicit memory, 137–38
Indirect-behavioral tasks, 203
Indirect-nonbehavioral tasks, 203
Influencing techniques, 135, 170
Inspiration, moments of, 152–53
Insurance companies, demands of, 25
Interpersonal perspective, 115
Interpretation, 29
Interventions
    custom-designed, 210
    engineering change, 23
    reinvention of, 3
Intimacy *versus* detachment, 47
Introspection, 103
Intuition pumps, 139
Inventory, taking, 77
Inverted-U relationship, emotions,
    131
Investigator role, 226
Invitations, waiting for, 237
Involuntary clients
    acknowledging, 235
    Carl Rogers with a Twist, 235–36
    checklist, 244–45
    client-therapist-goal relationship,
        228–33
    complaints, deconstructing, 236
    encouragement triad, 241–42
    exceptions, looking for, 239
    externalizing problems, 240–41
    finding the pony, 241
    first session, 233–34
    goals, 227–28, 237
    helping person role, 226
    hypotheticals, 238
    impact on counselor, 225–26
    investigator role, 226
    invitations, waiting for, 237
    manager role, 226

Involuntary clients (*cont.*)
    metaphors, 236
    miracle question, 240
    relationships, analyzing, 242–43
    reporter role, 226
    scaling, 238–39
    session openings, 227–28
    task types, 243
    third-party perspective, 239–40
Involuntary directives, 11
Involuntary-jailer-goal relationship,
    229–30

Jackson, Don, 8
Jefferson, Thomas, 245

Kant, Immanuel, 4, 207
Kopp, Sheldon, 31

Labels, 209
Laing, R. D., 86
Language
    brief attitude, 210
    Eastern *versus* Western views of,
        78–79
    meaning and, 103
Lazarus, Arnold, 43
Learned helplessness, 179
Letters
    from exotic audiences, 149
    importance of, 160, 162–63
Lewin, Kurt, 133
Liar paradox, 177
Life concerns *versus* problems, 210
Listening
    behaviors, 50
    importance of, 44–46
Locke, John, 84
Longing, 150–52
Long-term memory, 138
Lorenx, Edward, 168
LUV triangle, 40, 49–50, 52–53, 180

Magician, viewing counselor as, 42
Magritte, Rene, 83
Manager role, 226
Marmor, Judd, 43
Mead, Margaret, 8
Meaning
    brief attitude, 208
    importance of, 102
    problem of, 102–3
Meaning-making process, 86
Medical model, 109
Meditation, as stress-reduction
    technique, 136
Memory
    emotions and, 137–38
    loss, 126–26
    short-term, 146
    stress and, 130

Mental processes, 87–88
Mental Research Institute (MRI), 5,
    9–10
Metaphors
    brief attitude, 211
    charismatic use of, 37–38
    client, 33–37
    constructing, 31–32
    definition, 31
    dramatic hold, 155–56
    enchanting, 155
    importance of, 19
    involuntary clients, 237
    life stories, 33
    rigid *versus* fresh, 32
    types, 156
Metcalf, Linda, 154–55
Michenbaum, Donald, 192
Miller, Gale, 42
Miller, George, 146
Miller, Scott, 42, 44
Miracle question, 102, 113–14,
    151, 240
Misunderstanding, creative, 107
Mnemonic, Henry, 126–27
Moments of inspiration, 152–53
Moral model, 108
MRI. *See* Mental Research Institute
Mystery metaphors, 156
Mystification, 148–49

Narrative therapy
    coping question, 118–20
    development of, 106–7
    encouragement triad, 117–18
    externalization, 110–12
    fantasy process, 112–13
    goal statement, 112–13
    hypothetical solution, 112–13
    implications for counselors, 109
    importance of, 103–4
    interpersonal perspective, 115
    miracle question, 113–14
    responsibility, 108–9
    stories, types of, 105–6
Negative practice, 177
Negentropy, 169, 190
Newton, Sir Isaac, 5
Nose brain, 125
Not knowing, adopting posture of, 23

Objective reality, 83
Observing for positives, 116
Ocularcentrism, 159
O'Hanlon, Bill, 4
Open-ended leads, 95
Openings, session, 227–28
Oppositional defiant, 138
Order and chaos, 166
Other view, 115
Outdated stories, 105

Palo Alto Group. *See* Mental Research Institute
Pappenheim, Bertha, 159
Paradigmatic knowing, 103
Paradox, 165, 176–78, 180–81
Paradoxical Attendance Contract, 180
Parkinson's law, 27
Past tense phrases, 51
Period log, 140
Personal meaning, 103
Positive changes, 220–21
Possibility phrases, 51–52
Possibility Therapy, 5
Post-Modern Therapy, 5
Posttraumatic stress disorder, 127
Praise, 115–17
Preferred view, client's, 90–91
Prescribing symptoms, 179–80
Presumptive questions, 99
Primary clients, 225–28
Primary emotions, 129
Problems
    deconstructing, 24
    defining, 11–12
    destigmatizing, 236
    reality *versus* perception, 236
    relabeling, 236
    universals *versus* episodes, 236
Progress, recognizing, 78
Psychodrama, 140

Questions
    circular, 98–99
    deconstruction tools, 92–93
    getting by, 95–96
    presumptive, 99
    start-up, 95
    use of, 93–94
    when to avoid, 94–95
Quieting techniques, 134

Rationalist view, of mental processes, 87–88
Reacknowledgement, 199
Reality, location of, 83–84
Referrals, solution-centered, 73
Referring clients, 71, 225–28, 229
Reflecting team, 186–88, 193–94
Reframing, 23, 152–55, 212
Reinforcement *versus* remediation, 3
Relabeling technique, 154
Relational concerns, 48
Relational questions, 98–99
Relaxation training, 136
Reluctance, utilizing, 178
Reorganization, 172
Repetition compulsion, 21
Reporter role, 226
Representation, 85–86

Resistance
    brief attitude, 208
    dealing with, 29
    death of, 28
Resolution
    achieving, 7
    conceptual theme, 6
    promoting process of, 24
Responsibility, 108
Restraining, 178
Reverse empathy, 129–30
Rigidified stories, 105
Rogers, Carl, 235–36. *See also* Carl Rogers with a Twist
    change, belief in human ability to, 28
    empathy, 129–30
    listening, importance of, 45
    misunderstanding of, 50–51
    unconditional positive regard, 90
Ruesch, Jurgen, 8
Rules, brief attitude, 211

Satir, Virginia, 9
Saying goodbye, 221–22
Scaling
    client expectations, 77
    involuntary clients, 238–39
    reasons to use, 76–77
Schizophrenia, double-bind theory, 9
School counselors, 26, 138
Secondary qualities, 84
Second session, 213–14
Self-reflective recall, 103
Self view, 115
Seligman, Martin, 62
Sense of resolve, 6
Session openings, 227–28
SFBT. *See* solution-focused brief therapy
Simplicity, 209
Single-session counseling, 209
Situational concerns, 48
Skepticism, regarding therapeutic fads, 1–2
Solution-Building Therapy, 5
Solution-centered referral sheet, 73
Solution-focused brief therapy (SFBT)
    conceptual themes, 6
    history, 5
Solution-focused model
    impact on counseling practices, 15
    origins, 13
Solution-Focused Therapy, 5
Solution-Oriented Therapy, 5
Spontaneous self-organization, 169
Start-up questions, 95

Statistical analysis, 103
Stein, Gertrude, 85
Stories
    client's, 89–90
    deconstructing and co-construction, 92
    reconstructing, 74
Strategic therapy, 9–11, 22–24
Stress
    hippocampus and, 127
    reduction techniques, 136–37
SUDS (subjective units of distress technique), 79
Suggestions, 186, 189–92, 196–97, 199–200
Sullivan, Harry Stack, 9
Surprise/shock metaphors, 156
Suspense metaphors, 156
Symptoms, prescribing, 179–80
Symptom substitution, 190–91

Talking cure, 159
Task assignment, 195–96
Task construction paradigm, 203
Task types, 243
Teleology
    brief attitude, 210
    etiology, compared to, 60–62
Teleponding, 63
Temper Tamers' Club, 162–63
Termination
    client anxiety, 219–20
    follow-up, 220–21
    saying goodbye, 221–22
    when to end, 218–19
TFA (thinking-feeling-acting) matrix system, 197–99
Thalamus, 125
Theory
    counseling, relationship to, 4–5
    importance of, 3
    technique and, striking balance between, 3
Therapeutic distance, 47
Therapeutic fads, 1–2
Therapeutic paradox, 176–78
Third-party perspective, 239–40
Third-party referrals, 72–74
Time-Effective Therapy, 5
Tipping the balance, 63–64
Tolman, Edward, 62
Tools, ways to use this book, 16–18
Tragic stories, 105
Trance, common everyday, 147–48
Transderivational search, 146–47
Trauma, memory loss and, 127
Traveling Salesperson Problem, 25–26
Triadic relationship styles, 228–30

Unconscious memory, 137–38
Understanding, communicating to
    clients, 50
Unfinished business, 150–52
Universal price code problem,
    13–14
Utilization, 29–30

Validating behaviors, 50
Victims, 69, 236
Visitor-host-goal relationship, 229

Visitors, 69
Voluntary directives,

Watzlawick, Paul, 9
Weakland, John H., 8
Weather models, 168
Weiner-Davis, Michele, 220
White, Michael, 106, 188
Why questions, 94
Wiener, Norbert, 7
Window shoppers, 69

Witnessing, 107
Wittgenstein, Ludwig, 6
Working alliance, 47
World hypothesis-conjecture, 104
Writing
    importance of, 159–60
    as stress-reduction technique, 136

Yerkes-Dodson effect, 130–32

Zeigarnik, Bluma, 149